# THE wallflower

YAMATONADESHIKO SHICHIHENGE

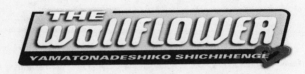

## 20

**Tomoko Hayakawa**

Translated and adapted by
David Ury

Lettered by
North Market Street Graphics

KC
KODANSHA COMICS

A Kodansha Comics Trade Paperback Original.

*The Wallflower* volume 20 copyright © 2008 Tomoko Hayakawa
English translation copyright © 2009, 2013 Tomoko Hayakawa

Published in the United States by Kodansha Comics, an imprint of Kodansha USA Publishing, LLC., New York.

Publication rights for this English edition arranged through Kodansha Ltd., Tokyo.

First published in Japan in 2008 by Kodansha Ltd., Tokyo,
as *Yamatonadeshiko Shichihenge*, volume 20.

ISBN 978-1-61262-332-0

Printed in Canada.

www.kodanshacomics.com

9 8 7 6 5 4 3 2 1

Translator/Adapter—David Ury
Lettering—North Market Street Graphics

# Contents

# A Note from the Author

♥ I WENT TO THE WRAP PARTY FOR *THE WALLFLOWER* ANIME. YOU CAN READ ALL ABOUT IT IN THE "BEHIND THE SCENES" SECTION. IT WAS REALLY FUN, BUT IT WAS SAD KNOWING THAT IT WAS ALL OVER. I COULD REALLY TELL THAT EVERYBODY PUT A LOT OF LOVE INTO THEIR WORK, AND IT MADE ME SO HAPPY. THANK YOU ALL SO MUCH. ♥ AND THANK YOU FOR YOUR SUPPORT. ♥

—Tomoko Hayakawa

# Honorifics Explained

Throughout the Kodansha Comics books, you will find Japanese honorifics left intact in the translations. For those not familiar with how the Japanese use honorifics and, more important, how they differ from American honorifics, we present this brief overview.

Politeness has always been a critical facet of Japanese culture. Ever since the feudal era, when Japan was a highly stratified society, use of honorifics—which can be defined as polite speech that indicates relationship or status—has played an essential role in the Japanese language. When addressing someone in Japanese, an honorific usually takes the form of a suffix attached to one's name (example: "Asuna-san"), is used as a title at the end of one's name, or appears in place of the name itself (example: "Negi-sensei," or simply "Sensei!").

Honorifics can be expressions of respect or endearment. In the context of manga and anime, honorifics give insight into the nature of the relationship between characters. Many English translations leave out these important honorifics and therefore distort the feel of the original Japanese. Because Japanese honorifics contain nuances that English honorifics lack, it is our policy at Kodansha not to translate them. Here, instead, is a guide to some of the honorifics you may encounter in Kodansha Comics.

-*san*: This is the most common honorific and is equivalent to Mr., Miss, Ms., or Mrs. It is the all-purpose honorific and can be used in any situation where politeness is required.

-*sama*: This is one level higher than "-san" and is used to confer great respect.

-*dono*: This comes from the word "tono," which means "lord." It is an even higher level than "-sama" and confers utmost respect.

**-kun:** This suffix is used at the end of boys' names to express familiarity or endearment. It is also sometimes used by men among friends, or when addressing someone younger or of a lower station.

**-chan:** This is used to express endearment, mostly toward girls. It is also used for little boys, pets, and even among lovers. It gives a sense of childish cuteness.

**Bozu:** This is an informal way to refer to a boy, similar to the English terms "kid" and "squirt."

**Sempai/
Senpai:** This title suggests that the addressee is one's senior in a group or organization. It is most often used in a school setting, where underclassmen refer to their upperclassmen as "sempai." It can also be used in the workplace, such as when a newer employee addresses an employee who has seniority in the company.

**Kohai:** This is the opposite of "sempai" and is used toward underclassmen in school or newcomers in the workplace. It connotes that the addressee is of a lower station.

**Sensei:** Literally meaning "one who has come before," this title is used for teachers, doctors, or masters of any profession or art.

**-[blank]:** This is usually forgotten in these lists, but it is perhaps the most significant difference between Japanese and English. The lack of honorific means that the speaker has permission to address the person in a very intimate way. Usually, only family, spouses, or very close friends have this kind of permission. Known as *yobisute*, it can be gratifying when someone who has earned the intimacy starts to call one by one's name without an honorific. But when that intimacy hasn't been earned, it can be very insulting.

THE wallflower

YAMATONADESHIKO SHICHIHENGE

ヤマトナデシコ七変化♡

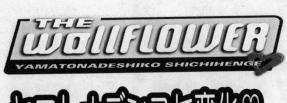

# CONTENTS

KYOHEI TAKANO—
A STRONG FIGHTER,
"I'M THE KING"

TAKENAGA ODA—
A CARING FEMINIST

RANMARU MORII—
A TRUE LADY'S MAN

YUKINOJO TOYAMA—
A GENTLE, CHEERFUL, AND
VERY EMOTIONAL GUY

SUNAKO NAKAHARA

## WALLFLOWER'S BEAUTIFUL CAST OF CHARACTERS (?)

SUNAKO IS A DARK LONER WHO LOVES HORROR MOVIES. WHEN HER AUNT, THE LANDLADY OF A BOARDINGHOUSE, LEAVES TOWN WITH HER BOYFRIEND, SUNAKO IS FORCED TO LIVE WITH FOUR HANDSOME GUYS. SUNAKO'S AUNT MAKES A DEAL WITH THE BOYS, WHICH CAUSES NOTHING BUT HEADACHES FOR SUNAKO: "MAKE SUNAKO INTO A LADY, AND YOU CAN LIVE RENT-FREE FOR THREE YEARS. THE ROAD TO TURNING SUNAKO INTO A LADY MAY GO ON FOREVER, BUT AT LEAST HER RELATIONSHIP WITH KYOHEI FINALLY SEEMS TO BE MOVING FORWARD. YET, NO MATTER HOW CLOSE THEY GET IT WILL NEVER LEAD TO LOVE . . . OR WILL IT?

# Chapter 79

## STEAL THE PRINCESS

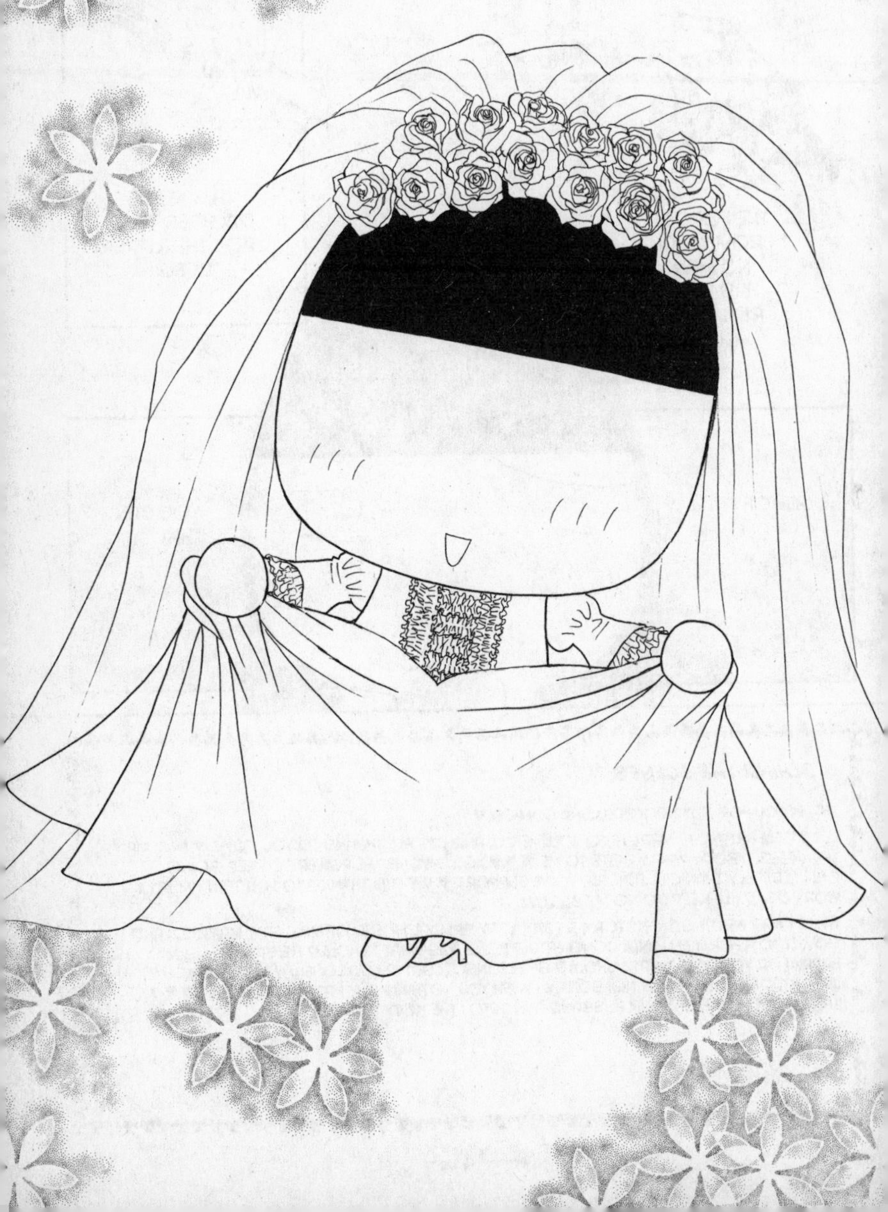

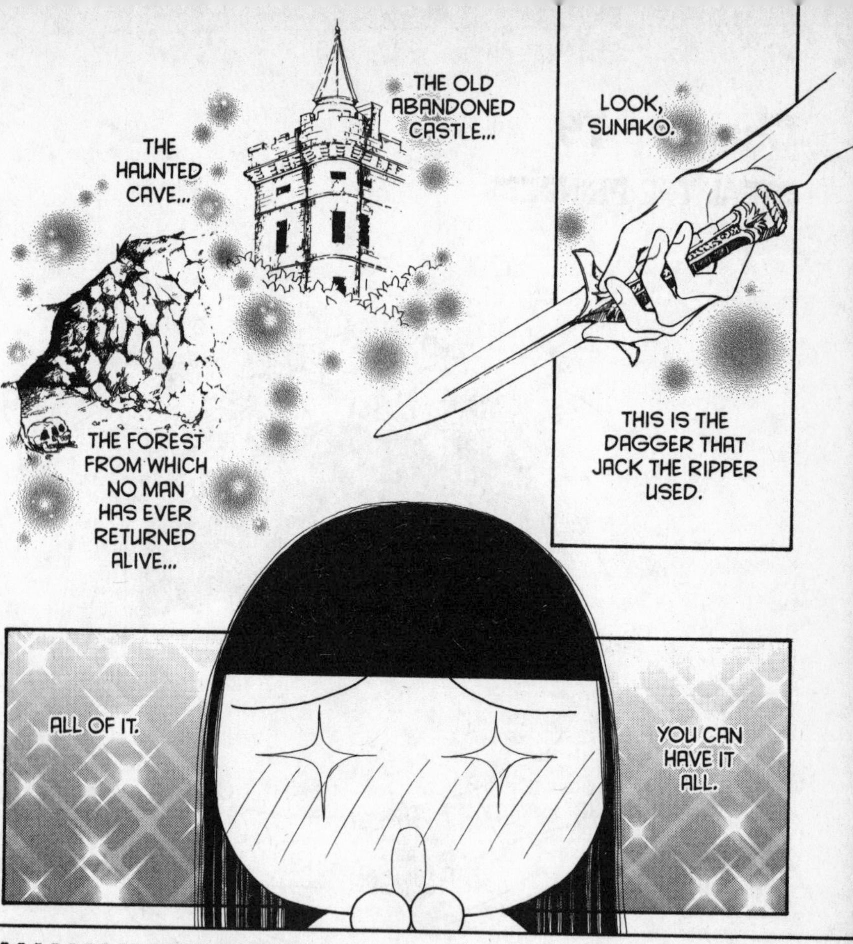
LOOK, SUNAKO.
THIS IS THE DAGGER THAT JACK THE RIPPER USED.
THE OLD ABANDONED CASTLE...
THE HAUNTED CAVE...
THE FOREST FROM WHICH NO MAN HAS EVER RETURNED ALIVE...
YOU CAN HAVE IT ALL.
ALL OF IT.

***BEHIND THE SCENES***

THANK YOU FOR BUYING KODANSHA COMICS. ♥

LET'S CELEBRATE. WE MADE IT TO VOLUME 20, AND IT'S ALL THANKS TO YOU GUYS. ♥ I WANNA THANK EVERYBODY WHO WROTE TO ME. ♥♥♥ YOU GIVE ME THE POWER TO KEEP GOING ON. I'M REALLY THANKFUL FOR ALL YOUR SUPPORT. ♥♥♥ IT'S THANKS TO YOU THAT I'M STILL WORKING!!! I'LL KEEP DOING MY BEST!!!

WHILE I WAS WRITING THIS STORY, A VERY, VERY SPECIAL FRIEND OF MINE GOT MARRIED, AND MOVED TO A FOREIGN LAND. CONGRATULATIONS ♥ IS WHAT I SHOULD BE SAYING . . . I'M SO HAPPY FOR YOU . . . IS WHAT I SHOULD BE FEELING . . . BUT I'M SO LONELY!!! COME BACK!!! JUST KIDDING. JUST KIDDING. SORRY. I WISH YOU NOTHING BUT HAPPINESS, M-SAN. ♥♥♥ TAKE GOOD CARE OF YOUR HUSBAND AND TETO (THE KITTY ♥) ♥♥♥

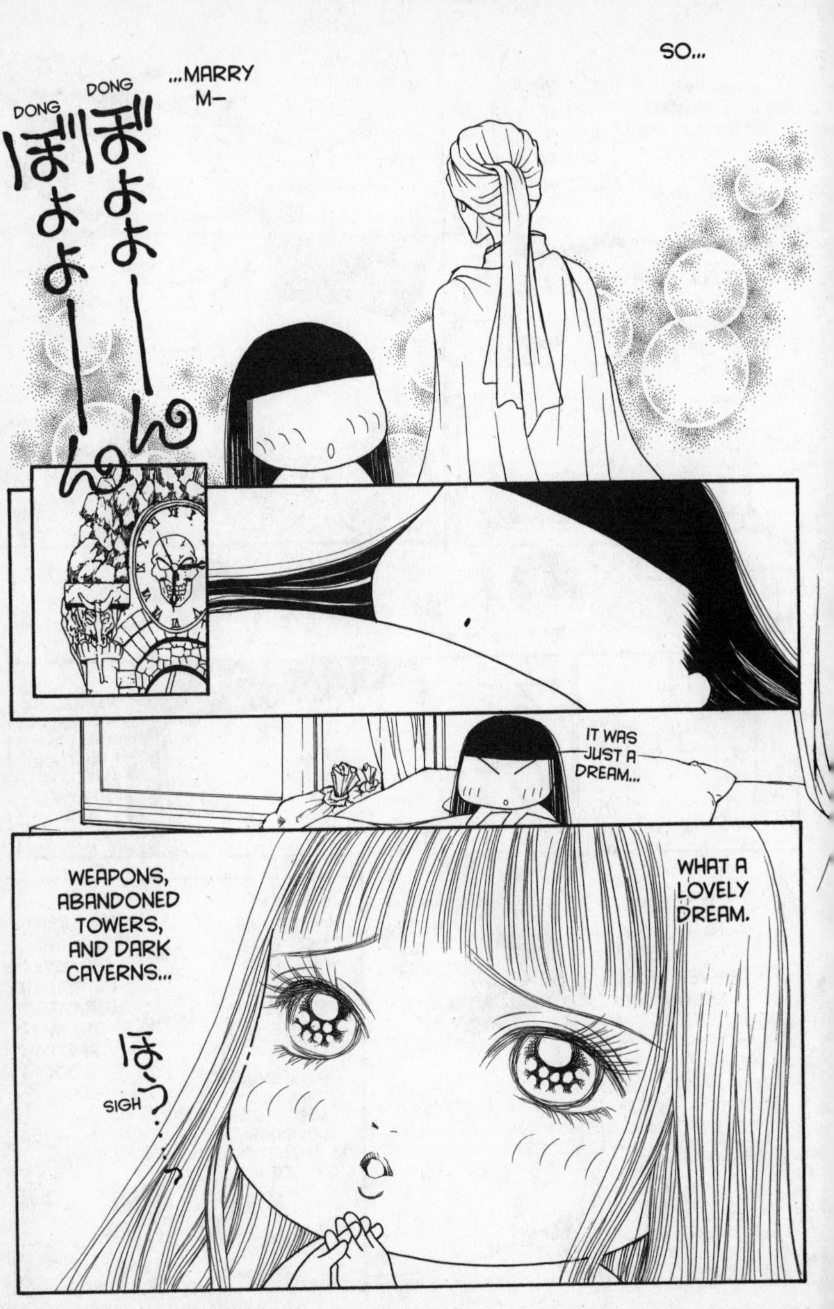
SO...
...MARRY M–
ぼよーん ぼよーん
DONG DONG
IT WAS JUST A DREAM...
WHAT A LOVELY DREAM.
WEAPONS, ABANDONED TOWERS, AND DARK CAVERNS...
ほう
SIGH

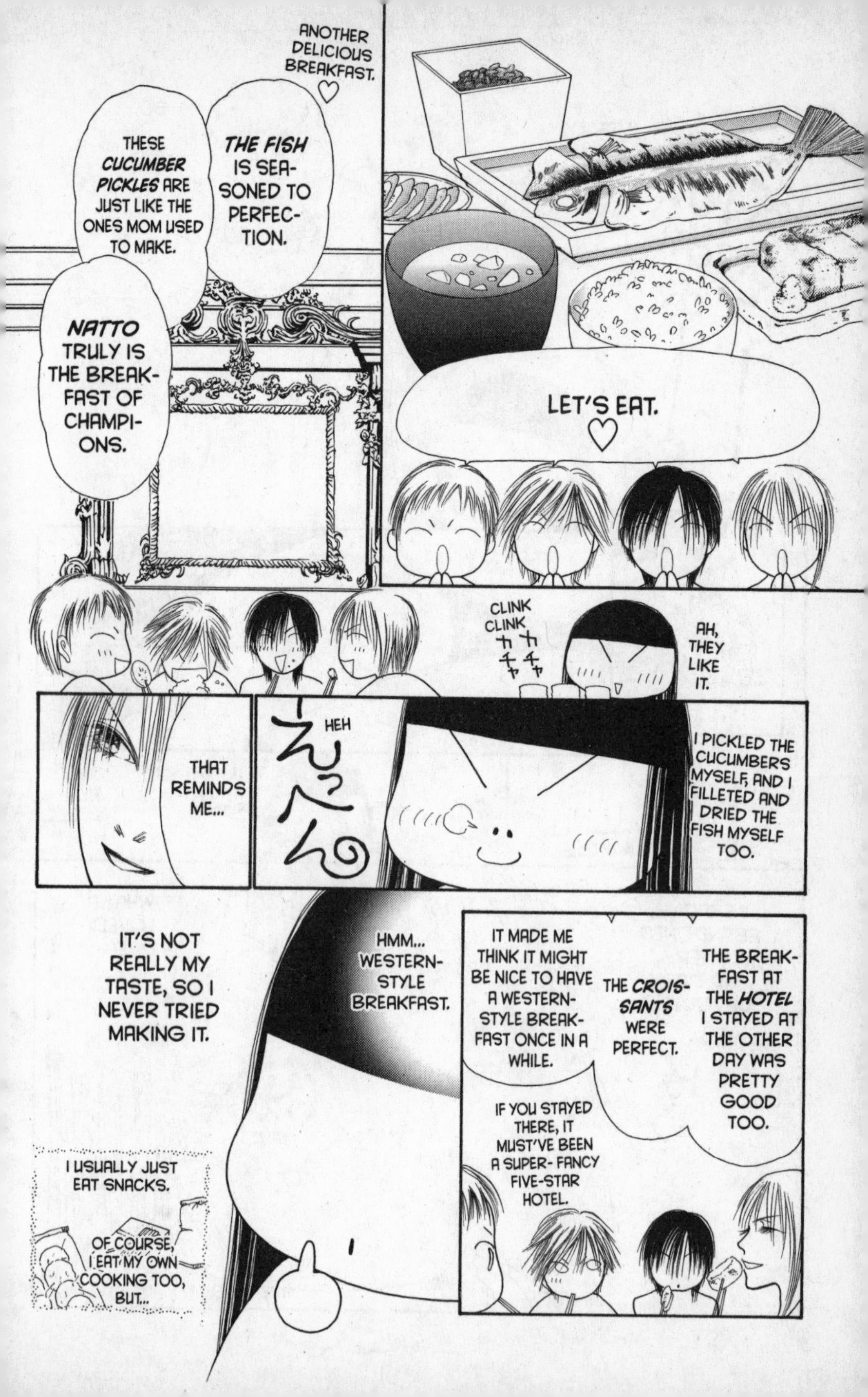

LET'S EAT. ♡
ANOTHER DELICIOUS BREAKFAST. ♡
THE FISH IS SEASONED TO PERFECTION.
THESE CUCUMBER PICKLES ARE JUST LIKE THE ONES MOM USED TO MAKE.
NATTO TRULY IS THE BREAKFAST OF CHAMPIONS.
AH, THEY LIKE IT.
CLINK CLINK
カチャ カチャ
I PICKLED THE CUCUMBERS MYSELF, AND I FILLETED AND DRIED THE FISH MYSELF TOO.
HEH
えっへん
THAT REMINDS ME...
THE BREAKFAST AT THE HOTEL I STAYED AT THE OTHER DAY WAS PRETTY GOOD TOO.
THE CROISSANTS WERE PERFECT.
IT MADE ME THINK IT MIGHT BE NICE TO HAVE A WESTERN-STYLE BREAKFAST ONCE IN A WHILE.
IF YOU STAYED THERE, IT MUST'VE BEEN A SUPER-FANCY FIVE-STAR HOTEL.
HMM... WESTERN-STYLE BREAKFAST.
IT'S NOT REALLY MY TASTE, SO I NEVER TRIED MAKING IT.
I USUALLY JUST EAT SNACKS.
OF COURSE, I EAT MY OWN COOKING TOO, BUT...

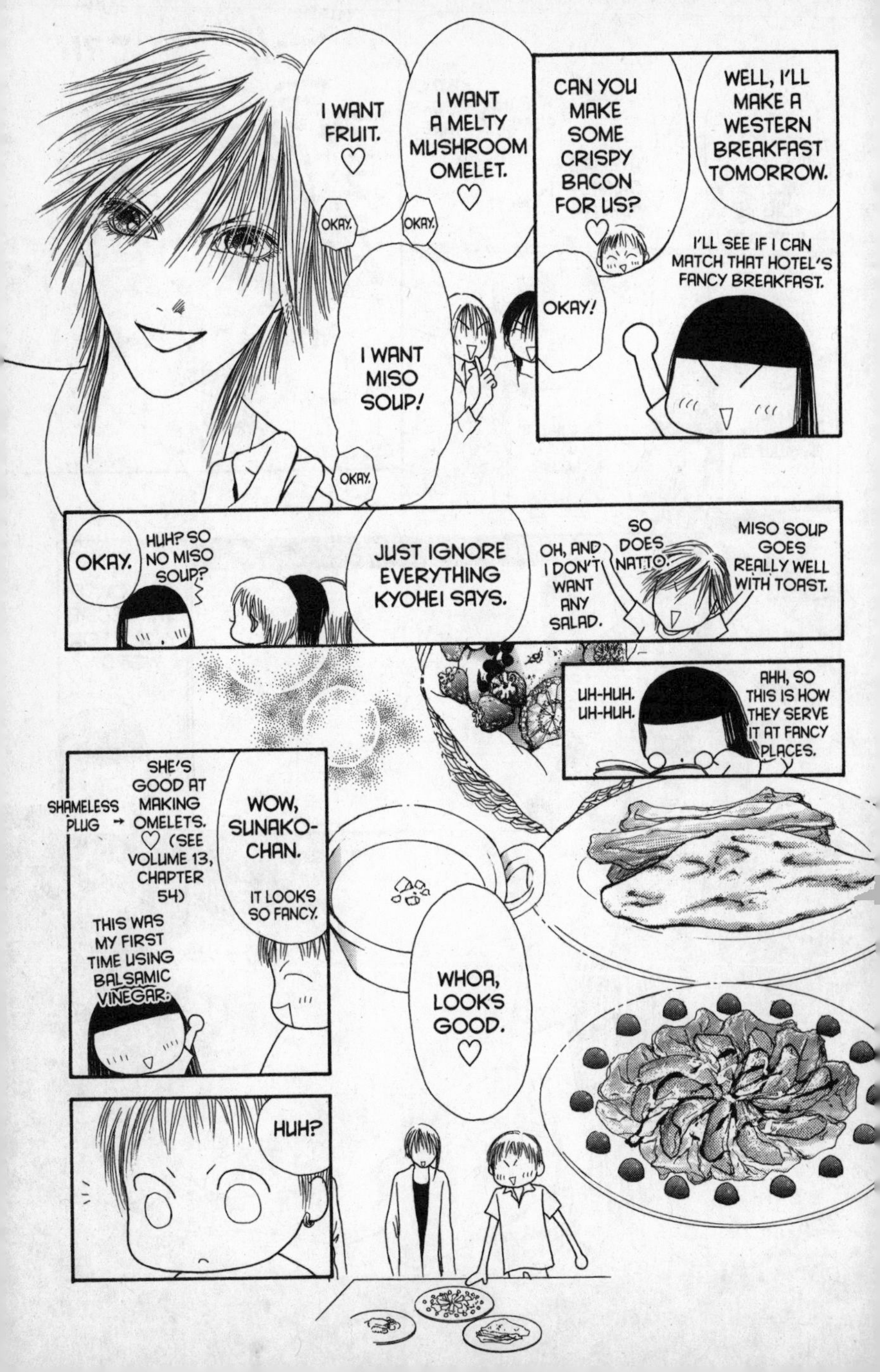

WELL, I'LL MAKE A WESTERN BREAKFAST TOMORROW.
I'LL SEE IF I CAN MATCH THAT HOTEL'S FANCY BREAKFAST.
CAN YOU MAKE SOME CRISPY BACON FOR US? ♡
OKAY!
I WANT A MELTY MUSHROOM OMELET. ♡
OKAY.
I WANT FRUIT. ♡
OKAY.
I WANT MISO SOUP!
OKAY.
MISO SOUP GOES REALLY WELL WITH TOAST.
SO DOES NATTO.
OH, AND I DON'T WANT ANY SALAD.
JUST IGNORE EVERYTHING KYOHEI SAYS.
HUH? SO NO MISO SOUP?
OKAY.
AHH, SO THIS IS HOW THEY SERVE IT AT FANCY PLACES.
UH-HUH. UH-HUH.
WHOA, LOOKS GOOD. ♡
WOW, SUNAKO-CHAN.
IT LOOKS SO FANCY.
SHE'S GOOD AT MAKING OMELETS. ♡ (SEE VOLUME 13, CHAPTER 54)
SHAMELESS PLUG →
THIS WAS MY FIRST TIME USING BALSAMIC VINEGAR.
HUH?

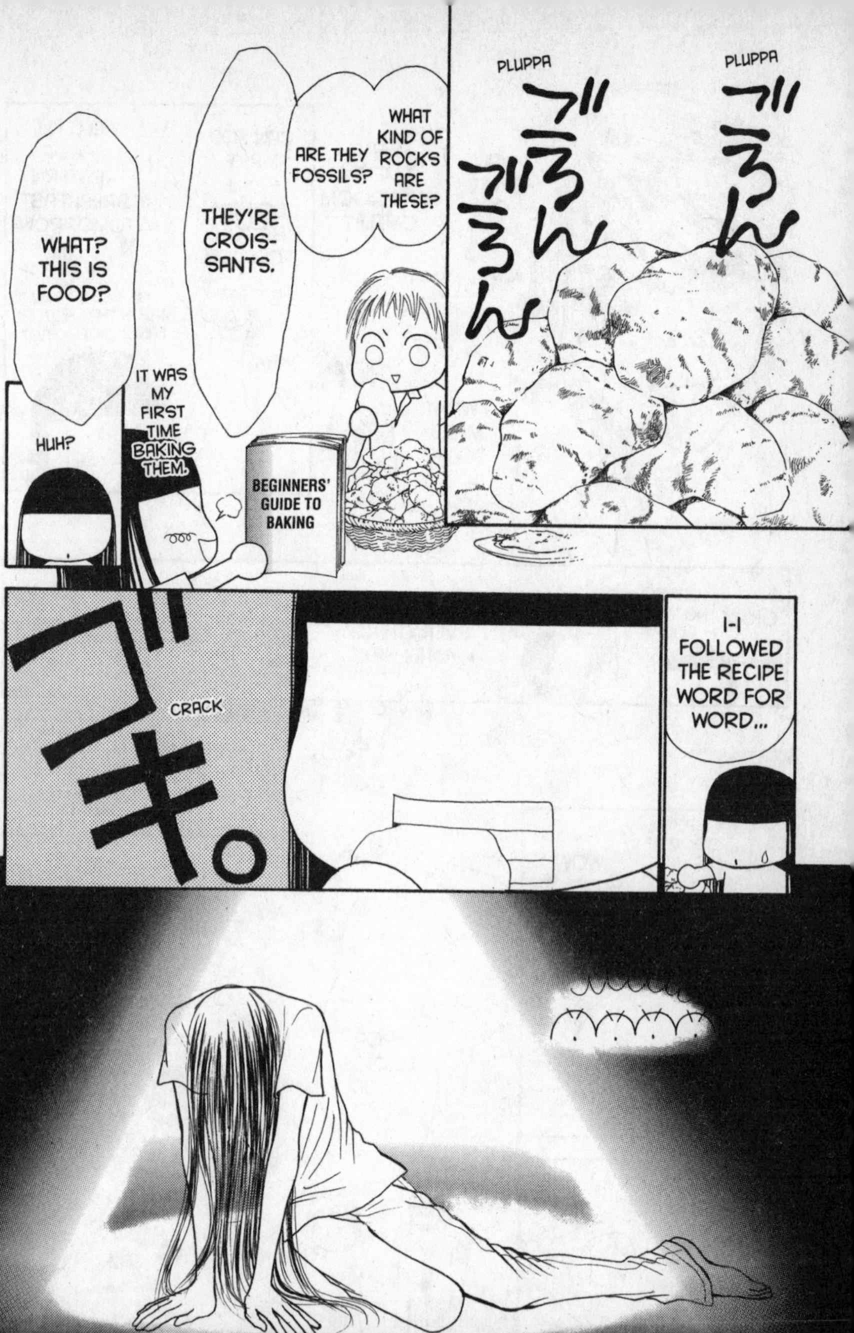
PLUPPA
ごろん
PLUPPA
ごろん
WHAT KIND OF ROCKS ARE THESE?
ARE THEY FOSSILS?
THEY'RE CROIS-SANTS.
WHAT? THIS IS FOOD?
IT WAS MY FIRST TIME BAKING THEM.
HUH?
BEGINNERS' GUIDE TO BAKING
I-I FOLLOWED THE RECIPE WORD FOR WORD...
CRACK
ゴキ。

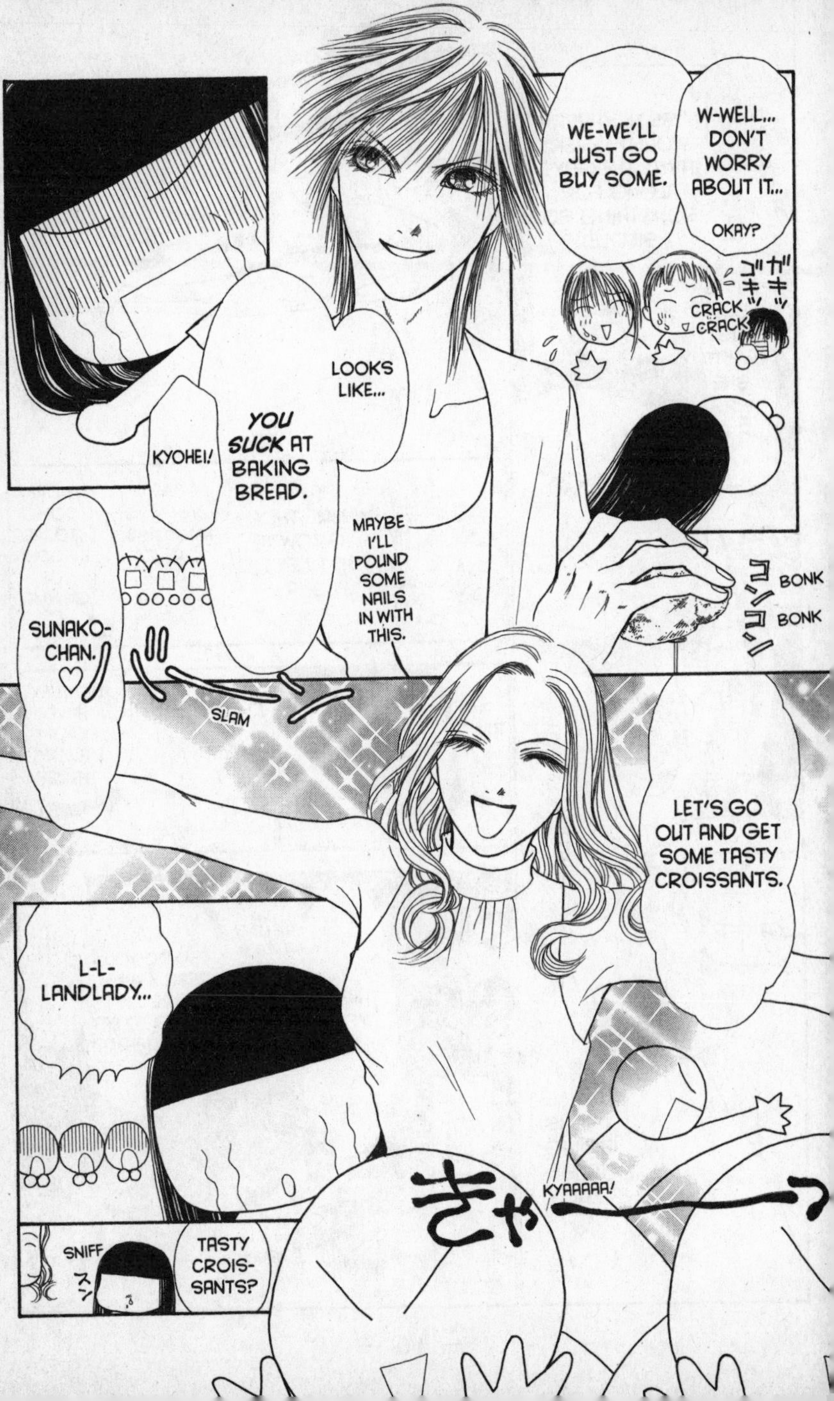
W-WELL... DON'T WORRY ABOUT IT... OKAY?
WE-WE'LL JUST GO BUY SOME.
ガキッ ゴキッ
CRACK CRACK
LOOKS LIKE...
YOU SUCK AT BAKING BREAD.
MAYBE I'LL POUND SOME NAILS IN WITH THIS.
コンコン
BONK BONK
KYOHEI!
SUNAKO-CHAN. ♡
SLAM
LET'S GO OUT AND GET SOME TASTY CROISSANTS.
きゃーっ
KYAAAAA!
L-L-LANDLADY...
TASTY CROIS-SANTS?
スン
SNIFF

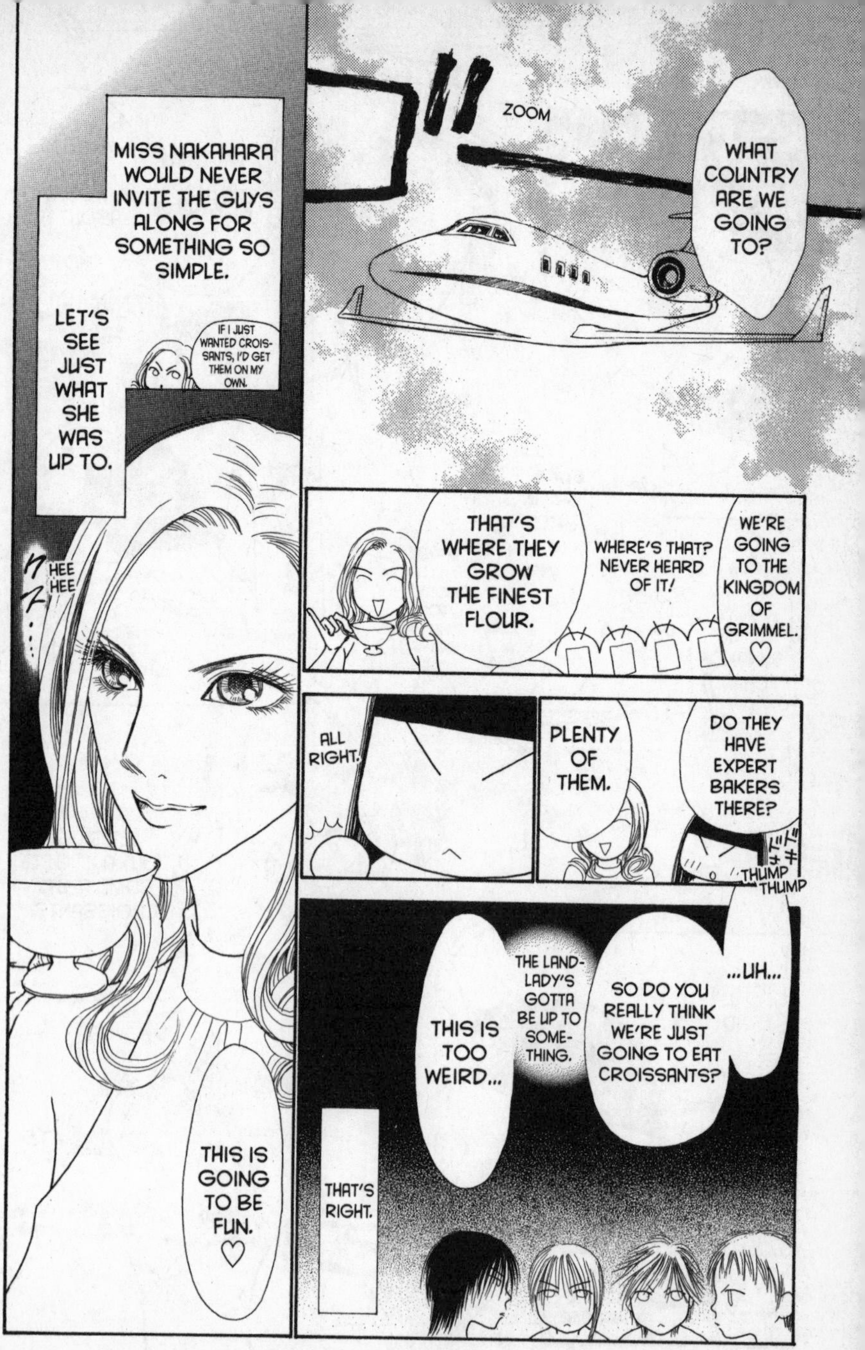
ZOOM
WHAT COUNTRY ARE WE GOING TO?
WE'RE GOING TO THE KINGDOM OF GRIMMEL. ♡
WHERE'S THAT? NEVER HEARD OF IT!
THAT'S WHERE THEY GROW THE FINEST FLOUR.
DO THEY HAVE EXPERT BAKERS THERE?
PLENTY OF THEM.
THUMP THUMP
ALL RIGHT.
...UH...
SO DO YOU REALLY THINK WE'RE JUST GOING TO EAT CROISSANTS?
THE LANDLADY'S GOTTA BE UP TO SOMETHING.
THIS IS TOO WEIRD...
THAT'S RIGHT.
MISS NAKAHARA WOULD NEVER INVITE THE GUYS ALONG FOR SOMETHING SO SIMPLE.
IF I JUST WANTED CROISSANTS, I'D GET THEM ON MY OWN.
LET'S SEE JUST WHAT SHE WAS UP TO.
HEE HEE
THIS IS GOING TO BE FUN. ♡

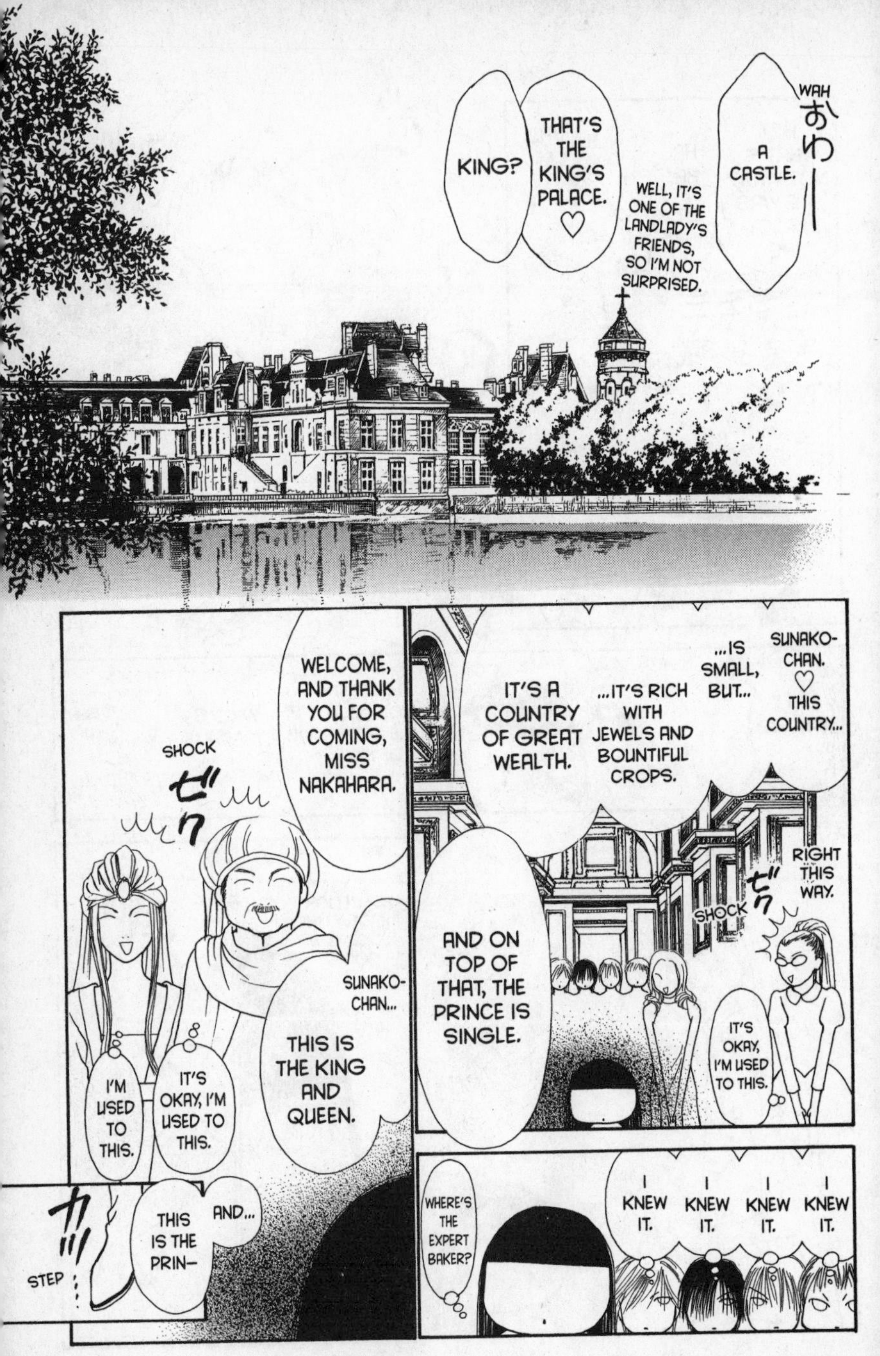

WAH
おわー
A CASTLE.
WELL, IT'S ONE OF THE LANDLADY'S FRIENDS, SO I'M NOT SURPRISED.
THAT'S THE KING'S PALACE. ♡
KING?
SUNAKO-CHAN. ♡ THIS COUNTRY...
...IS SMALL, BUT...
...IT'S RICH WITH JEWELS AND BOUNTIFUL CROPS.
IT'S A COUNTRY OF GREAT WEALTH.
RIGHT THIS WAY.
SHOCK
ゼク
AND ON TOP OF THAT, THE PRINCE IS SINGLE.
IT'S OKAY, I'M USED TO THIS.
WELCOME, AND THANK YOU FOR COMING, MISS NAKAHARA.
SHOCK
ゼク
SUNAKO-CHAN...
THIS IS THE KING AND QUEEN.
IT'S OKAY, I'M USED TO THIS.
I'M USED TO THIS.
I KNEW IT.
I KNEW IT.
I KNEW IT.
I KNEW IT.
WHERE'S THE EXPERT BAKER?
AND...
THIS IS THE PRIN-
STEP
カッ

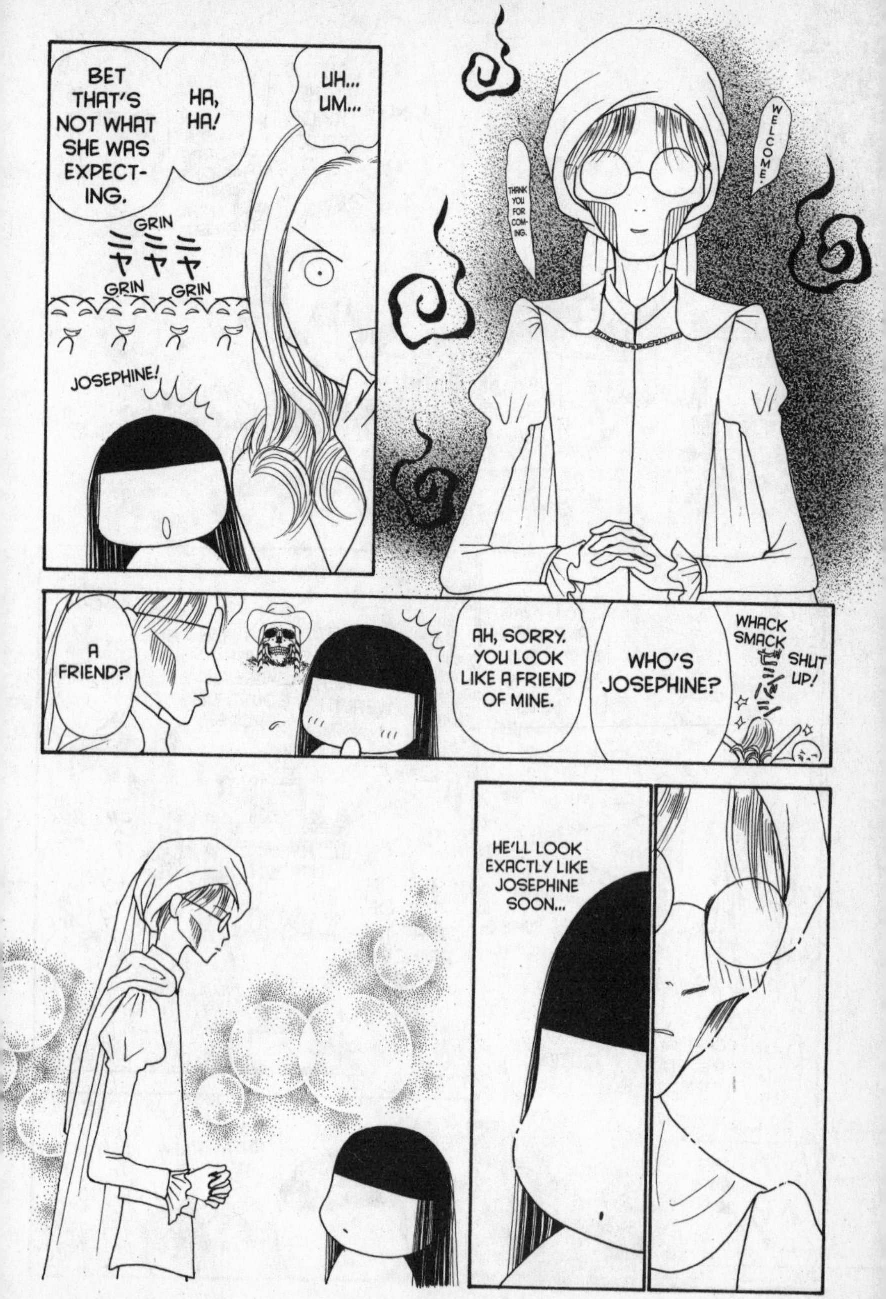
WELCOME.
THANK YOU FOR COMING.
UH... UM...
HA, HA!
BET THAT'S NOT WHAT SHE WAS EXPECT-ING.
GRIN
ニヤニヤニヤ
GRIN GRIN
JOSEPHINE!
WHACK SMACK
SHUT UP!
WHO'S JOSEPHINE?
AH, SORRY. YOU LOOK LIKE A FRIEND OF MINE.
A FRIEND?
HE'LL LOOK EXACTLY LIKE JOSEPHINE SOON...

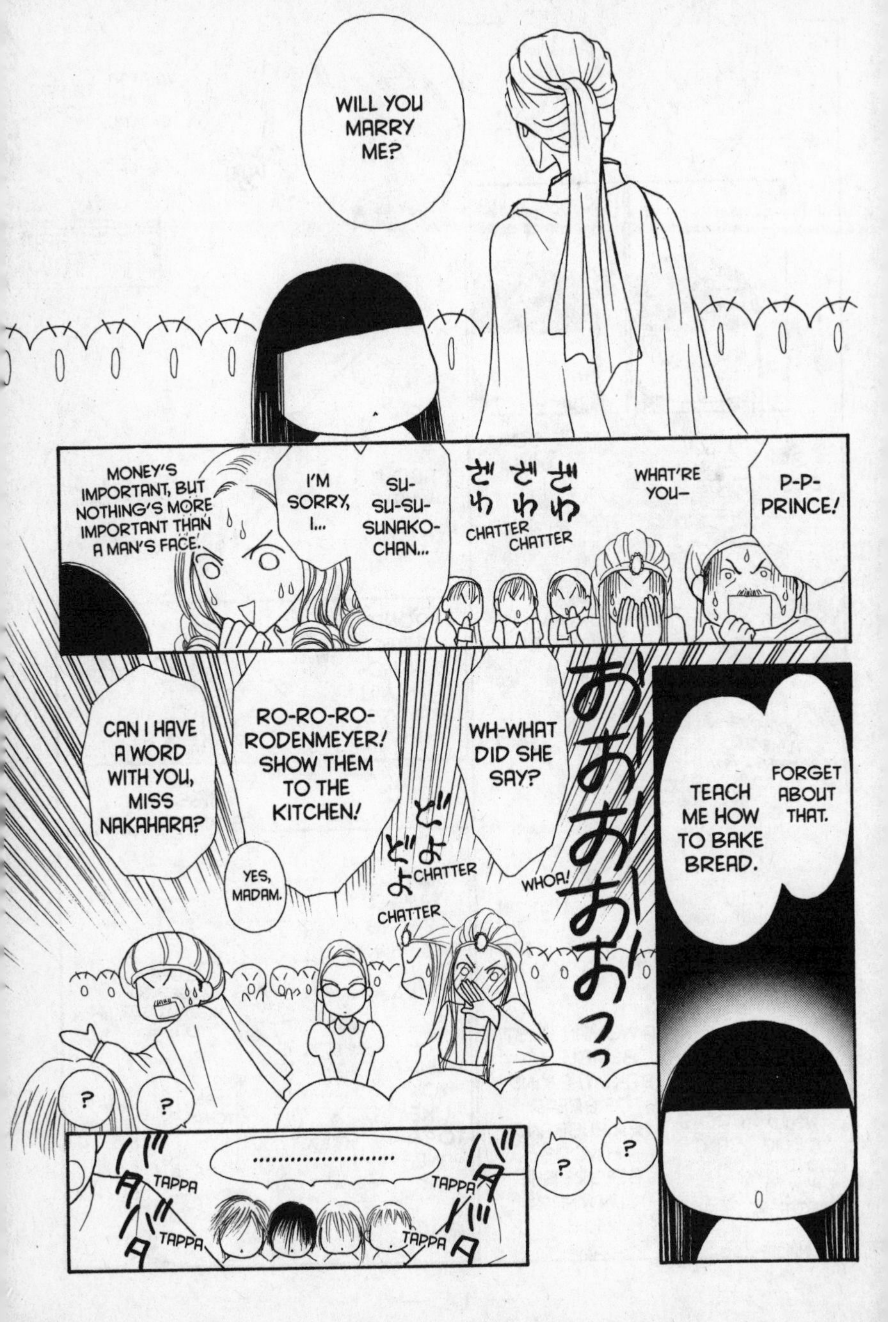
WILL YOU MARRY ME?
P-P-PRINCE!
WHAT'RE YOU–
ざわざわざわ
CHATTER CHATTER
SU-SU-SU-SUNAKO-CHAN...
I'M SORRY, I...
MONEY'S IMPORTANT, BUT NOTHING'S MORE IMPORTANT THAN A MAN'S FACE!
FORGET ABOUT THAT.
TEACH ME HOW TO BAKE BREAD.
おおおおおっ
WH-WHAT DID SHE SAY?
WHOA!
RO-RO-RO-RODENMEYER! SHOW THEM TO THE KITCHEN!
どよどよ
CHATTER CHATTER
YES, MADAM.
CAN I HAVE A WORD WITH YOU, MISS NAKAHARA?
?
?
?
?
バタバタ
TAPPA TAPPA
......................
バタバタ
TAPPA TAPPA

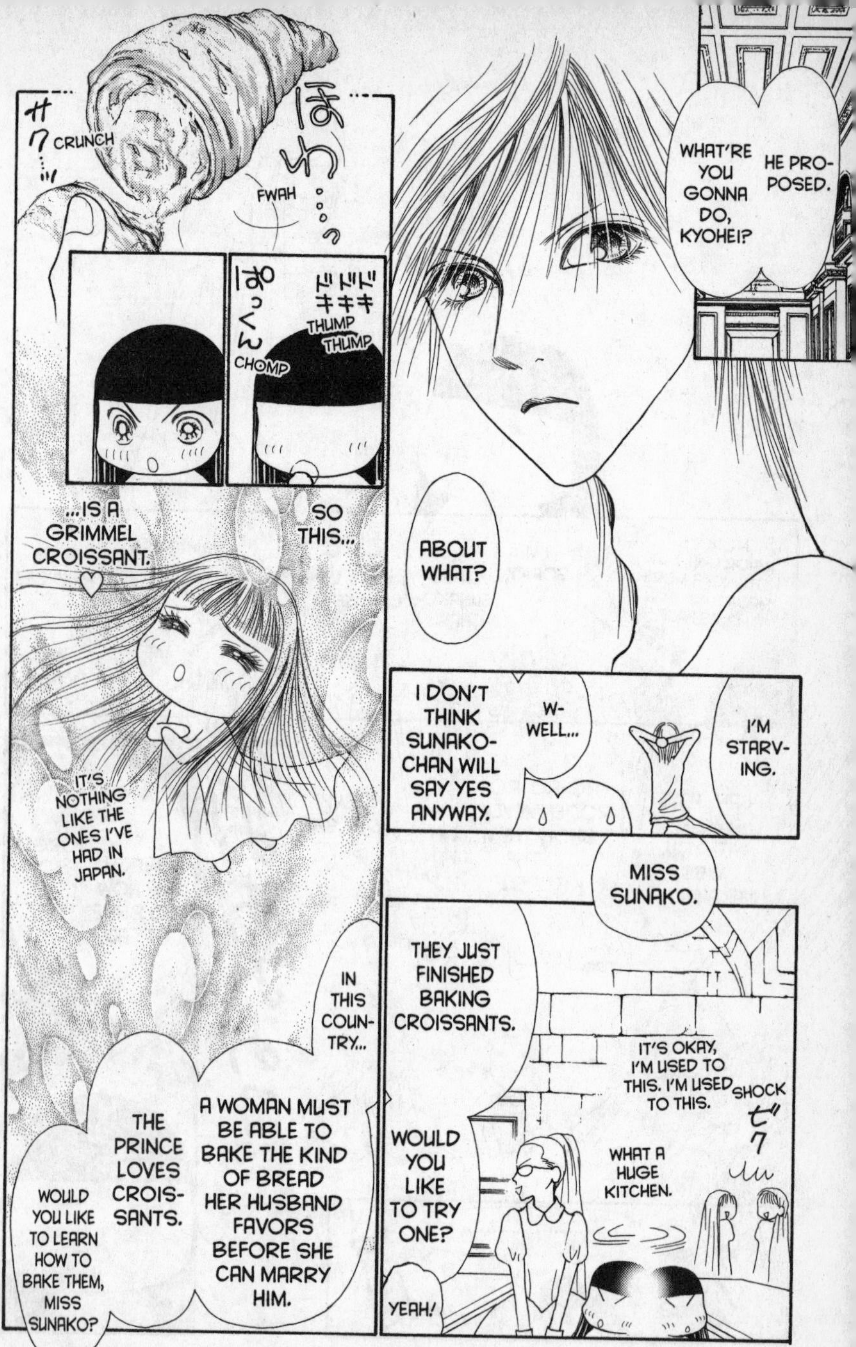
HE PROPOSED.
WHAT'RE YOU GONNA DO, KYOHEI?
ABOUT WHAT?
I'M STARVING.
W-WELL...
I DON'T THINK SUNAKO-CHAN WILL SAY YES ANYWAY.
MISS SUNAKO.
THEY JUST FINISHED BAKING CROISSANTS.
WOULD YOU LIKE TO TRY ONE?
YEAH!
ビク
SHOCK
IT'S OKAY, I'M USED TO THIS. I'M USED TO THIS.
WHAT A HUGE KITCHEN.
ほわ…っ
FWAH
サク…
CRUNCH
ドキドキドキ
THUMP THUMP
ぱっくん
CHOMP
SO THIS...
...IS A GRIMMEL CROISSANT.
IT'S NOTHING LIKE THE ONES I'VE HAD IN JAPAN.
IN THIS COUNTRY...
THE PRINCE LOVES CROISSANTS.
A WOMAN MUST BE ABLE TO BAKE THE KIND OF BREAD HER HUSBAND FAVORS BEFORE SHE CAN MARRY HIM.
WOULD YOU LIKE TO LEARN HOW TO BAKE THEM, MISS SUNAKO?

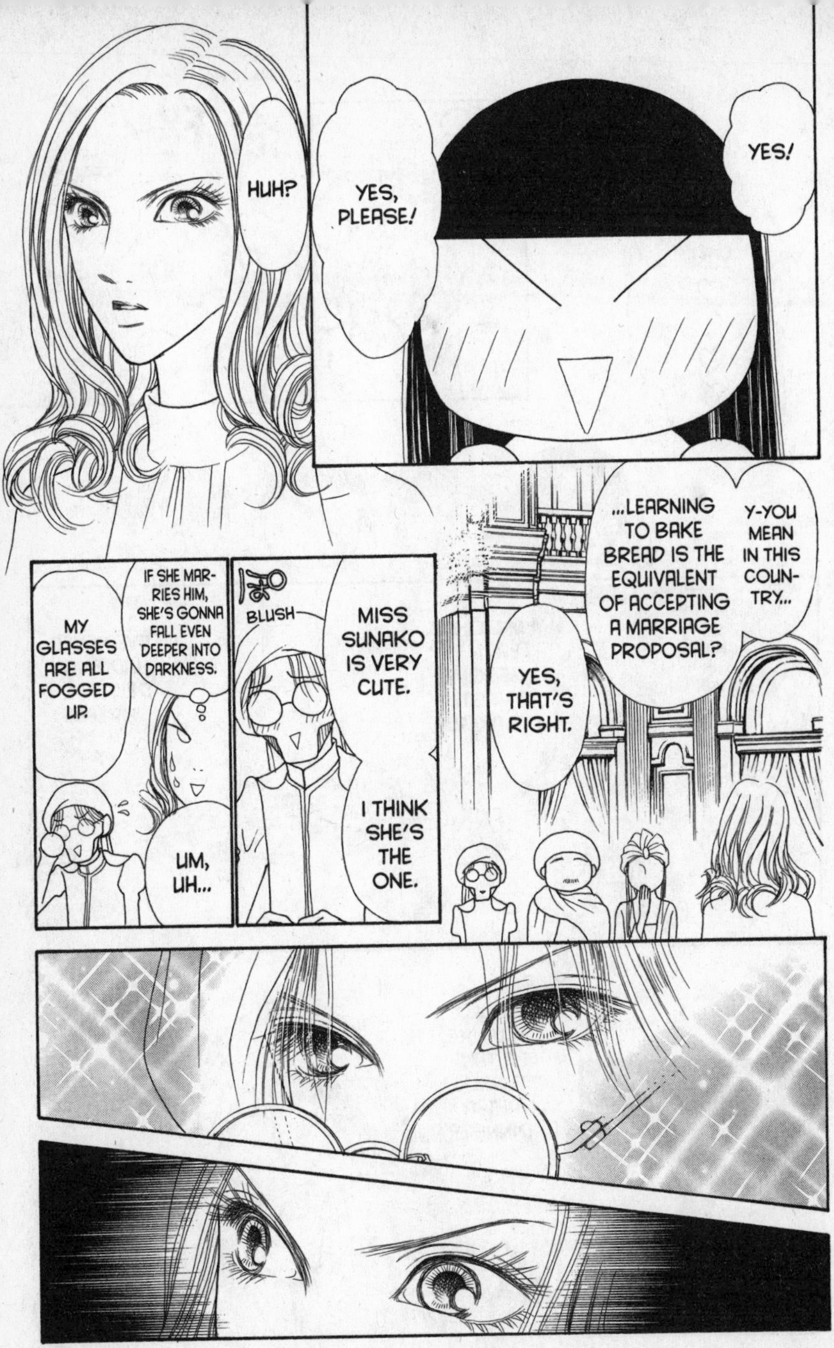
YES!
YES, PLEASE!
HUH?
Y-YOU MEAN IN THIS COUNTRY...
...LEARNING TO BAKE BREAD IS THE EQUIVALENT OF ACCEPTING A MARRIAGE PROPOSAL?
YES, THAT'S RIGHT.
MISS SUNAKO IS VERY CUTE.
BLUSH
I THINK SHE'S THE ONE.
IF SHE MARRIES HIM, SHE'S GONNA FALL EVEN DEEPER INTO DARKNESS.
MY GLASSES ARE ALL FOGGED UP.
UM, UH...

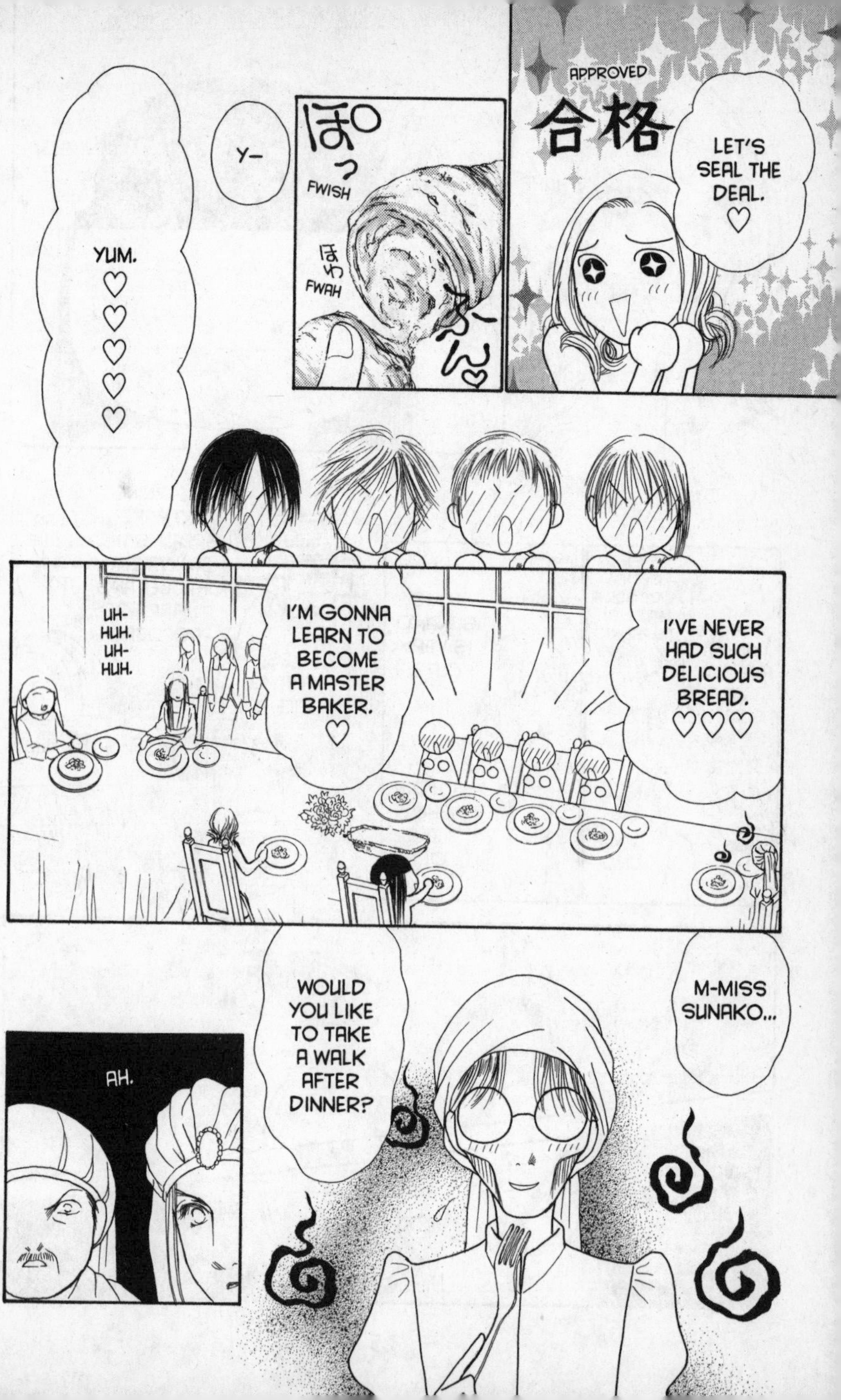
APPROVED
合格
LET'S SEAL THE DEAL. ♡
ぽっ
FWISH
ほわ
FWAH
ふ～ん♡
Y-
YUM. ♡ ♡ ♡ ♡ ♡
I'VE NEVER HAD SUCH DELICIOUS BREAD. ♡♡♡
I'M GONNA LEARN TO BECOME A MASTER BAKER. ♡
UH-HUH. UH-HUH.
M-MISS SUNAKO...
WOULD YOU LIKE TO TAKE A WALK AFTER DINNER?
AH.

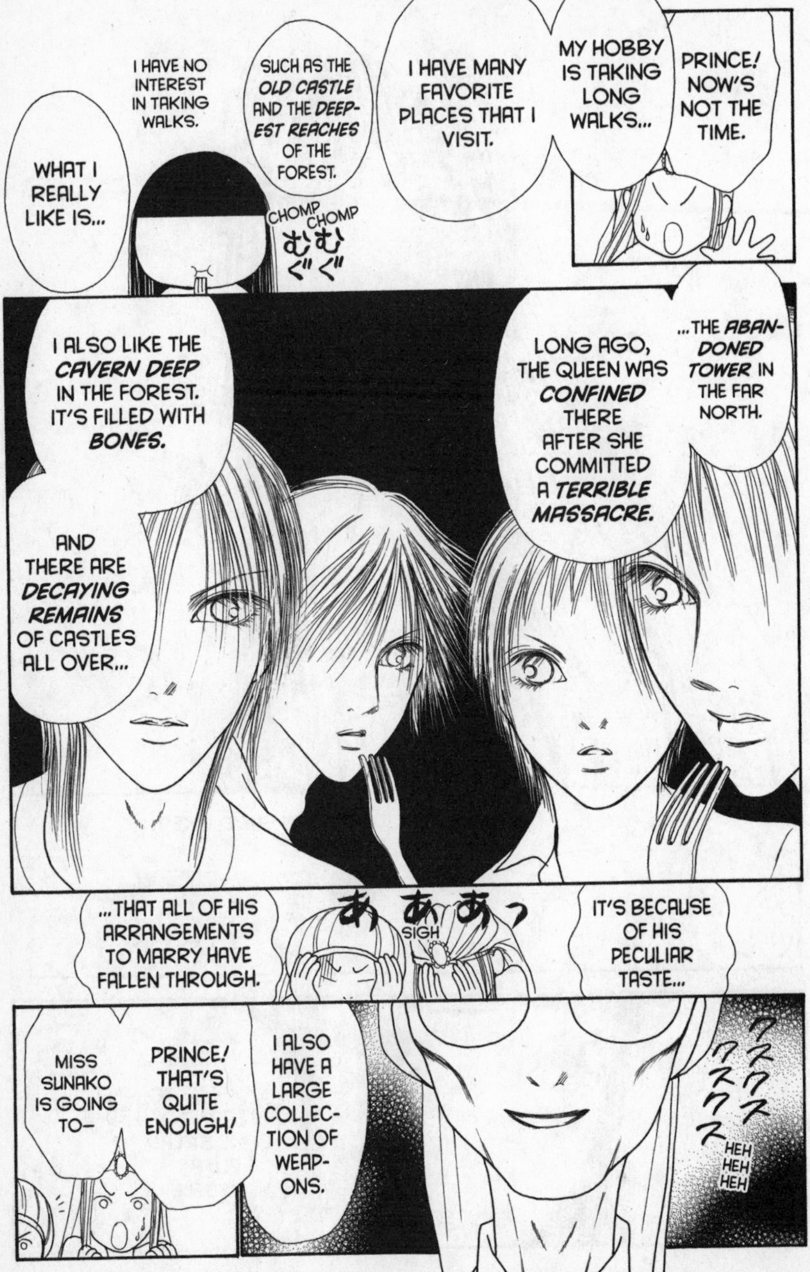
PRINCE! NOW'S NOT THE TIME.
MY HOBBY IS TAKING LONG WALKS...
I HAVE MANY FAVORITE PLACES THAT I VISIT.
SUCH AS THE OLD CASTLE AND THE DEEPEST REACHES OF THE FOREST.
I HAVE NO INTEREST IN TAKING WALKS.
むぐむぐ
CHOMP CHOMP
WHAT I REALLY LIKE IS...
...THE ABANDONED TOWER IN THE FAR NORTH.
LONG AGO, THE QUEEN WAS CONFINED THERE AFTER SHE COMMITTED A TERRIBLE MASSACRE.
I ALSO LIKE THE CAVERN DEEP IN THE FOREST. IT'S FILLED WITH BONES.
AND THERE ARE DECAYING REMAINS OF CASTLES ALL OVER...
IT'S BECAUSE OF HIS PECULIAR TASTE...
あああっ
SIGH
...THAT ALL OF HIS ARRANGEMENTS TO MARRY HAVE FALLEN THROUGH.
HEH HEH HEH
I ALSO HAVE A LARGE COLLECTION OF WEAPONS.
PRINCE! THAT'S QUITE ENOUGH!
MISS SUNAKO IS GOING TO—

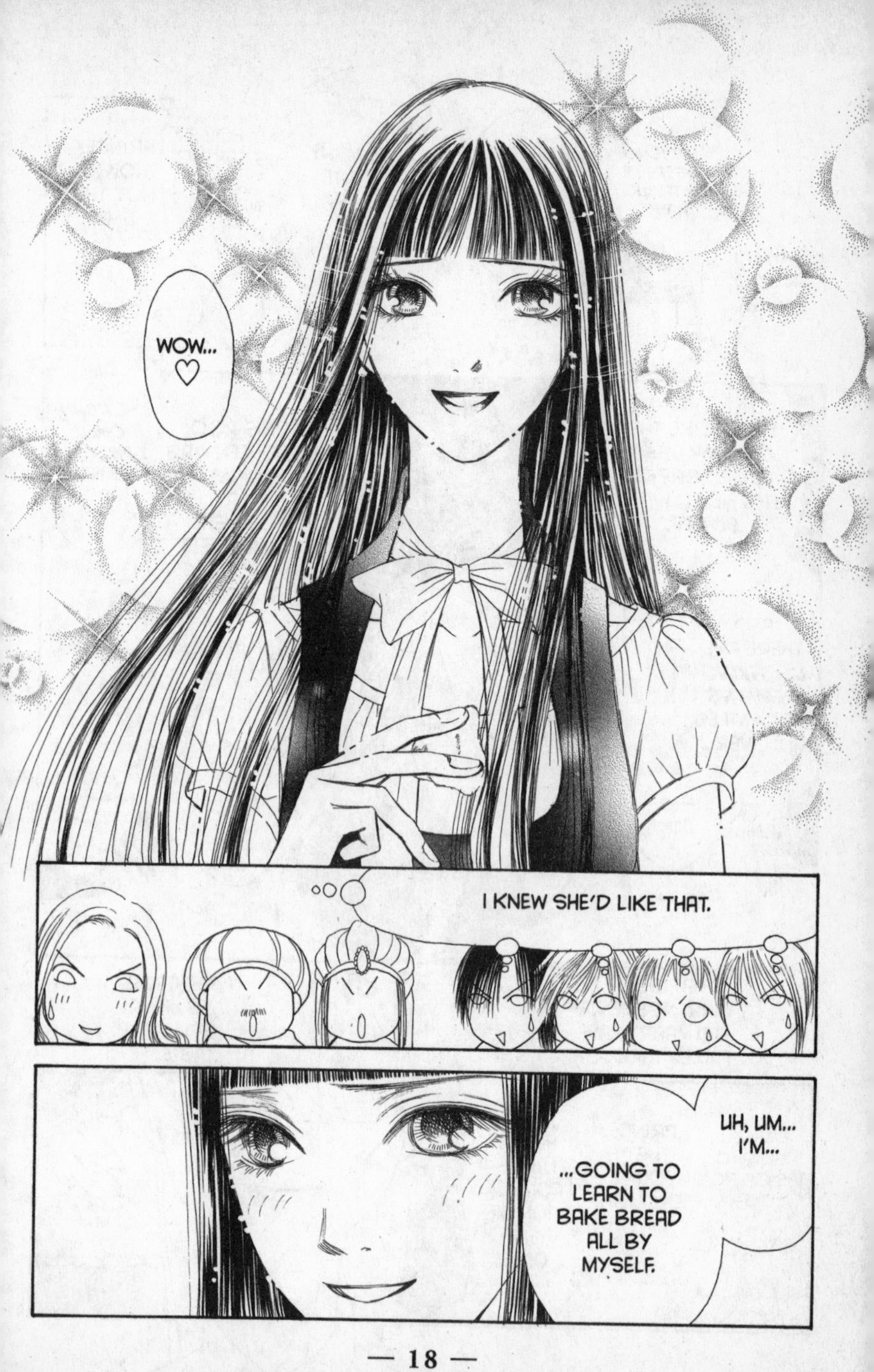

WOW... ♡
I KNEW SHE'D LIKE THAT.
UH, UM... I'M...
...GOING TO LEARN TO BAKE BREAD ALL BY MYSELF.

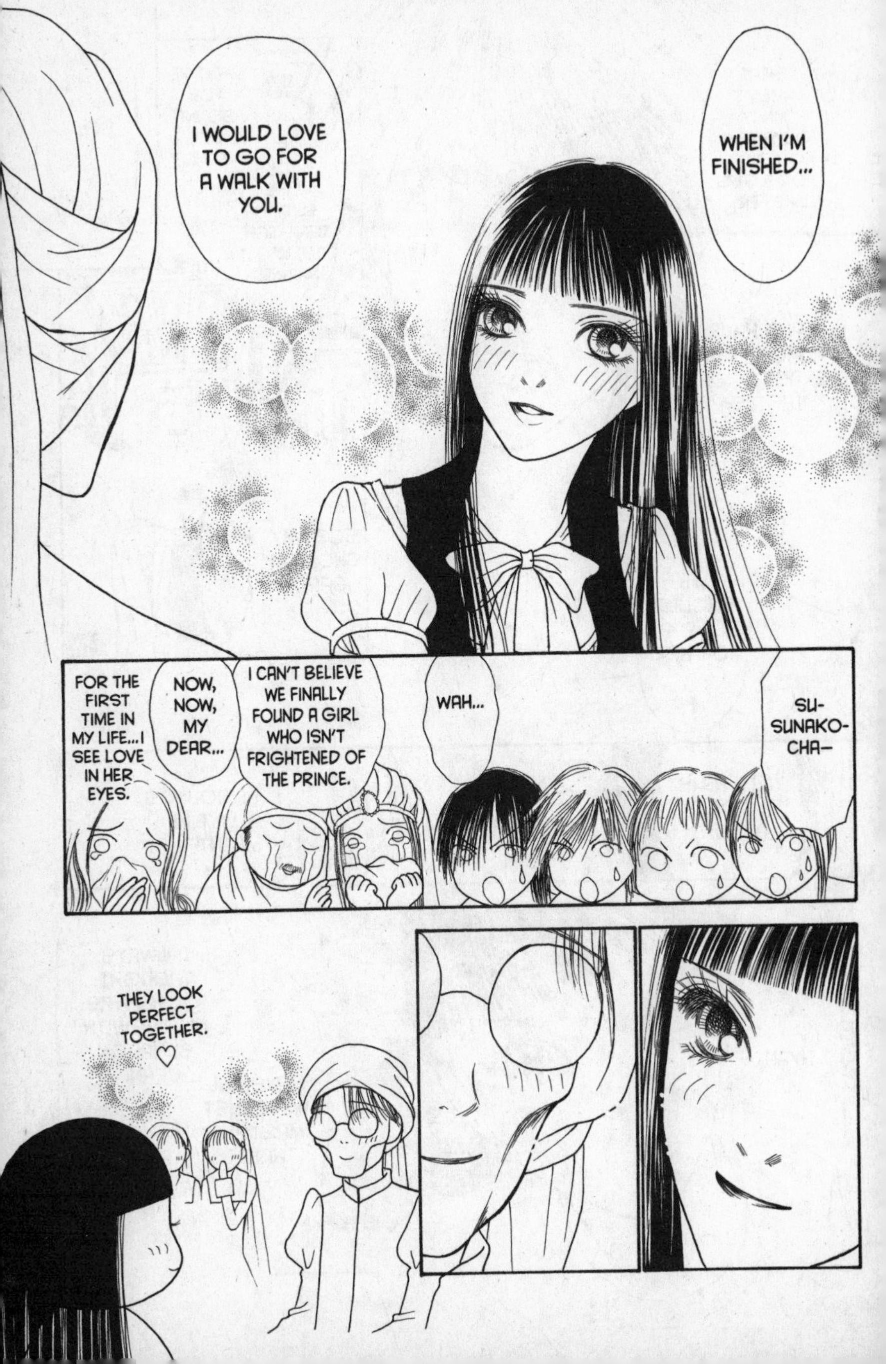
WHEN I'M FINISHED...
I WOULD LOVE TO GO FOR A WALK WITH YOU.
SU-SUNAKO-CHA-
WAH...
I CAN'T BELIEVE WE FINALLY FOUND A GIRL WHO ISN'T FRIGHTENED OF THE PRINCE.
NOW, NOW, MY DEAR...
FOR THE FIRST TIME IN MY LIFE...I SEE LOVE IN HER EYES.
THEY LOOK PERFECT TOGETHER. ♡

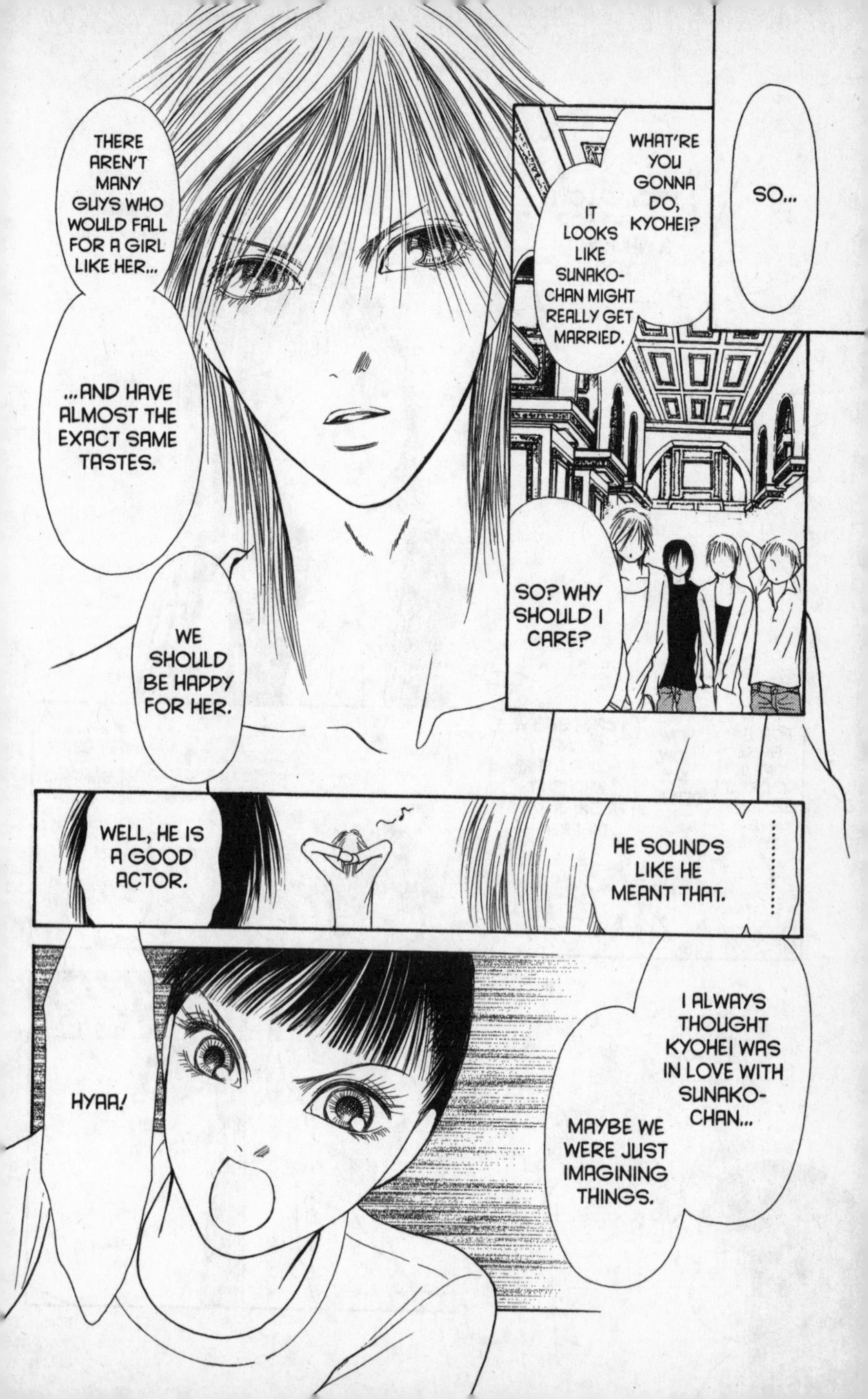
SO...
WHAT'RE YOU GONNA DO, KYOHEI?
IT LOOKS LIKE SUNAKO-CHAN MIGHT REALLY GET MARRIED.
SO? WHY SHOULD I CARE?
THERE AREN'T MANY GUYS WHO WOULD FALL FOR A GIRL LIKE HER...
...AND HAVE ALMOST THE EXACT SAME TASTES.
WE SHOULD BE HAPPY FOR HER.
......
HE SOUNDS LIKE HE MEANT THAT.
WELL, HE IS A GOOD ACTOR.
I ALWAYS THOUGHT KYOHEI WAS IN LOVE WITH SUNAKO-CHAN...
MAYBE WE WERE JUST IMAGINING THINGS.
HYAA!

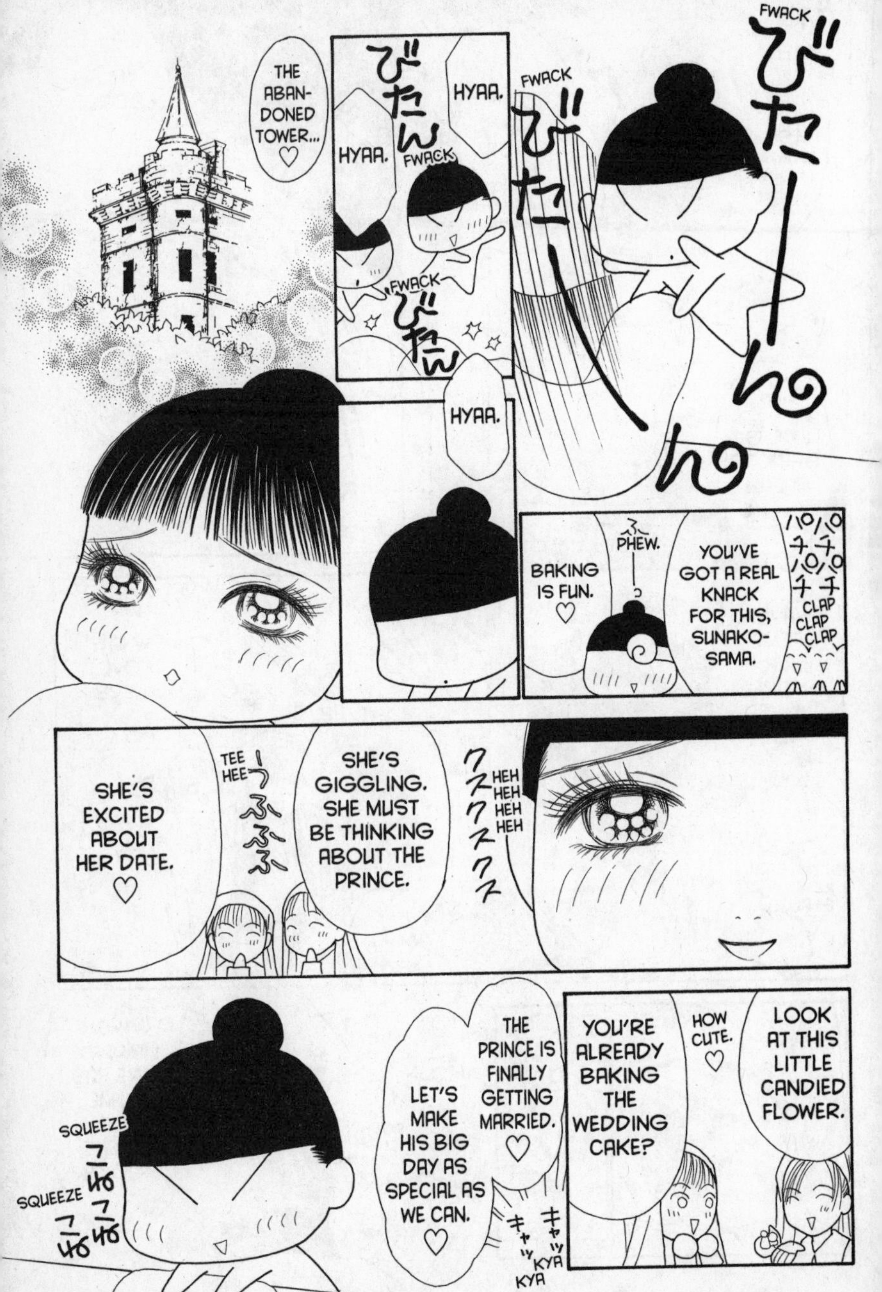

FWACK
びたーん
FWACK
びたーん
HYAA.
びたん
HYAA.
FWACK
FWACK
びたん
THE ABANDONED TOWER... ♡
HYAA.
YOU'VE GOT A REAL KNACK FOR THIS, SUNAKO-SAMA.
パチパチパチパチ
CLAP CLAP CLAP
ふ
PHEW.
BAKING IS FUN. ♡
ククククク
HEH HEH HEH HEH
SHE'S GIGGLING. SHE MUST BE THINKING ABOUT THE PRINCE.
うふふ
TEE HEE
SHE'S EXCITED ABOUT HER DATE. ♡
LOOK AT THIS LITTLE CANDIED FLOWER.
HOW CUTE. ♡
YOU'RE ALREADY BAKING THE WEDDING CAKE?
THE PRINCE IS FINALLY GETTING MARRIED. ♡
LET'S MAKE HIS BIG DAY AS SPECIAL AS WE CAN. ♡
キャッキャッ
KYA KYA
SQUEEZE
SQUEEZE

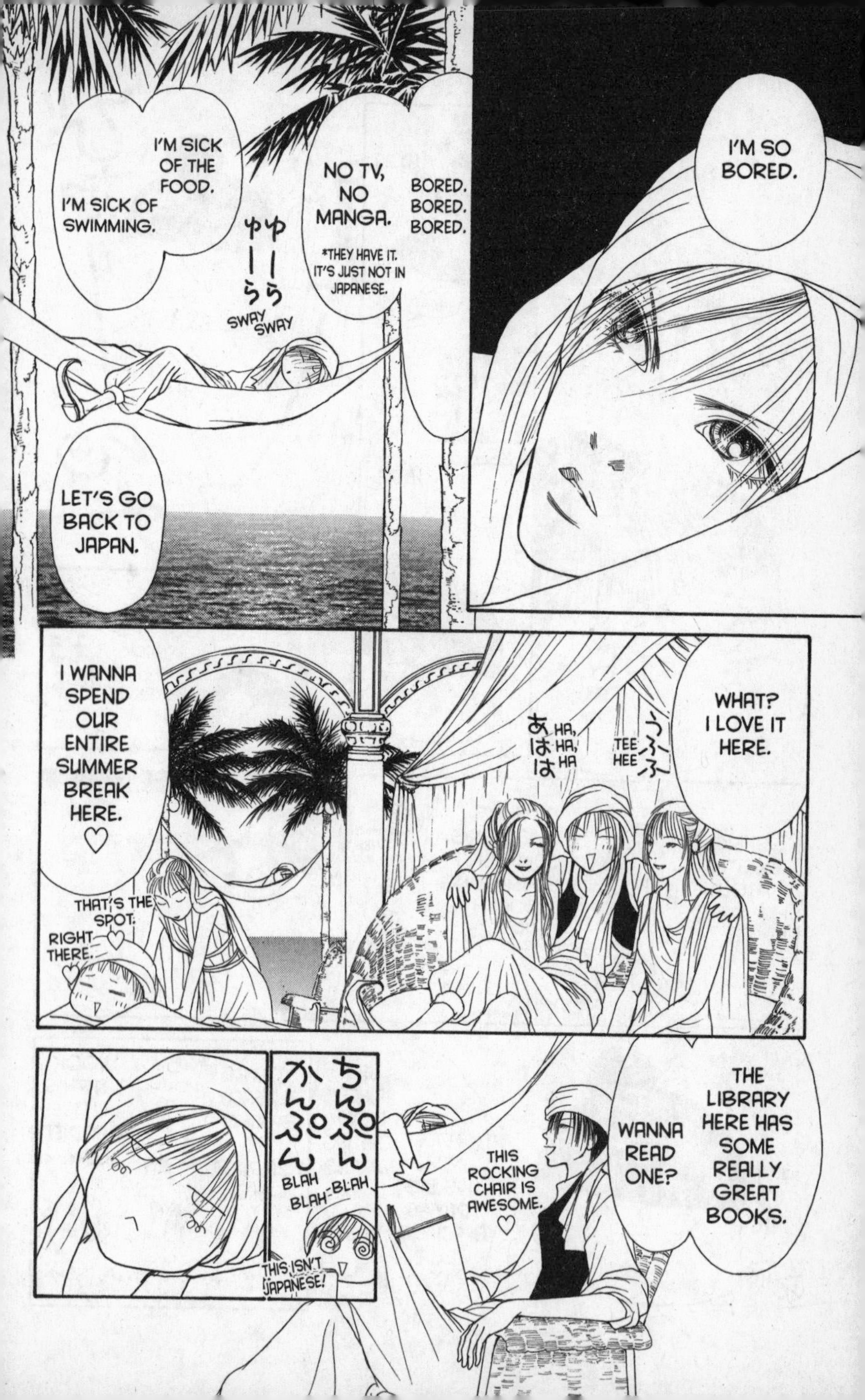
I'M SO BORED.
BORED. BORED. BORED.
NO TV, NO MANGA.
*THEY HAVE IT. IT'S JUST NOT IN JAPANESE.
I'M SICK OF THE FOOD.
I'M SICK OF SWIMMING.
ゆーらゆーら
SWAY SWAY
LET'S GO BACK TO JAPAN.
WHAT? I LOVE IT HERE.
うふふ
TEE HEE
あはは
HA, HA, HA
I WANNA SPEND OUR ENTIRE SUMMER BREAK HERE. ♡
THAT'S THE SPOT.
RIGHT THERE. ♡
THE LIBRARY HERE HAS SOME REALLY GREAT BOOKS.
WANNA READ ONE?
THIS ROCKING CHAIR IS AWESOME. ♡
ちんぷんかんぷん
BLAH BLAH BLAH
THIS ISN'T JAPANESE!

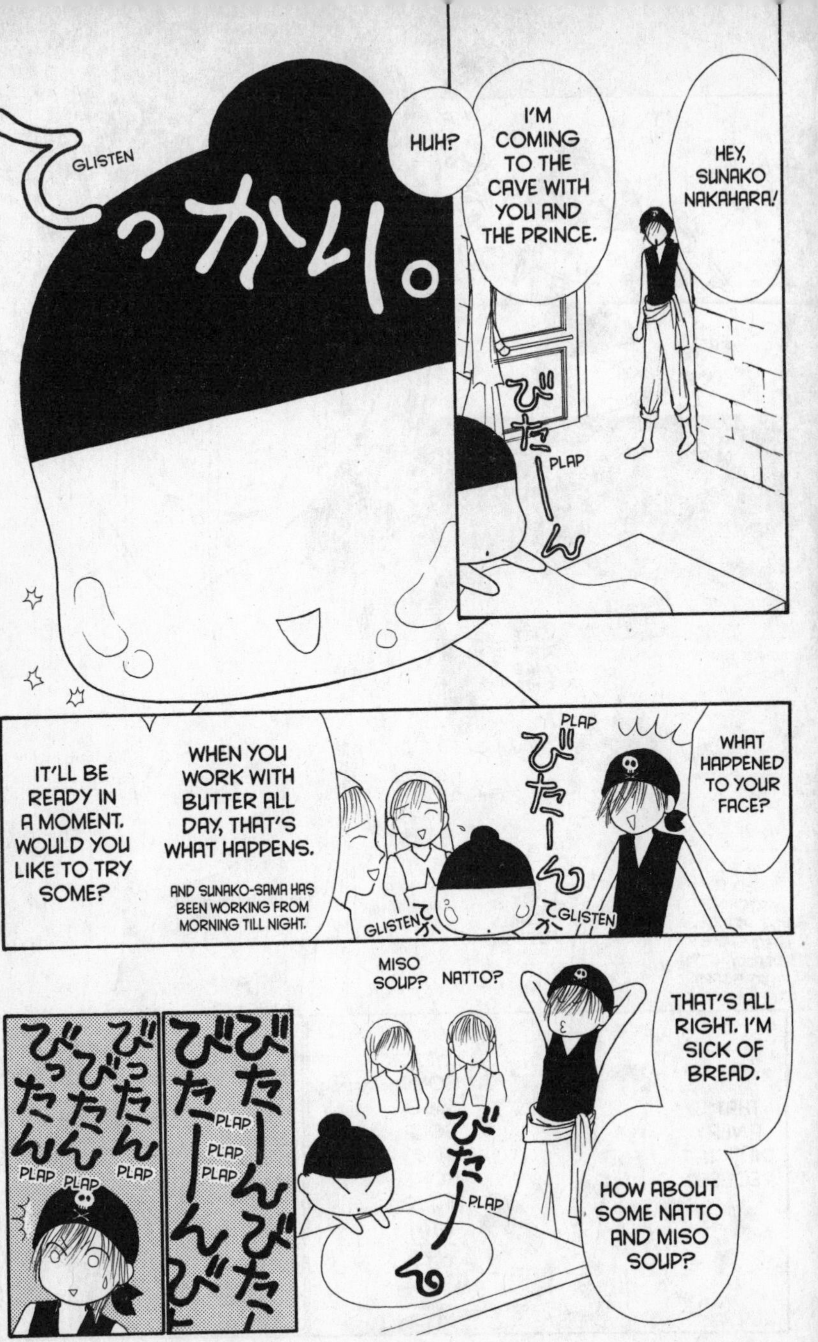
HEY, SUNAKO NAKAHARA!
I'M COMING TO THE CAVE WITH YOU AND THE PRINCE.
HUH?
びたーん
PLAP
てっかり。
GLISTEN
WHAT HAPPENED TO YOUR FACE?
びたーん
PLAP
てか
GLISTEN
てか
GLISTEN
WHEN YOU WORK WITH BUTTER ALL DAY, THAT'S WHAT HAPPENS.
AND SUNAKO-SAMA HAS BEEN WORKING FROM MORNING TILL NIGHT.
IT'LL BE READY IN A MOMENT. WOULD YOU LIKE TO TRY SOME?
THAT'S ALL RIGHT. I'M SICK OF BREAD.
NATTO?
MISO SOUP?
HOW ABOUT SOME NATTO AND MISO SOUP?
びたーん
PLAP
びたーんびたーんびたーんび
PLAP
PLAP
PLAP
びったんびったんびったん
PLAP
PLAP
PLAP

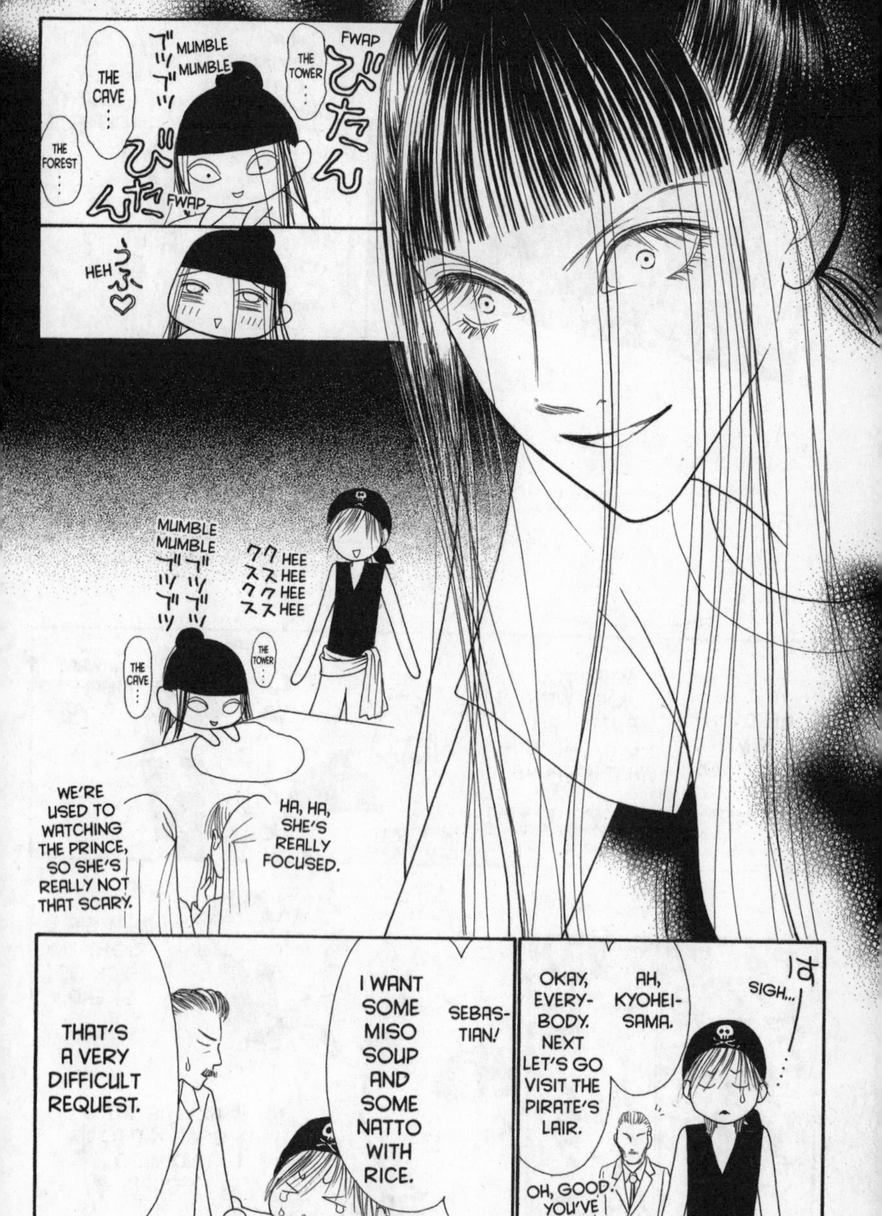
FWAP びたん
THE TOWER...
MUMBLE MUMBLE ブツブツ
THE CAVE...
THE FOREST...
びたん FWAP
HEH うふ♡
ククスス HEE HEE HEE HEE
MUMBLE MUMBLE ブツブツ ブツブツ
THE TOWER...
THE CAVE...
HA, HA, SHE'S REALLY FOCUSED.
WE'RE USED TO WATCHING THE PRINCE, SO SHE'S REALLY NOT THAT SCARY.
す SIGH...
AH, KYOHEI-SAMA.
OKAY, EVERYBODY. NEXT LET'S GO VISIT THE PIRATE'S LAIR.
OH, GOOD. YOU'VE ALREADY CHANGED.
SEBASTIAN!
I WANT SOME MISO SOUP AND SOME NATTO WITH RICE.
THAT'S A VERY DIFFICULT REQUEST.

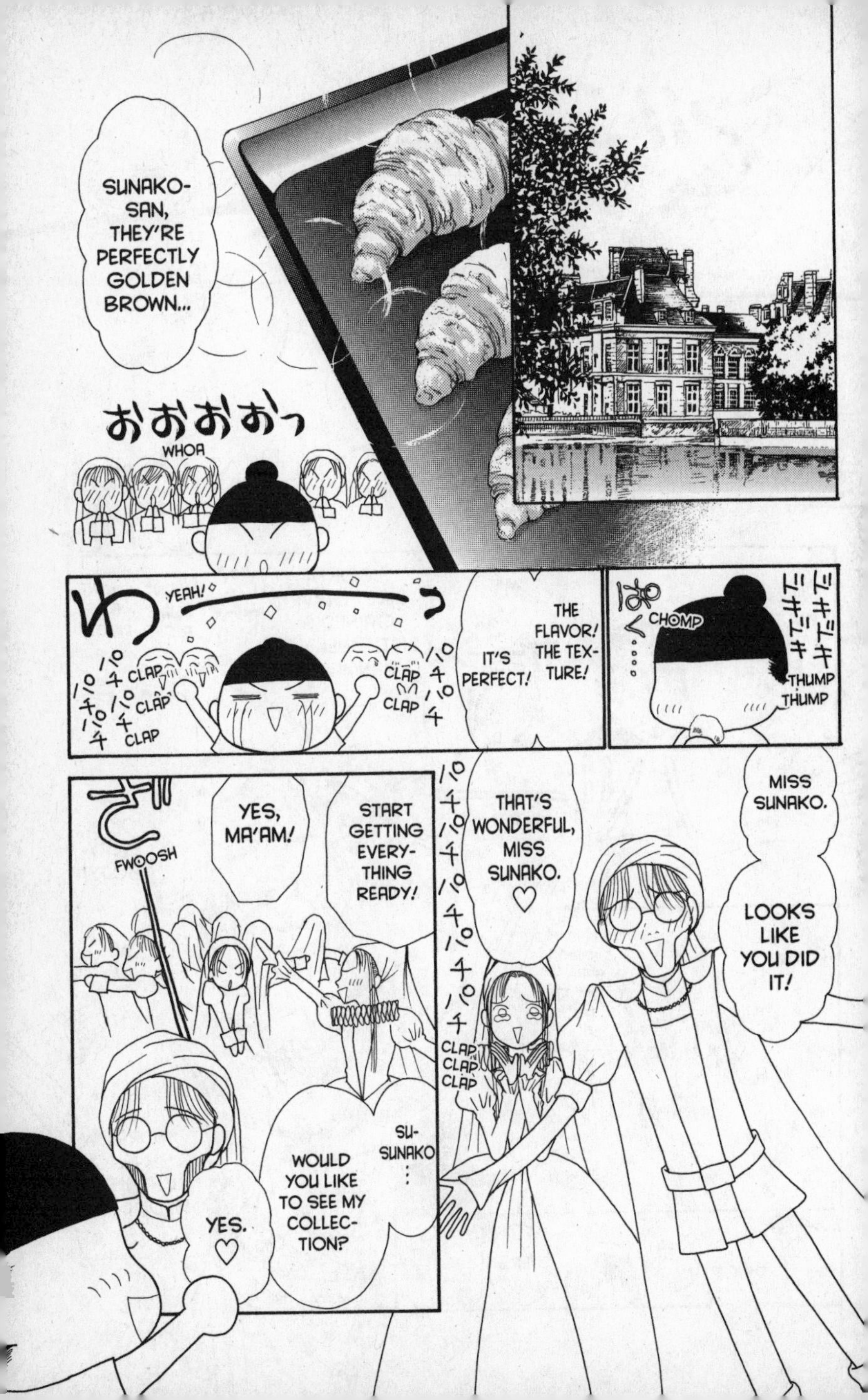
SUNAKO-SAN, THEY'RE PERFECTLY GOLDEN BROWN...
おおおおっ
WHOA
ドキドキ
THUMP THUMP
ぱく…
CHOMP
THE FLAVOR! THE TEXTURE!
IT'S PERFECT!
わーっ
YEAH!
パチパチ
CLAP CLAP
パチパチ
CLAP CLAP
パチパチ
CLAP
MISS SUNAKO.
LOOKS LIKE YOU DID IT!
THAT'S WONDERFUL, MISS SUNAKO. ♡
パチパチパチパチパチ
CLAP CLAP CLAP
START GETTING EVERYTHING READY!
YES, MA'AM!
さっ
FWOOSH
SU-SUNAKO...
WOULD YOU LIKE TO SEE MY COLLECTION?
YES. ♡

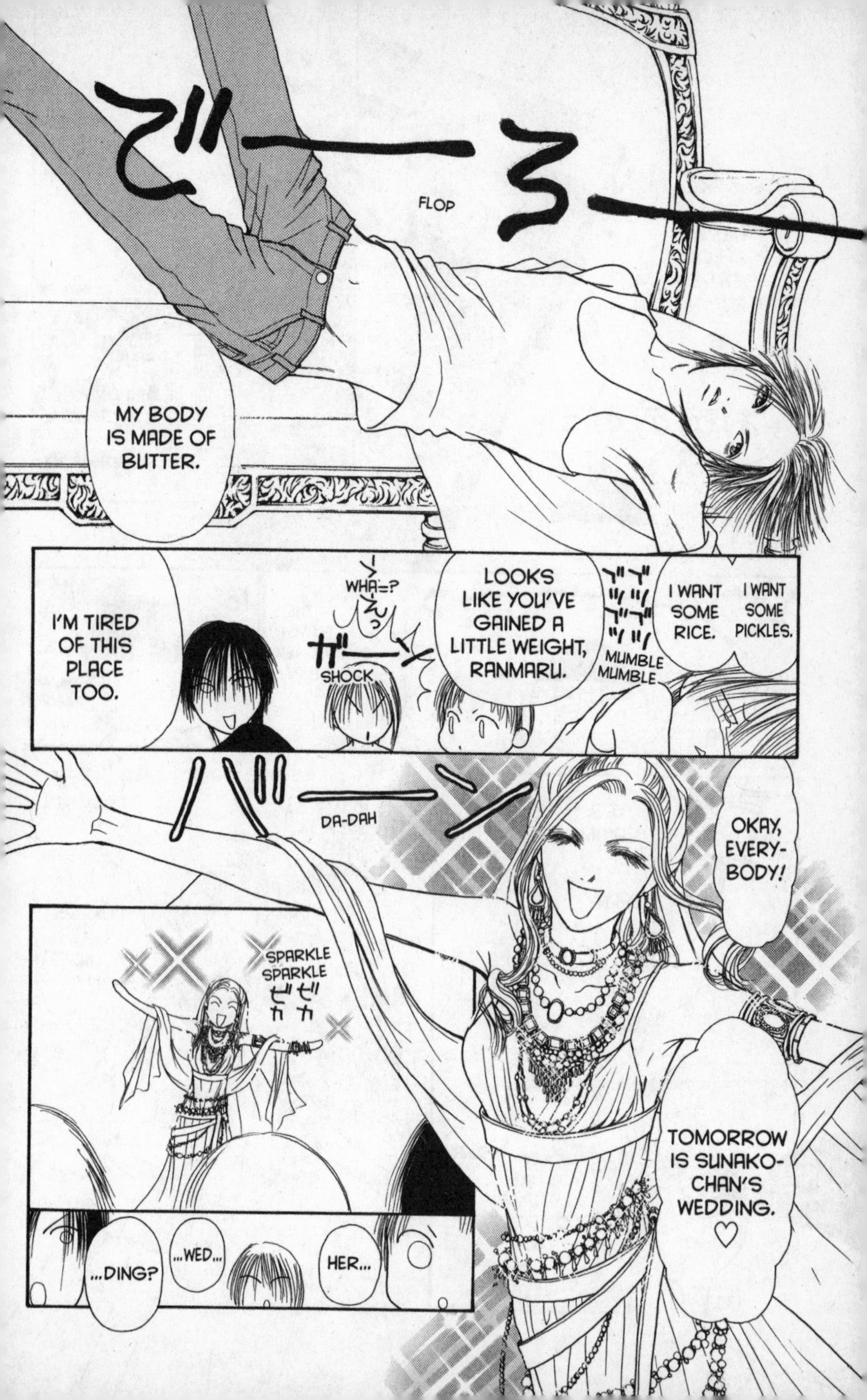
でーろー
FLOP
MY BODY IS MADE OF BUTTER.
I WANT SOME RICE.
I WANT SOME PICKLES.
ブツブツ
MUMBLE MUMBLE
LOOKS LIKE YOU'VE GAINED A LITTLE WEIGHT, RANMARU.
ガーン
SHOCK
えっ
WHA=?
I'M TIRED OF THIS PLACE TOO.
パーン
DA-DAH
OKAY, EVERY-BODY!
TOMORROW IS SUNAKO-CHAN'S WEDDING. ♡
SPARKLE SPARKLE
ピカピカ
HER...
...WED...
...DING?

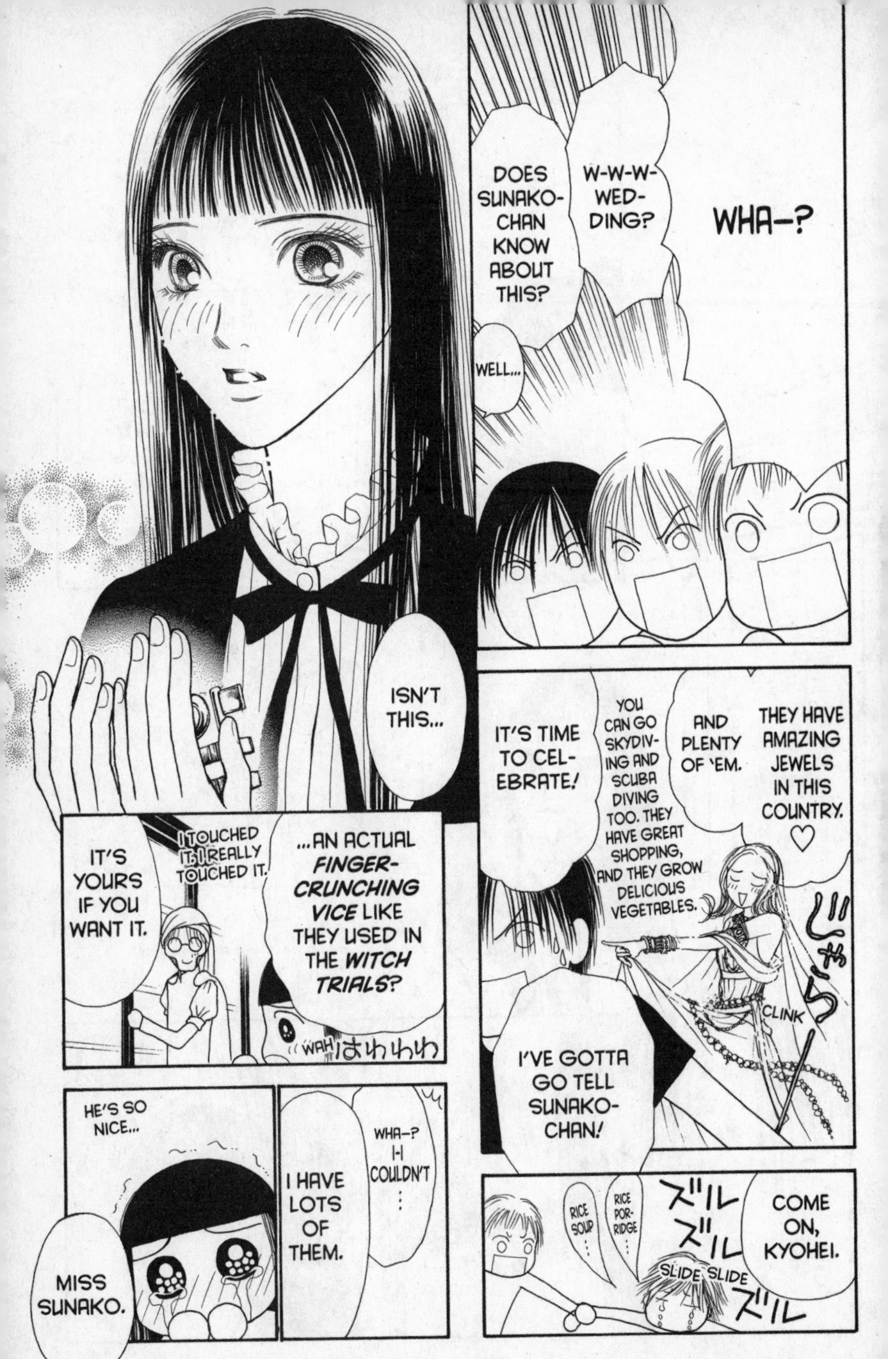
WHA–?
W-W-W-WED-DING?
DOES SUNAKO-CHAN KNOW ABOUT THIS?
WELL...
THEY HAVE AMAZING JEWELS IN THIS COUNTRY. ♡
AND PLENTY OF 'EM.
YOU CAN GO SKYDIVING AND SCUBA DIVING TOO. THEY HAVE GREAT SHOPPING, AND THEY GROW DELICIOUS VEGETABLES.
IT'S TIME TO CELEBRATE!
じゃら
CLINK
I'VE GOTTA GO TELL SUNAKO-CHAN!
COME ON, KYOHEI.
ズル ズル
SLIDE SLIDE
ズル
RICE PORRIDGE...
RICE SOUP...
ISN'T THIS...
...AN ACTUAL *FINGER-CRUNCHING VICE* LIKE THEY USED IN THE *WITCH TRIALS?*
I TOUCHED IT. I REALLY TOUCHED IT.
IT'S YOURS IF YOU WANT IT.
WAH
はわわわ
WHA–? I-I COULDN'T...
I HAVE LOTS OF THEM.
HE'S SO NICE...
MISS SUNAKO.

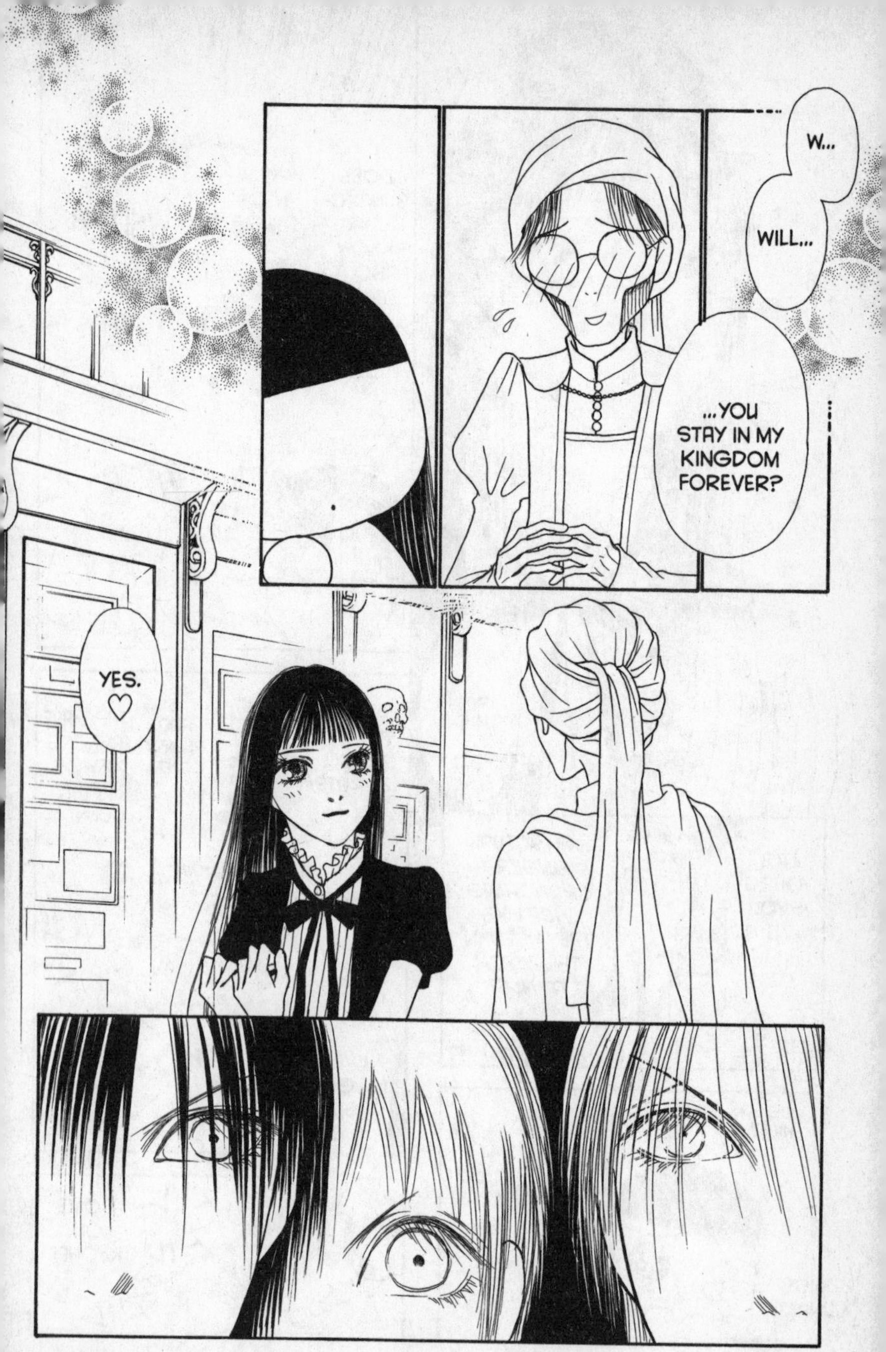
W...
WILL...
...YOU STAY IN MY KINGDOM FOREVER?
YES. ♡

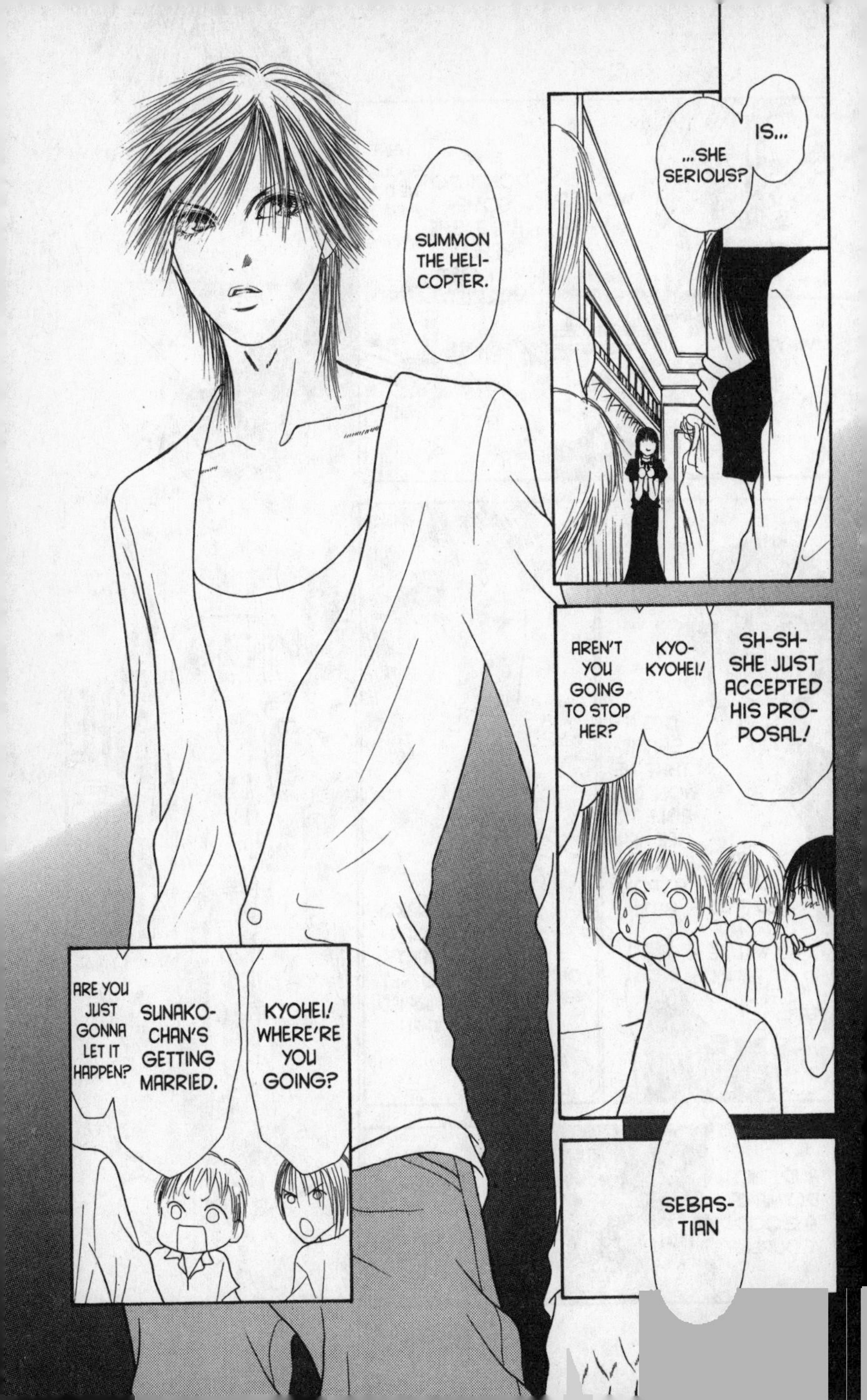
IS...
...SHE SERIOUS?
SH-SH-SHE JUST ACCEPTED HIS PROPOSAL!
KYO-KYOHEI!
AREN'T YOU GOING TO STOP HER?
SEBASTIAN
SUMMON THE HELICOPTER.
KYOHEI! WHERE'RE YOU GOING?
SUNAKO-CHAN'S GETTING MARRIED.
ARE YOU JUST GONNA LET IT HAPPEN?

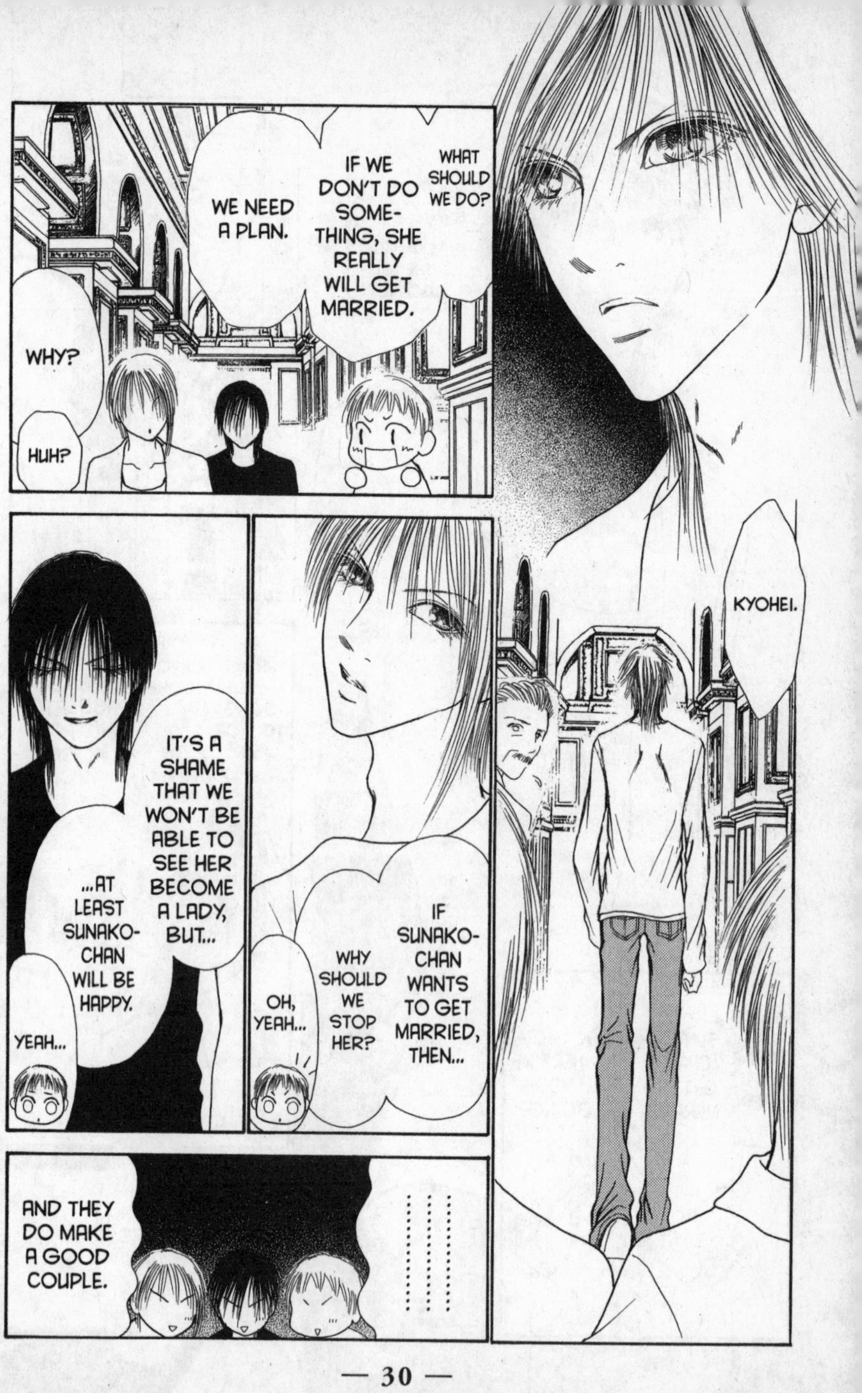
KYOHEI.
WHAT SHOULD WE DO?
IF WE DON'T DO SOME-THING, SHE REALLY WILL GET MARRIED.
WE NEED A PLAN.
WHY?
HUH?
IF SUNAKO-CHAN WANTS TO GET MARRIED, THEN...
WHY SHOULD WE STOP HER?
OH, YEAH...
IT'S A SHAME THAT WE WON'T BE ABLE TO SEE HER BECOME A LADY, BUT...
...AT LEAST SUNAKO-CHAN WILL BE HAPPY.
YEAH...
......
AND THEY DO MAKE A GOOD COUPLE.

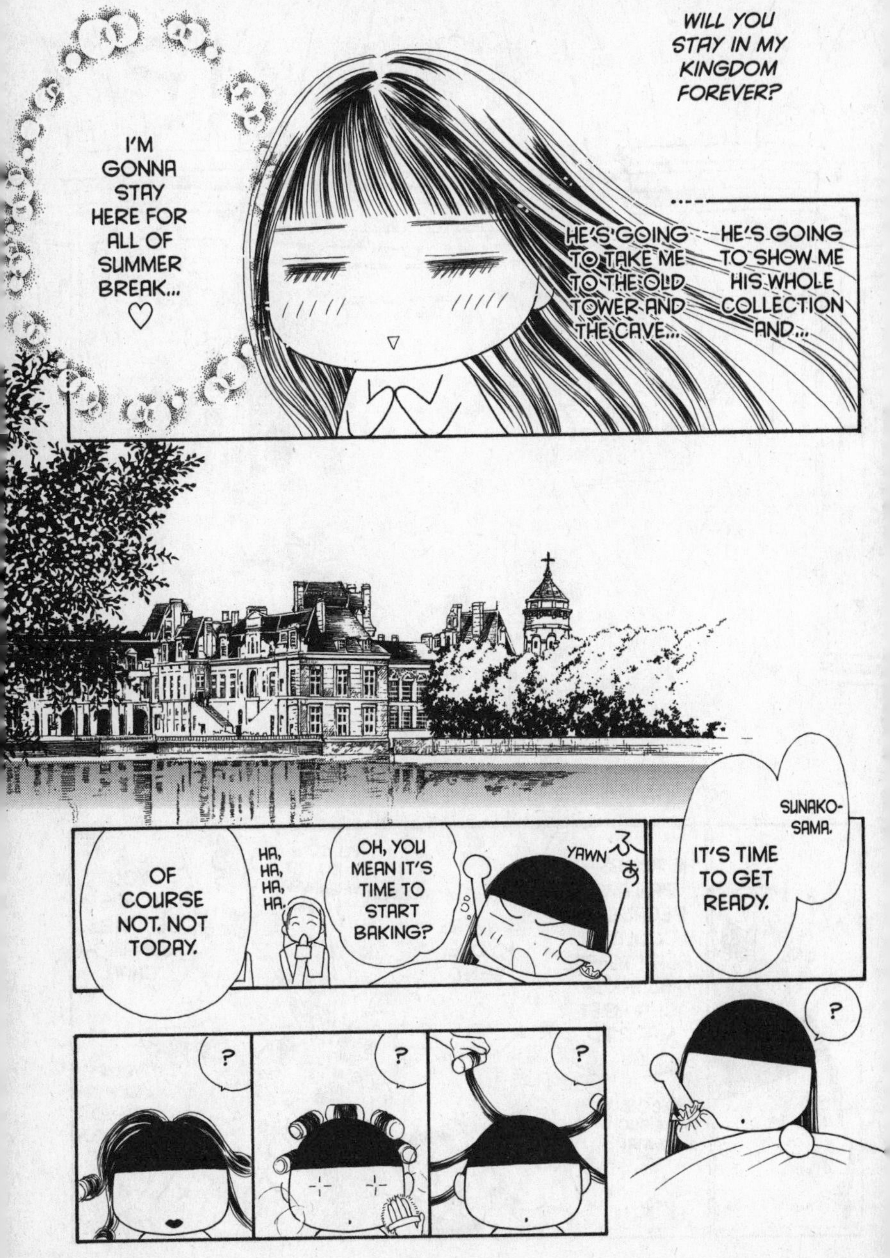
WILL YOU STAY IN MY KINGDOM FOREVER?
....HE'S GOING TO SHOW ME HIS WHOLE COLLECTION AND...
HE'S GOING TO TAKE ME TO THE OLD TOWER AND THE CAVE...
I'M GONNA STAY HERE FOR ALL OF SUMMER BREAK... ♡
SUNAKO-SAMA.
IT'S TIME TO GET READY.
ふあ
YAWN
OH, YOU MEAN IT'S TIME TO START BAKING?
HA, HA, HA, HA.
OF COURSE NOT. NOT TODAY.
?
?
?
?

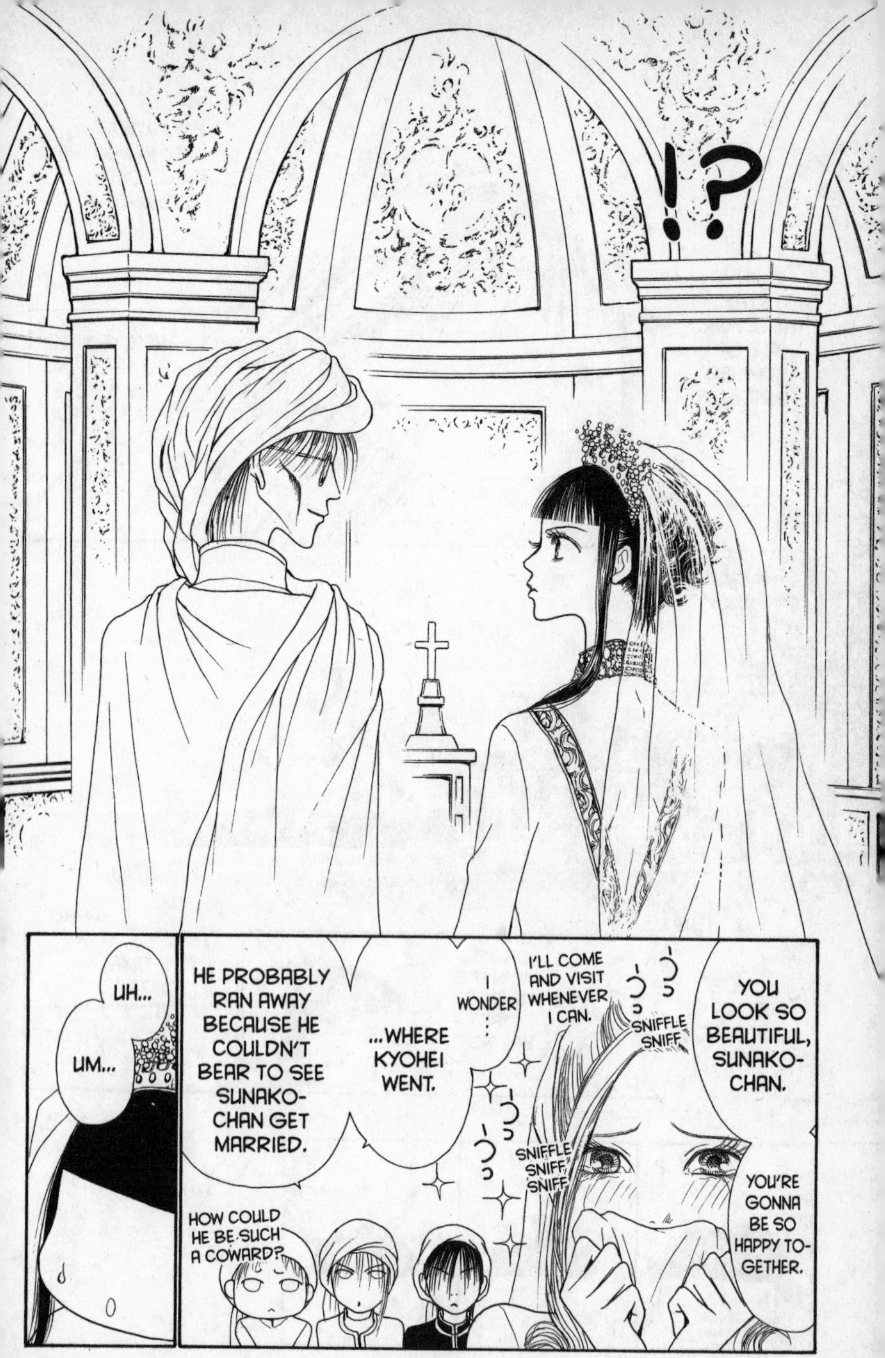
!?
YOU LOOK SO BEAUTIFUL, SUNAKO-CHAN.
SNIFFLE SNIFF
I'LL COME AND VISIT WHENEVER I CAN.
I WONDER...
...WHERE KYOHEI WENT.
HE PROBABLY RAN AWAY BECAUSE HE COULDN'T BEAR TO SEE SUNAKO-CHAN GET MARRIED.
SNIFFLE SNIFF SNIFF
YOU'RE GONNA BE SO HAPPY TO-GETHER.
HOW COULD HE BE SUCH A COWARD?
UH...
UM...

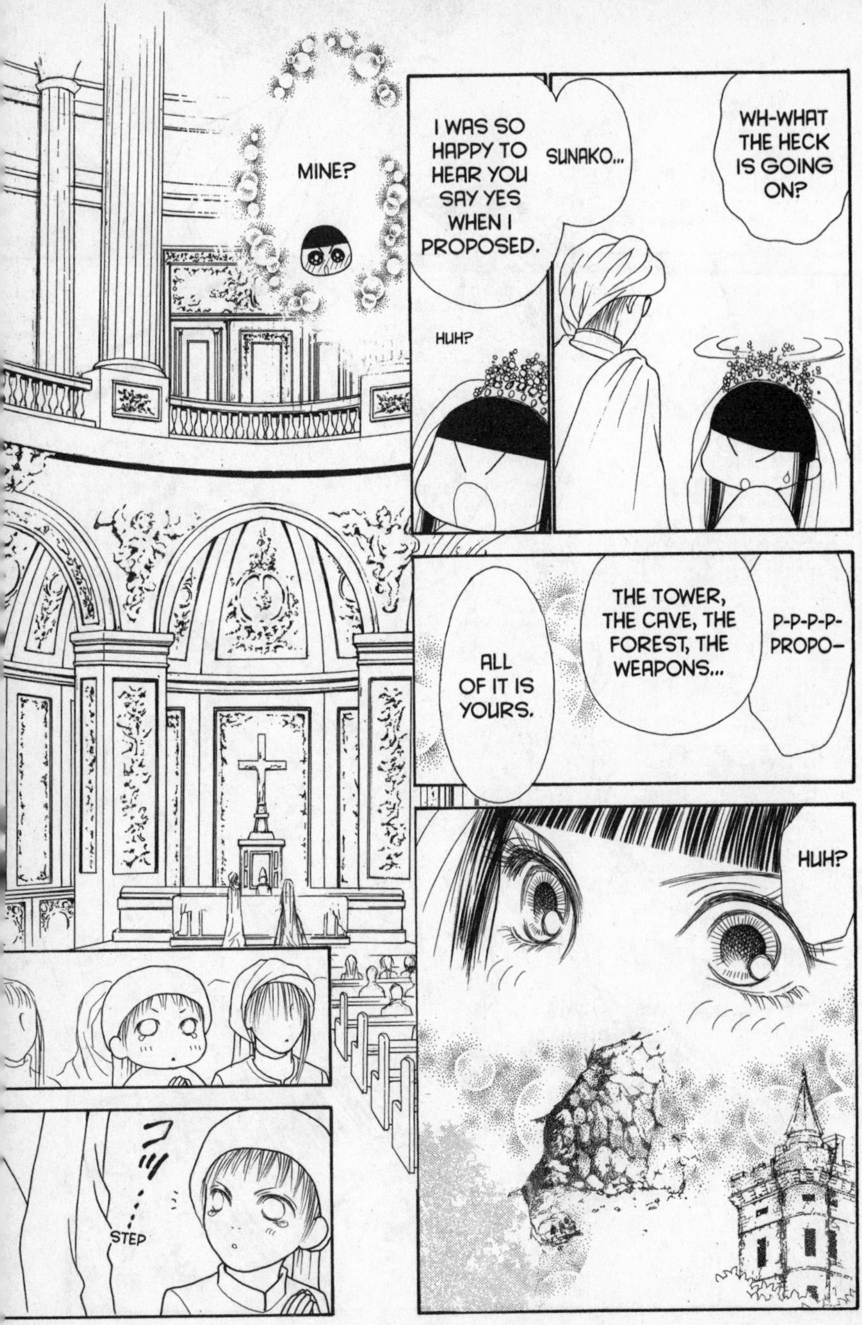
WH-WHAT THE HECK IS GOING ON?
SUNAKO...
I WAS SO HAPPY TO HEAR YOU SAY YES WHEN I PROPOSED.
HUH?
P-P-P-P-PROPO-
THE TOWER, THE CAVE, THE FOREST, THE WEAPONS...
ALL OF IT IS YOURS.
HUH?
MINE?
コツ...
STEP

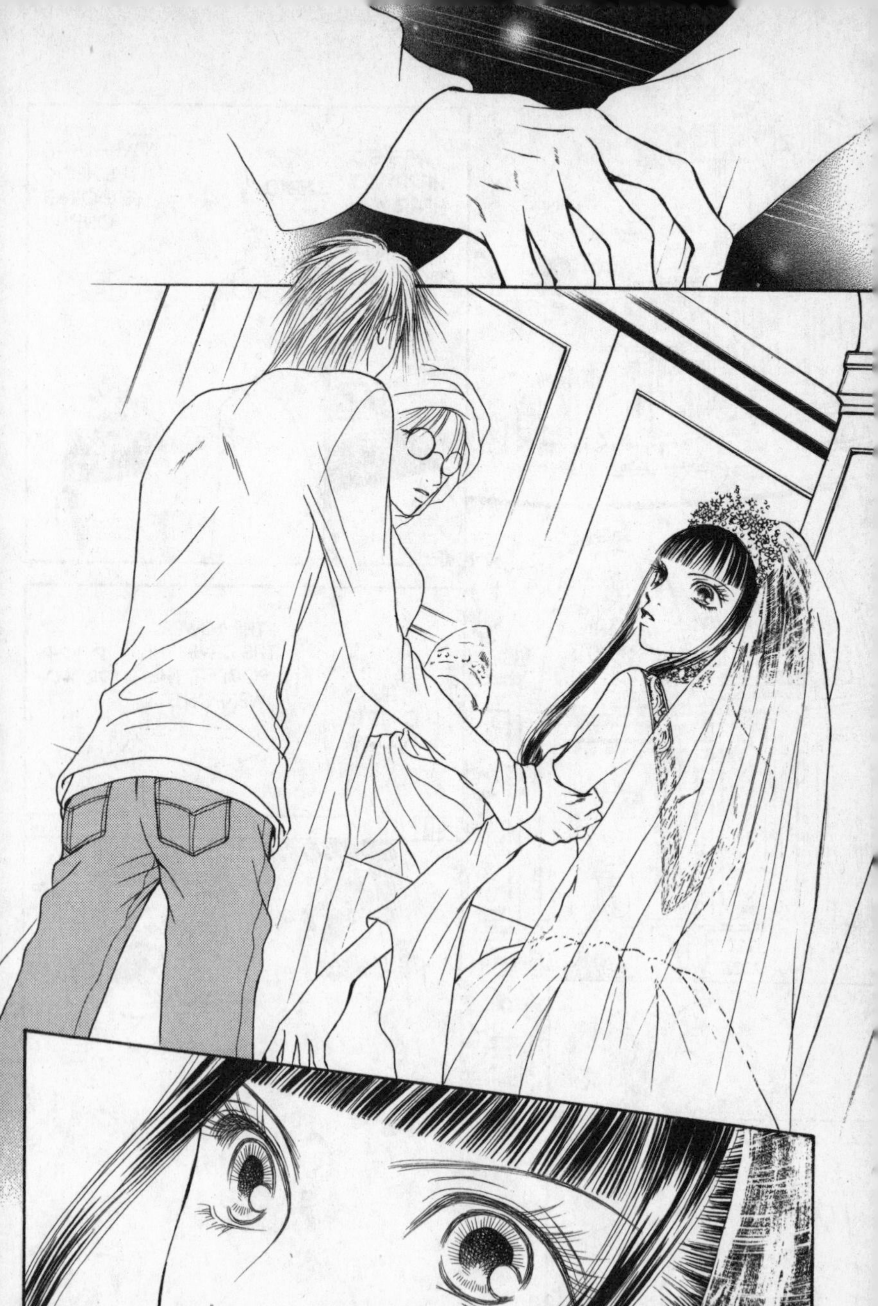

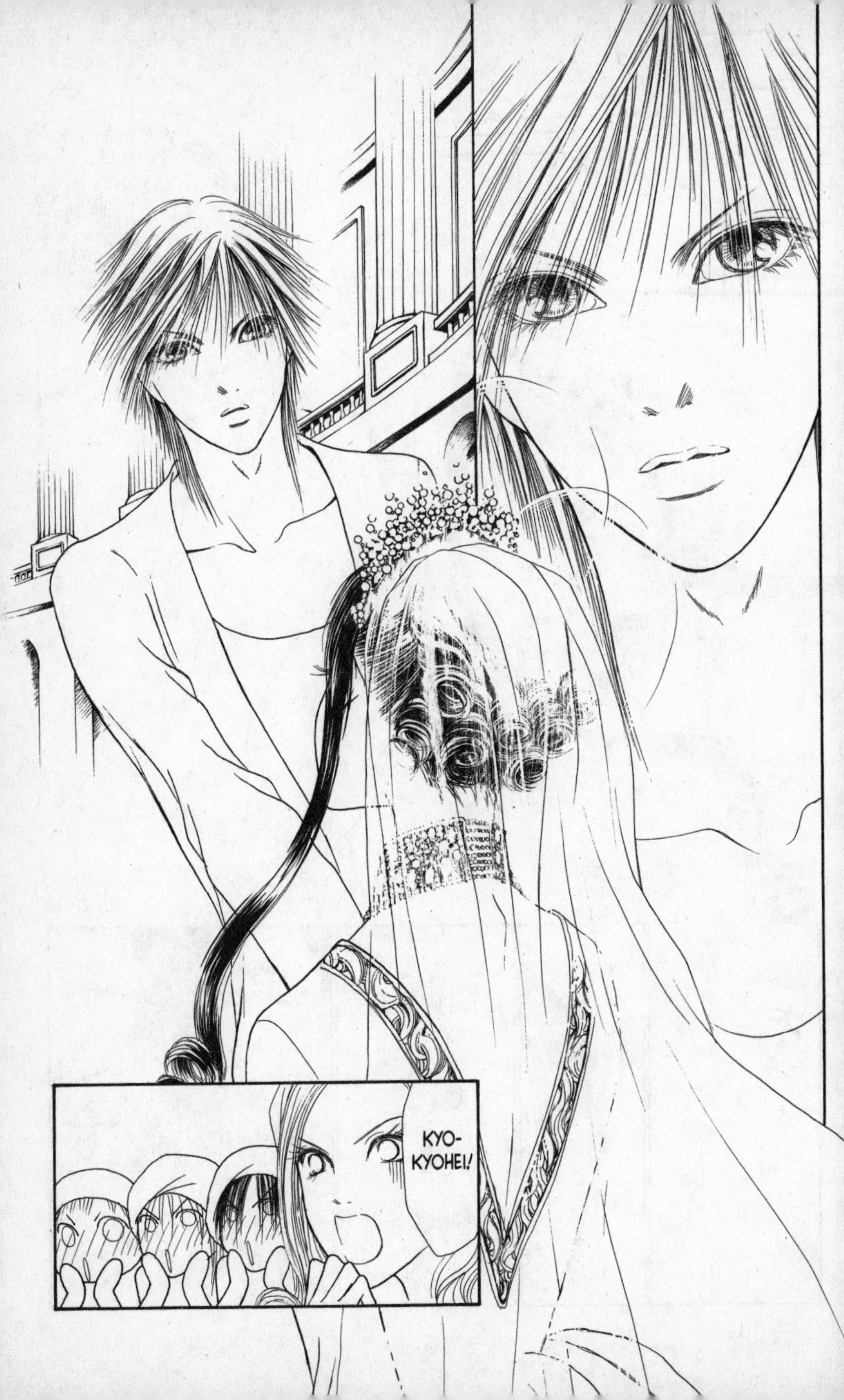
KYO-
KYOHEI!

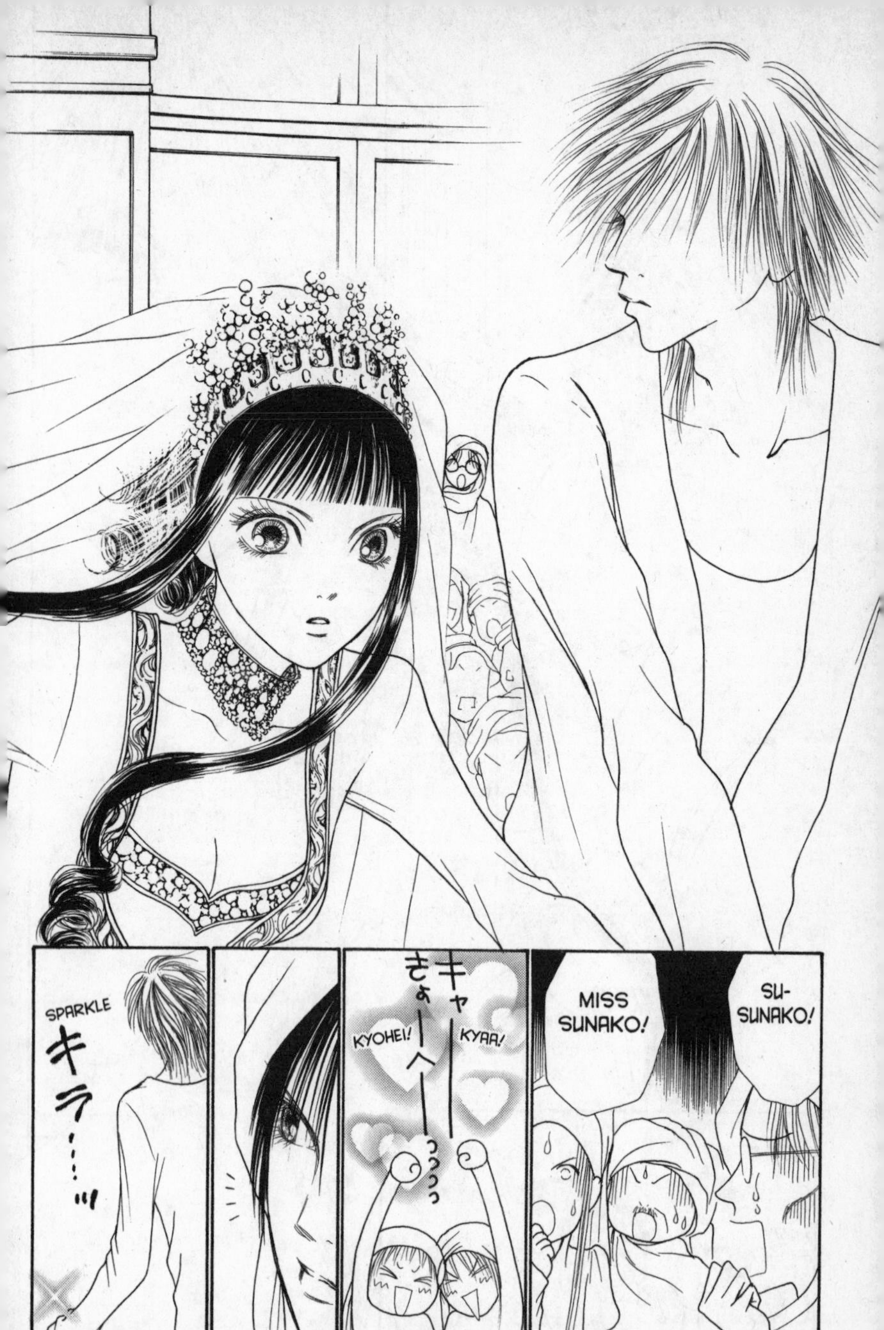
SU-SUNAKO!
MISS SUNAKO!
キャ
KYAA!
きょーへーっっっ
KYOHEI!
SPARKLE
キラ・・・!!

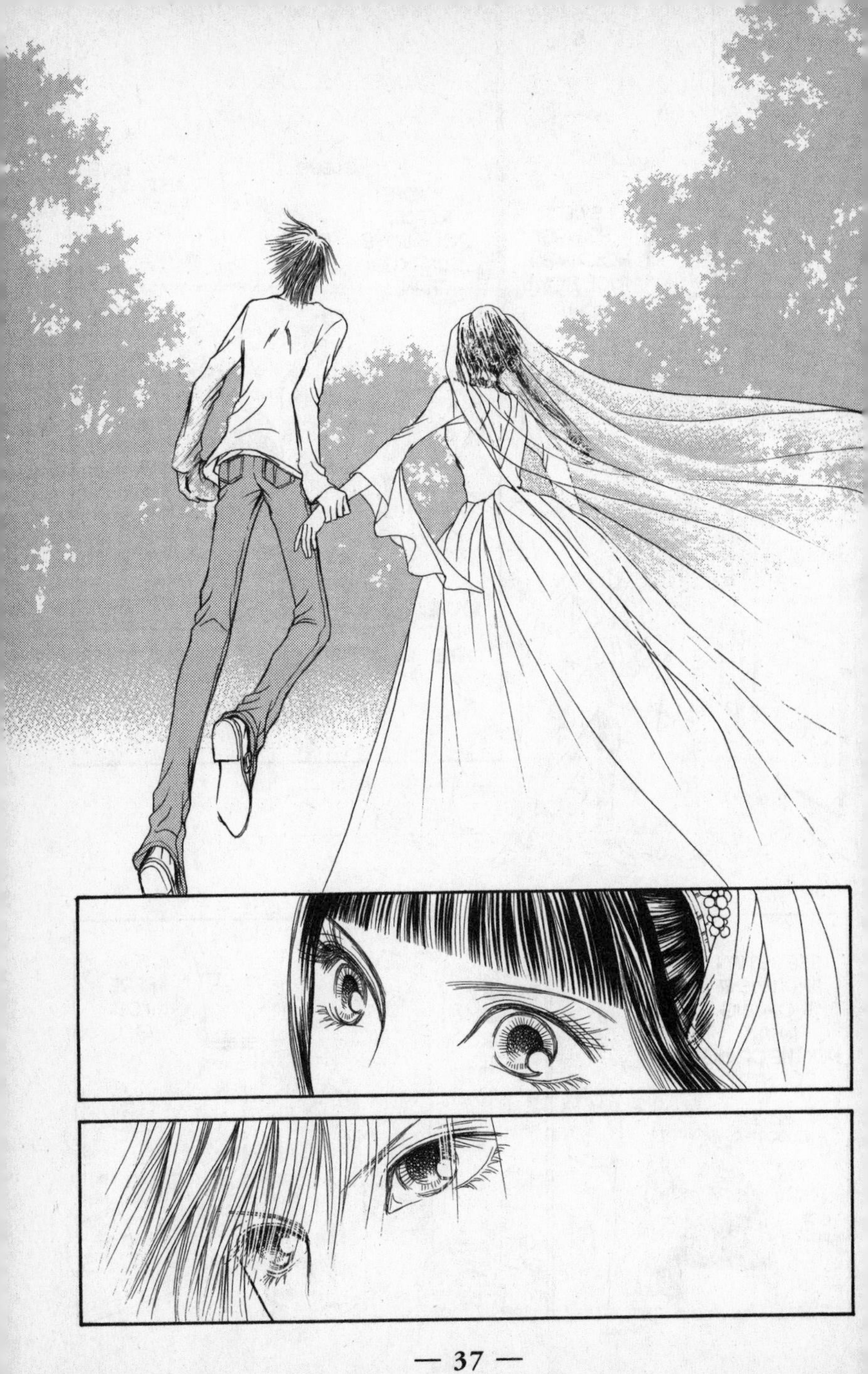

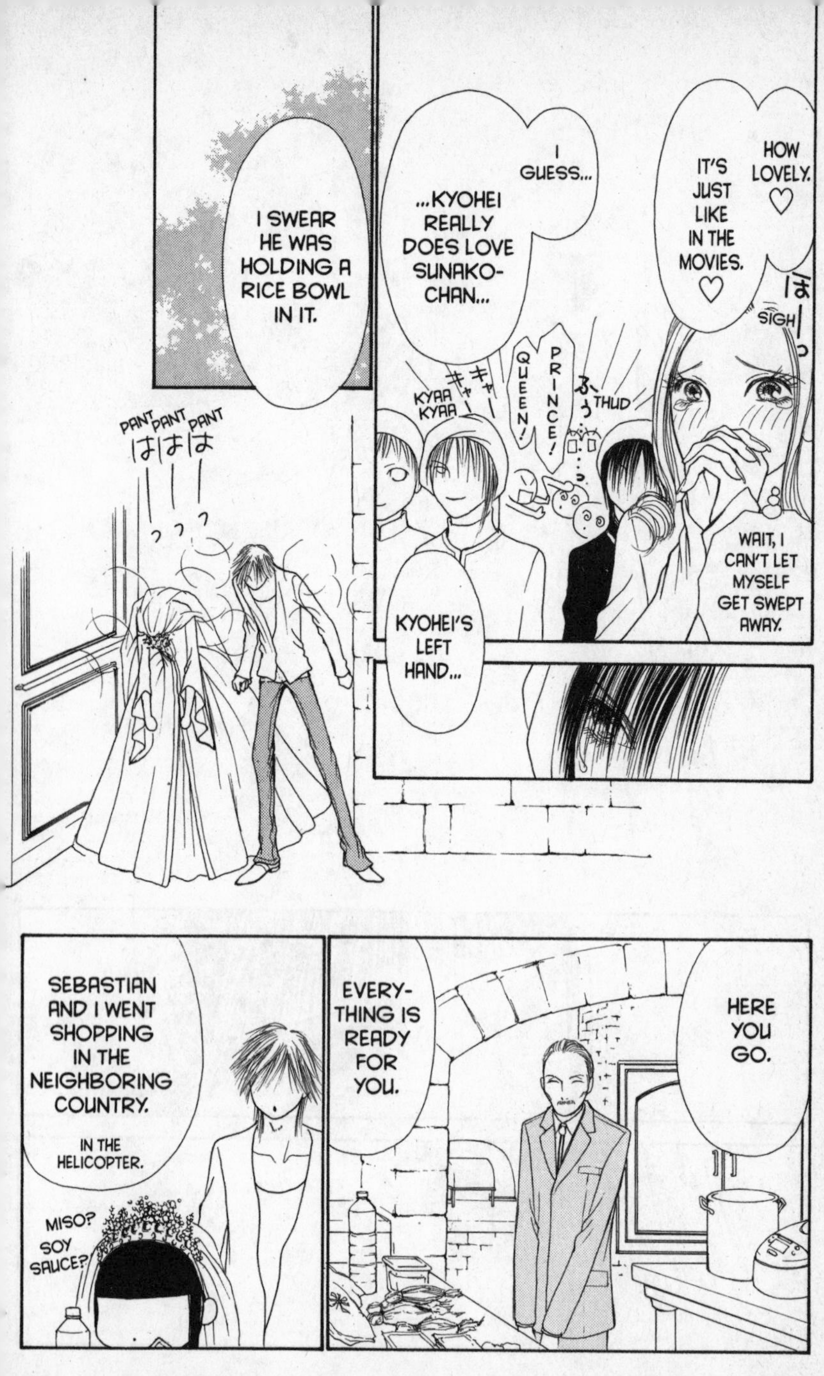

HOW LOVELY. ♡
IT'S JUST LIKE IN THE MOVIES. ♡
はーっ
SIGH
I GUESS...
...KYOHEI REALLY DOES LOVE SUNAKO-CHAN...
キャー キャー
KYAA KYAA
QUEEN!
PRINCE!
THUD
WAIT, I CAN'T LET MYSELF GET SWEPT AWAY.
KYOHEI'S LEFT HAND...
I SWEAR HE WAS HOLDING A RICE BOWL IN IT.
ははは
PANT PANT PANT
HERE YOU GO.
EVERY-THING IS READY FOR YOU.
SEBASTIAN AND I WENT SHOPPING IN THE NEIGHBORING COUNTRY.
IN THE HELICOPTER.
MISO? SOY SAUCE?

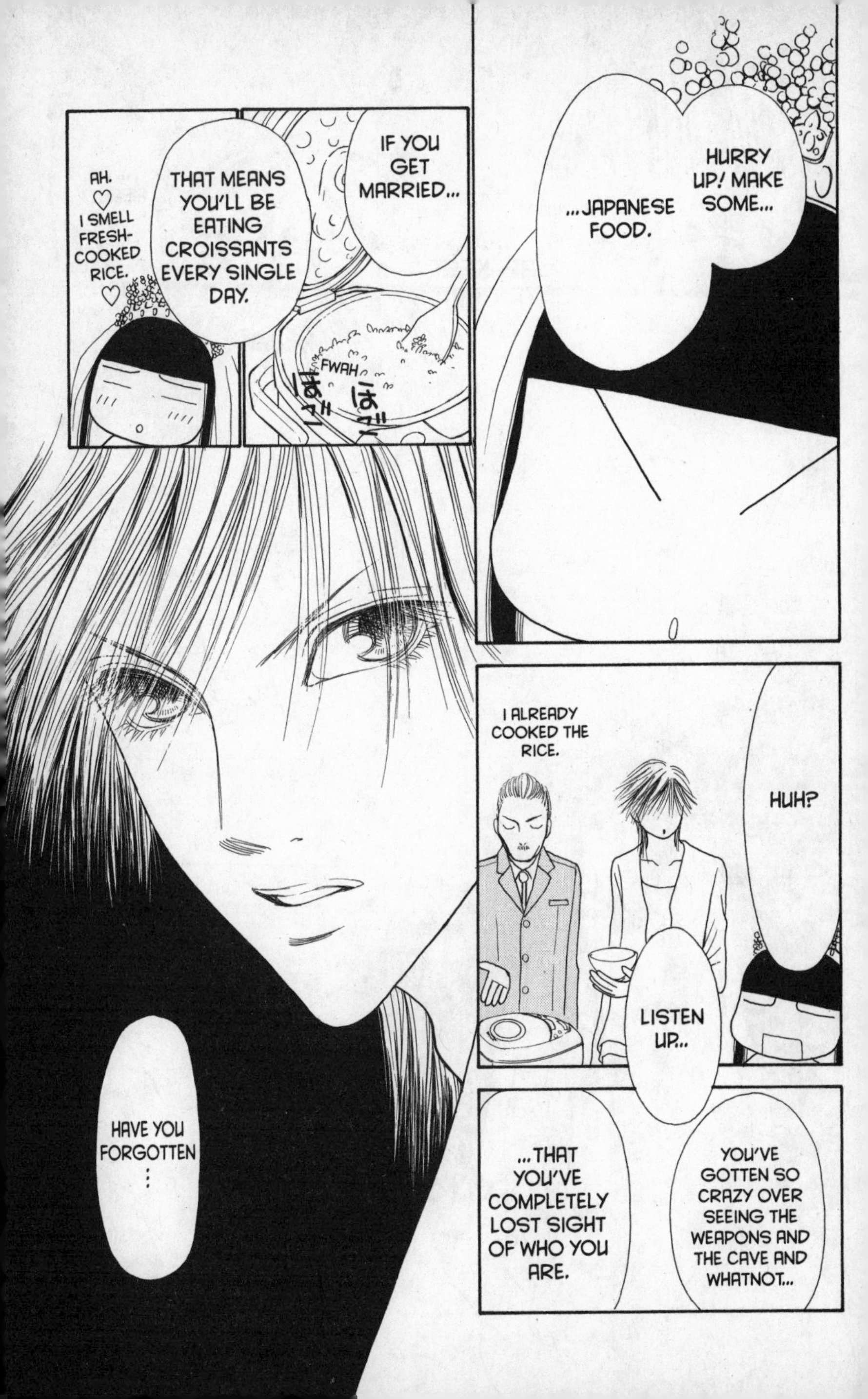

HURRY UP! MAKE SOME...
...JAPANESE FOOD.
IF YOU GET MARRIED...
FWAH
THAT MEANS YOU'LL BE EATING CROISSANTS EVERY SINGLE DAY.
AH. ♡ I SMELL FRESH-COOKED RICE. ♡
HUH?
I ALREADY COOKED THE RICE.
HAVE YOU FORGOTTEN ...
LISTEN UP...
YOU'VE GOTTEN SO CRAZY OVER SEEING THE WEAPONS AND THE CAVE AND WHATNOT...
...THAT YOU'VE COMPLETELY LOST SIGHT OF WHO YOU ARE.

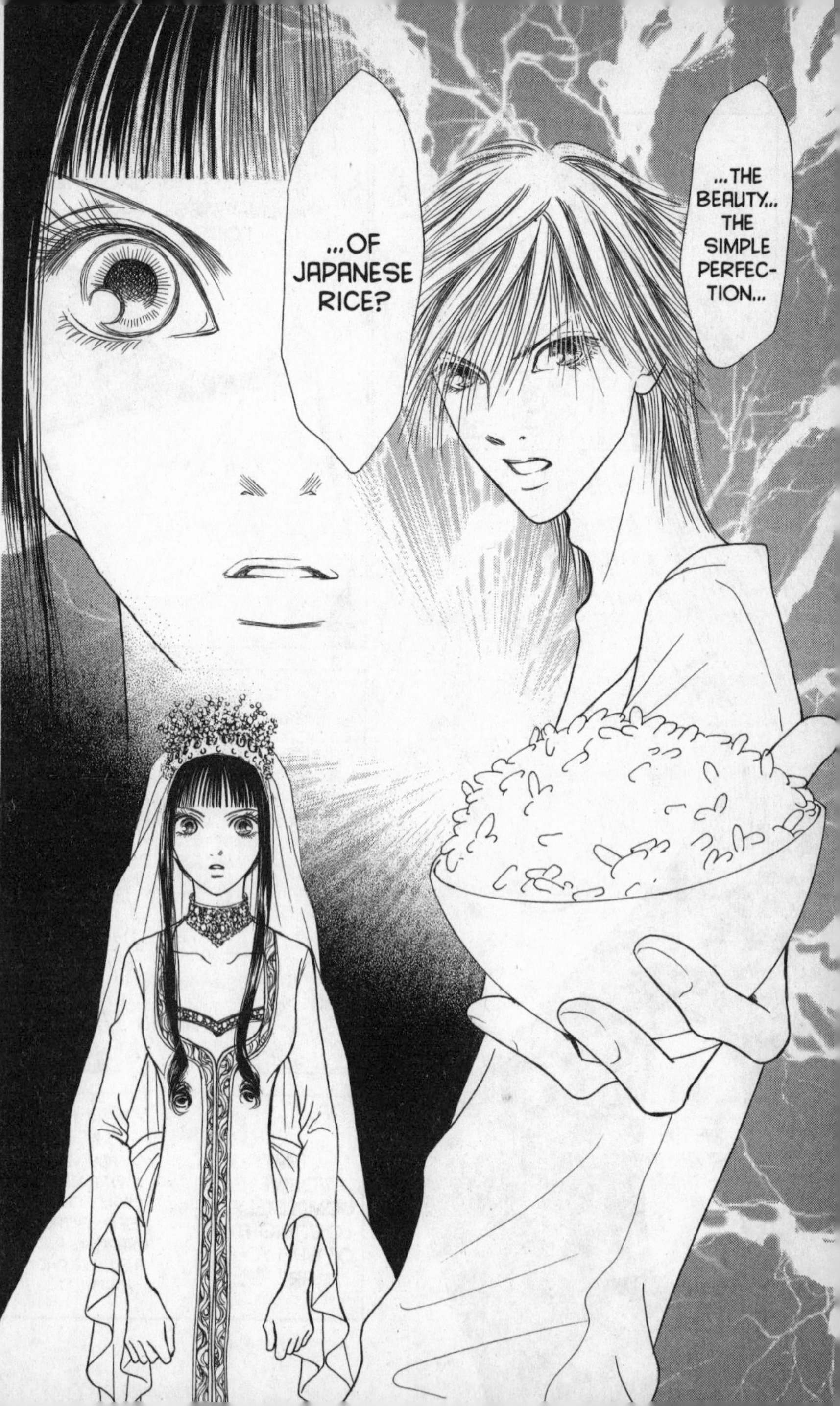
...THE BEAUTY... THE SIMPLE PERFEC-TION...
...OF JAPANESE RICE?

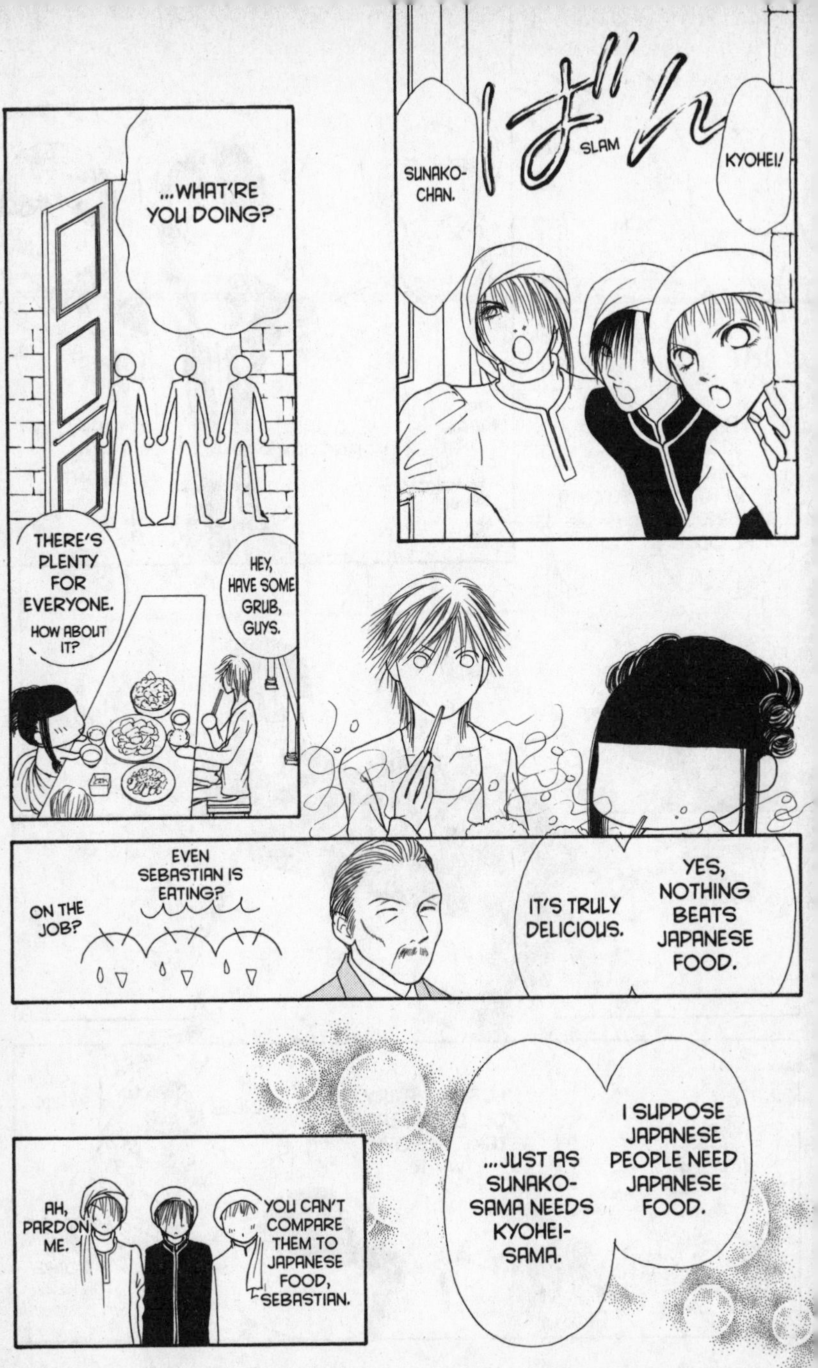
ばん
SLAM
KYOHEI!
SUNAKO-CHAN.
...WHAT'RE YOU DOING?
HEY, HAVE SOME GRUB, GUYS.
THERE'S PLENTY FOR EVERYONE.
HOW ABOUT IT?
YES, NOTHING BEATS JAPANESE FOOD.
IT'S TRULY DELICIOUS.
EVEN SEBASTIAN IS EATING?
ON THE JOB?
I SUPPOSE JAPANESE PEOPLE NEED JAPANESE FOOD.
...JUST AS SUNAKO-SAMA NEEDS KYOHEI-SAMA.
YOU CAN'T COMPARE THEM TO JAPANESE FOOD, SEBASTIAN.
AH, PARDON ME.

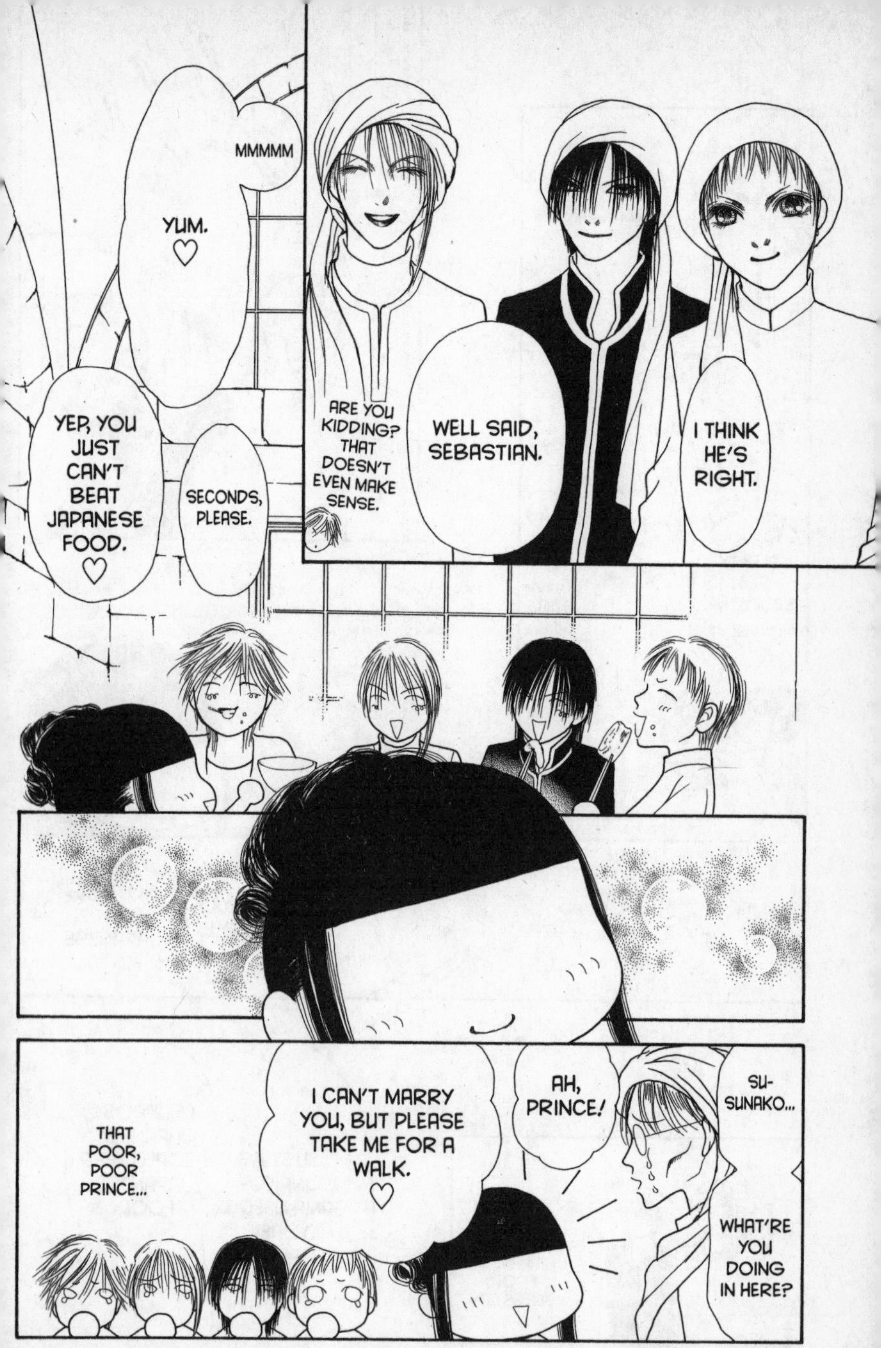
I THINK HE'S RIGHT.
WELL SAID, SEBASTIAN.
ARE YOU KIDDING? THAT DOESN'T EVEN MAKE SENSE.
MMMMM
YUM. ♡
SECONDS, PLEASE.
YEP, YOU JUST CAN'T BEAT JAPANESE FOOD. ♡
SU-SUNAKO...
WHAT'RE YOU DOING IN HERE?
AH, PRINCE!
I CAN'T MARRY YOU, BUT PLEASE TAKE ME FOR A WALK. ♡
THAT POOR, POOR PRINCE...

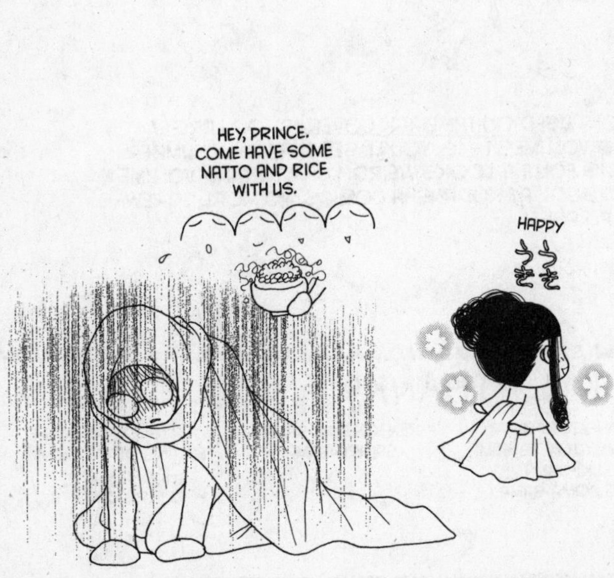
HEY, PRINCE. COME HAVE SOME NATTO AND RICE WITH US.
HAPPY

# ALL ABOUT VOLUME 19

THERE WAS ANOTHER PRINTING ERROR.
TAKE A LOOK AT VOLUME 19, PAGE 84.

CORRECT

ALL RIGHT, LET'S PARTY!
OKAY.
I WONDER IF THERE'S SUCH A THING...
...AS LOVE THAT ISN'T AN ILLUSION.

WRONG

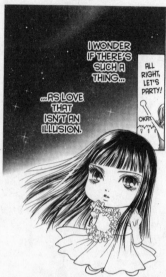

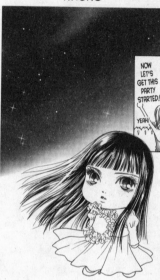

NOW LET'S GET THIS PARTY STARTED!
YEAH!

ALSO, THE FONT USED ON THE BACK COVER IS TOO LARGE! IF YOU LINE UP VOLUMES 1 - 19, YOU'LL SEE THAT ONLY NUMBER 19 HAS THE BIG FONT. IT LOOKS WEIRD. I CAN'T STAND VOLUME 19. HEY, EVERYBODY AT KODANSHA COMICS, NO MORE SCREW-UPS, OKAY? PLEASE!!

## SPECIAL THANKS

TAEKO CHOBIN HATORI-SAMA
YOUICHIROU TOMMY TOMITA-SAMA
MIEKO SUZUKI-SAMA
HARUKA MATSUYAMA-SAMA

REN KOIZUMI-SAMA
SAKIRA-SAMA

EVERYBODY FROM THE EDITING DEPARTMENT
EVERYBODY WHO'S READING THIS RIGHT NOW
♡ ♡ ♡

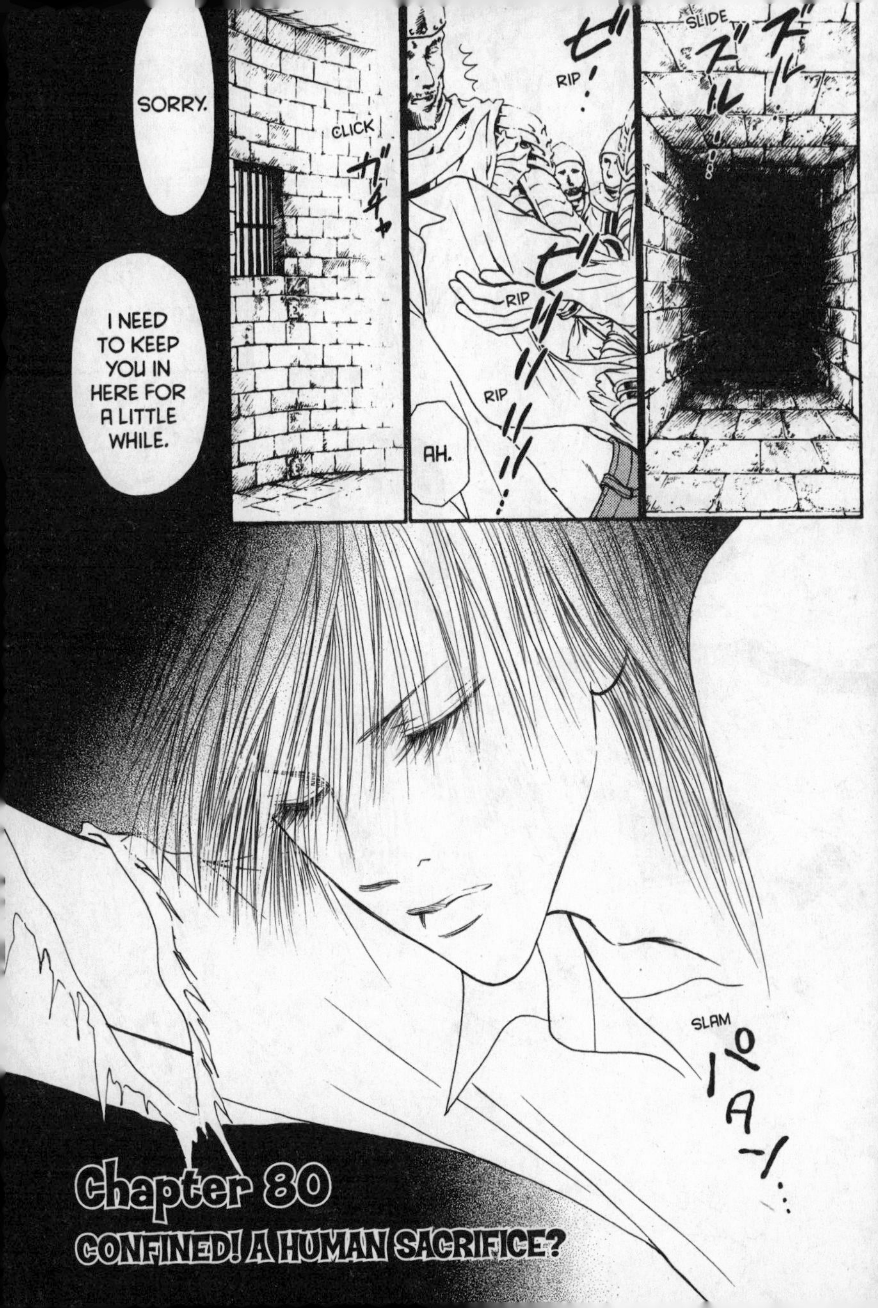
SLIDE
RIP
RIP
RIP
AH.
CLICK
SORRY.
I NEED TO KEEP YOU IN HERE FOR A LITTLE WHILE.
SLAM
Chapter 80
CONFINED! A HUMAN SACRIFICE?

# Chapter 80
## CONFINED! A HUMAN SACRIFICE?

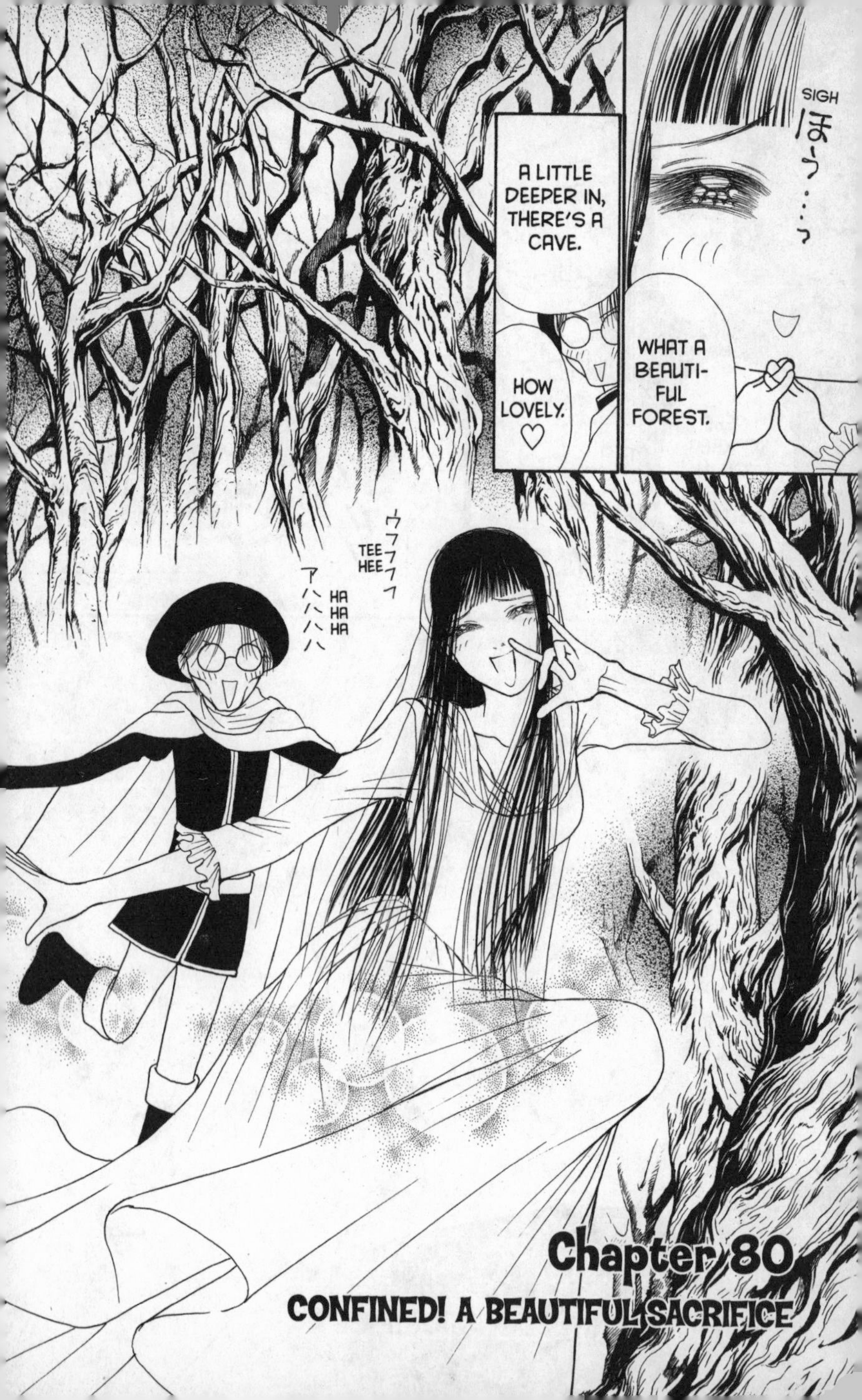
SIGH
ほう…
WHAT A BEAUTIFUL FOREST.
A LITTLE DEEPER IN, THERE'S A CAVE.
HOW LOVELY. ♡
TEE HEE
ウフフフ
HA HA HA
アハハハ
Chapter 80
CONFINED! A BEAUTIFUL SACRIFICE

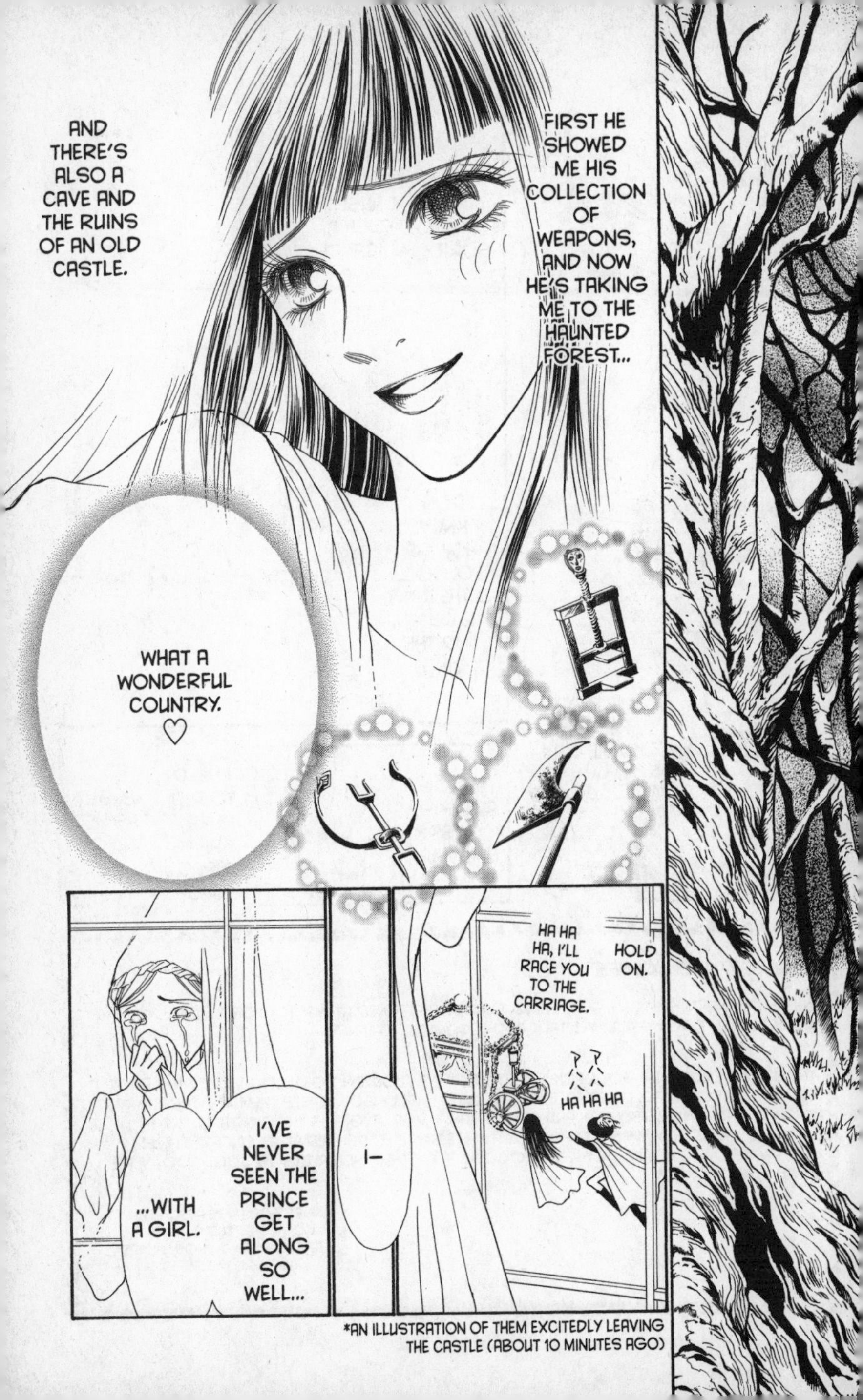
FIRST HE SHOWED ME HIS COLLECTION OF WEAPONS, AND NOW HE'S TAKING ME TO THE HAUNTED FOREST...
AND THERE'S ALSO A CAVE AND THE RUINS OF AN OLD CASTLE.
WHAT A WONDERFUL COUNTRY. ♡
HOLD ON.
HA HA HA, I'LL RACE YOU TO THE CARRIAGE.
HA HA HA
I—
I'VE NEVER SEEN THE PRINCE GET ALONG SO WELL...
...WITH A GIRL.
*AN ILLUSTRATION OF THEM EXCITEDLY LEAVING THE CASTLE (ABOUT 10 MINUTES AGO)

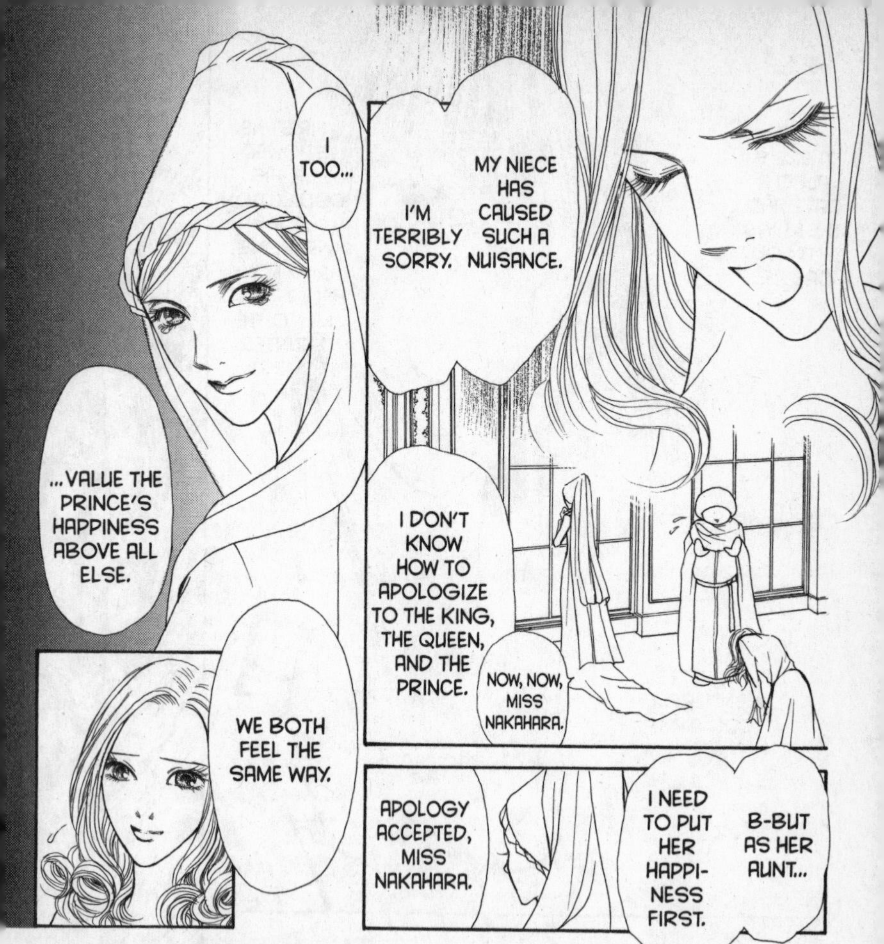
MY NIECE HAS CAUSED SUCH A NUISANCE.
I'M TERRIBLY SORRY.
I DON'T KNOW HOW TO APOLOGIZE TO THE KING, THE QUEEN, AND THE PRINCE.
NOW, NOW, MISS NAKAHARA.
I TOO...
...VALUE THE PRINCE'S HAPPINESS ABOVE ALL ELSE.
B-BUT AS HER AUNT...
I NEED TO PUT HER HAPPINESS FIRST.
APOLOGY ACCEPTED, MISS NAKAHARA.
WE BOTH FEEL THE SAME WAY.

***BEHIND THE SCENES***

WHILE WRITING THIS STORY, SOMETHING TERRIBLE HAPPENED AT WORK. I DON'T EVEN WANNA THINK ABOUT IT, SO INSTEAD I'LL TALK ABOUT SOMETHING FUN. ♥

THE BAND D'ERLANGER GOT BACK TOGETHER. ♥♥♥ I COULDN'T GET TICKETS TO THEIR FIRST SHOW, SO OF COURSE I CRIED MY EYES OUT, BUT I FINALLY GOT TO SEE THEM AT A THREE-BAND SHOW ALONG WITH MERRY-SAN AND MUKKU-SAN. ♥ D'ERLANGER IS THE GREATEST. ♥♥♥ I DANCED LIKE CRAZY. ♥♥♥ (IT HAD BEEN A WHILE SINCE I'D DANCED AT A CONCERT.) I FELT LIKE I WAS YOUNG AGAIN. THEY WERE SO COOL. ♥♥♥ THEIR NEW ALBUM IS GOOD TOO. ♥♥♥ REALLY GOOD. ♥♥♥

MERRY-SAN WAS ALSO REALLY COOL. THEY DID COVERS OF D'ERLANGER SONGS! IT WAS AN AWESOME EVENT. ♥

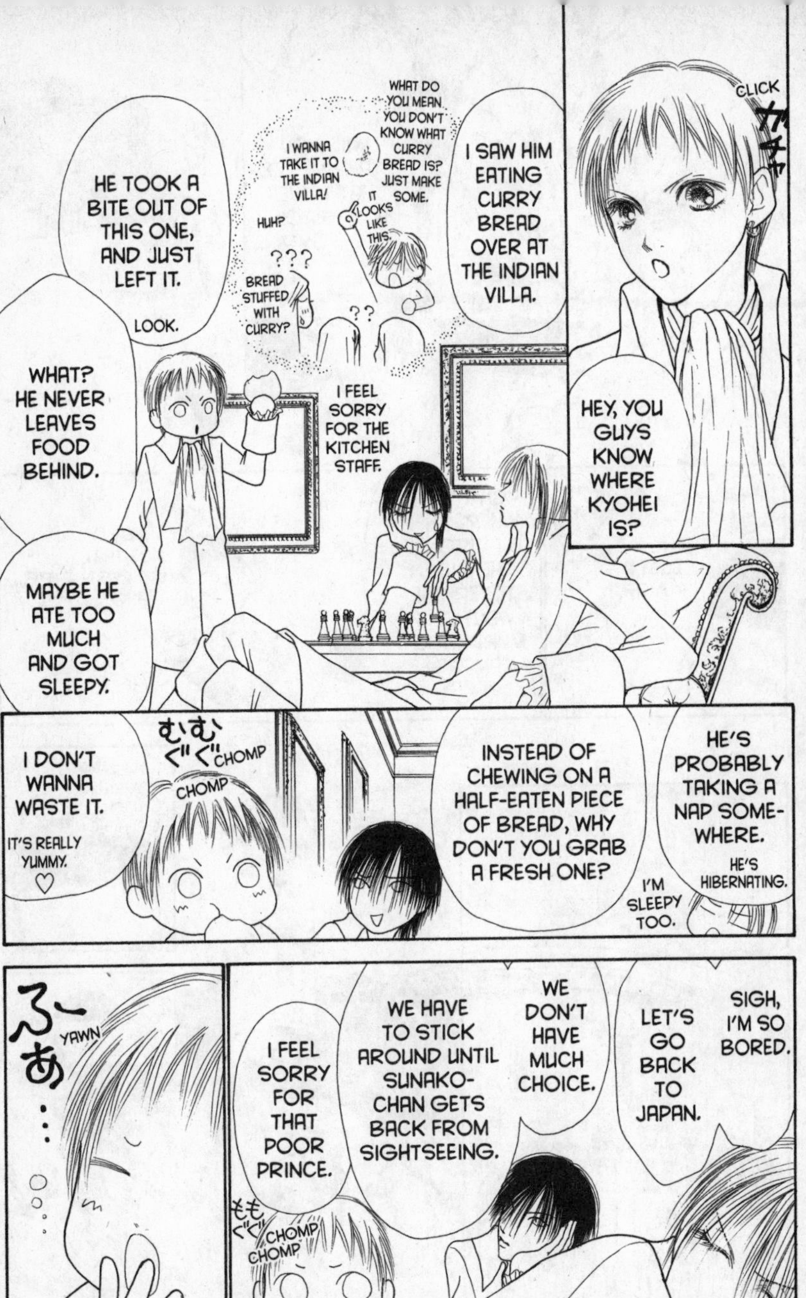
CLICK
ガチャ
HEY, YOU GUYS KNOW WHERE KYOHEI IS?
I SAW HIM EATING CURRY BREAD OVER AT THE INDIAN VILLA.
WHAT DO YOU MEAN, YOU DON'T KNOW WHAT CURRY BREAD IS? JUST MAKE SOME.
I WANNA TAKE IT TO THE INDIAN VILLA!
IT LOOKS LIKE THIS.
HUH?
???
BREAD STUFFED WITH CURRY?
??
HE TOOK A BITE OUT OF THIS ONE, AND JUST LEFT IT.
LOOK.
I FEEL SORRY FOR THE KITCHEN STAFF.
WHAT? HE NEVER LEAVES FOOD BEHIND.
MAYBE HE ATE TOO MUCH AND GOT SLEEPY.
HE'S PROBABLY TAKING A NAP SOME-WHERE.
HE'S HIBERNATING.
I'M SLEEPY TOO.
INSTEAD OF CHEWING ON A HALF-EATEN PIECE OF BREAD, WHY DON'T YOU GRAB A FRESH ONE?
むぐむぐ
CHOMP
CHOMP
I DON'T WANNA WASTE IT.
IT'S REALLY YUMMY. ♡
SIGH, I'M SO BORED.
LET'S GO BACK TO JAPAN.
WE DON'T HAVE MUCH CHOICE.
WE HAVE TO STICK AROUND UNTIL SUNAKO-CHAN GETS BACK FROM SIGHTSEEING.
I FEEL SORRY FOR THAT POOR PRINCE.
もぐもぐ
CHOMP CHOMP
ふぁ
YAWN
...

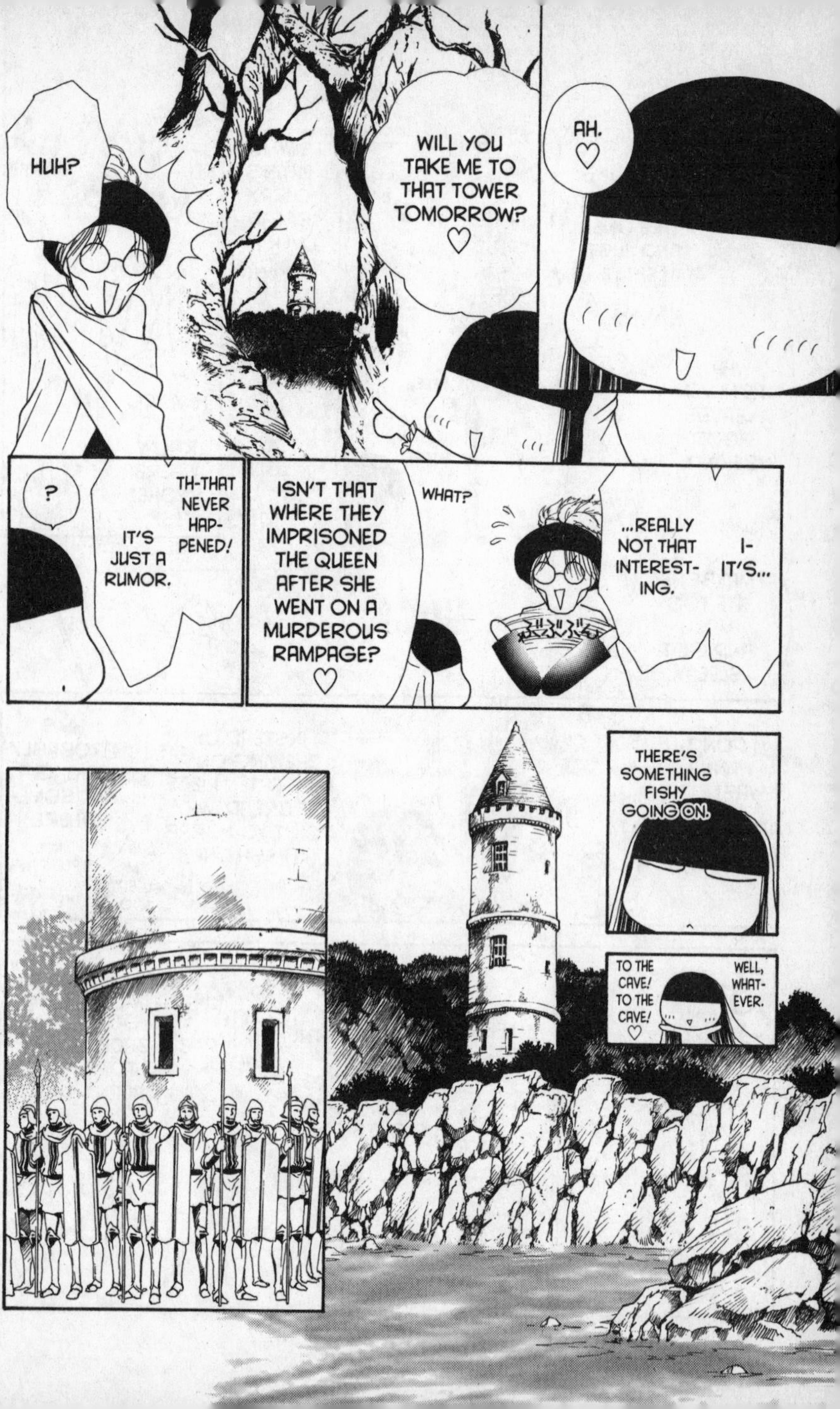
AH. ♡
WILL YOU TAKE ME TO THAT TOWER TOMORROW? ♡
HUH?
I- IT'S...
...REALLY NOT THAT INTEREST-ING.
WHAT?
ISN'T THAT WHERE THEY IMPRISONED THE QUEEN AFTER SHE WENT ON A MURDEROUS RAMPAGE? ♡
TH-THAT NEVER HAP-PENED!
IT'S JUST A RUMOR.
?
THERE'S SOMETHING FISHY GOING ON.
WELL, WHAT-EVER.
TO THE CAVE! TO THE CAVE! ♡

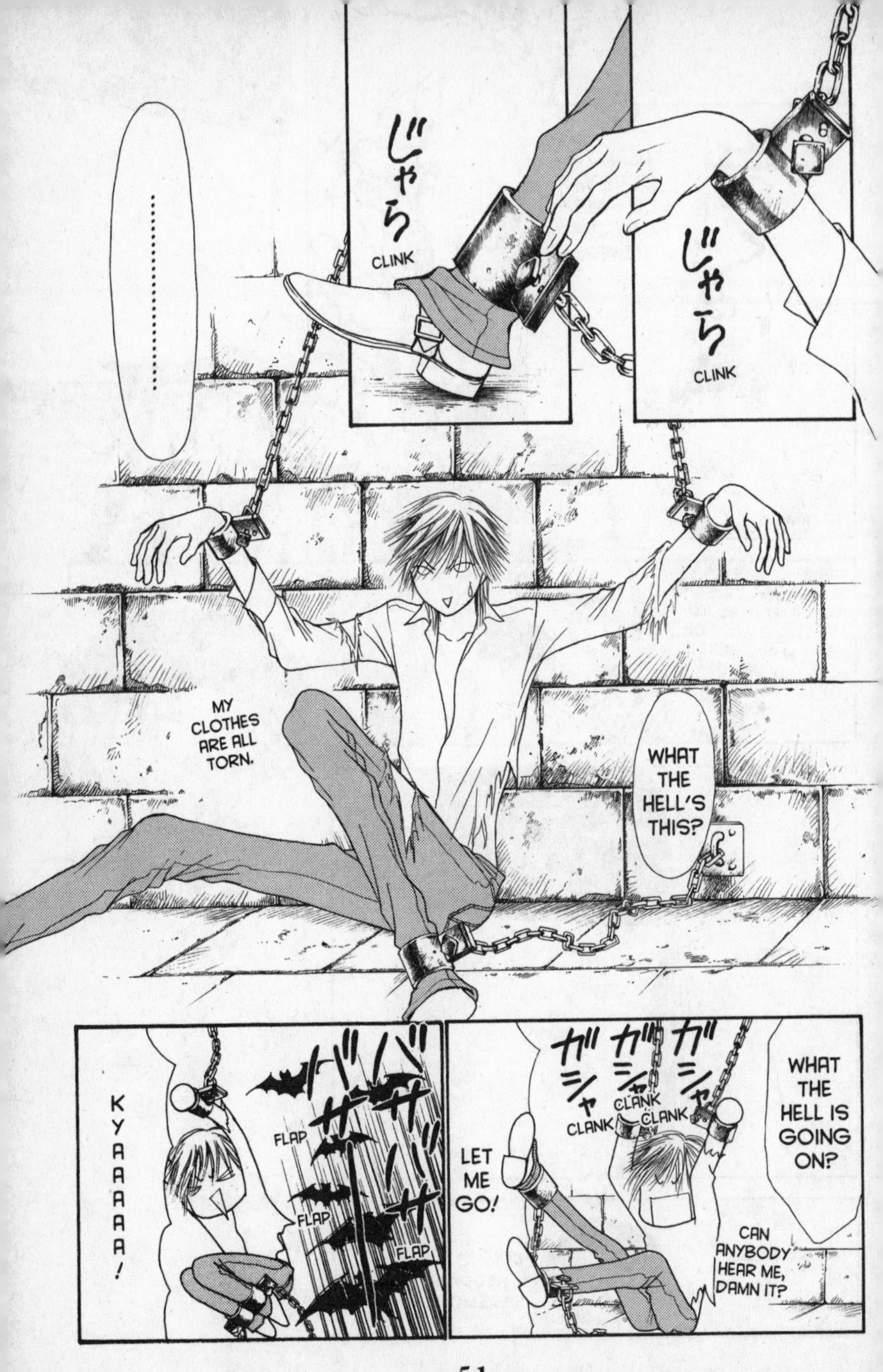
じゃら
CLINK
じゃら
CLINK
......
WHAT THE HELL'S THIS?
MY CLOTHES ARE ALL TORN.
WHAT THE HELL IS GOING ON?
ガシャ ガシャ ガシャ
CLANK CLANK CLANK
CAN ANYBODY HEAR ME, DAMN IT?
LET ME GO!
バサバサ
FLAP FLAP FLAP
KYAAAAAA!

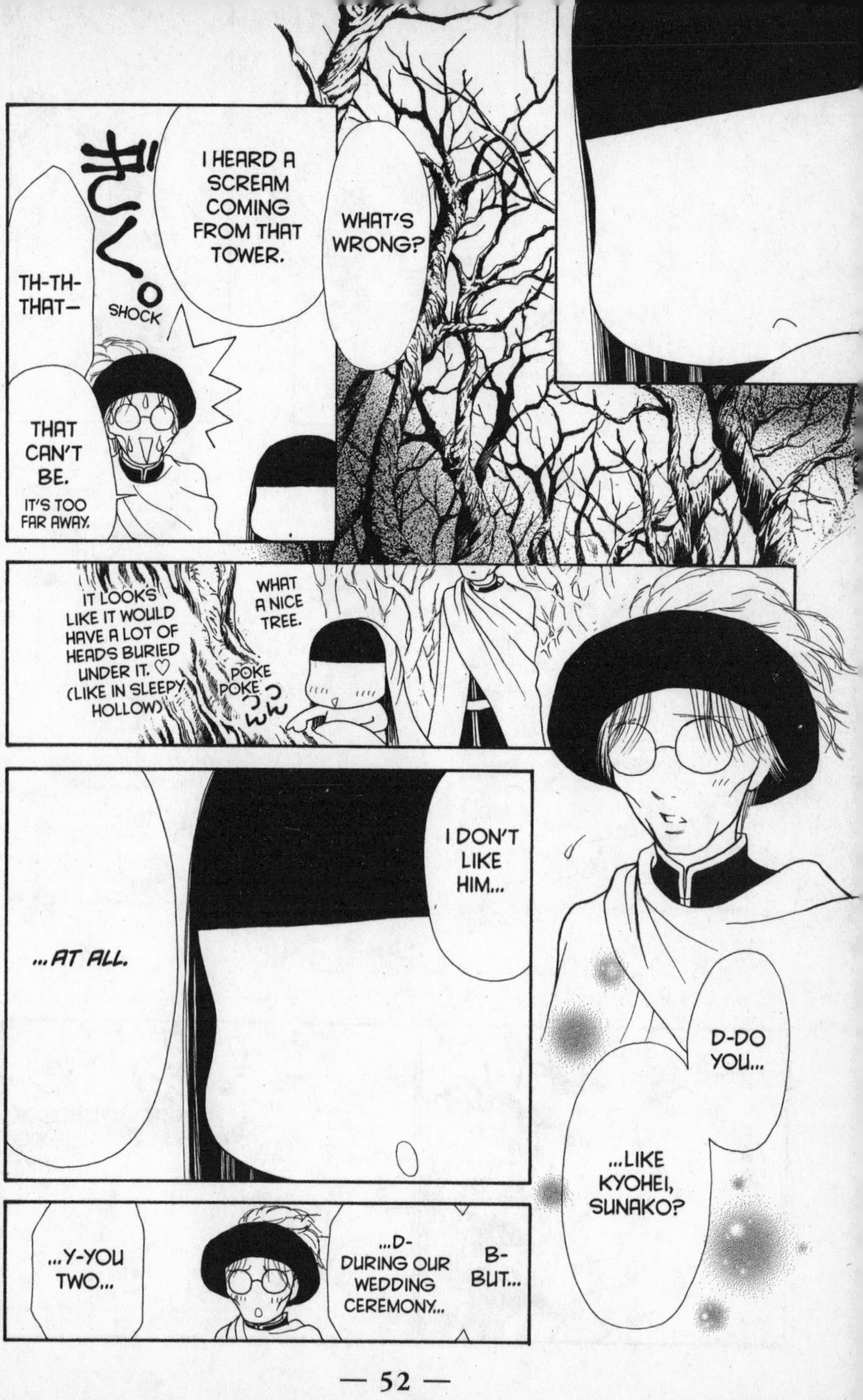
WHAT'S WRONG?
I HEARD A SCREAM COMING FROM THAT TOWER.
SHOCK
TH-TH-THAT—
THAT CAN'T BE.
IT'S TOO FAR AWAY.
WHAT A NICE TREE.
IT LOOKS LIKE IT WOULD HAVE A LOT OF HEADS BURIED UNDER IT. ♡ (LIKE IN SLEEPY HOLLOW)
POKE POKE
D-DO YOU...
...LIKE KYOHEI, SUNAKO?
I DON'T LIKE HIM...
...AT ALL.
B-BUT...
...D-DURING OUR WEDDING CEREMONY...
...Y-YOU TWO...

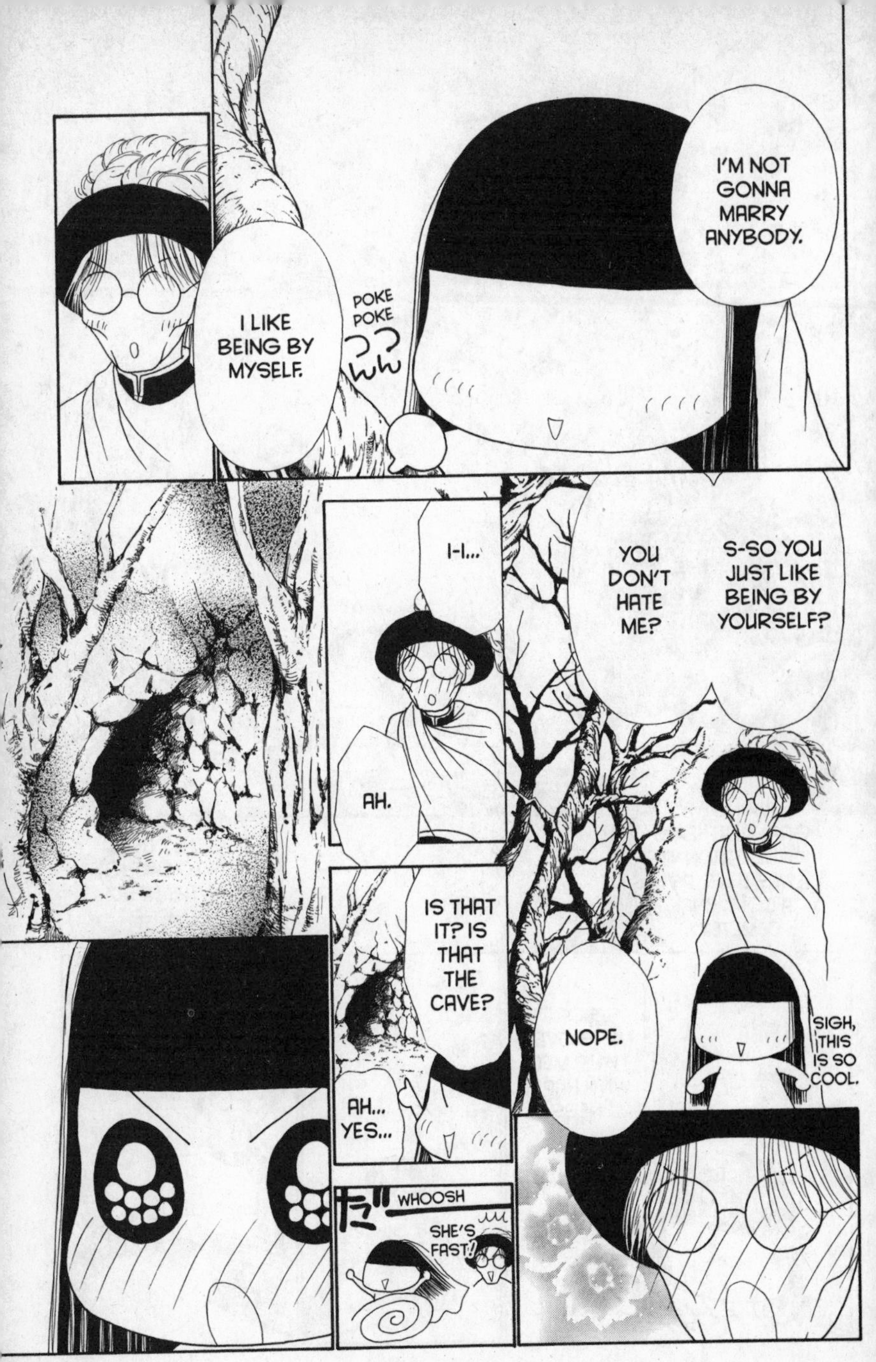
I'M NOT GONNA MARRY ANYBODY.
POKE POKE
I LIKE BEING BY MYSELF.
S-SO YOU JUST LIKE BEING BY YOURSELF?
YOU DON'T HATE ME?
I-I...
AH.
NOPE.
SIGH, THIS IS SO COOL.
IS THAT IT? IS THAT THE CAVE?
AH... YES...
WHOOSH
SHE'S FAST!

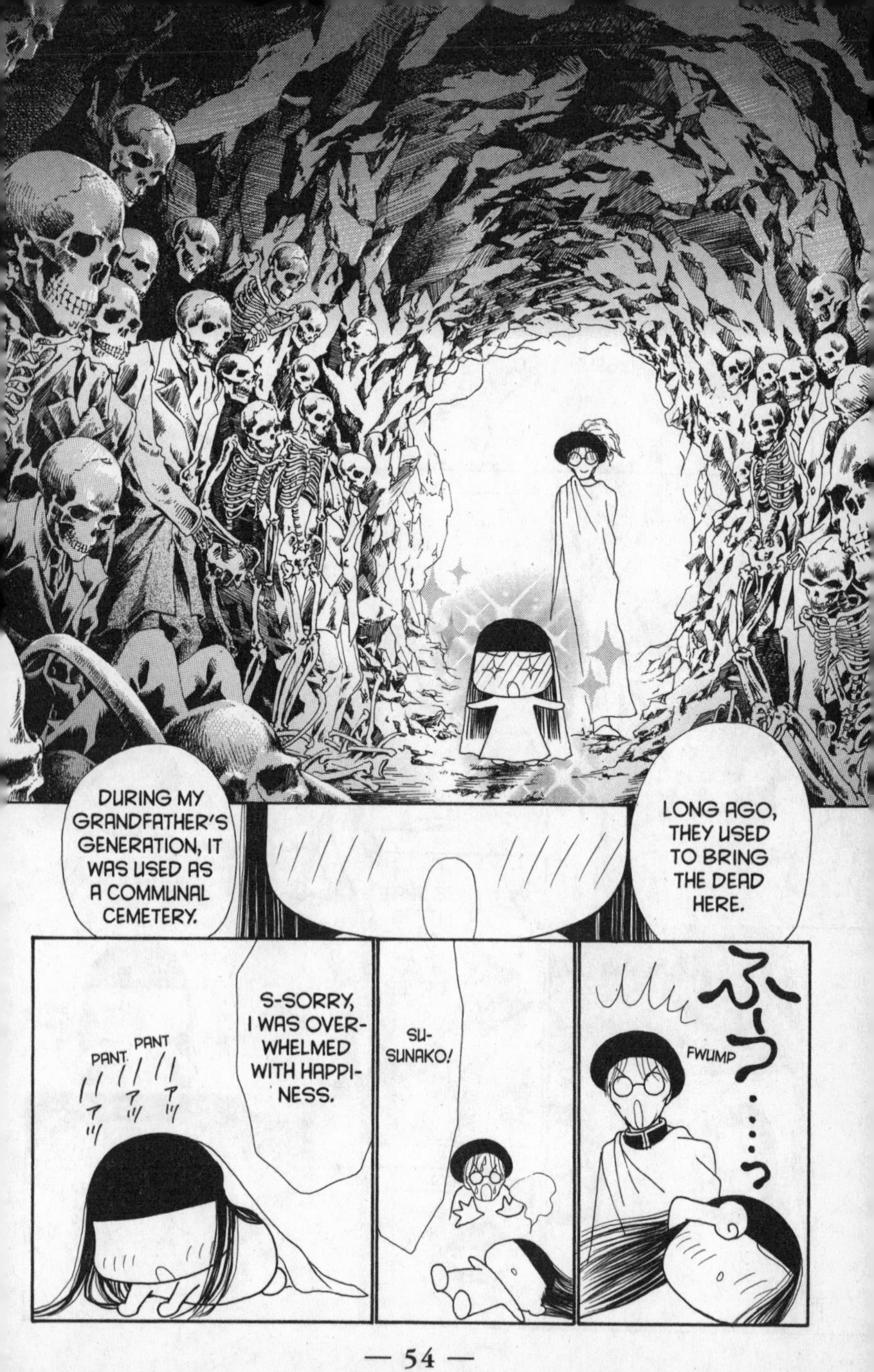

LONG AGO, THEY USED TO BRING THE DEAD HERE.
DURING MY GRANDFATHER'S GENERATION, IT WAS USED AS A COMMUNAL CEMETERY.
ふ〜っ…
FWUMP
SU-SUNAKO!
S-SORRY, I WAS OVER-WHELMED WITH HAPPI-NESS.
PANT PANT
アッ アッ アッ

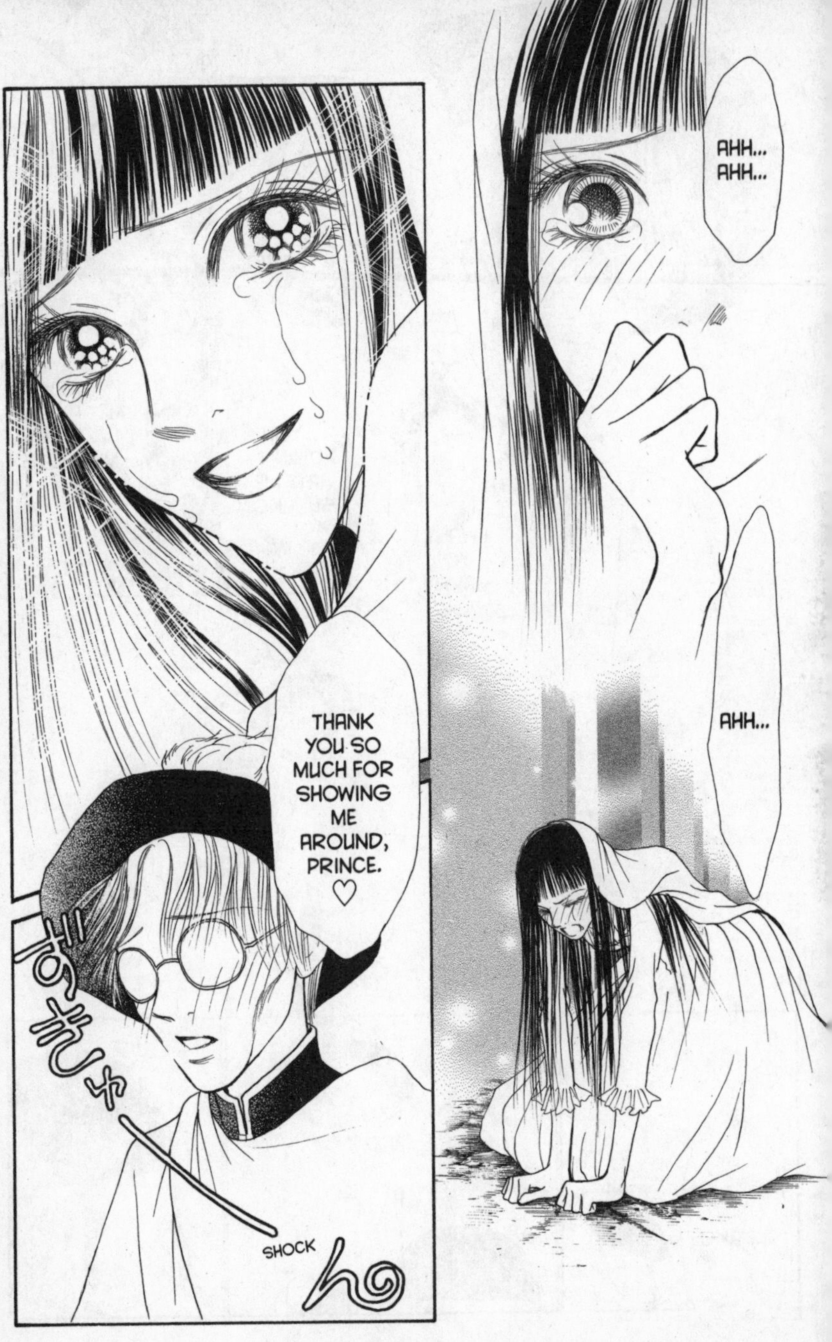
AHH... AHH...
AHH...
THANK YOU SO MUCH FOR SHOWING ME AROUND, PRINCE. ♡
SHOCK

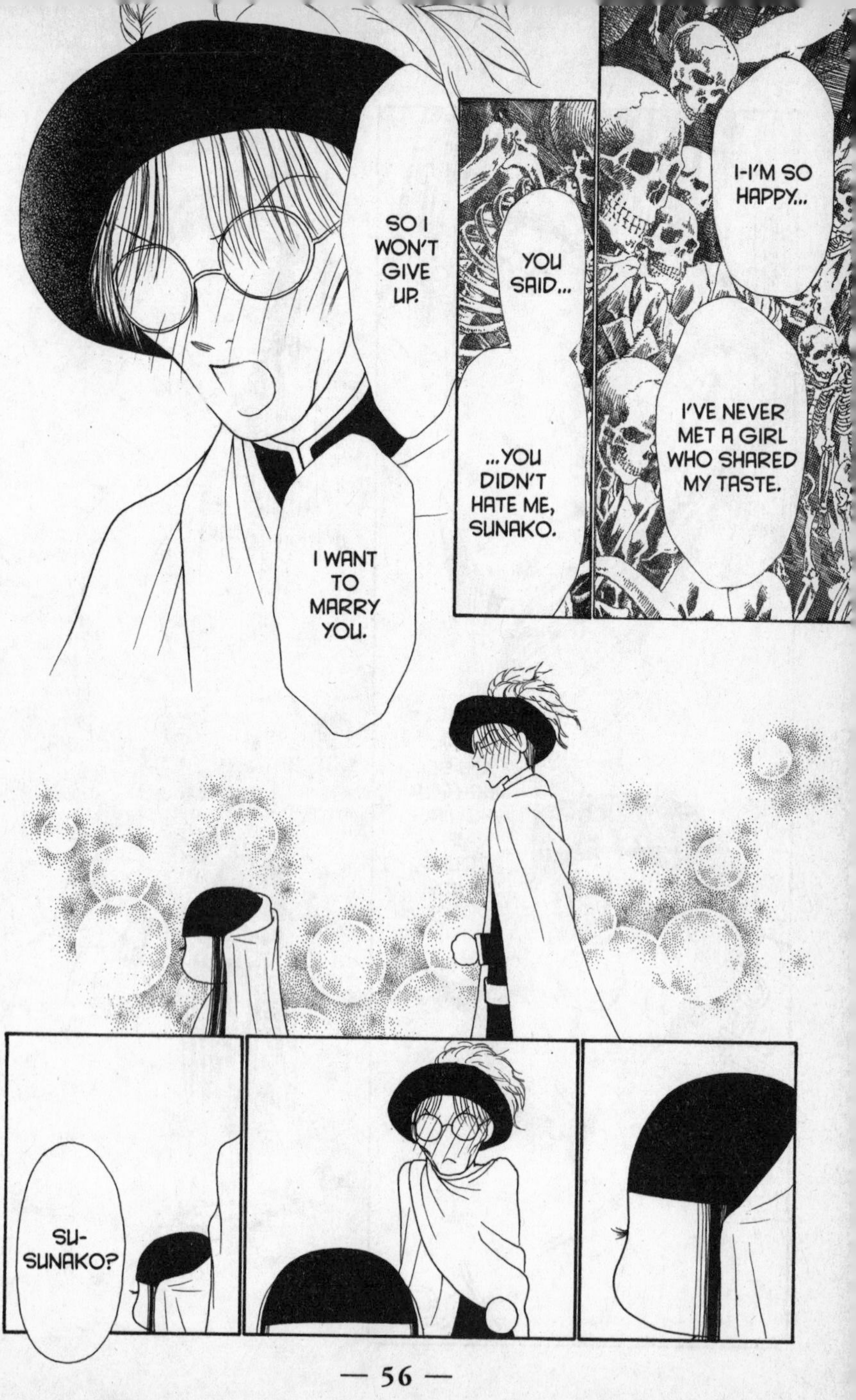
I-I'M SO HAPPY...
I'VE NEVER MET A GIRL WHO SHARED MY TASTE.
YOU SAID...
...YOU DIDN'T HATE ME, SUNAKO.
SO I WON'T GIVE UP.
I WANT TO MARRY YOU.
SU-SUNAKO?

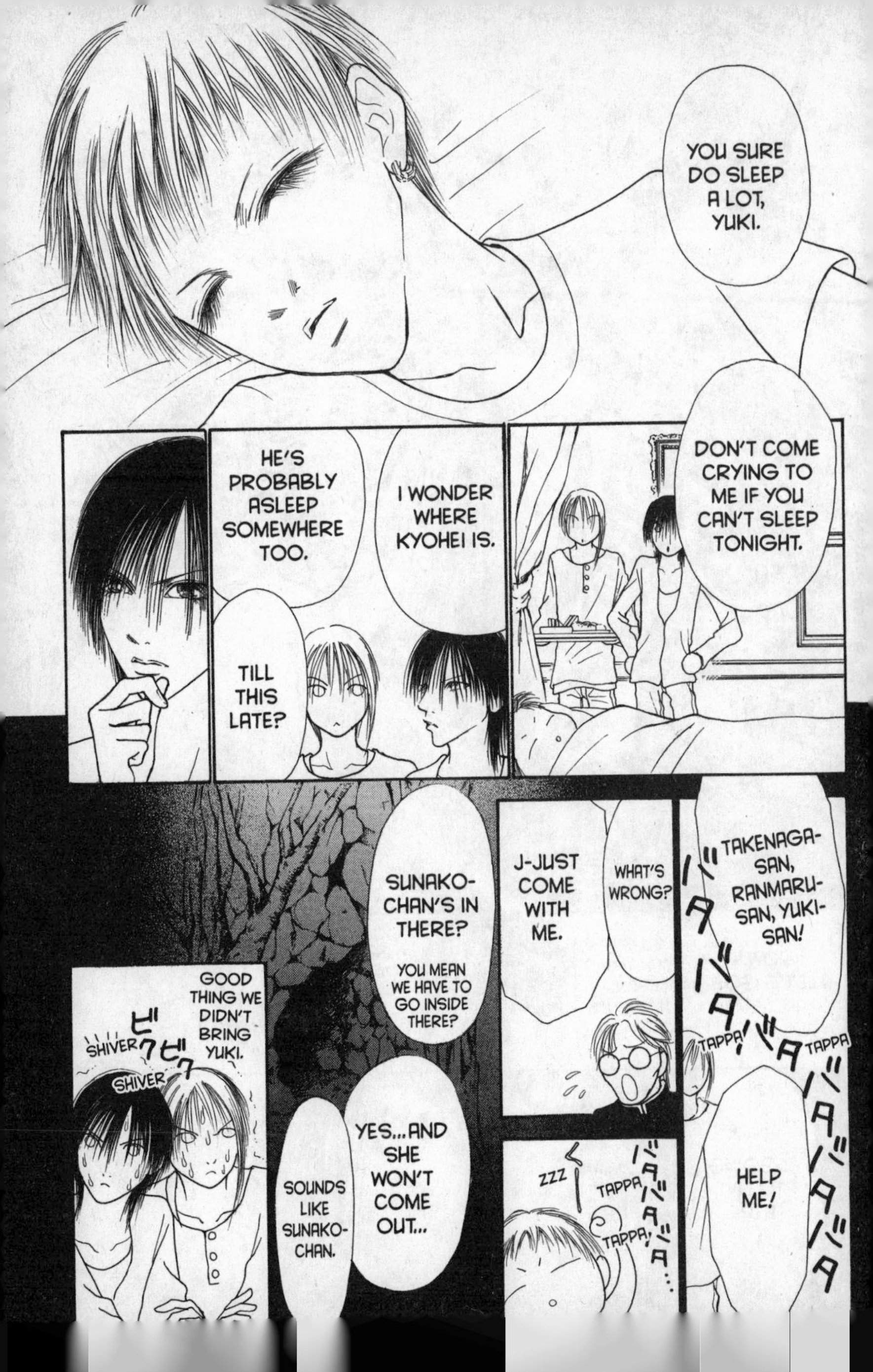
YOU SURE DO SLEEP A LOT, YUKI.
DON'T COME CRYING TO ME IF YOU CAN'T SLEEP TONIGHT.
I WONDER WHERE KYOHEI IS.
HE'S PROBABLY ASLEEP SOMEWHERE TOO.
TILL THIS LATE?
TAKENAGA-SAN, RANMARU-SAN, YUKI-SAN!
バタバタ
TAPPA
TAPPA
HELP ME!
WHAT'S WRONG?
J-JUST COME WITH ME.
ZZZ
バタバタ...
TAPPA
TAPPA
SUNAKO-CHAN'S IN THERE?
YOU MEAN WE HAVE TO GO INSIDE THERE?
YES...AND SHE WON'T COME OUT...
SOUNDS LIKE SUNAKO-CHAN.
GOOD THING WE DIDN'T BRING YUKI.
ビクビク
SHIVER
SHIVER

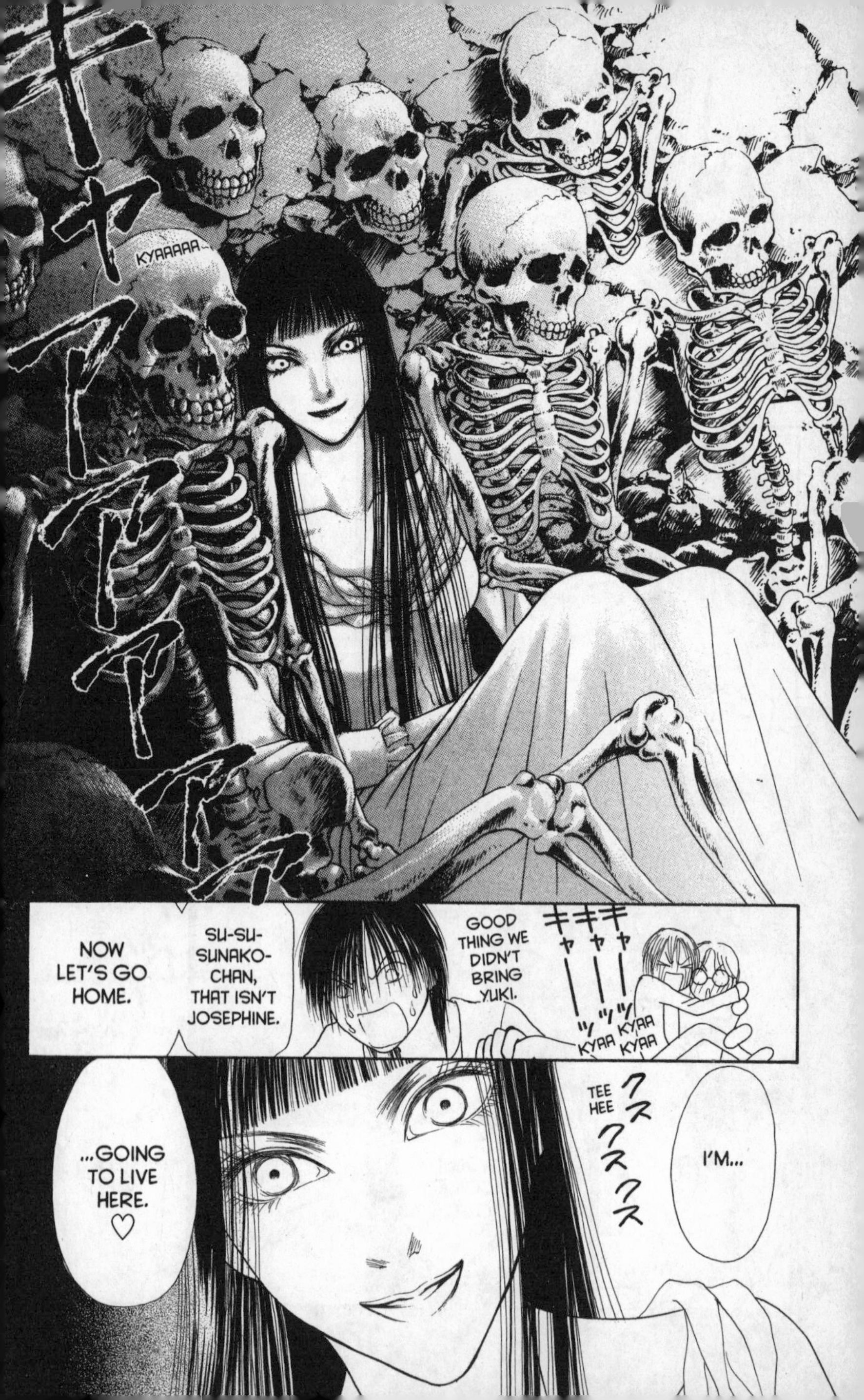
キャアアアアア
KYAAAAA...
キャーッ キャーッ キャーッ
KYAA KYAA KYAA
GOOD THING WE DIDN'T BRING YUKI.
SU-SU-SUNAKO-CHAN, THAT ISN'T JOSEPHINE.
NOW LET'S GO HOME.
I'M...
クスクスクスクス
TEE HEE
...GOING TO LIVE HERE. ♡

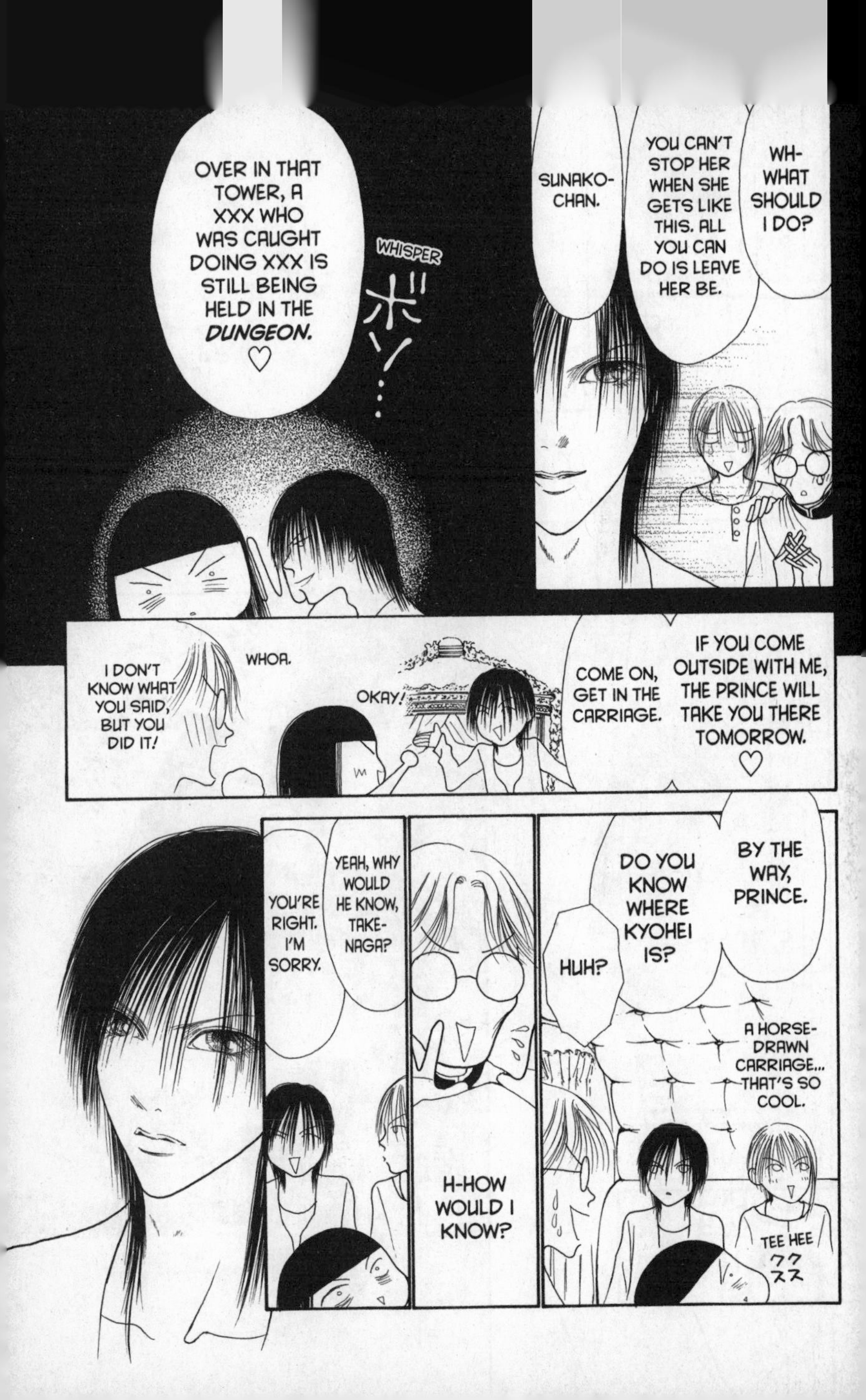
WH- WHAT SHOULD I DO?
YOU CAN'T STOP HER WHEN SHE GETS LIKE THIS. ALL YOU CAN DO IS LEAVE HER BE.
SUNAKO-CHAN.
OVER IN THAT TOWER, A XXX WHO WAS CAUGHT DOING XXX IS STILL BEING HELD IN THE ***DUNGEON.*** ♡
WHISPER
ボソ…
IF YOU COME OUTSIDE WITH ME, THE PRINCE WILL TAKE YOU THERE TOMORROW. ♡
COME ON, GET IN THE CARRIAGE.
OKAY!
WHOA.
I DON'T KNOW WHAT YOU SAID, BUT YOU DID IT!
BY THE WAY, PRINCE.
DO YOU KNOW WHERE KYOHEI IS?
HUH?
A HORSE-DRAWN CARRIAGE... THAT'S SO COOL.
TEE HEE
ククスス
H-HOW WOULD I KNOW?
YEAH, WHY WOULD HE KNOW, TAKE-NAGA?
YOU'RE RIGHT. I'M SORRY.

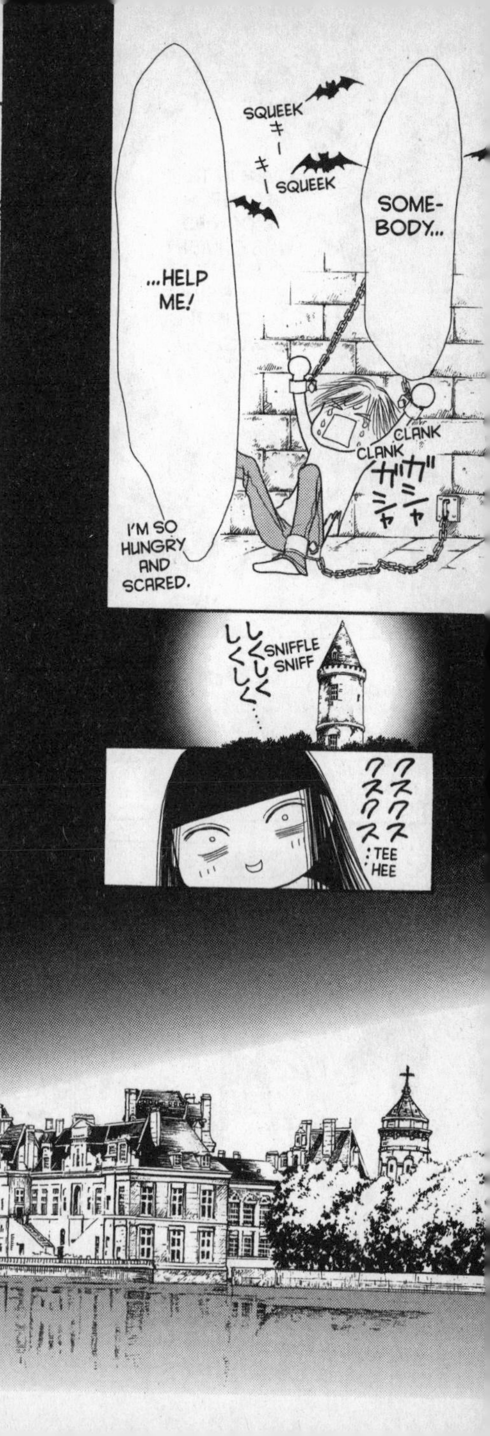
SOME-BODY...
SQUEEK
キーキー
SQUEEK
...HELP ME!
I'M SO HUNGRY AND SCARED.
CLANK CLANK
ガシャガシャ
しくしくしくしく
SNIFFLE SNIFF
クスクスクスクス
TEE HEE
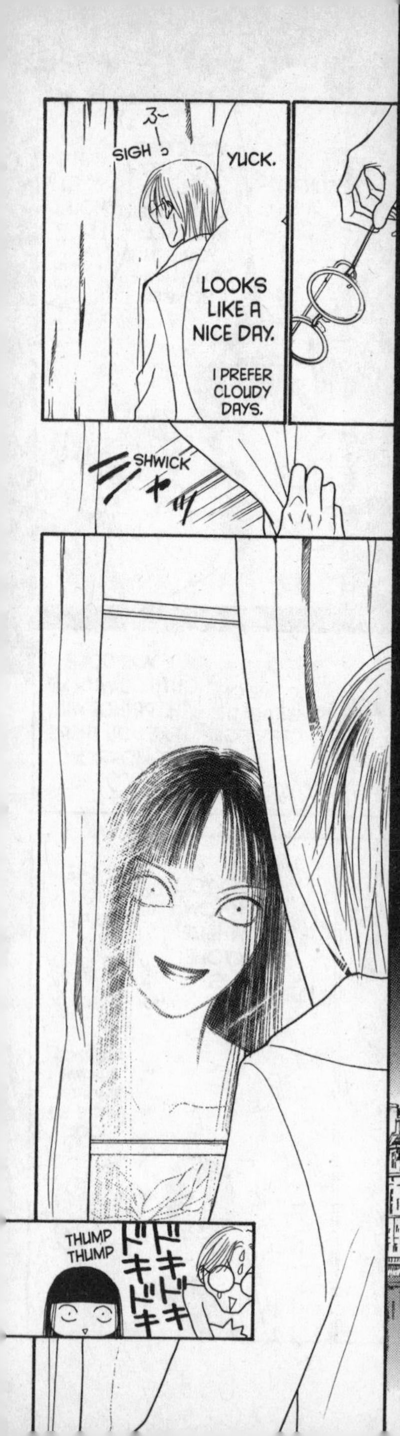
ふ～っ
SIGH
YUCK.
LOOKS LIKE A NICE DAY.
I PREFER CLOUDY DAYS.
SHWICK
シャッ
THUMP THUMP
ドキドキドキドキ

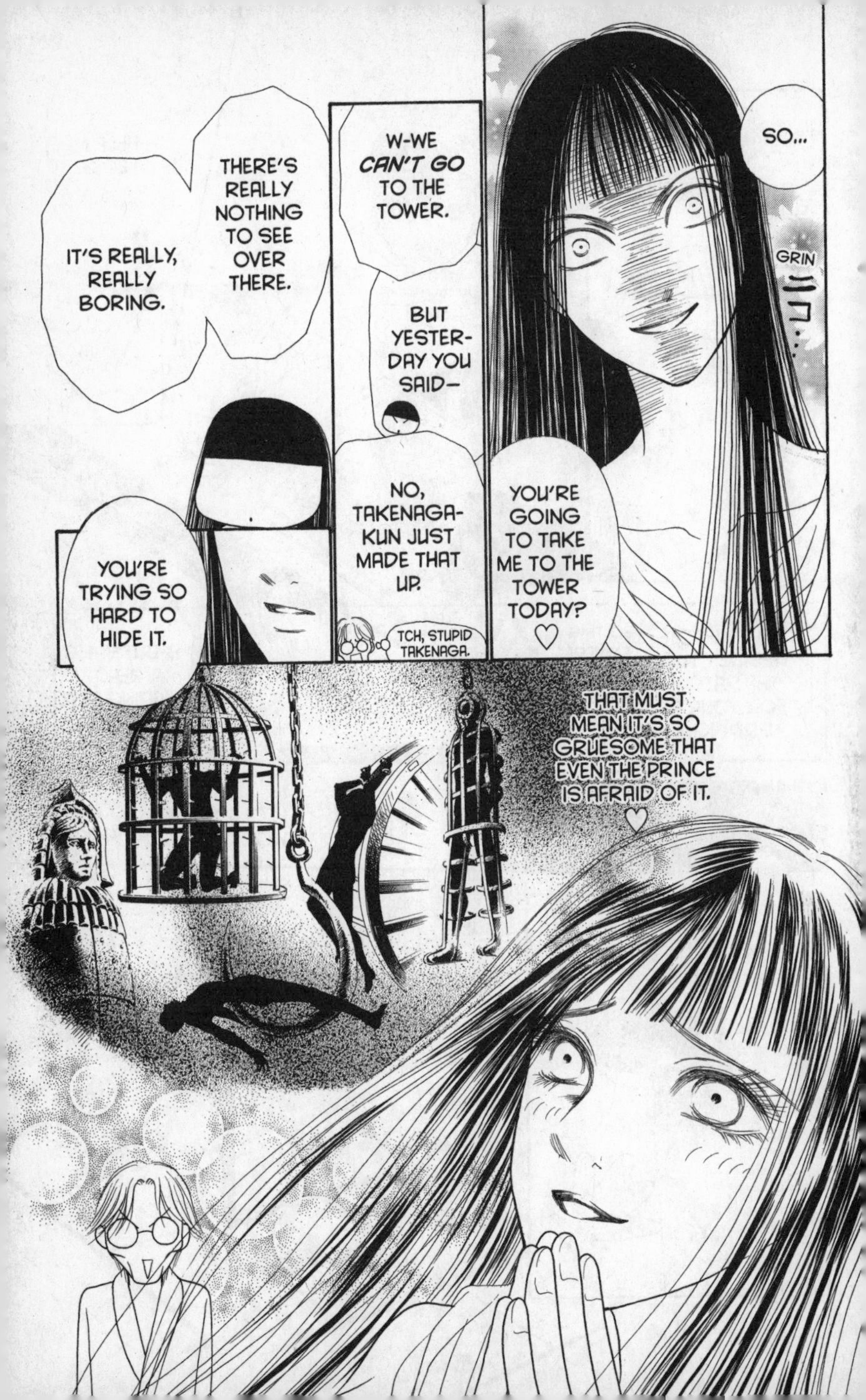
SO...
GRIN
YOU'RE GOING TO TAKE ME TO THE TOWER TODAY? ♡
W-WE *CAN'T GO* TO THE TOWER.
BUT YESTERDAY YOU SAID—
NO, TAKENAGA-KUN JUST MADE THAT UP.
TCH, STUPID TAKENAGA.
THERE'S REALLY NOTHING TO SEE OVER THERE.
IT'S REALLY, REALLY BORING.
YOU'RE TRYING SO HARD TO HIDE IT.
THAT MUST MEAN IT'S SO GRUESOME THAT EVEN THE PRINCE IS AFRAID OF IT. ♡

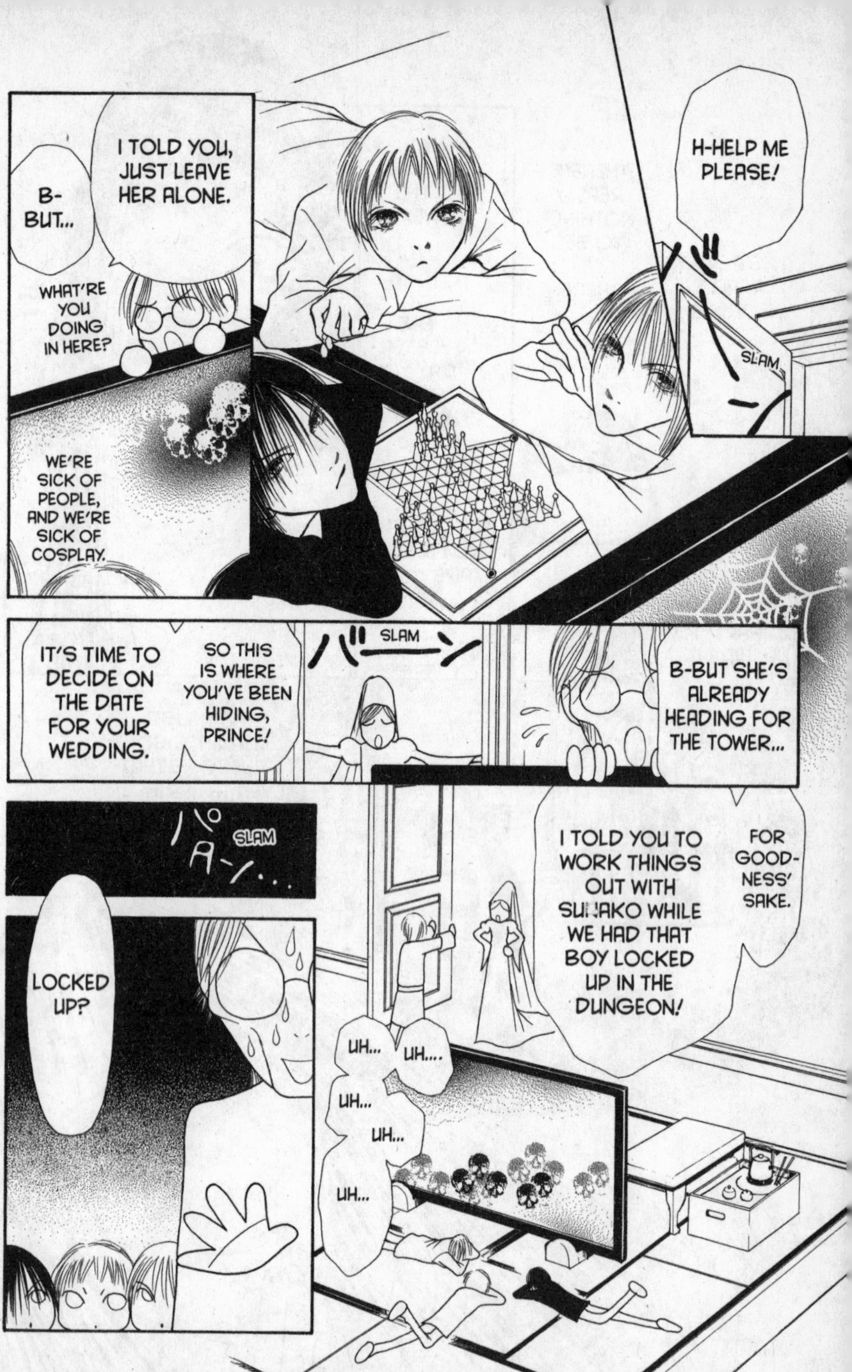
H-HELP ME PLEASE!
SLAM
I TOLD YOU, JUST LEAVE HER ALONE.
B-BUT...
WHAT'RE YOU DOING IN HERE?
WE'RE SICK OF PEOPLE, AND WE'RE SICK OF COSPLAY.
B-BUT SHE'S ALREADY HEADING FOR THE TOWER...
SLAM
SO THIS IS WHERE YOU'VE BEEN HIDING, PRINCE!
IT'S TIME TO DECIDE ON THE DATE FOR YOUR WEDDING.
FOR GOODNESS' SAKE.
I TOLD YOU TO WORK THINGS OUT WITH SUNAKO WHILE WE HAD THAT BOY LOCKED UP IN THE DUNGEON!
UH...
UH....
UH...
UH...
UH...
SLAM
LOCKED UP?

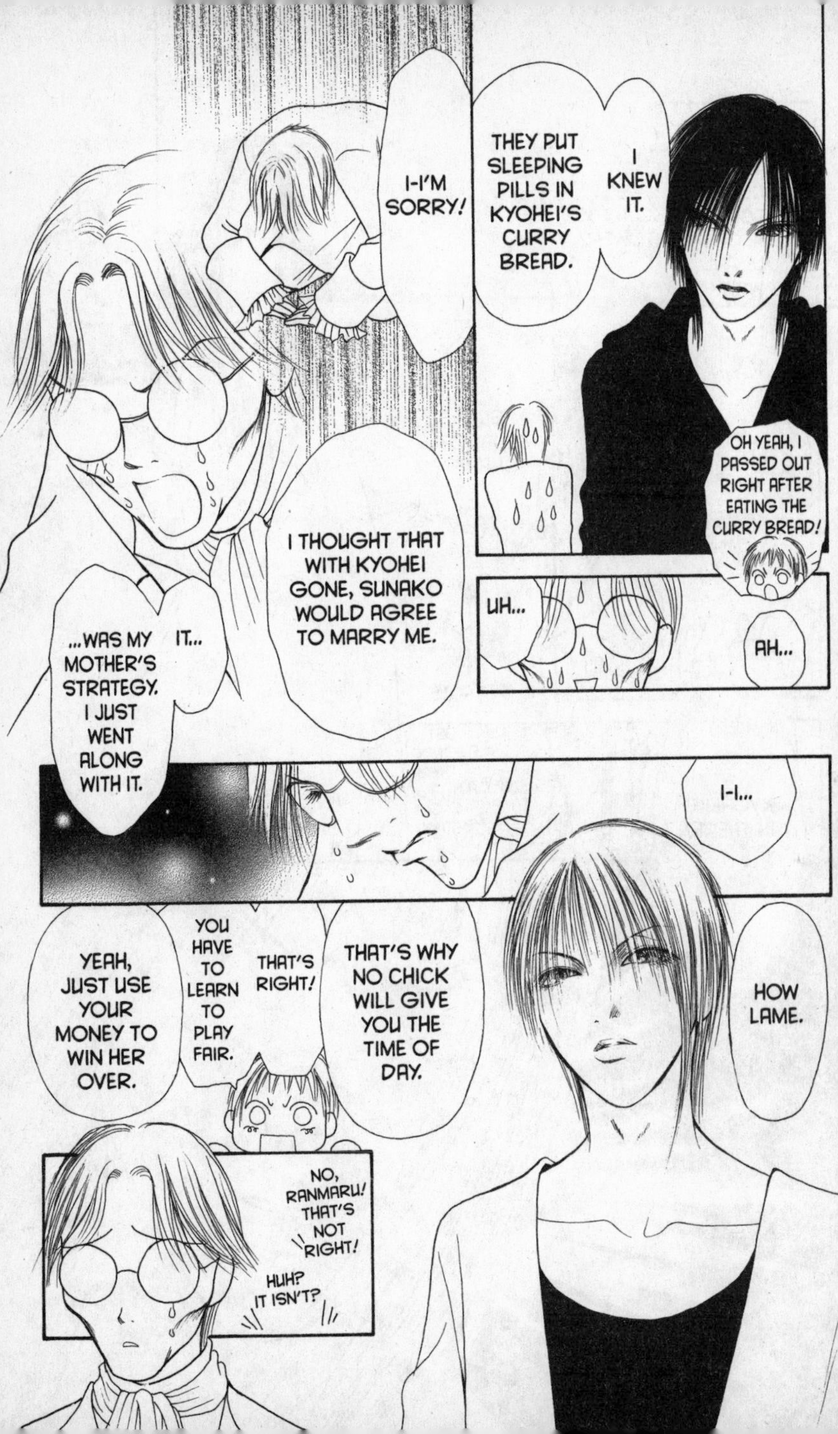
I KNEW IT.
THEY PUT SLEEPING PILLS IN KYOHEI'S CURRY BREAD.
OH YEAH, I PASSED OUT RIGHT AFTER EATING THE CURRY BREAD!
AH...
UH...
I-I'M SORRY!
I THOUGHT THAT WITH KYOHEI GONE, SUNAKO WOULD AGREE TO MARRY ME.
IT...
...WAS MY MOTHER'S STRATEGY. I JUST WENT ALONG WITH IT.
I-I...
HOW LAME.
THAT'S WHY NO CHICK WILL GIVE YOU THE TIME OF DAY.
THAT'S RIGHT!
YOU HAVE TO LEARN TO PLAY FAIR.
YEAH, JUST USE YOUR MONEY TO WIN HER OVER.
NO, RANMARU! THAT'S NOT RIGHT!
HUH? IT ISN'T?

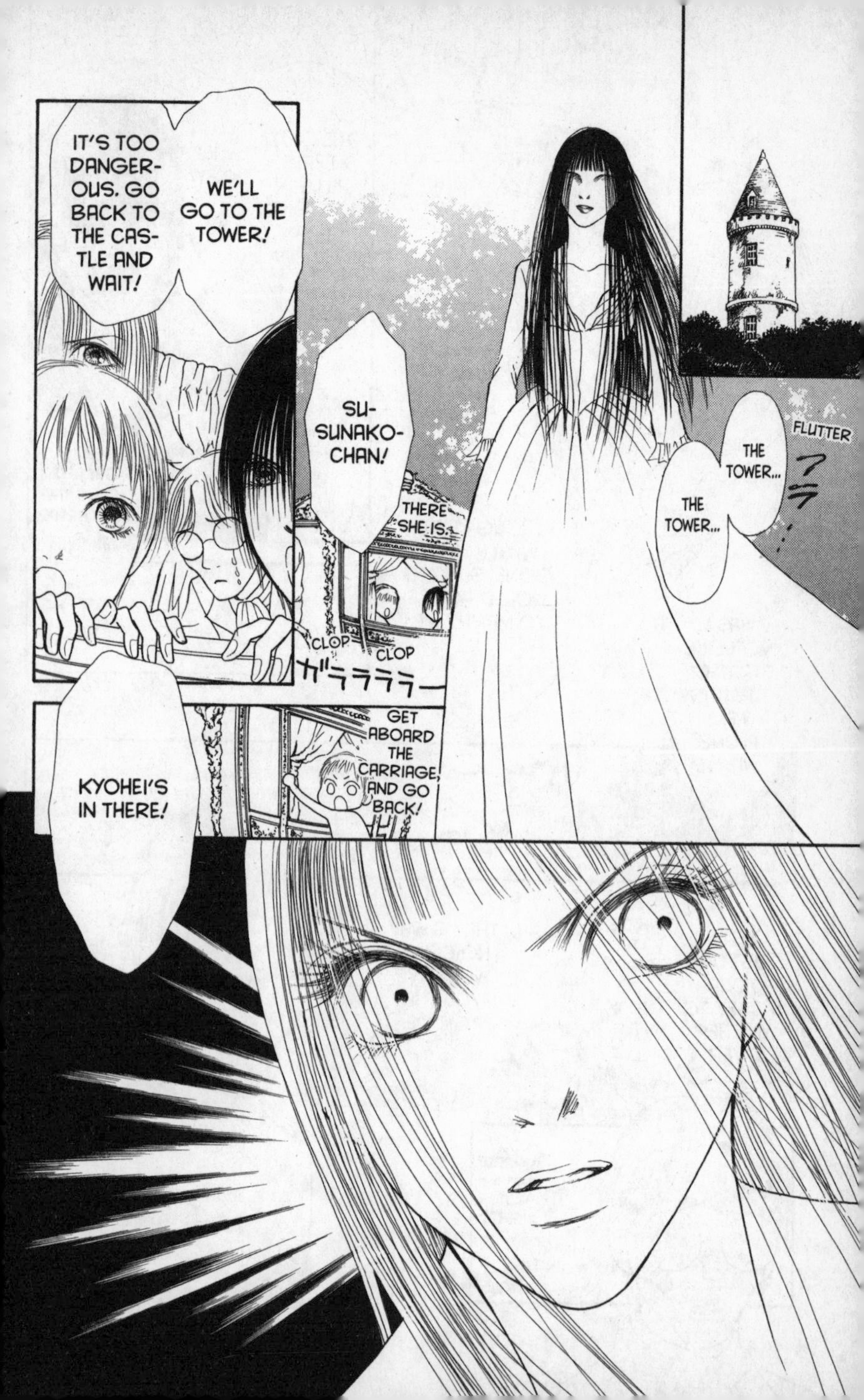
FLUTTER
フラ
THE TOWER...
THE TOWER...
WE'LL GO TO THE TOWER!
IT'S TOO DANGER-OUS. GO BACK TO THE CAS-TLE AND WAIT!
SU-SUNAKO-CHAN!
THERE SHE IS.
CLOP CLOP
ガラララララー
GET ABOARD THE CARRIAGE, AND GO BACK!
KYOHEI'S IN THERE!

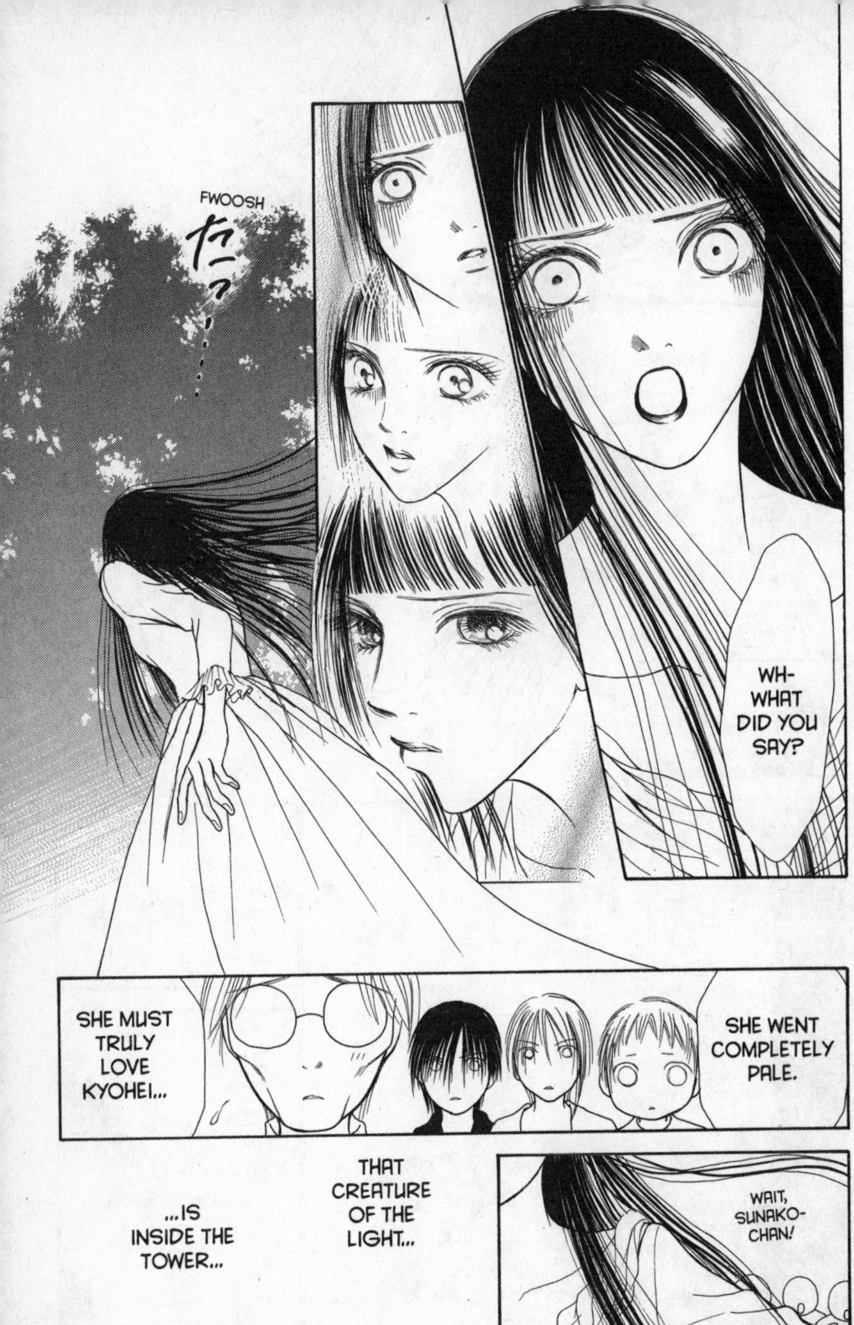
WH-WHAT DID YOU SAY?
FWOOSH
SHE WENT COMPLETELY PALE.
SHE MUST TRULY LOVE KYOHEI...
WAIT, SUNAKO-CHAN!
THAT CREATURE OF THE LIGHT...
...IS INSIDE THE TOWER...

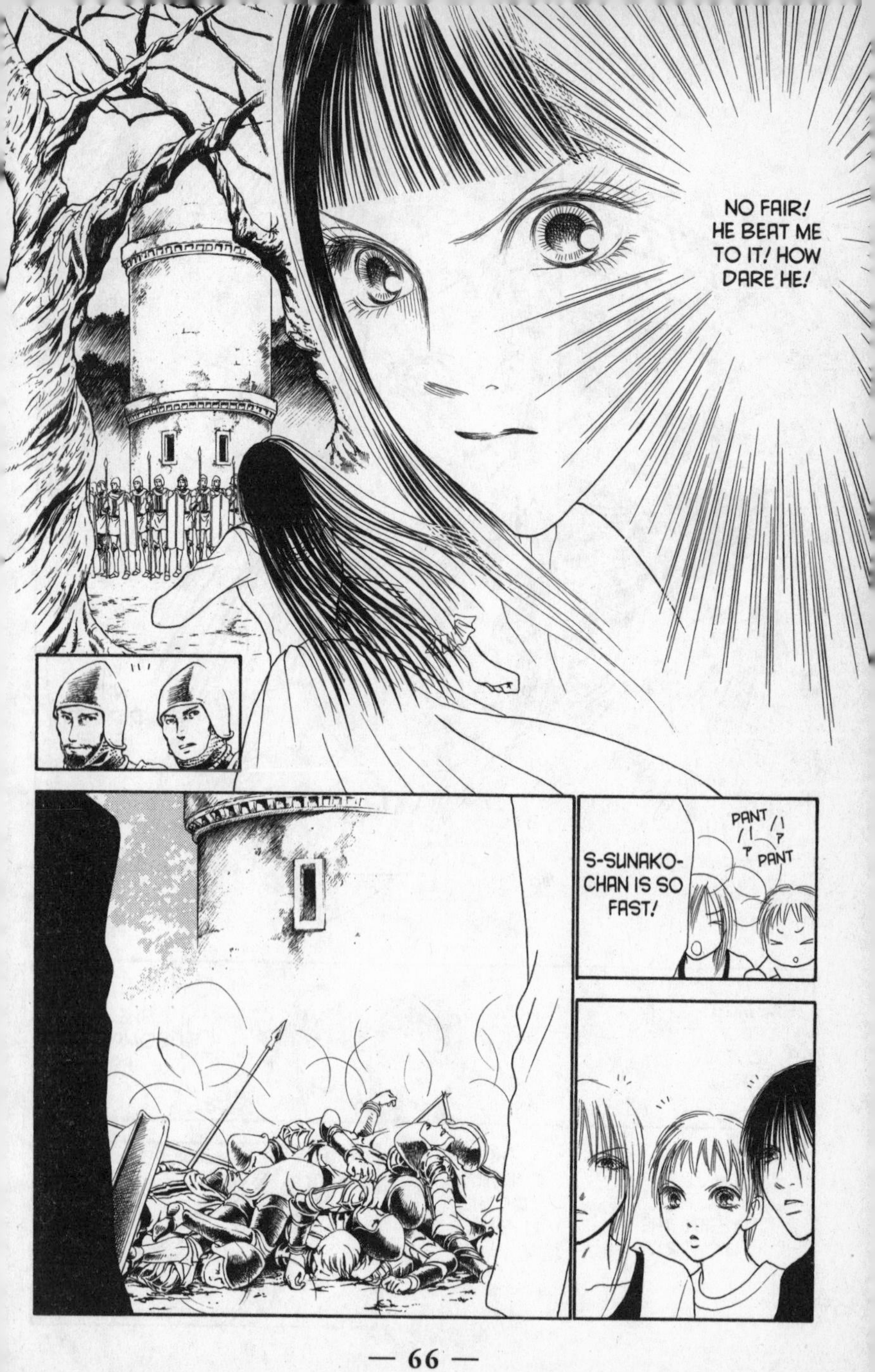
NO FAIR! HE BEAT ME TO IT! HOW DARE HE!
PANT PANT
S-SUNAKO-CHAN IS SO FAST!

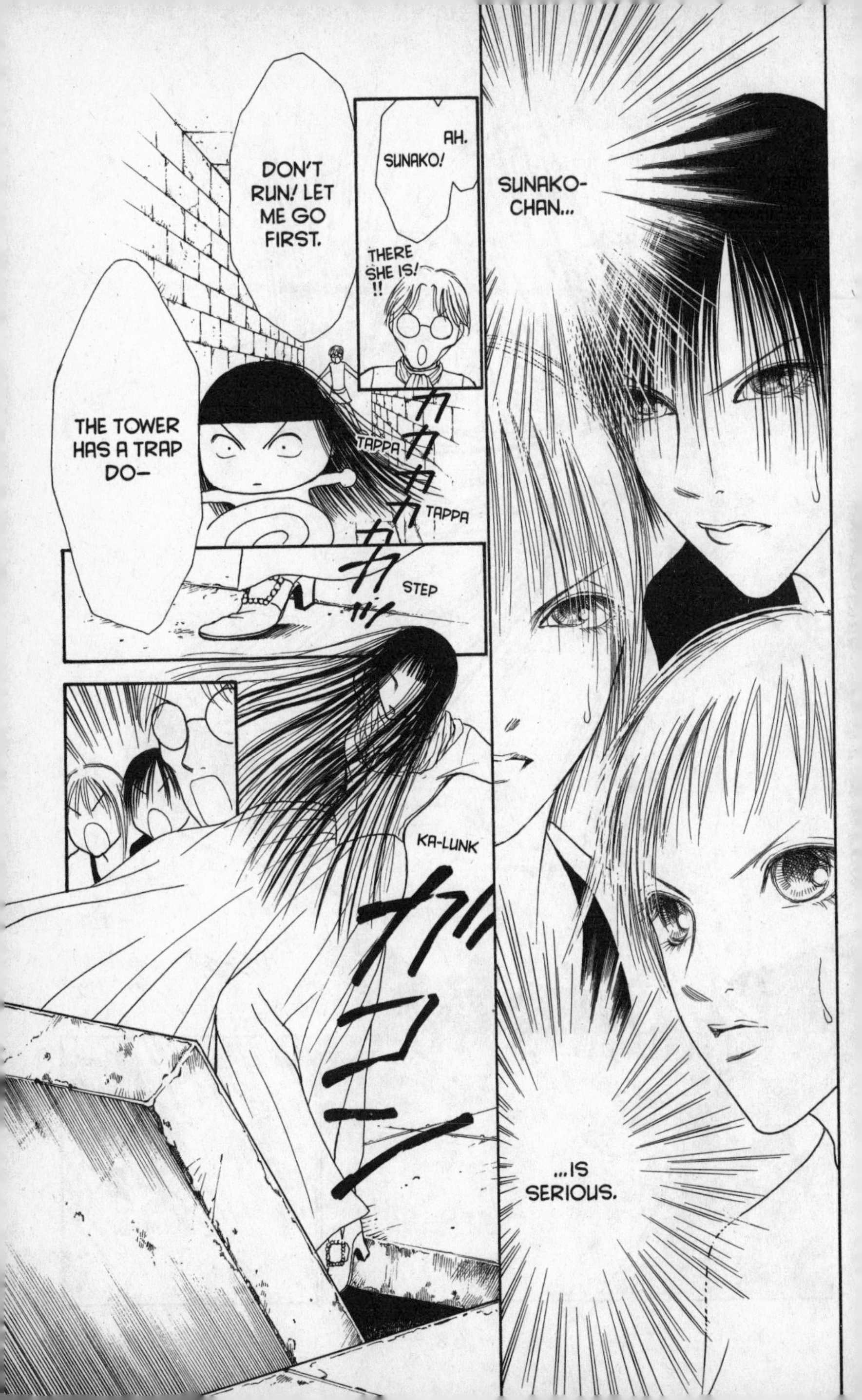
SUNAKO-CHAN...
...IS SERIOUS.
AH. SUNAKO!
THERE SHE IS!!
DON'T RUN! LET ME GO FIRST.
THE TOWER HAS A TRAP DO—
TAPPA
TAPPA
STEP
KA-LUNK

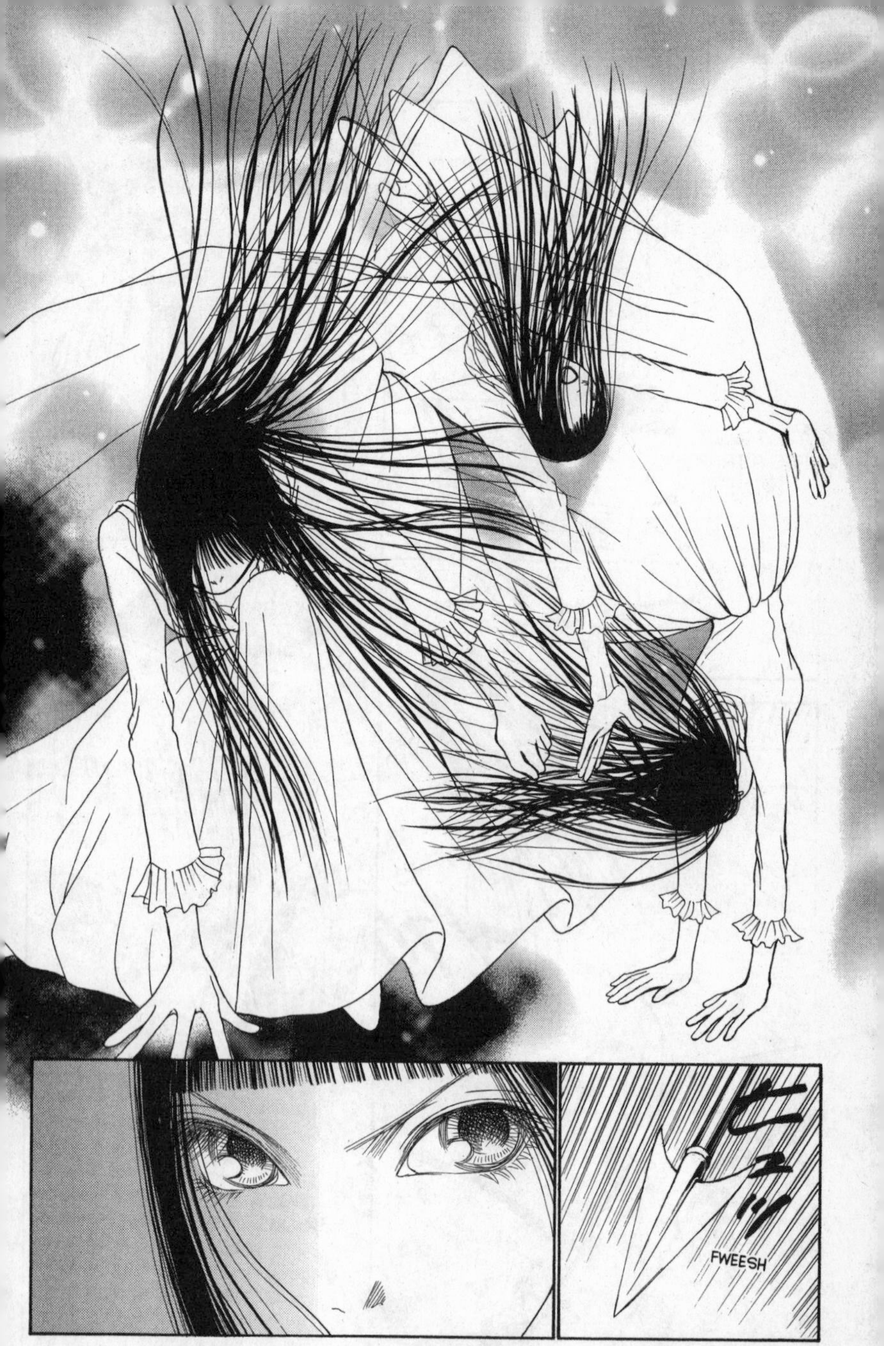
ヒュッ
FWEESH

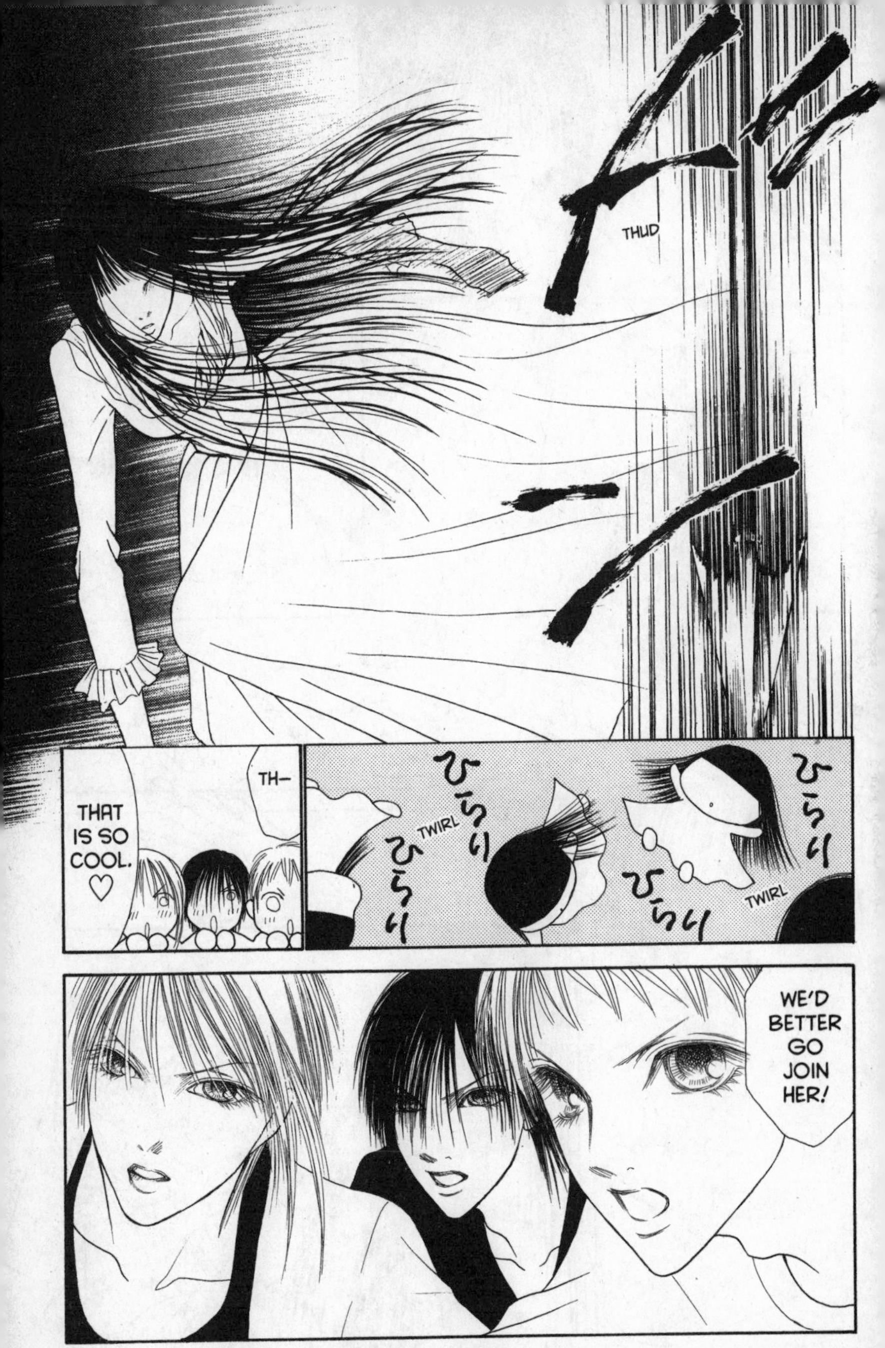
THUD
ひらり
ひらり
TWIRL
ひらり
TWIRL
ひらり
TH—
THAT IS SO COOL. ♡
WE'D BETTER GO JOIN HER!

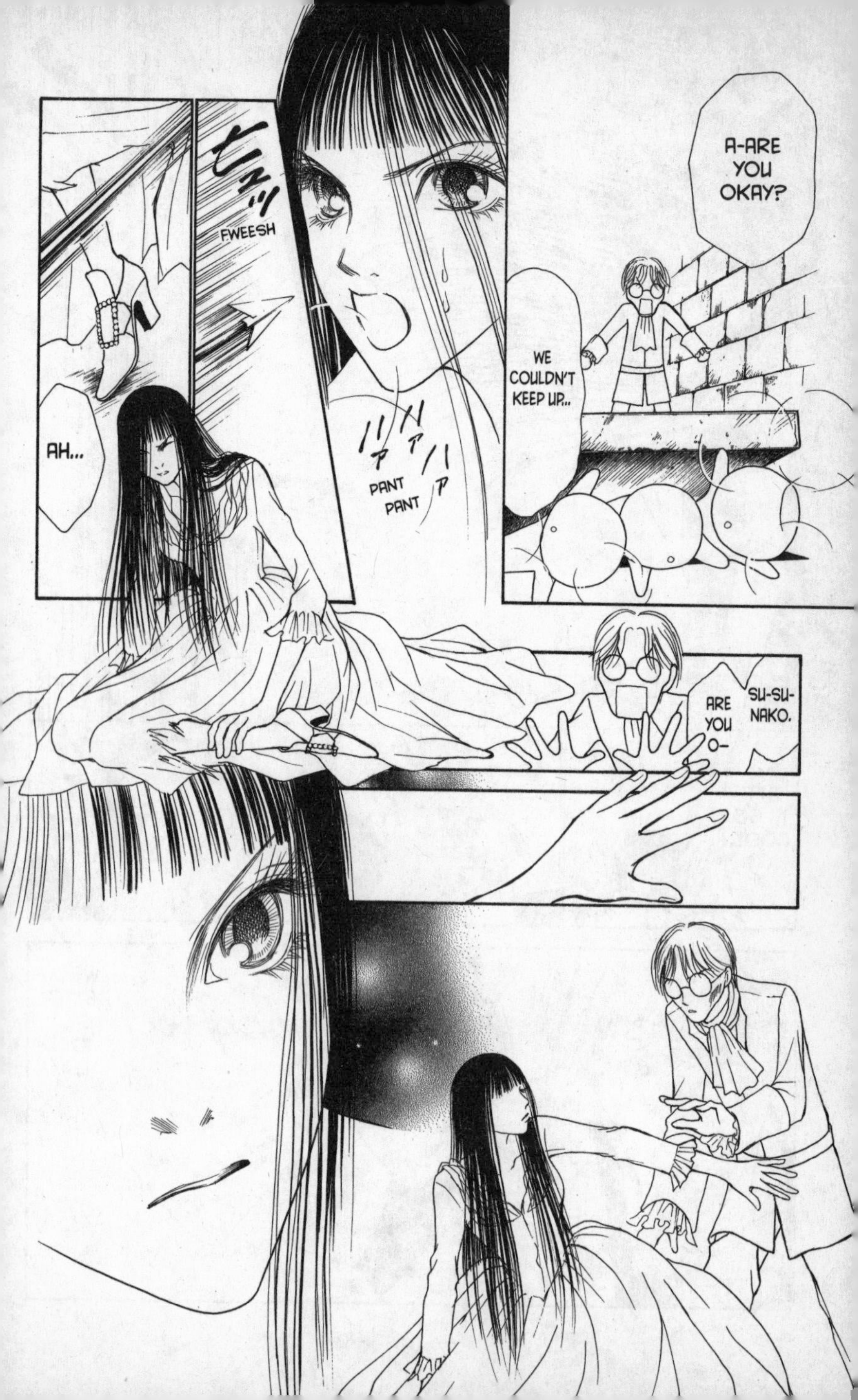
A-ARE YOU OKAY?
WE COULDN'T KEEP UP...
PANT PANT
FWEESH
AH...
SU-SU-NAKO.
ARE YOU O-

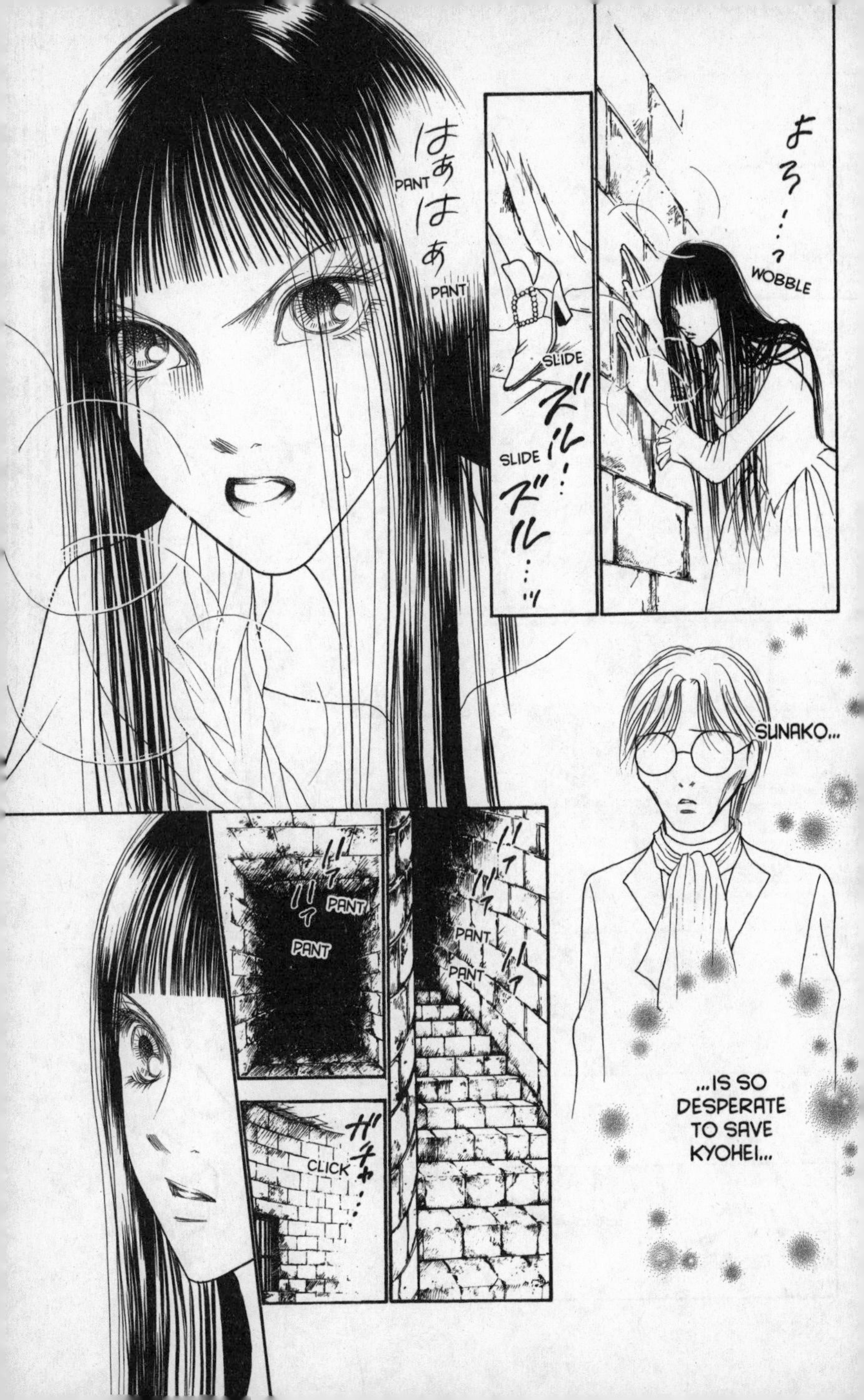

よろ…っ
WOBBLE
ズル…ズル…ッ
SLIDE
SLIDE
はぁはぁ
PANT
PANT
SUNAKO...
...IS SO DESPERATE TO SAVE KYOHEI...
PANT
PANT
PANT
PANT
ガチャ…
CLICK

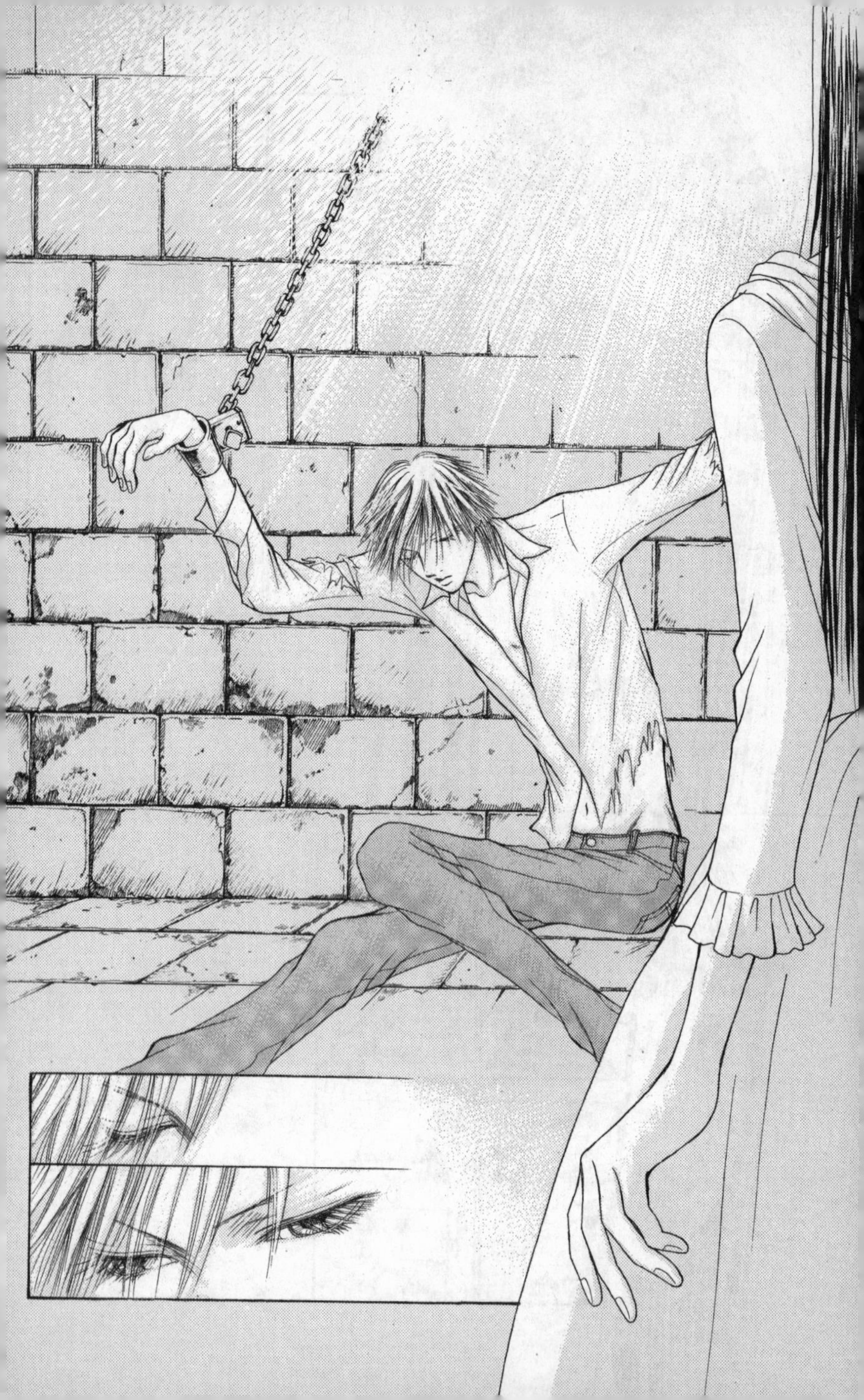

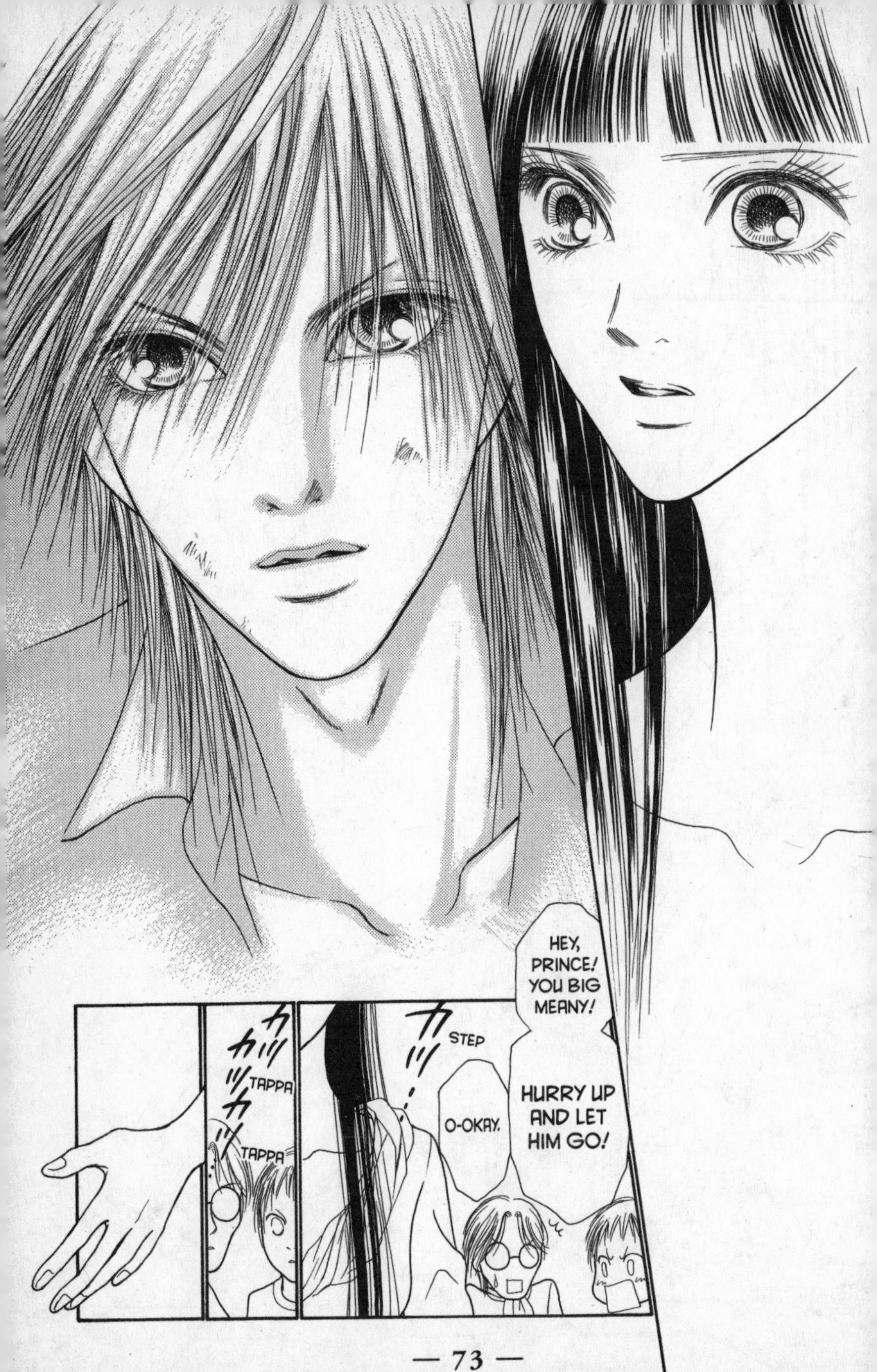
HEY, PRINCE! YOU BIG MEANY!
STEP
HURRY UP AND LET HIM GO!
O-OKAY.
TAPPA
TAPPA

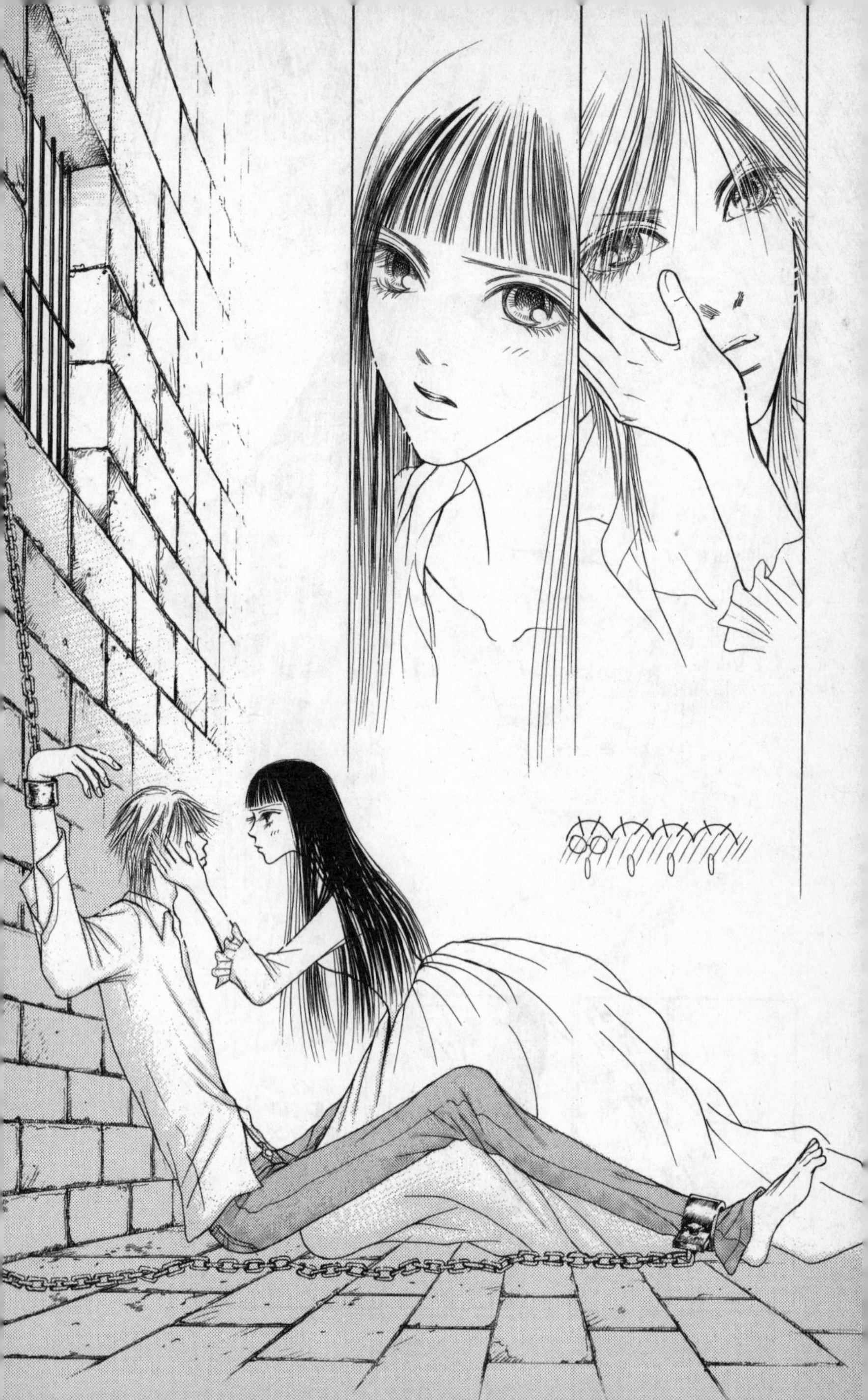

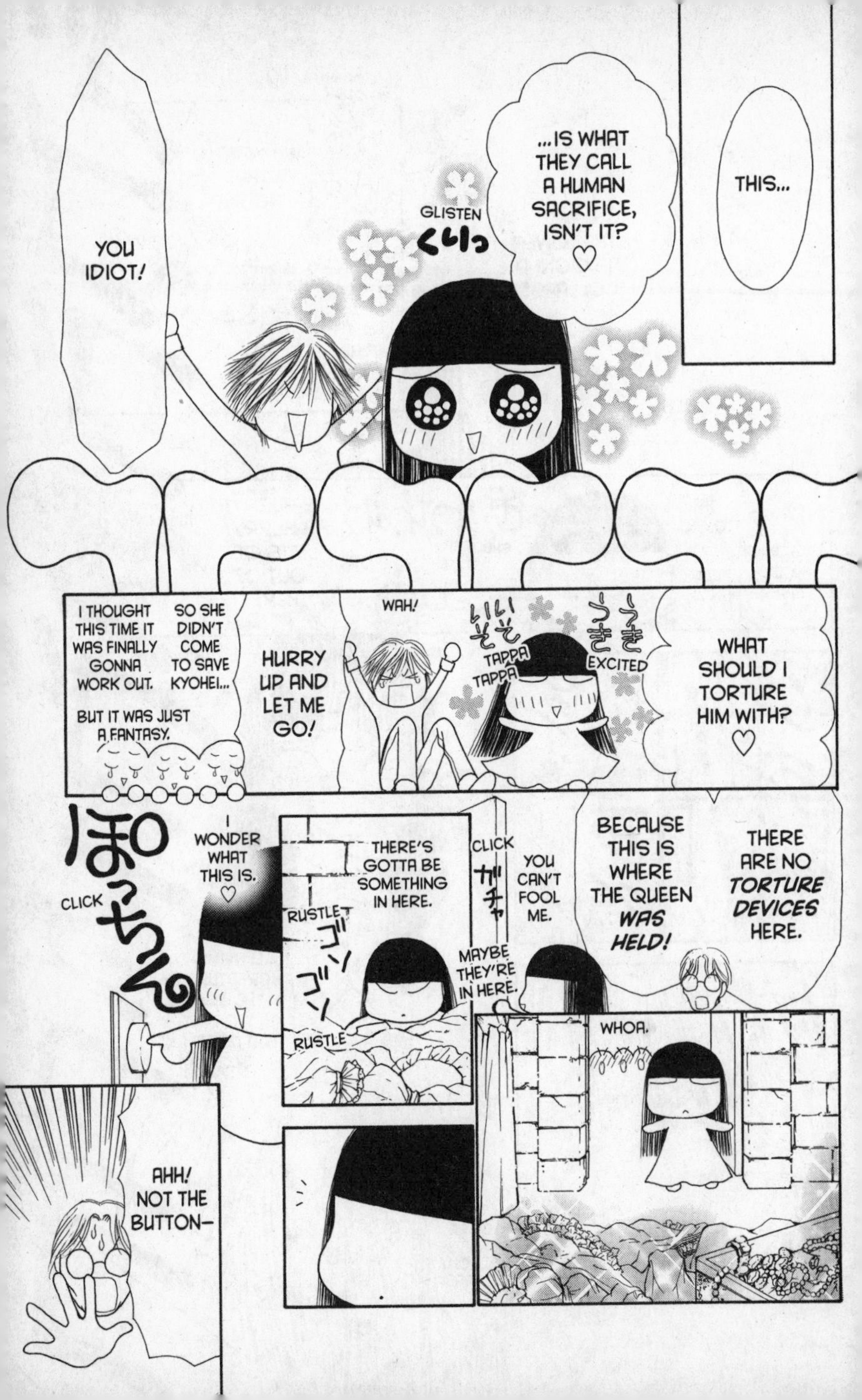
THIS...
...IS WHAT THEY CALL A HUMAN SACRIFICE, ISN'T IT? ♡
GLISTEN
くりっ
YOU IDIOT!
WHAT SHOULD I TORTURE HIM WITH? ♡
うきうき
EXCITED
いそいそ
TAPPA TAPPA
WAH!
HURRY UP AND LET ME GO!
SO SHE DIDN'T COME TO SAVE KYOHEI...
I THOUGHT THIS TIME IT WAS FINALLY GONNA WORK OUT.
BUT IT WAS JUST A FANTASY.
THERE ARE NO *TORTURE DEVICES* HERE.
BECAUSE THIS IS WHERE THE QUEEN *WAS HELD!*
YOU CAN'T FOOL ME.
CLICK
ガチャ
MAYBE THEY'RE IN HERE.
WHOA.
THERE'S GOTTA BE SOMETHING IN HERE.
RUSTLE
ゴソゴソ
RUSTLE
I WONDER WHAT THIS IS. ♡
CLICK
ぽっちん
AHH! NOT THE BUTTON—

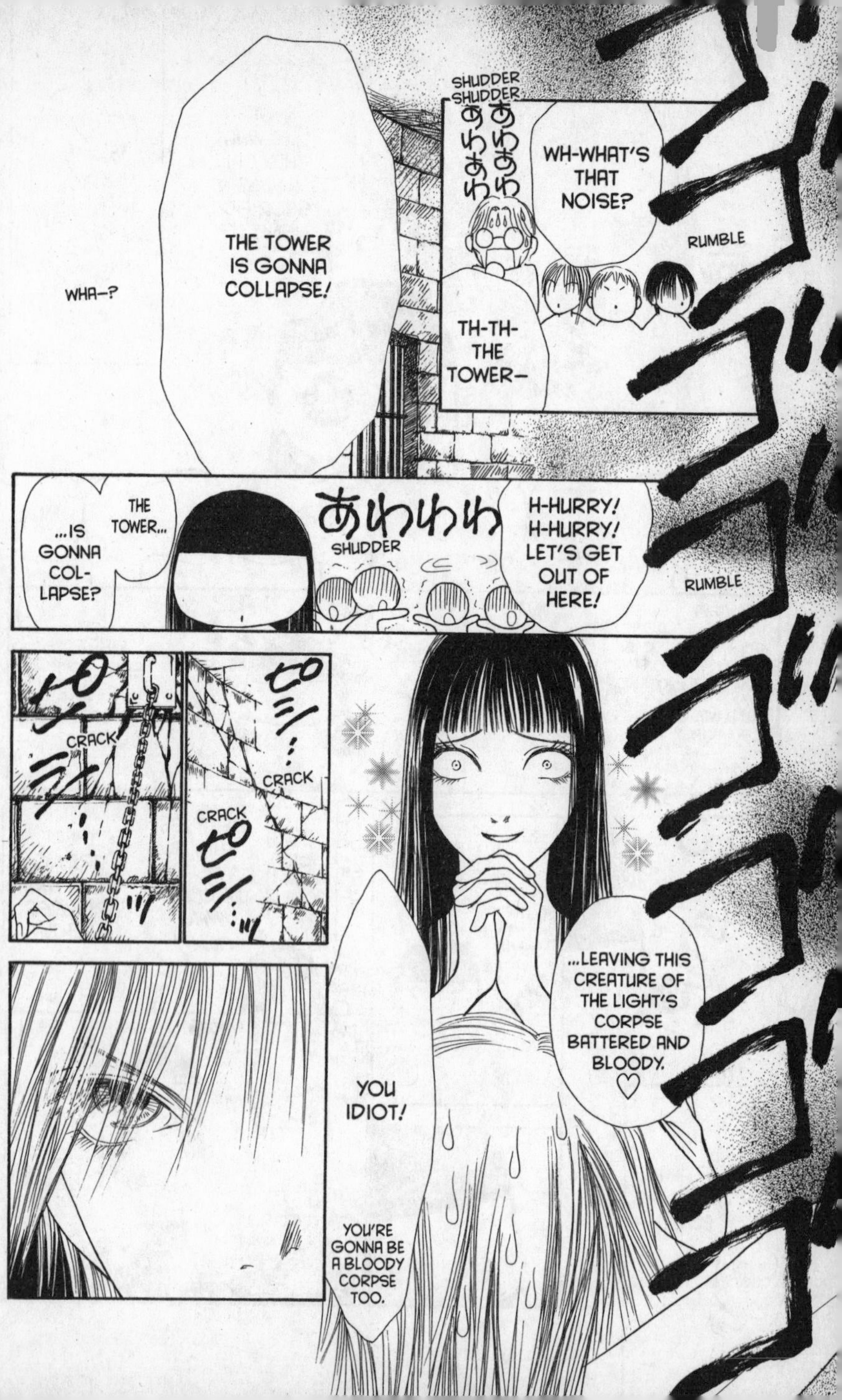
SHUDDER SHUDDER
あわあわ あわあわ
WH-WHAT'S THAT NOISE?
TH-TH-THE TOWER—
RUMBLE
THE TOWER IS GONNA COLLAPSE!
WHA-?
H-HURRY! H-HURRY! LET'S GET OUT OF HERE!
RUMBLE
あわわわ
SHUDDER
THE TOWER...
...IS GONNA COL-LAPSE?
...LEAVING THIS CREATURE OF THE LIGHT'S CORPSE BATTERED AND BLOODY. ♡
ピシ
CRACK
CRACK
ピシ
ピシ
CRACK
YOU IDIOT!
YOU'RE GONNA BE A BLOODY CORPSE TOO.

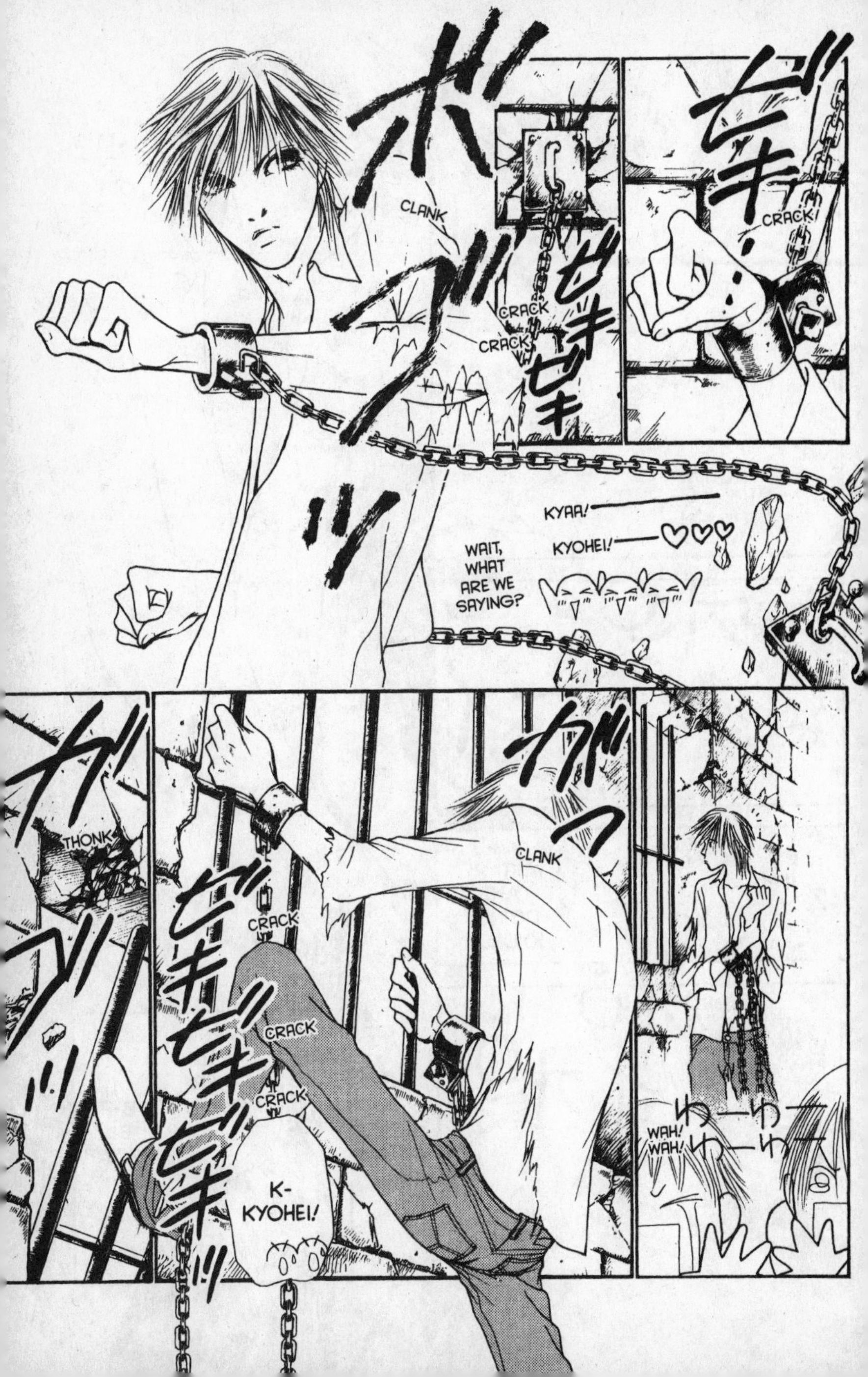
CRACK
CLANK
CRACK
CRACK
KYAA!
KYOHEI!
WAIT, WHAT ARE WE SAYING?
WAH! WAH!
CLANK
CRACK
CRACK
CRACK
K-KYOHEI!
THONK

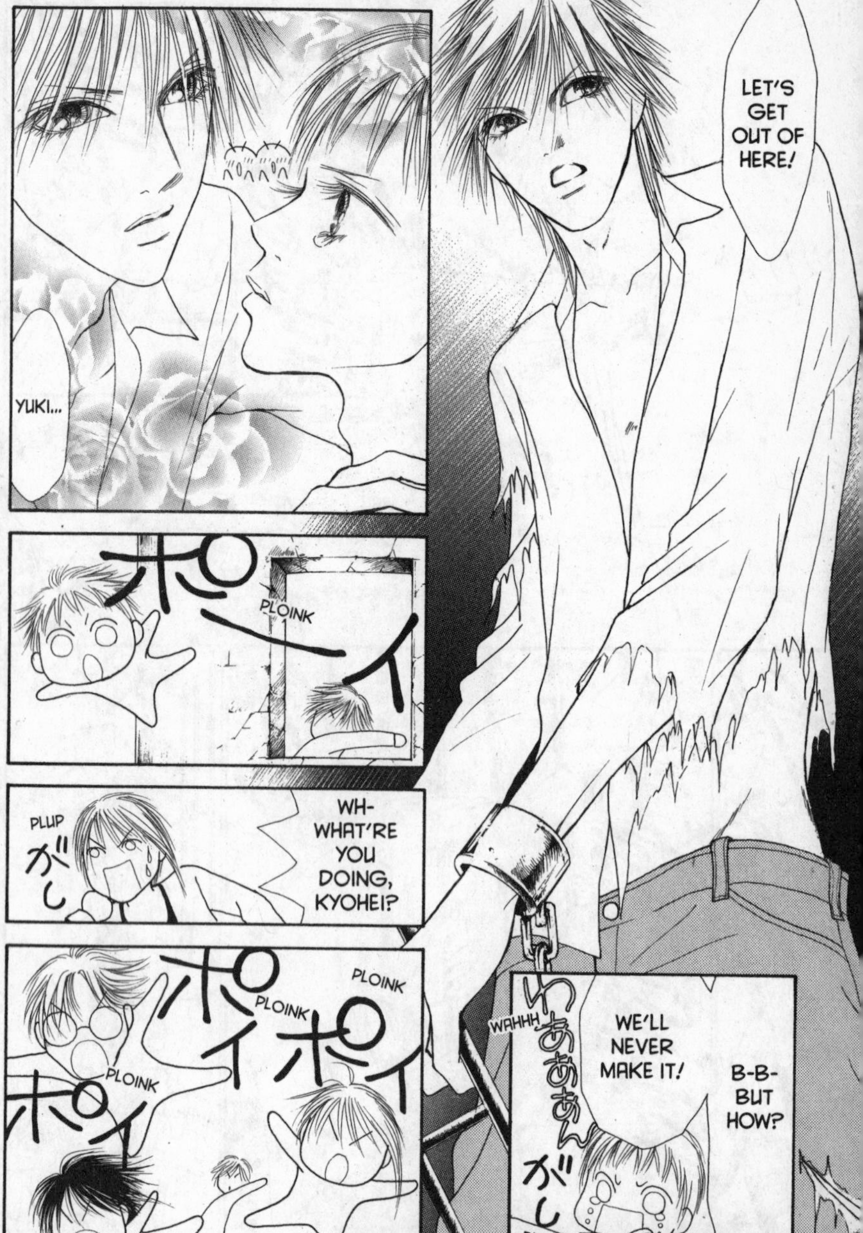
LET'S GET OUT OF HERE!
B-B-BUT HOW?
わあああん
WAHHH
WE'LL NEVER MAKE IT!
がし
PLUP
YUKI...
ポーイ
PLOINK
WH-WHAT'RE YOU DOING, KYOHEI?
がし
PLUP
ポイポイ
PLOINK
PLOINK
ポイ
PLOINK

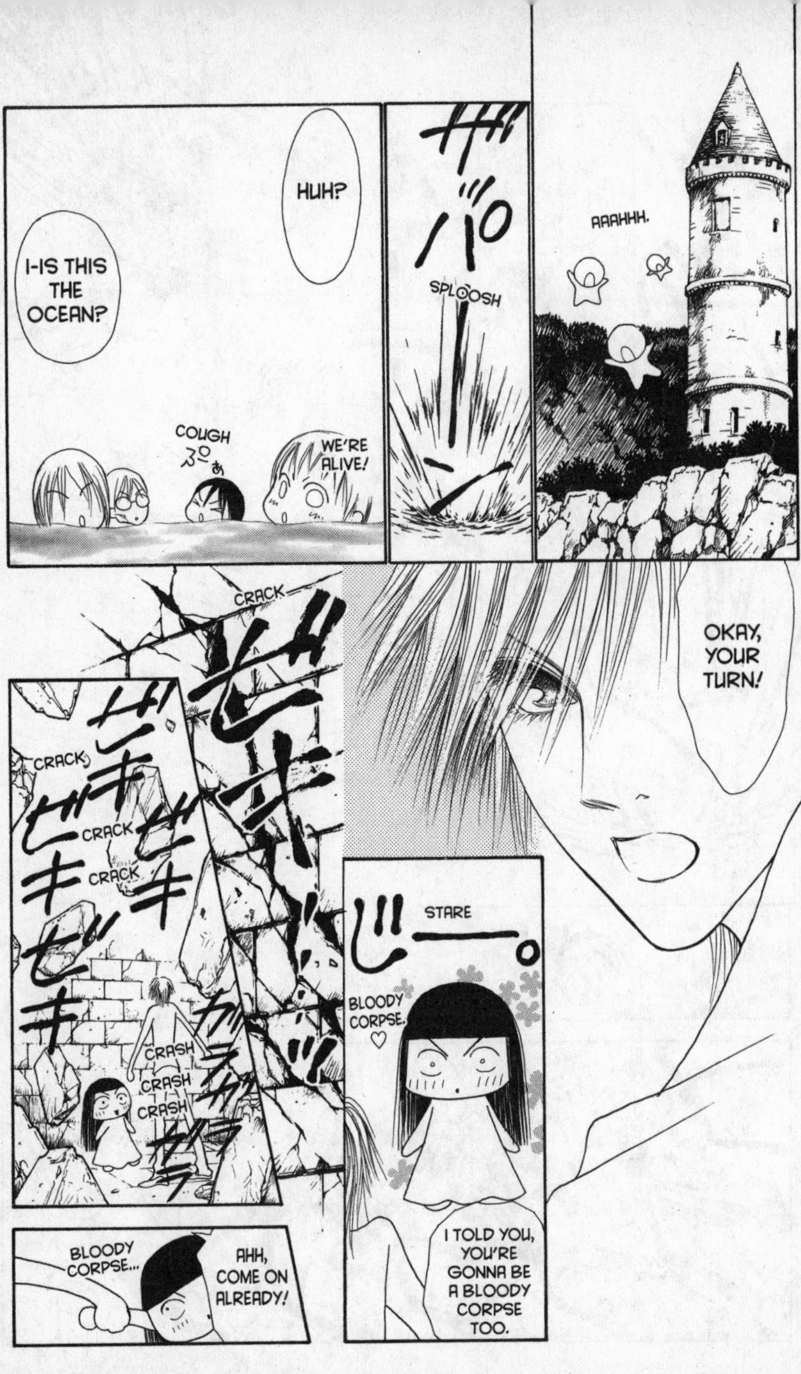
AAAHHH.
ザバ
SPLOOSH
HUH?
I-IS THIS THE OCEAN?
WE'RE ALIVE!
COUGH
OKAY, YOUR TURN!
CRACK
CRACK
CRACK
CRACK
CRASH
CRASH
CRASH
STARE
じー。
BLOODY CORPSE. ♡
I TOLD YOU, YOU'RE GONNA BE A BLOODY CORPSE TOO.
AHH, COME ON ALREADY!
BLOODY CORPSE...

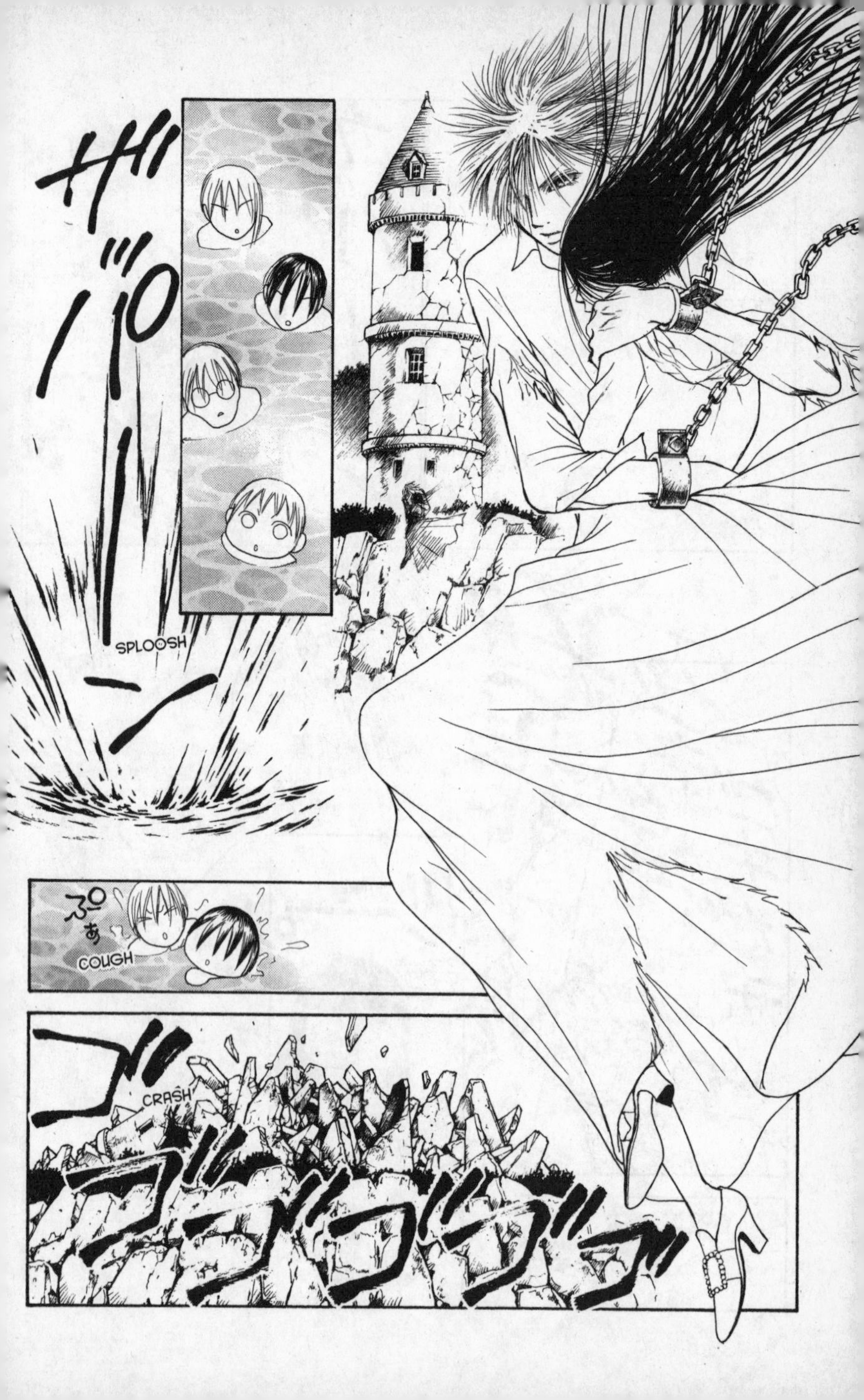
ザバーン
SPLOOSH
ぷあ
COUGH
ゴゴゴゴゴゴ
CRASH

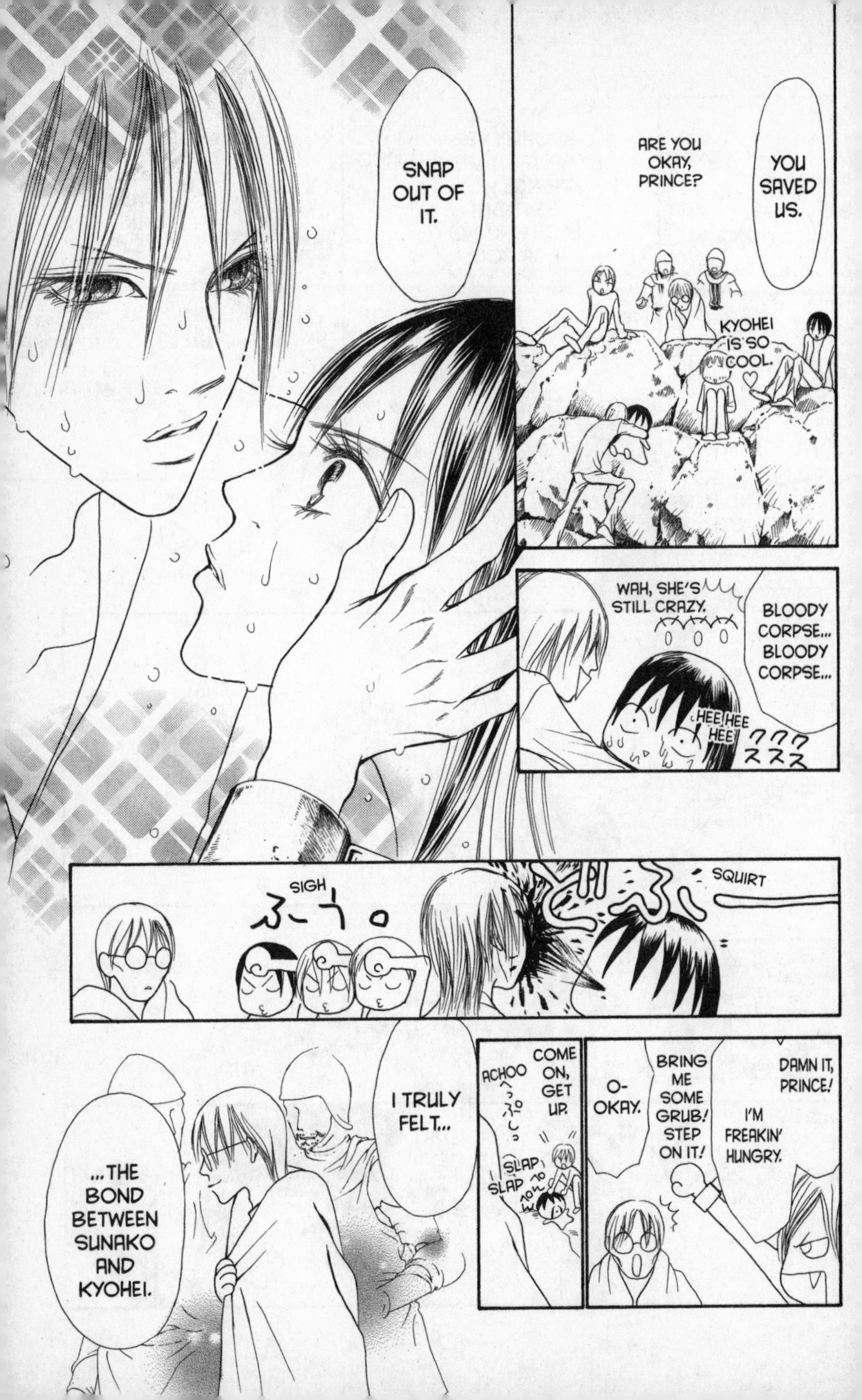
YOU SAVED US.
ARE YOU OKAY, PRINCE?
KYOHEI IS SO COOL.
BLOODY CORPSE... BLOODY CORPSE...
WAH, SHE'S STILL CRAZY.
HEE HEE HEE
SNAP OUT OF IT.
SQUIRT
SIGH
DAMN IT, PRINCE!
I'M FREAKIN' HUNGRY.
BRING ME SOME GRUB! STEP ON IT!
O-OKAY.
COME ON, GET UP.
ACHOO
SLAP SLAP
I TRULY FELT...
...THE BOND BETWEEN SUNAKO AND KYOHEI.

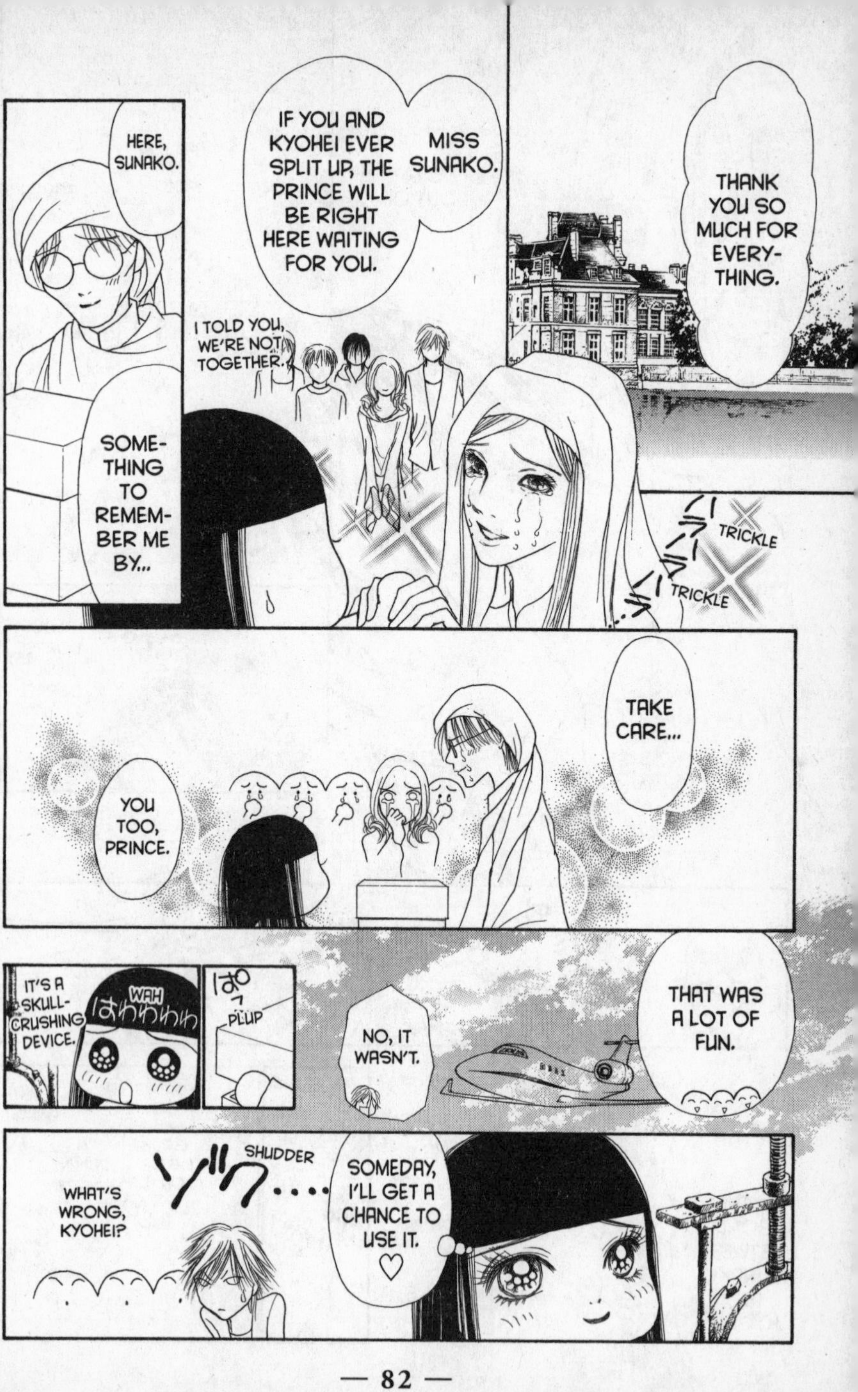
THANK YOU SO MUCH FOR EVERY-THING.
MISS SUNAKO.
IF YOU AND KYOHEI EVER SPLIT UP, THE PRINCE WILL BE RIGHT HERE WAITING FOR YOU.
TRICKLE
TRICKLE
I TOLD YOU, WE'RE NOT TOGETHER.
HERE, SUNAKO.
SOME-THING TO REMEM-BER ME BY...
TAKE CARE...
YOU TOO, PRINCE.
THAT WAS A LOT OF FUN.
NO, IT WASN'T.
ぱっ
PLUP
はわわわわ
WAH
IT'S A SKULL-CRUSHING DEVICE.
SOMEDAY, I'LL GET A CHANCE TO USE IT. ♡
ゾワ
SHUDDER
WHAT'S WRONG, KYOHEI?

WHY DID KYOHEI TURN BLUE?
SHIVER
ざわわ

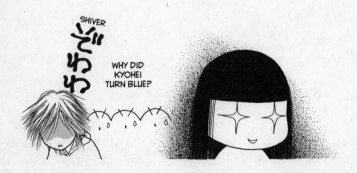

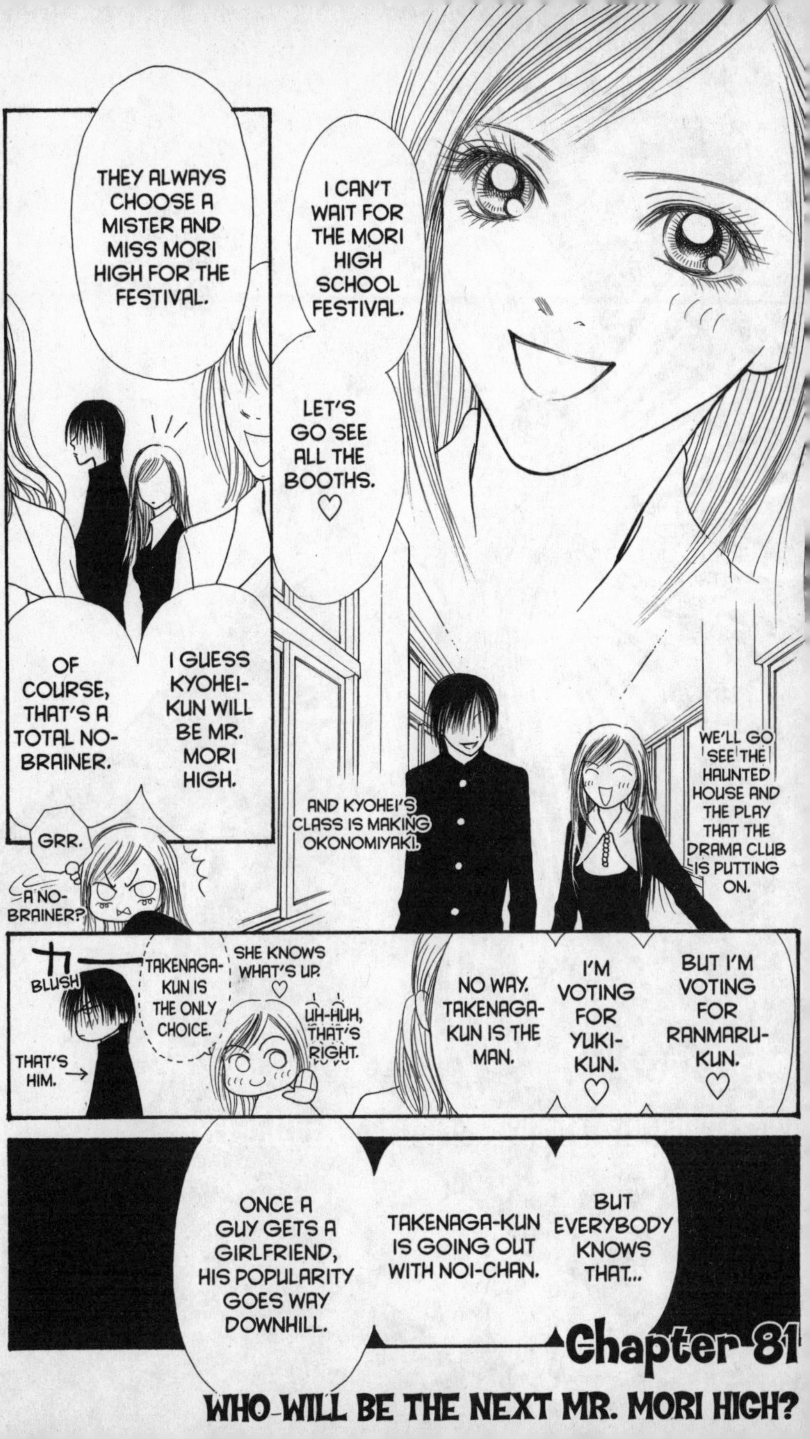
I CAN'T WAIT FOR THE MORI HIGH SCHOOL FESTIVAL.
LET'S GO SEE ALL THE BOOTHS. ♡
WE'LL GO SEE THE HAUNTED HOUSE AND THE PLAY THAT THE DRAMA CLUB IS PUTTING ON.
AND KYOHEI'S CLASS IS MAKING OKONOMIYAKI.
THEY ALWAYS CHOOSE A MISTER AND MISS MORI HIGH FOR THE FESTIVAL.
I GUESS KYOHEI-KUN WILL BE MR. MORI HIGH.
OF COURSE, THAT'S A TOTAL NO-BRAINER.
GRR.
A NO-BRAINER?
BUT I'M VOTING FOR RANMARU-KUN. ♡
I'M VOTING FOR YUKI-KUN. ♡
NO WAY. TAKENAGA-KUN IS THE MAN.
UH-HUH, THAT'S RIGHT.
SHE KNOWS WHAT'S UP. ♡
TAKENAGA-KUN IS THE ONLY CHOICE.
カー
BLUSH
THAT'S HIM. →
BUT EVERYBODY KNOWS THAT...
TAKENAGA-KUN IS GOING OUT WITH NOI-CHAN.
ONCE A GUY GETS A GIRLFRIEND, HIS POPULARITY GOES WAY DOWNHILL.
Chapter 81
WHO WILL BE THE NEXT MR. MORI HIGH?

# Chapter 81

## WHO WILL BE THE NEXT MR. MORI HIGH?

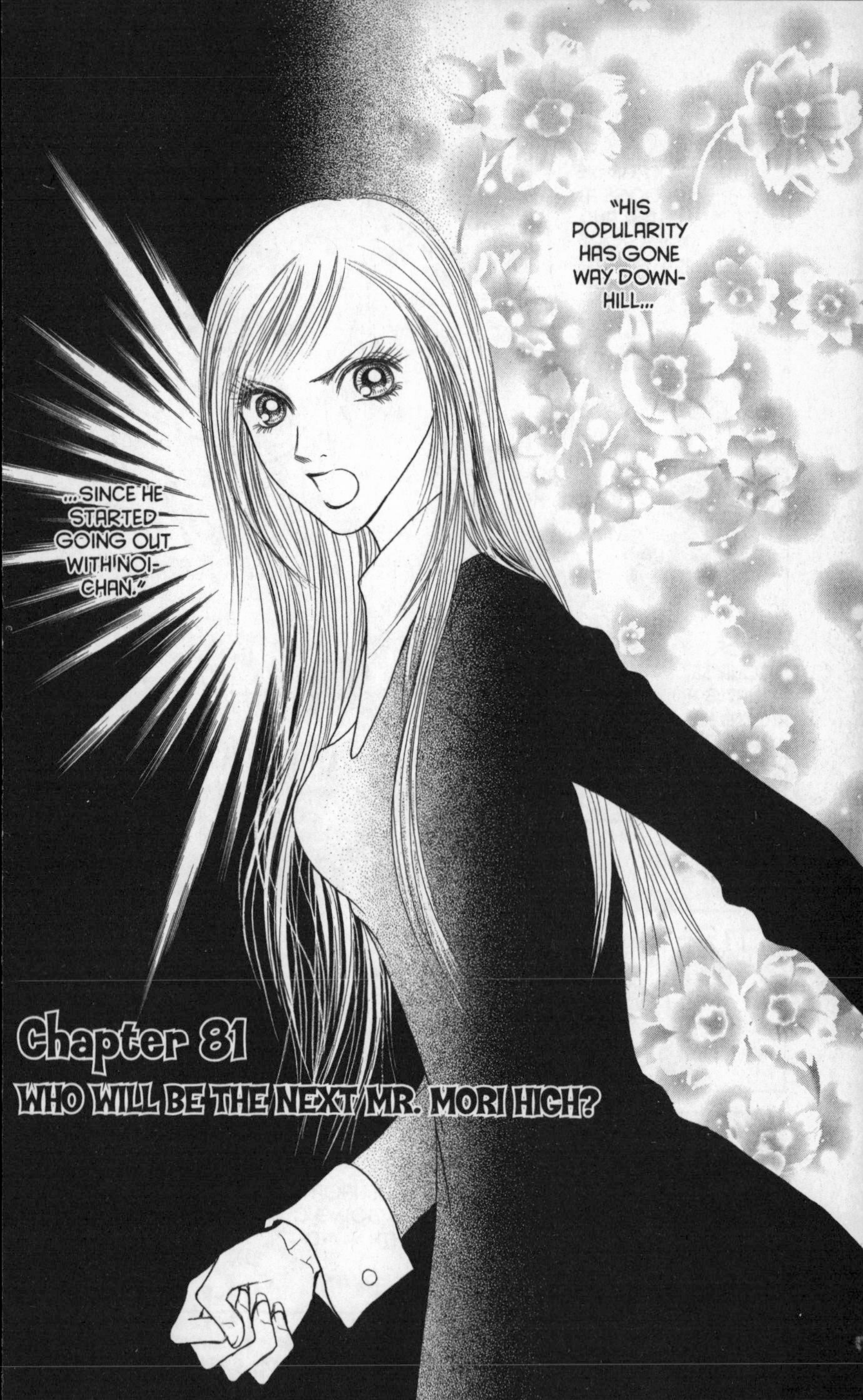
"HIS POPULARITY HAS GONE WAY DOWN-HILL...
...SINCE HE STARTED GOING OUT WITH NOI-CHAN."

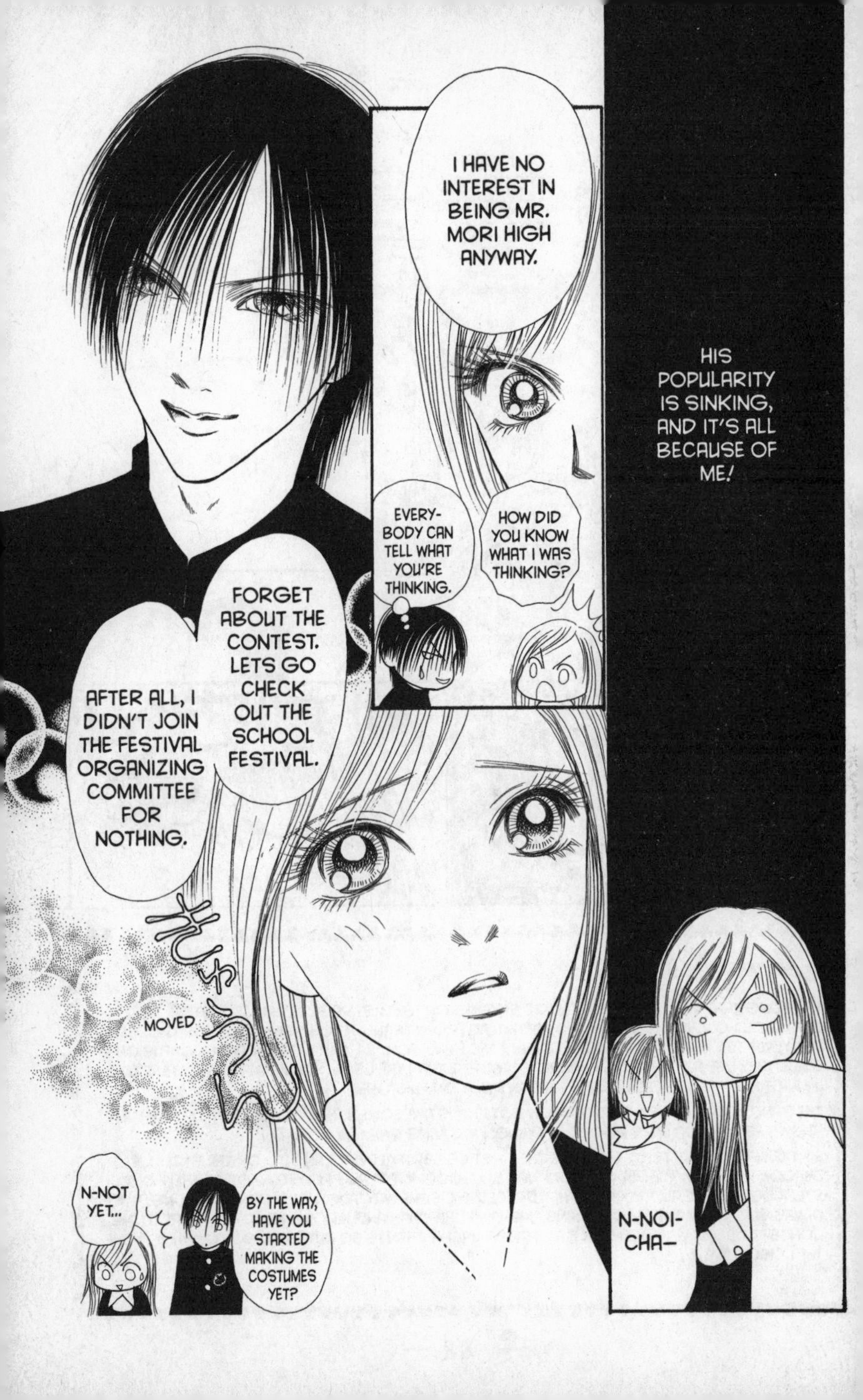

HIS POPULARITY IS SINKING, AND IT'S ALL BECAUSE OF ME!
N-NOI-CHA—
I HAVE NO INTEREST IN BEING MR. MORI HIGH ANYWAY.
HOW DID YOU KNOW WHAT I WAS THINKING?
EVERYBODY CAN TELL WHAT YOU'RE THINKING.
FORGET ABOUT THE CONTEST. LETS GO CHECK OUT THE SCHOOL FESTIVAL.
AFTER ALL, I DIDN'T JOIN THE FESTIVAL ORGANIZING COMMITTEE FOR NOTHING.
MOVED
BY THE WAY, HAVE YOU STARTED MAKING THE COSTUMES YET?
N-NOT YET...

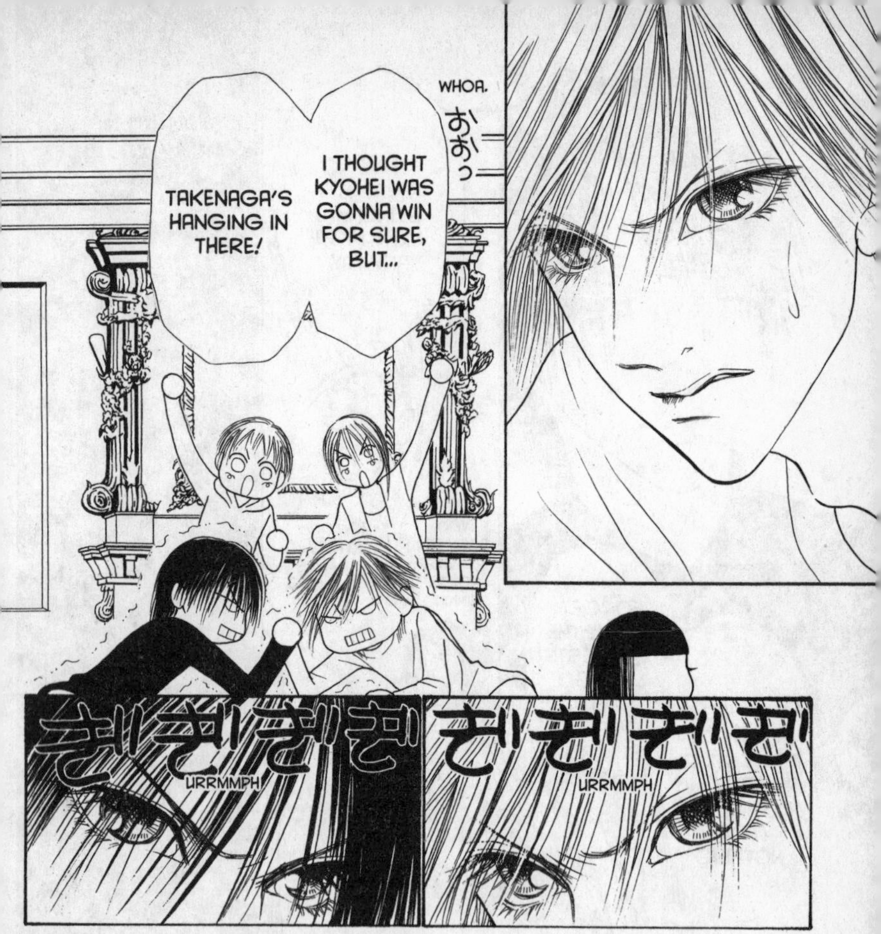
WHOA.
おおっ
I THOUGHT KYOHEI WAS GONNA WIN FOR SURE, BUT...
TAKENAGA'S HANGING IN THERE!
URRMMPH
URRMMPH

***BEHIND THE SCENES***

THE SONG THAT THE THREE OF THEM ARE SINGING ON THE LAST PAGE IS CALLED "ZETTAI ZETSUBOU NO PINCHI NI SHIPPO WO TAKAKU AGERO!" (TRANSLATION: WHEN YOU'RE IN TROUBLE LIFT YOUR TAIL HIGH). I WAS WORRIED THAT THE KANJI FOR "ZETTAI" WOULD CAUSE CONFUSION SINCE THEY USE AN OBSCURE CHARACTER RATHER THAN THE USUAL KANJI. THAT'S WHY I ENDED UP WRITING IT IN HIRAGANA. ROTE'KA-SAN DID IT ON PURPOSE.

THE BAND IS CALLED NEW ROTE'KA. NEW ROTE'KA IS AWESOME. I USED TO GO TO A LOT OF THEIR SHOWS ABOUT 20 YEARS AGO. ♥ ← OH NO, I'M GIVING AWAY MY AGE.

BY THE WAY, THE VOCALIST A-CHAN IS THE FIRST CELEBRITY I EVER RAN INTO ON THE STREET. ♥ I SHOOK HIS HAND. ♥ THEIR CONCERT WAS SO GOOD. ♥♥♥ THEY PLAYED A LOT OF THEIR OLD STUFF, SO I WAS REALLY HAPPY. ♥ THEY DANCED THE SAME WAY TOO. I EVEN DANCED ALONG. ♥♥♥ IT WAS SUPER FUN. ♥♥♥ COMEDIANS MACHA MACHA-CHAN AND HIROSHI NEKO-SAN WERE AT THE CONCERT TOO. IT WAS SO MUCH FUN. MACHA MACHA-CHAN IS SO CUTE. AND SO TOUGH. ♥ I LOVE THAT CHICK. ♥♥♥

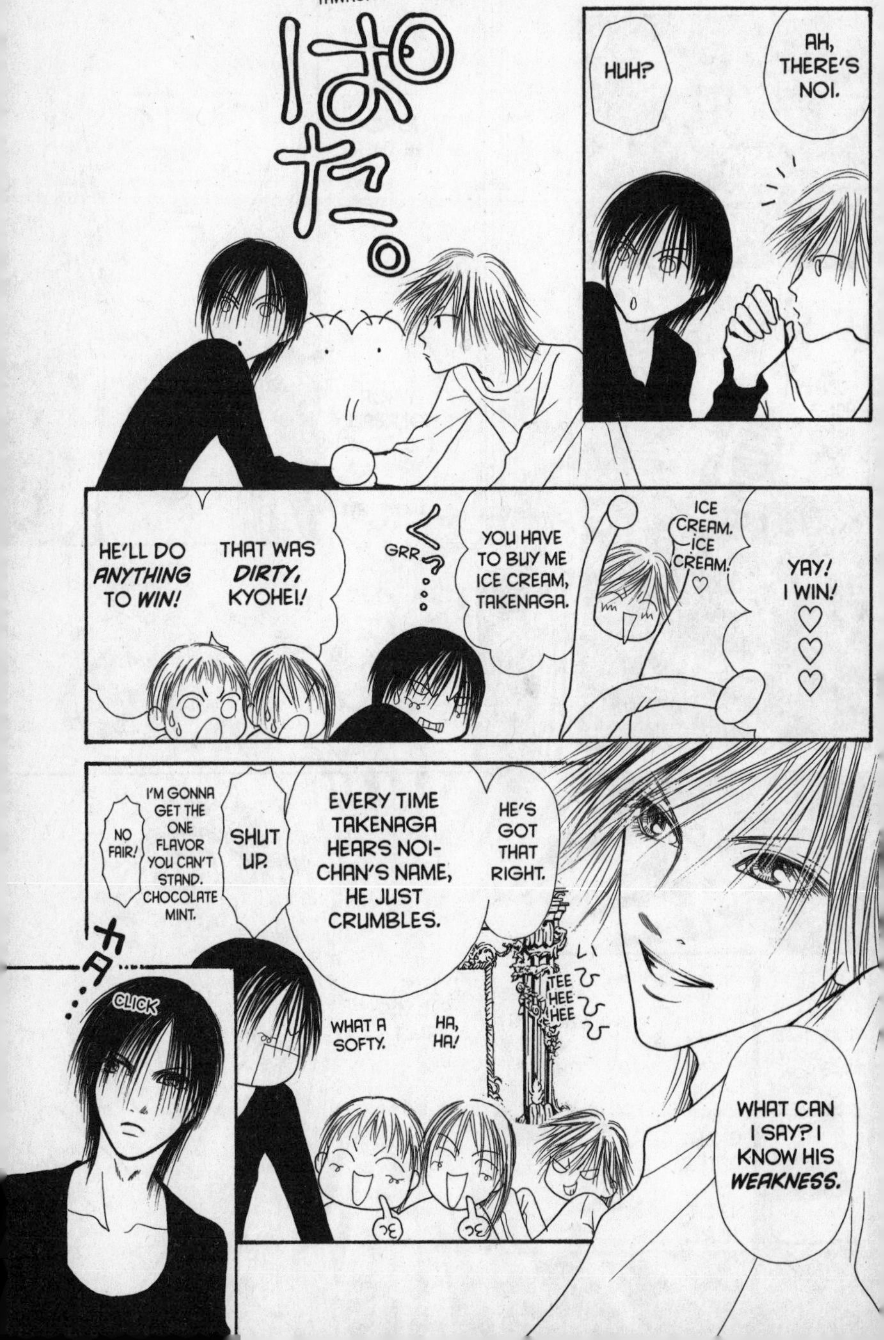
AH, THERE'S NOI.
HUH?
THWACK
ぱたー。
YAY! I WIN! ♡ ♡ ♡
ICE CREAM. ICE CREAM. ♡
YOU HAVE TO BUY ME ICE CREAM, TAKENAGA.
GRR
く…
THAT WAS *DIRTY*, KYOHEI!
HE'LL DO *ANYTHING* TO *WIN!*
WHAT CAN I SAY? I KNOW HIS *WEAKNESS.*
HE'S GOT THAT RIGHT.
EVERY TIME TAKENAGA HEARS NOI-CHAN'S NAME, HE JUST CRUMBLES.
いひひ
TEE HEE HEE
HA, HA!
WHAT A SOFTY.
SHUT UP.
I'M GONNA GET THE ONE FLAVOR YOU CAN'T STAND. CHOCOLATE MINT.
NO FAIR!
カタ…
CLICK

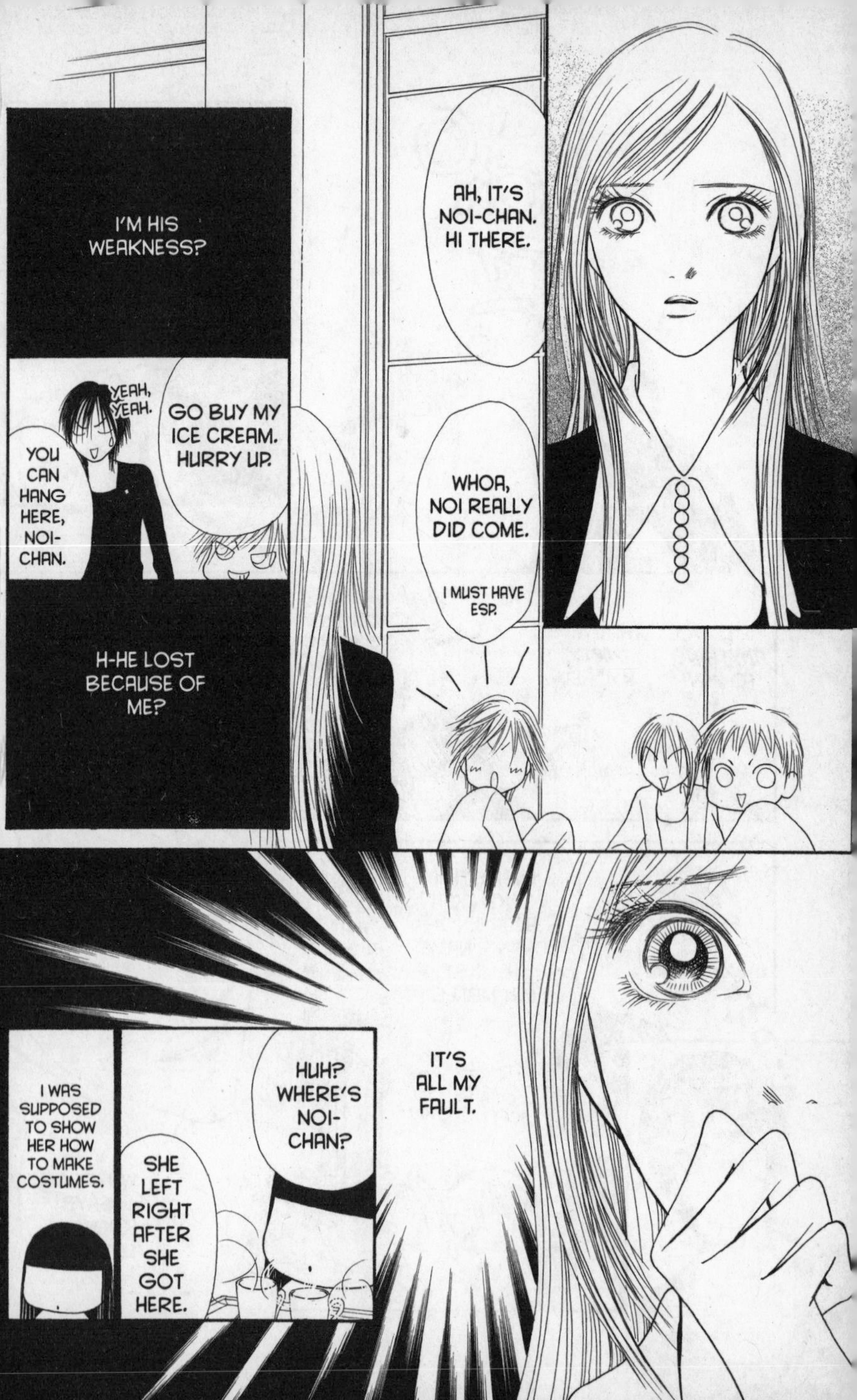
AH, IT'S NOI-CHAN. HI THERE.
WHOA, NOI REALLY DID COME.
I MUST HAVE ESP.
I'M HIS WEAKNESS?
GO BUY MY ICE CREAM. HURRY UP.
YEAH, YEAH.
YOU CAN HANG HERE, NOI-CHAN.
H-HE LOST BECAUSE OF ME?
IT'S ALL MY FAULT.
HUH? WHERE'S NOI-CHAN?
SHE LEFT RIGHT AFTER SHE GOT HERE.
I WAS SUPPOSED TO SHOW HER HOW TO MAKE COSTUMES.

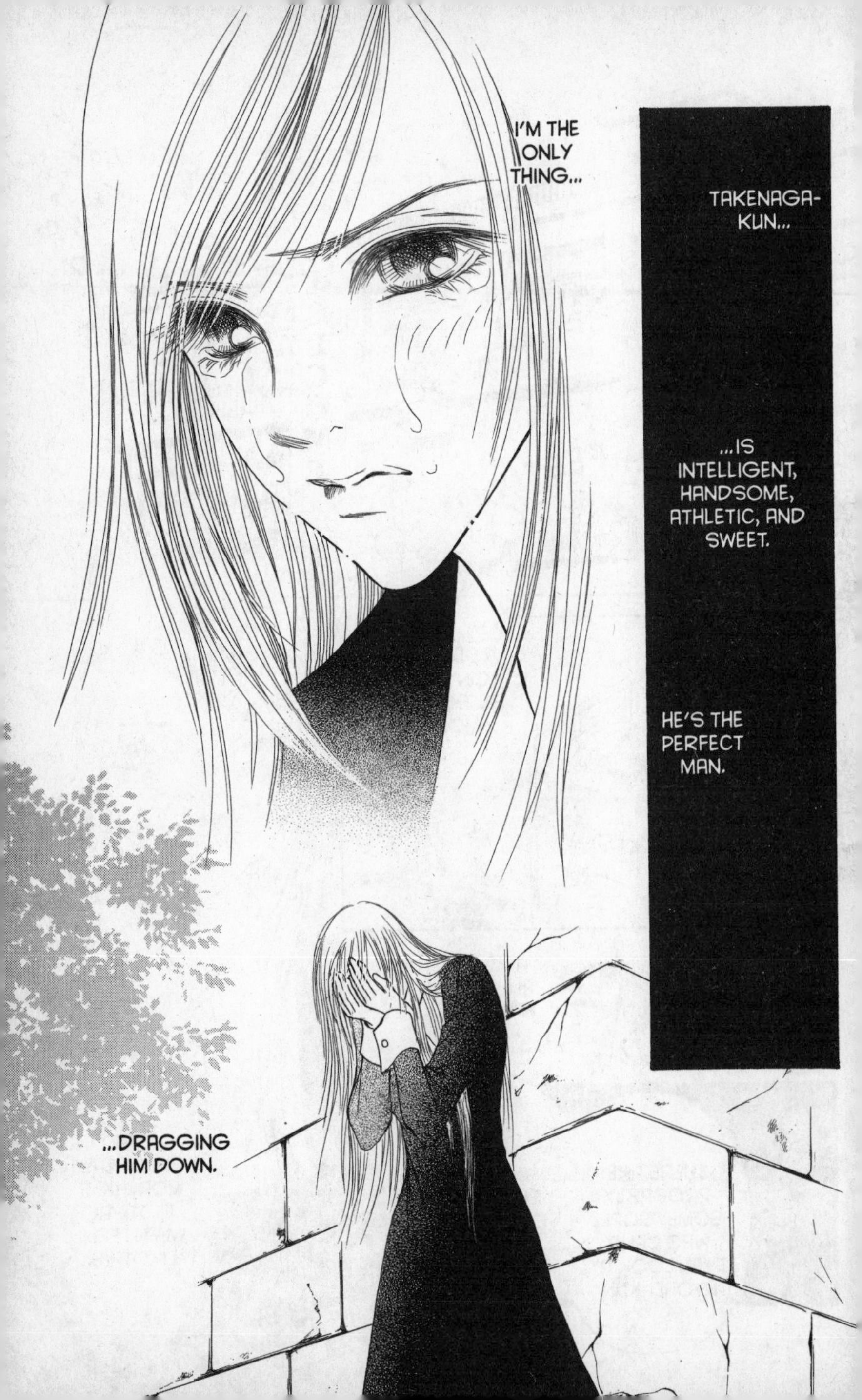
TAKENAGA-KUN...
...IS INTELLIGENT, HANDSOME, ATHLETIC, AND SWEET.
HE'S THE PERFECT MAN.
I'M THE ONLY THING...
...DRAGGING HIM DOWN.

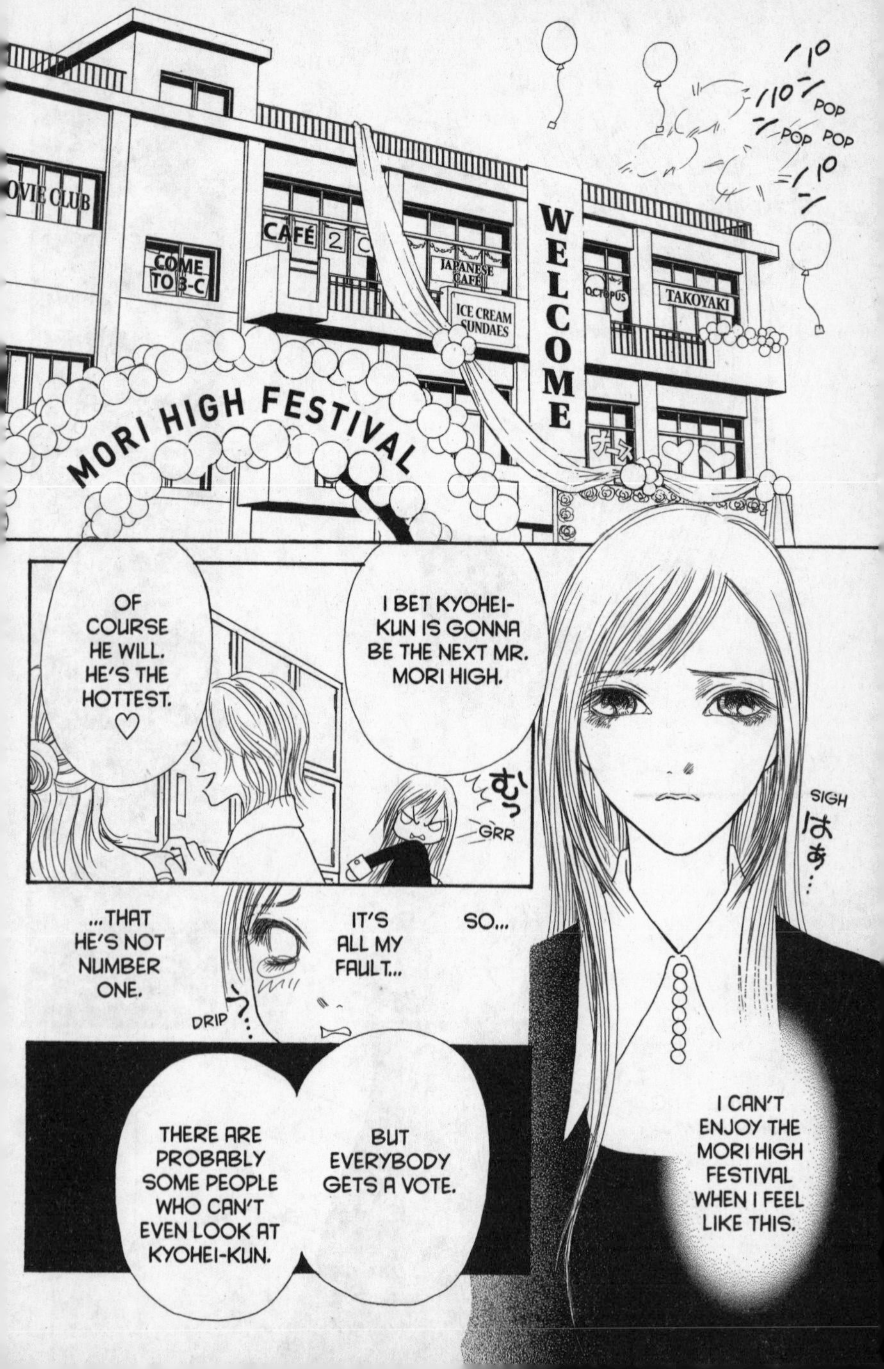
POP
POP POP
TAKOYAKI
OCTOPUS
WELCOME
ICE CREAM SUNDAES
JAPANESE CAFÉ
CAFÉ 2-C
MORI HIGH FESTIVAL
COME TO 3-C
OVIE CLUB
SIGH
I CAN'T ENJOY THE MORI HIGH FESTIVAL WHEN I FEEL LIKE THIS.
I BET KYOHEI-KUN IS GONNA BE THE NEXT MR. MORI HIGH.
OF COURSE HE WILL. HE'S THE HOTTEST. ♡
GRR
SO...
IT'S ALL MY FAULT...
...THAT HE'S NOT NUMBER ONE.
DRIP
BUT EVERYBODY GETS A VOTE.
THERE ARE PROBABLY SOME PEOPLE WHO CAN'T EVEN LOOK AT KYOHEI-KUN.

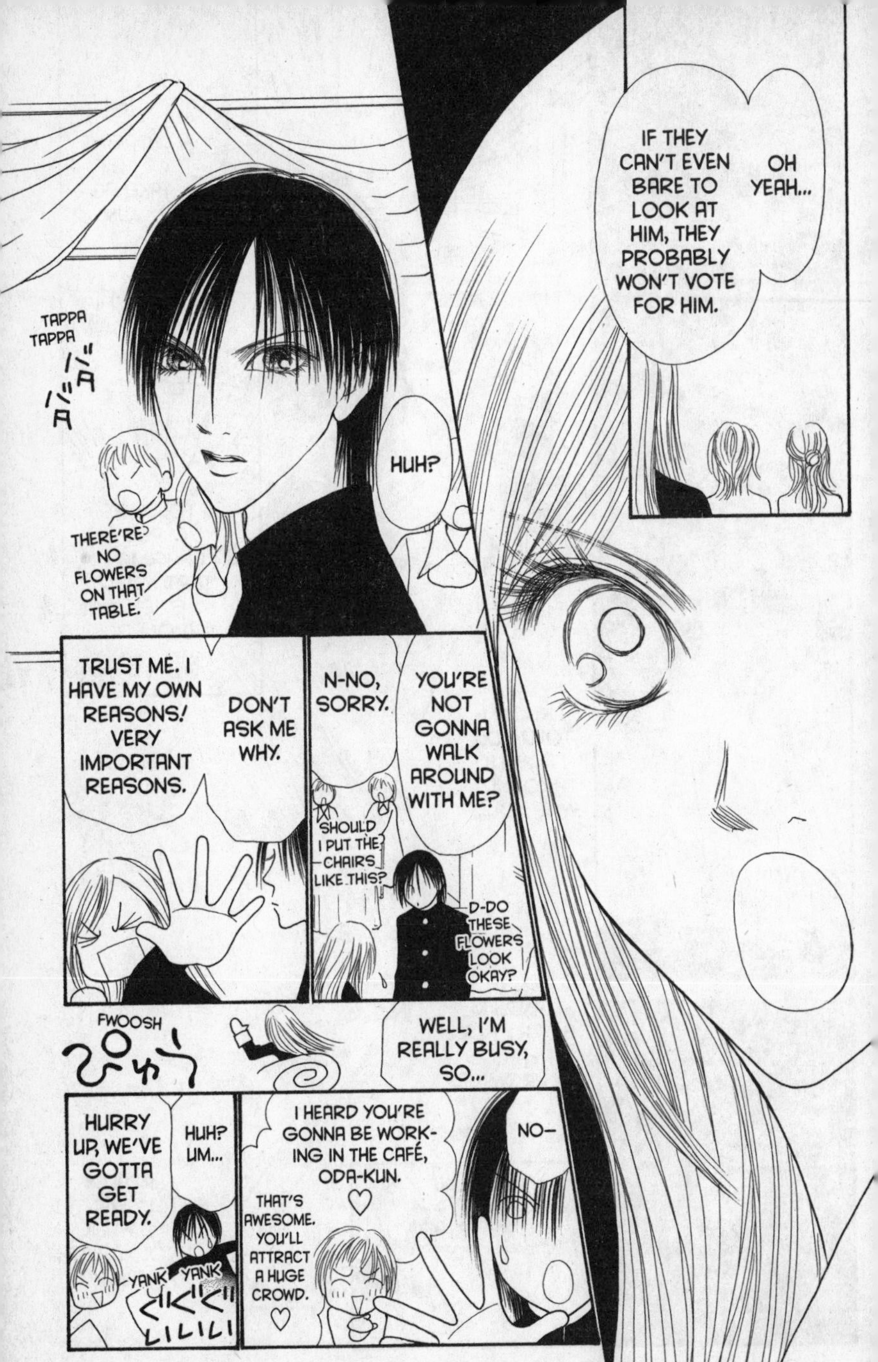
OH YEAH...
IF THEY CAN'T EVEN BARE TO LOOK AT HIM, THEY PROBABLY WON'T VOTE FOR HIM.
HUH?
TAPPA TAPPA
THERE'RE NO FLOWERS ON THAT TABLE.
YOU'RE NOT GONNA WALK AROUND WITH ME?
N-NO, SORRY.
D-DO THESE FLOWERS LOOK OKAY?
SHOULD I PUT THE CHAIRS LIKE THIS?
DON'T ASK ME WHY.
TRUST ME. I HAVE MY OWN REASONS! VERY IMPORTANT REASONS.
WELL, I'M REALLY BUSY, SO...
FWOOSH
NO–
I HEARD YOU'RE GONNA BE WORK-ING IN THE CAFÉ, ODA-KUN. ♡
THAT'S AWESOME. YOU'LL ATTRACT A HUGE CROWD. ♡
HUH? UM...
HURRY UP, WE'VE GOTTA GET READY.
YANK YANK

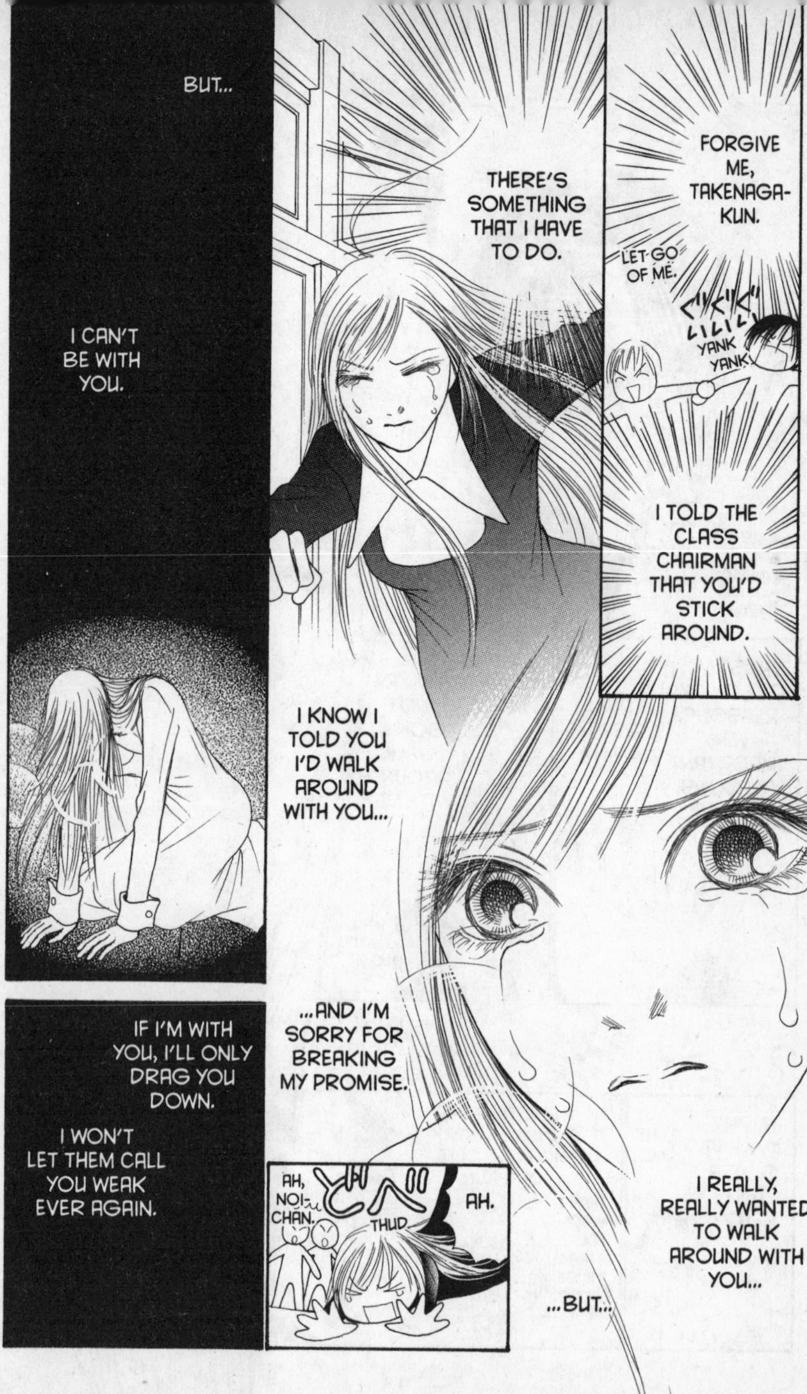
FORGIVE ME, TAKENAGA-KUN.
LET GO OF ME.
YANK YANK
I TOLD THE CLASS CHAIRMAN THAT YOU'D STICK AROUND.
THERE'S SOMETHING THAT I HAVE TO DO.
BUT...
I CAN'T BE WITH YOU.
I KNOW I TOLD YOU I'D WALK AROUND WITH YOU...
...AND I'M SORRY FOR BREAKING MY PROMISE.
I REALLY, REALLY WANTED TO WALK AROUND WITH YOU...
...BUT...
AH.
AH, NOI-CHAN.
THUD
IF I'M WITH YOU, I'LL ONLY DRAG YOU DOWN.
I WON'T LET THEM CALL YOU WEAK EVER AGAIN.

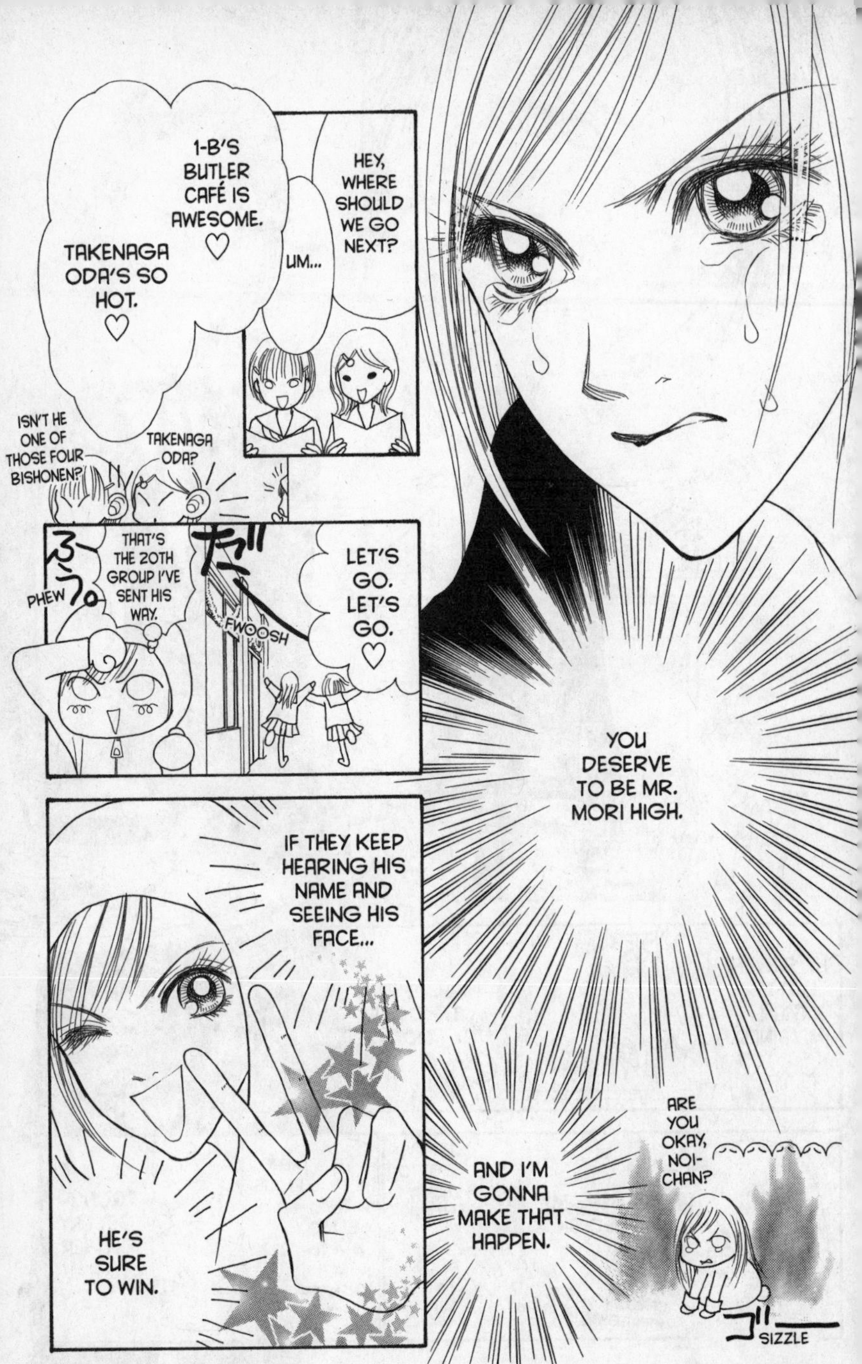
YOU DESERVE TO BE MR. MORI HIGH.
AND I'M GONNA MAKE THAT HAPPEN.
ARE YOU OKAY, NOI-CHAN?
SIZZLE
HEY, WHERE SHOULD WE GO NEXT?
UM...
1-B'S BUTLER CAFÉ IS AWESOME. ♡
TAKENAGA ODA'S SO HOT. ♡
TAKENAGA ODA?
ISN'T HE ONE OF THOSE FOUR BISHONEN?
LET'S GO. LET'S GO. ♡
FWOOSH
THAT'S THE 20TH GROUP I'VE SENT HIS WAY.
PHEW
IF THEY KEEP HEARING HIS NAME AND SEEING HIS FACE...
HE'S SURE TO WIN.

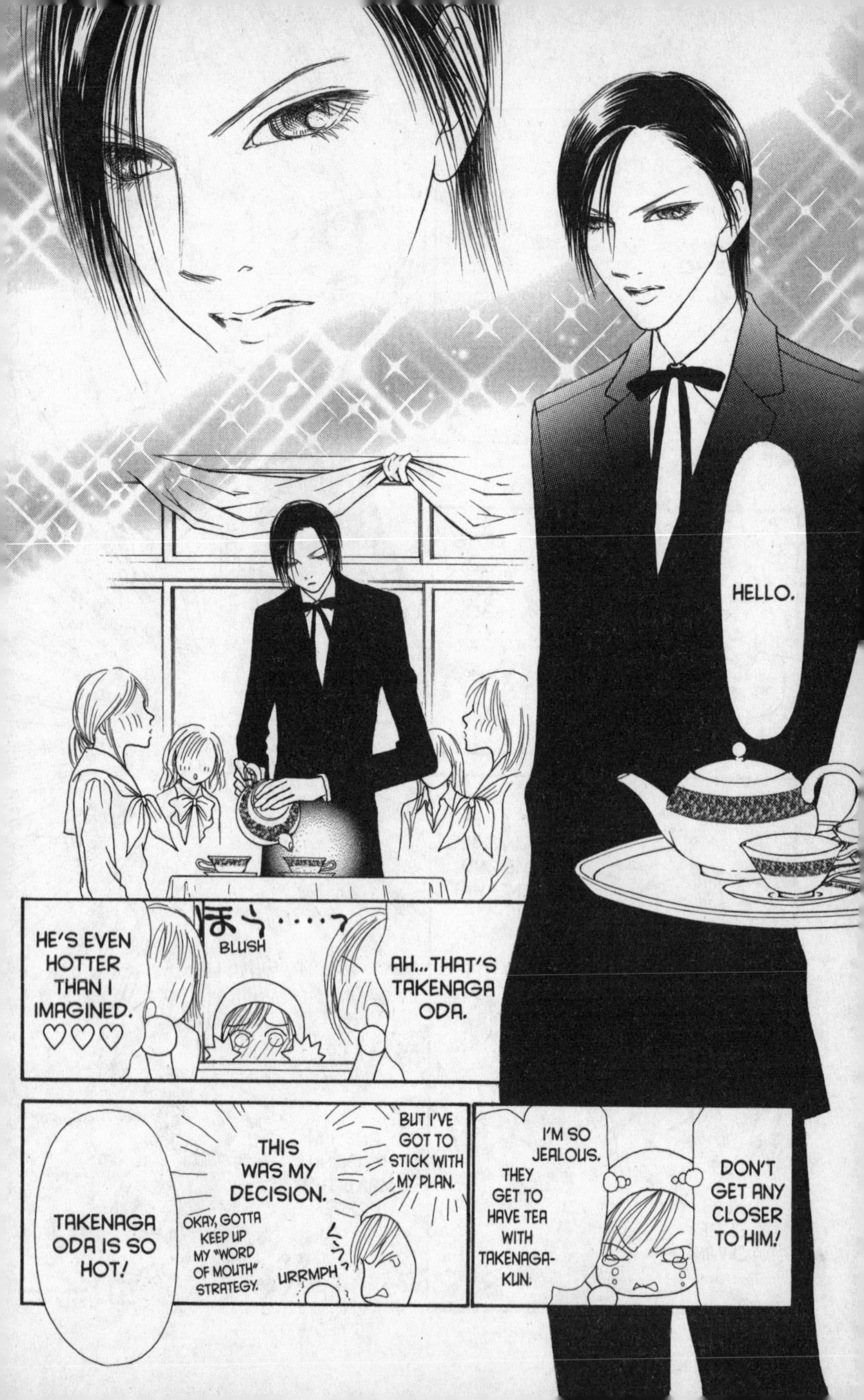
HELLO.
AH...THAT'S TAKENAGA ODA.
ほぅ....
BLUSH
HE'S EVEN HOTTER THAN I IMAGINED. ♡♡♡
DON'T GET ANY CLOSER TO HIM!
I'M SO JEALOUS.
THEY GET TO HAVE TEA WITH TAKENAGA-KUN.
BUT I'VE GOT TO STICK WITH MY PLAN.
THIS WAS MY DECISION.
URRMPH
OKAY, GOTTA KEEP UP MY "WORD OF MOUTH" STRATEGY.
TAKENAGA ODA IS SO HOT!

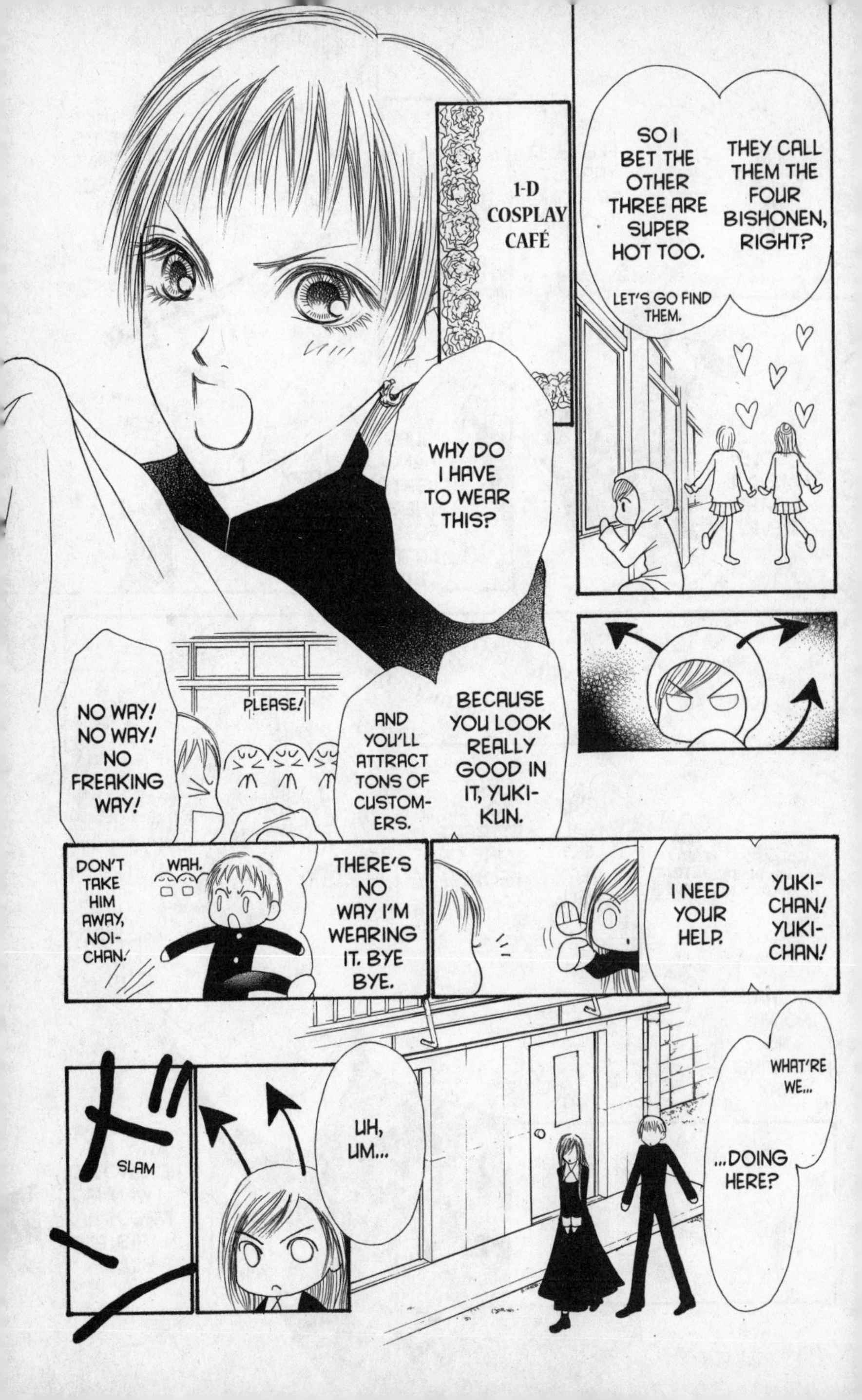
THEY CALL THEM THE FOUR BISHONEN, RIGHT?
SO I BET THE OTHER THREE ARE SUPER HOT TOO.
LET'S GO FIND THEM.
1-D COSPLAY CAFÉ
WHY DO I HAVE TO WEAR THIS?
BECAUSE YOU LOOK REALLY GOOD IN IT, YUKI-KUN.
AND YOU'LL ATTRACT TONS OF CUSTOMERS.
PLEASE!
NO WAY! NO WAY! NO FREAKING WAY!
YUKI-CHAN! YUKI-CHAN!
I NEED YOUR HELP.
THERE'S NO WAY I'M WEARING IT. BYE BYE.
WAH.
DON'T TAKE HIM AWAY, NOI-CHAN!
WHAT'RE WE...
...DOING HERE?
UH, UM...
SLAM

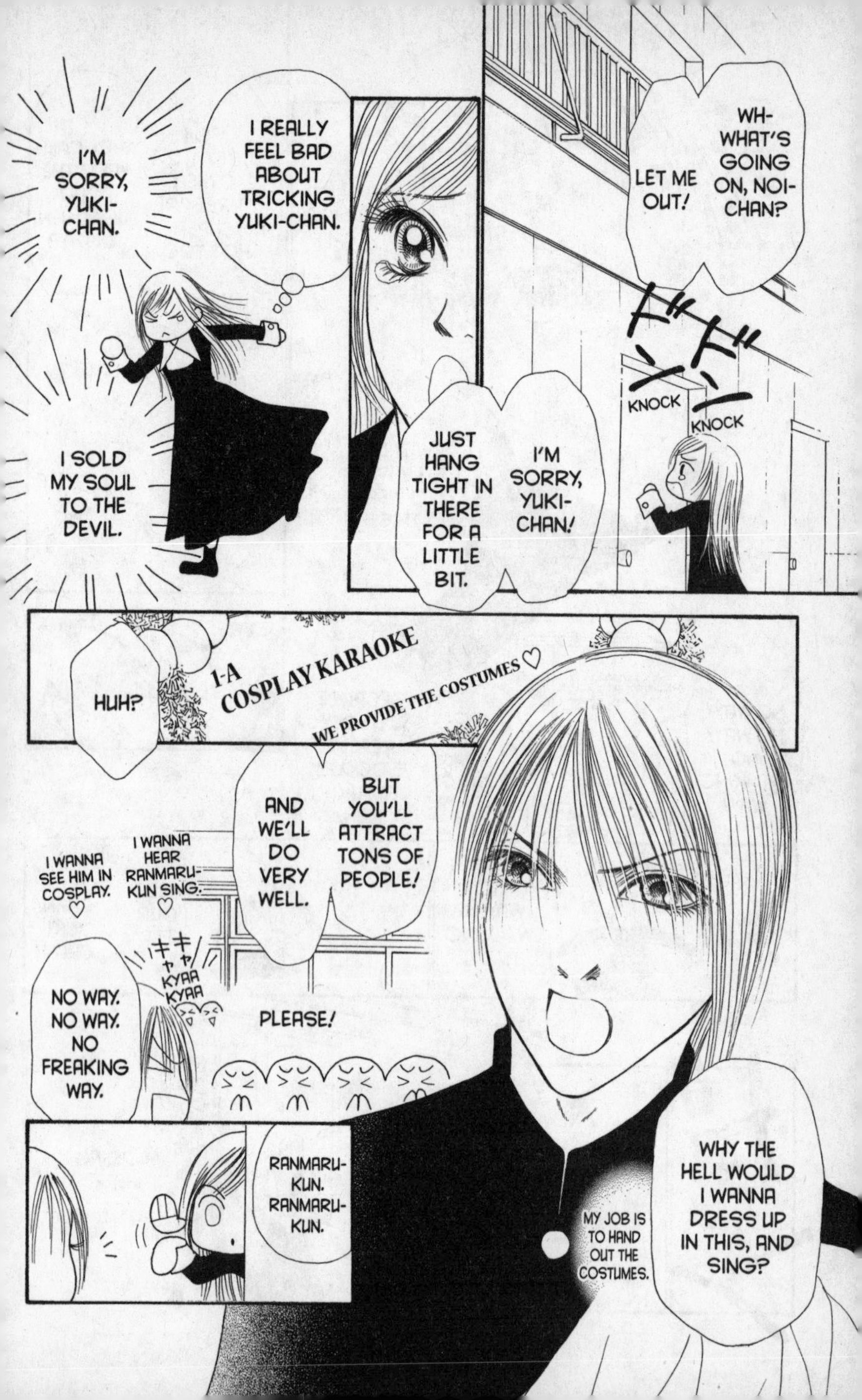
WH- WHAT'S GOING ON, NOI-CHAN?
LET ME OUT!
KNOCK
KNOCK
I'M SORRY, YUKI-CHAN!
JUST HANG TIGHT IN THERE FOR A LITTLE BIT.
I REALLY FEEL BAD ABOUT TRICKING YUKI-CHAN.
I'M SORRY, YUKI-CHAN.
I SOLD MY SOUL TO THE DEVIL.
1-A COSPLAY KARAOKE
WE PROVIDE THE COSTUMES ♡
HUH?
BUT YOU'LL ATTRACT TONS OF PEOPLE!
AND WE'LL DO VERY WELL.
I WANNA HEAR RANMARU-KUN SING. ♡
I WANNA SEE HIM IN COSPLAY. ♡
KYAA KYAA
PLEASE!
NO WAY. NO WAY. NO FREAKING WAY.
WHY THE HELL WOULD I WANNA DRESS UP IN THIS, AND SING?
MY JOB IS TO HAND OUT THE COSTUMES.
RANMARU-KUN. RANMARU-KUN.

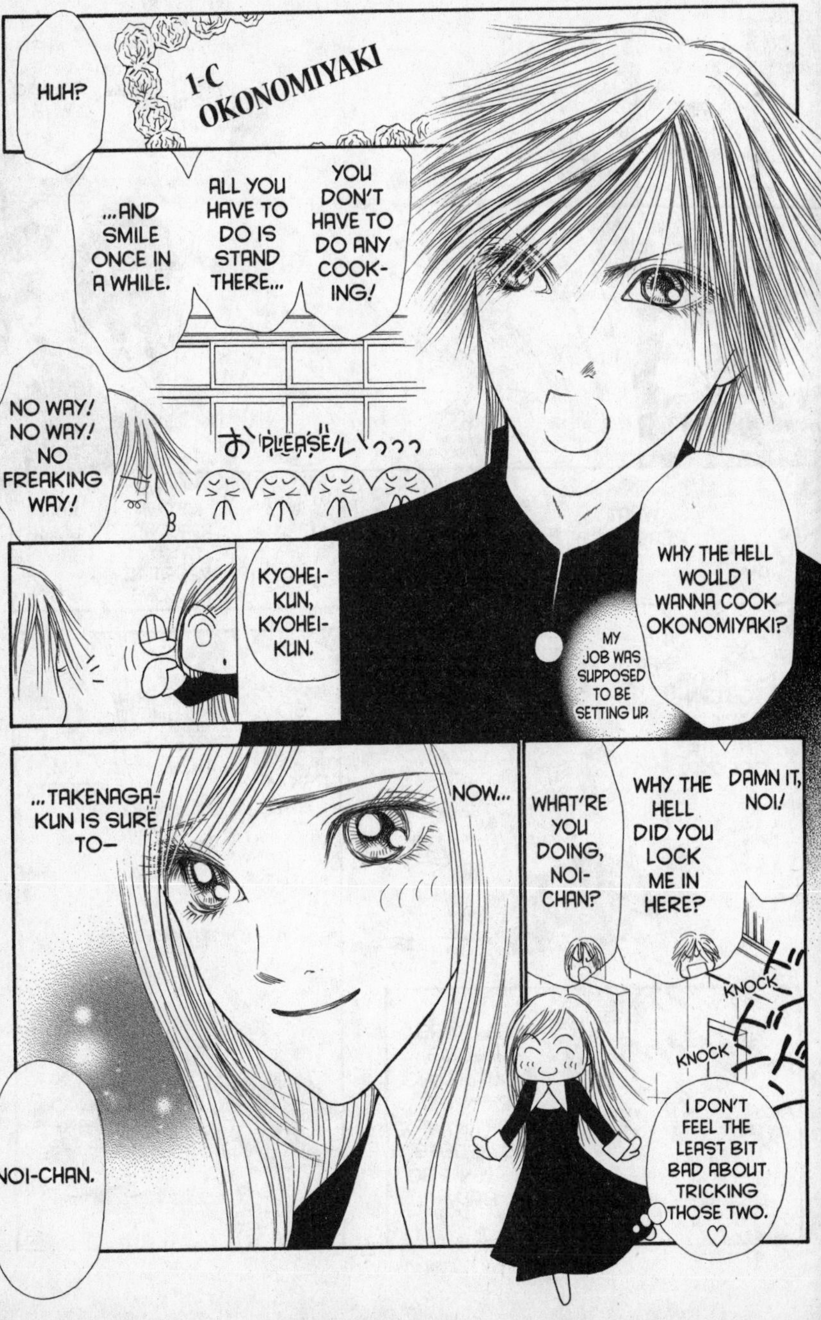
1-C OKONOMIYAKI
HUH?
YOU DON'T HAVE TO DO ANY COOKING!
ALL YOU HAVE TO DO IS STAND THERE...
...AND SMILE ONCE IN A WHILE.
NO WAY! NO WAY! NO FREAKING WAY!
PLEASE!
WHY THE HELL WOULD I WANNA COOK OKONOMIYAKI?
MY JOB WAS SUPPOSED TO BE SETTING UP.
KYOHEI-KUN, KYOHEI-KUN.
DAMN IT, NOI!
WHY THE HELL DID YOU LOCK ME IN HERE?
WHAT'RE YOU DOING, NOI-CHAN?
KNOCK
KNOCK
I DON'T FEEL THE LEAST BIT BAD ABOUT TRICKING THOSE TWO. ♡
NOW...
...TAKENAGA-KUN IS SURE TO—
NOI-CHAN.

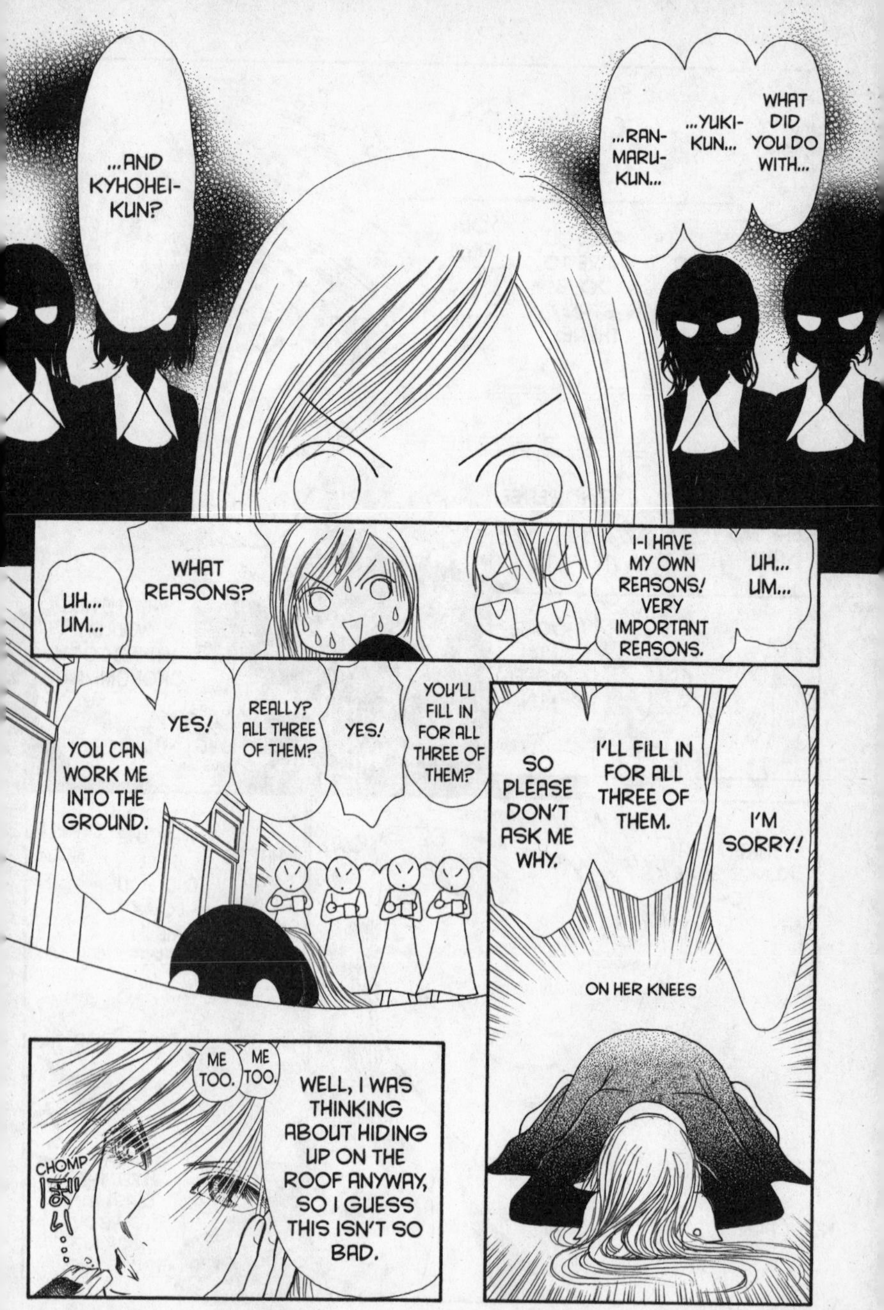
WHAT DID YOU DO WITH...
...YUKI-KUN...
...RAN-MARU-KUN...
...AND KYHOHEI-KUN?
UH... UM...
I-I HAVE MY OWN REASONS! VERY IMPORTANT REASONS.
WHAT REASONS?
UH... UM...
I'M SORRY!
I'LL FILL IN FOR ALL THREE OF THEM.
SO PLEASE DON'T ASK ME WHY.
ON HER KNEES
YOU'LL FILL IN FOR ALL THREE OF THEM?
YES!
REALLY? ALL THREE OF THEM?
YES!
YOU CAN WORK ME INTO THE GROUND.
WELL, I WAS THINKING ABOUT HIDING UP ON THE ROOF ANYWAY, SO I GUESS THIS ISN'T SO BAD.
ME TOO.
ME TOO.
CHOMP

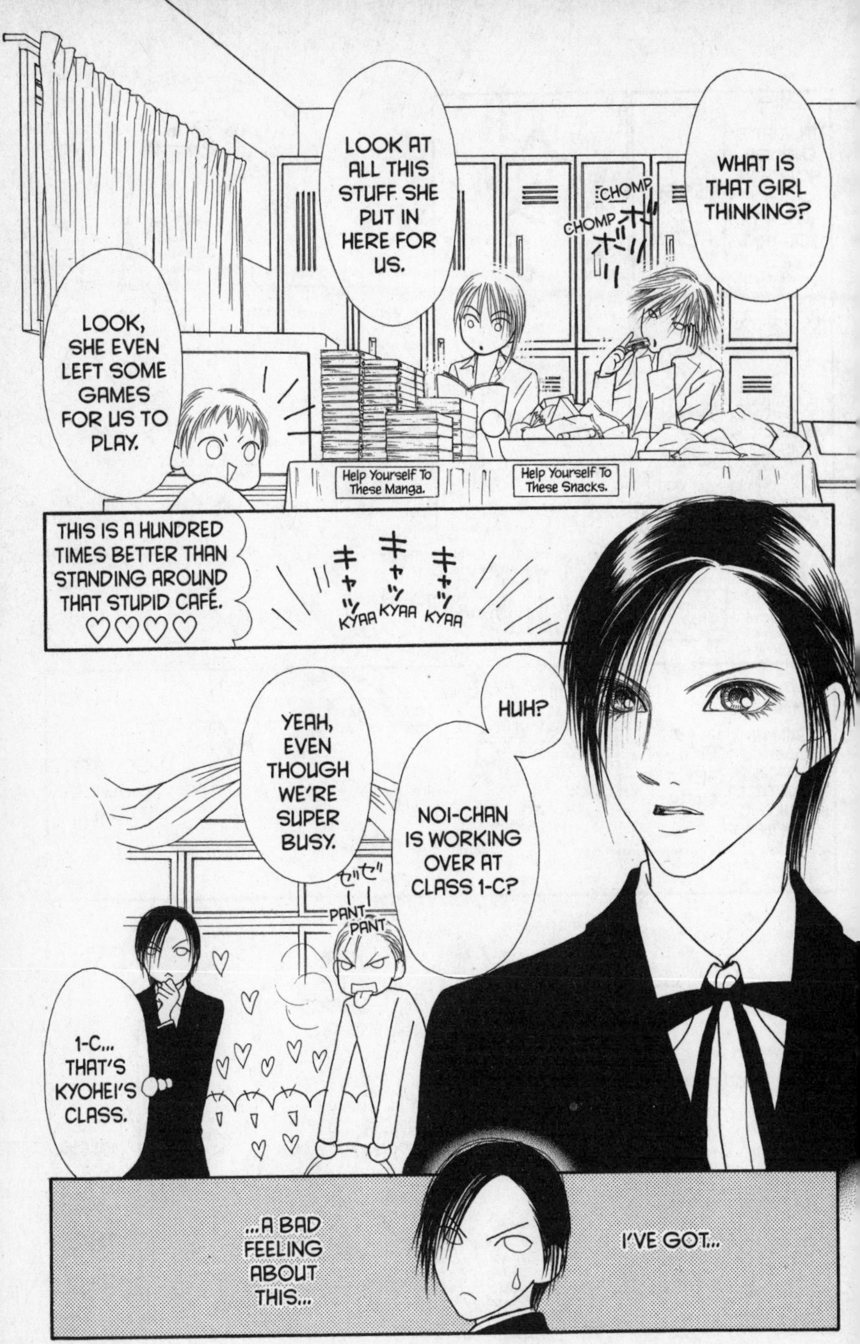
WHAT IS THAT GIRL THINKING?
CHOMP CHOMP
LOOK AT ALL THIS STUFF SHE PUT IN HERE FOR US.
LOOK, SHE EVEN LEFT SOME GAMES FOR US TO PLAY.
Help Yourself To These Snacks.
Help Yourself To These Manga.
HUH?
NOI-CHAN IS WORKING OVER AT CLASS 1-C?
キャッ KYAA キャッ KYAA キャッ KYAA
THIS IS A HUNDRED TIMES BETTER THAN STANDING AROUND THAT STUPID CAFÉ. ♡♡♡♡
YEAH, EVEN THOUGH WE'RE SUPER BUSY.
ゼゼ PANT PANT
1-C... THAT'S KYOHEI'S CLASS.
I'VE GOT...
...A BAD FEELING ABOUT THIS...

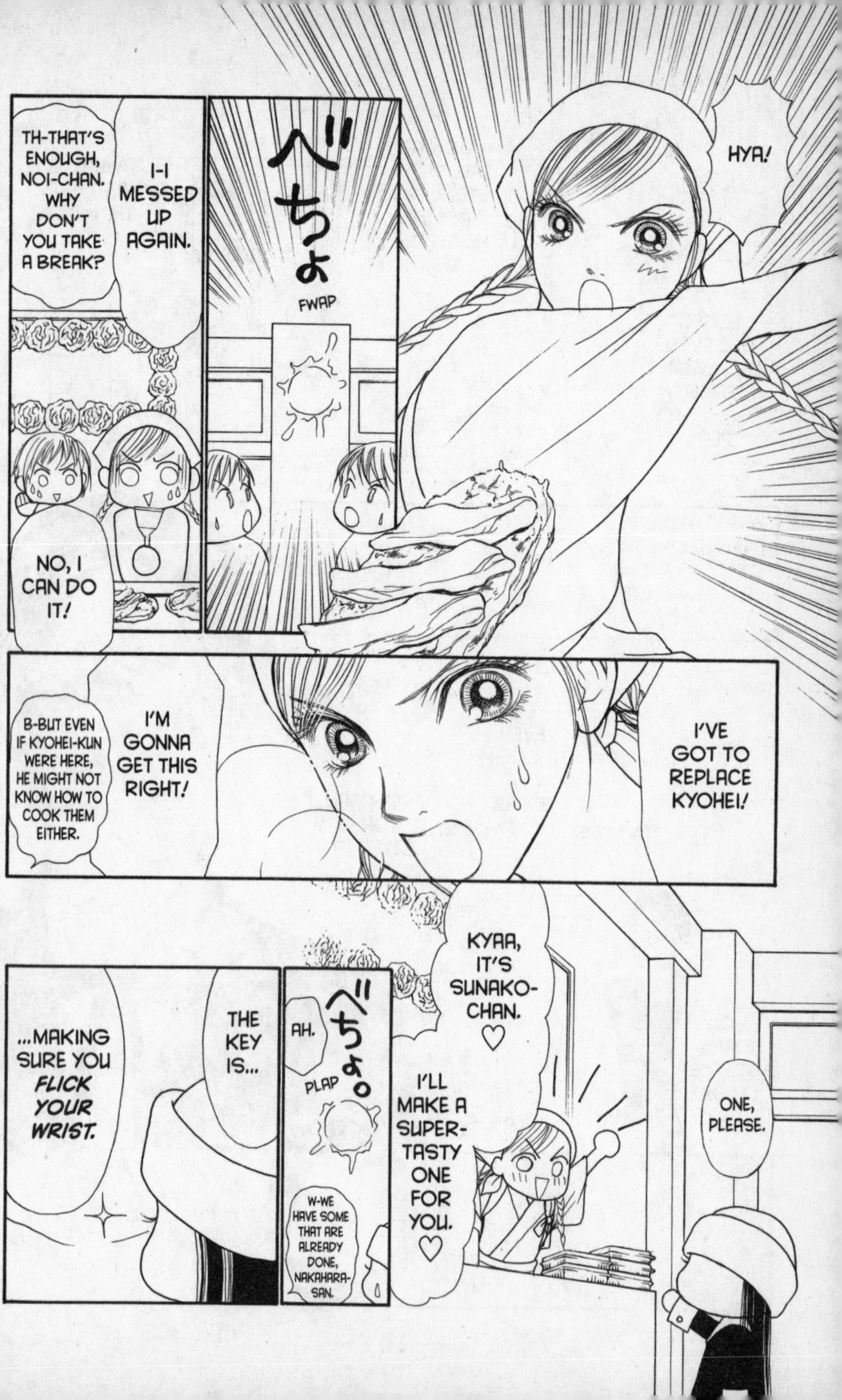
HYA!
べちょ
FWAP
I-I MESSED UP AGAIN.
TH-THAT'S ENOUGH, NOI-CHAN. WHY DON'T YOU TAKE A BREAK?
NO, I CAN DO IT!
I'VE GOT TO REPLACE KYOHEI!
I'M GONNA GET THIS RIGHT!
B-BUT EVEN IF KYOHEI-KUN WERE HERE, HE MIGHT NOT KNOW HOW TO COOK THEM EITHER.
KYAA, IT'S SUNAKO-CHAN. ♡
ONE, PLEASE.
I'LL MAKE A SUPER-TASTY ONE FOR YOU. ♡
べちょ
AH.
PLAP
W-WE HAVE SOME THAT ARE ALREADY DONE, NAKAHARA-SAN.
THE KEY IS...
...MAKING SURE YOU *FLICK YOUR WRIST.*

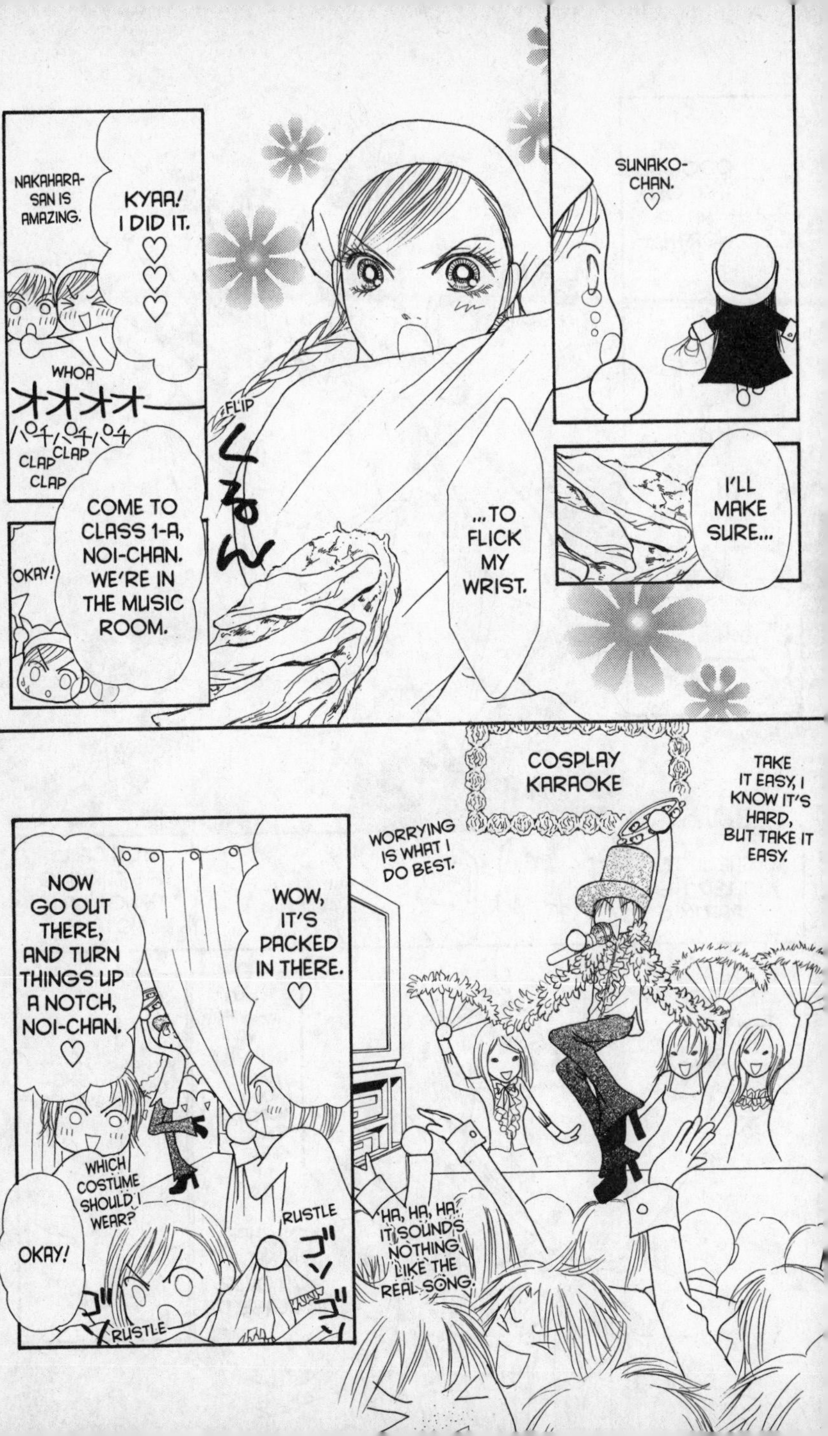

SUNAKO-CHAN. ♡
I'LL MAKE SURE...
...TO FLICK MY WRIST.
FLIP
くるん
KYAA! I DID IT. ♡ ♡ ♡
NAKAHARA-SAN IS AMAZING.
WHOA
オオオオー
パチパチパチ
CLAP CLAP CLAP
COME TO CLASS 1-A, NOI-CHAN. WE'RE IN THE MUSIC ROOM.
OKAY!
COSPLAY KARAOKE
TAKE IT EASY, I KNOW IT'S HARD, BUT TAKE IT EASY.
WORRYING IS WHAT I DO BEST.
HA, HA, HA. IT SOUNDS NOTHING LIKE THE REAL SONG.
WOW, IT'S PACKED IN THERE. ♡
NOW GO OUT THERE, AND TURN THINGS UP A NOTCH, NOI-CHAN. ♡
RUSTLE
ゴソ
ゴソ
WHICH COSTUME SHOULD I WEAR?
OKAY!
ゴソ
RUSTLE

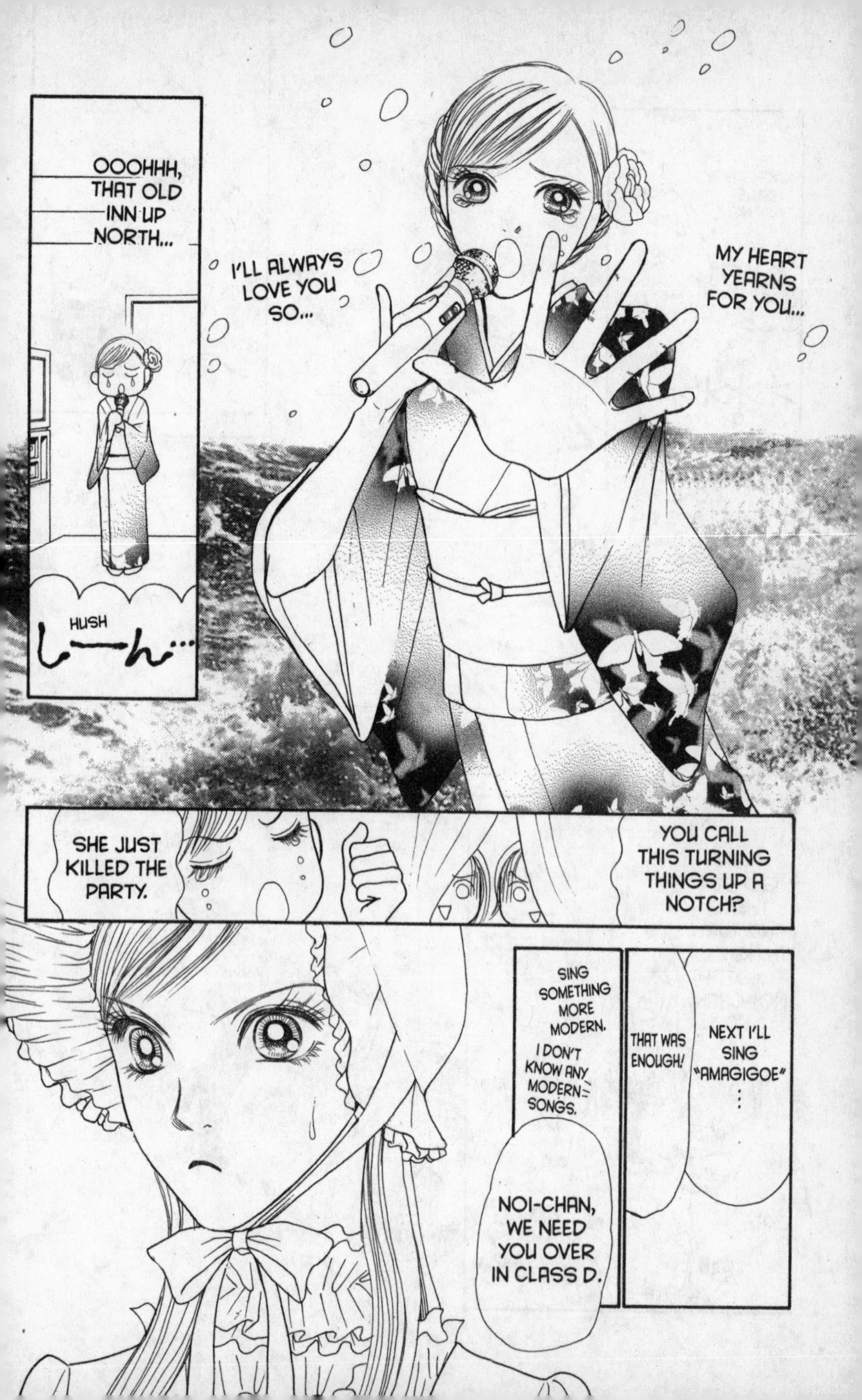
MY HEART YEARNS FOR YOU...
I'LL ALWAYS LOVE YOU SO...
OOOHHH, THAT OLD INN UP NORTH...
HUSH
しーん…
YOU CALL THIS TURNING THINGS UP A NOTCH?
SHE JUST KILLED THE PARTY.
NEXT I'LL SING "AMAGIGOE" ...
THAT WAS ENOUGH!
SING SOMETHING MORE MODERN.
I DON'T KNOW ANY MODERN SONGS.
NOI-CHAN, WE NEED YOU OVER IN CLASS D.

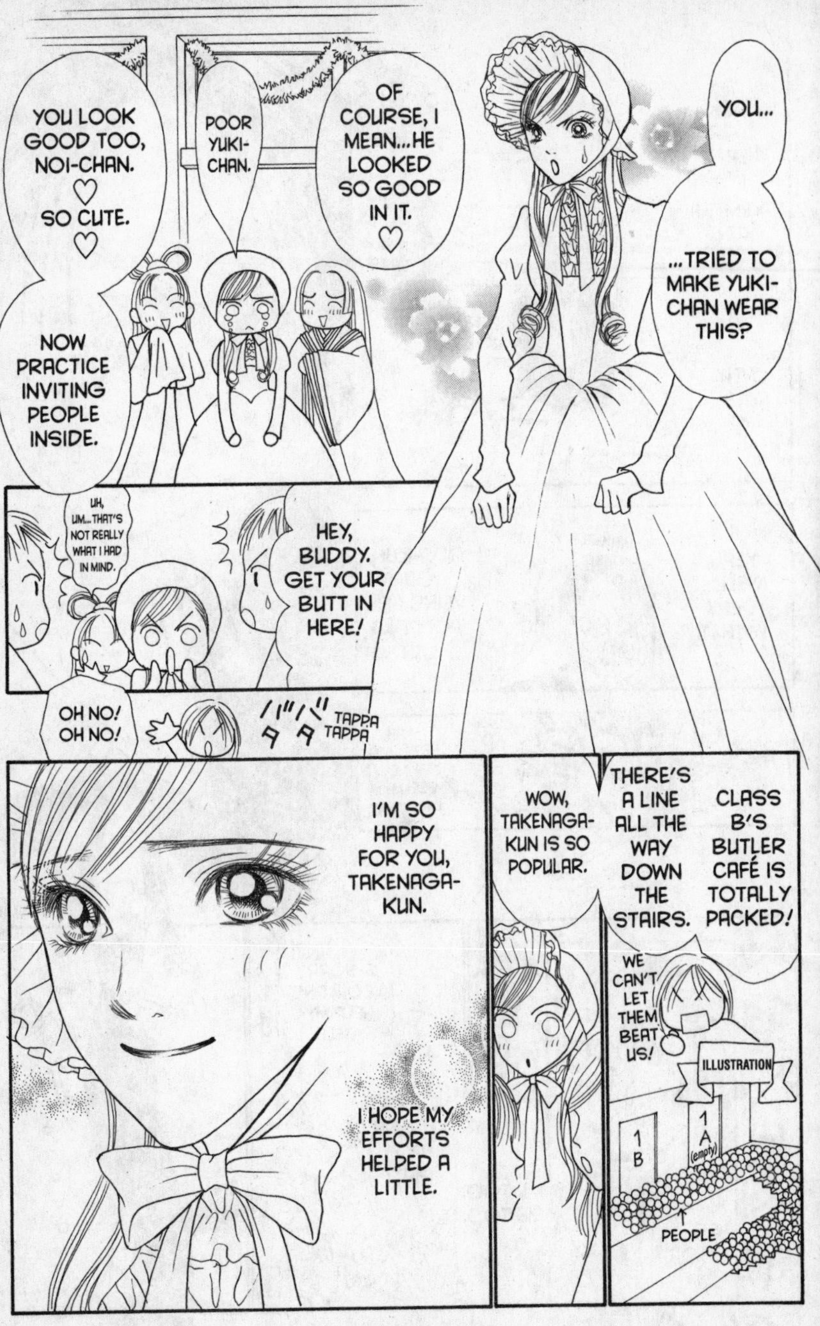
YOU...
...TRIED TO MAKE YUKI-CHAN WEAR THIS?
OF COURSE, I MEAN...HE LOOKED SO GOOD IN IT. ♡
POOR YUKI-CHAN.
YOU LOOK GOOD TOO, NOI-CHAN. ♡ SO CUTE. ♡
NOW PRACTICE INVITING PEOPLE INSIDE.
HEY, BUDDY. GET YOUR BUTT IN HERE!
UH, UM...THAT'S NOT REALLY WHAT I HAD IN MIND.
バタバタ TAPPA TAPPA
OH NO! OH NO!
CLASS B'S BUTLER CAFÉ IS TOTALLY PACKED!
THERE'S A LINE ALL THE WAY DOWN THE STAIRS.
WE CAN'T LET THEM BEAT US!
ILLUSTRATION
1 A (empty)
1 B
PEOPLE
WOW, TAKENAGA-KUN IS SO POPULAR.
I'M SO HAPPY FOR YOU, TAKENAGA-KUN.
I HOPE MY EFFORTS HELPED A LITTLE.

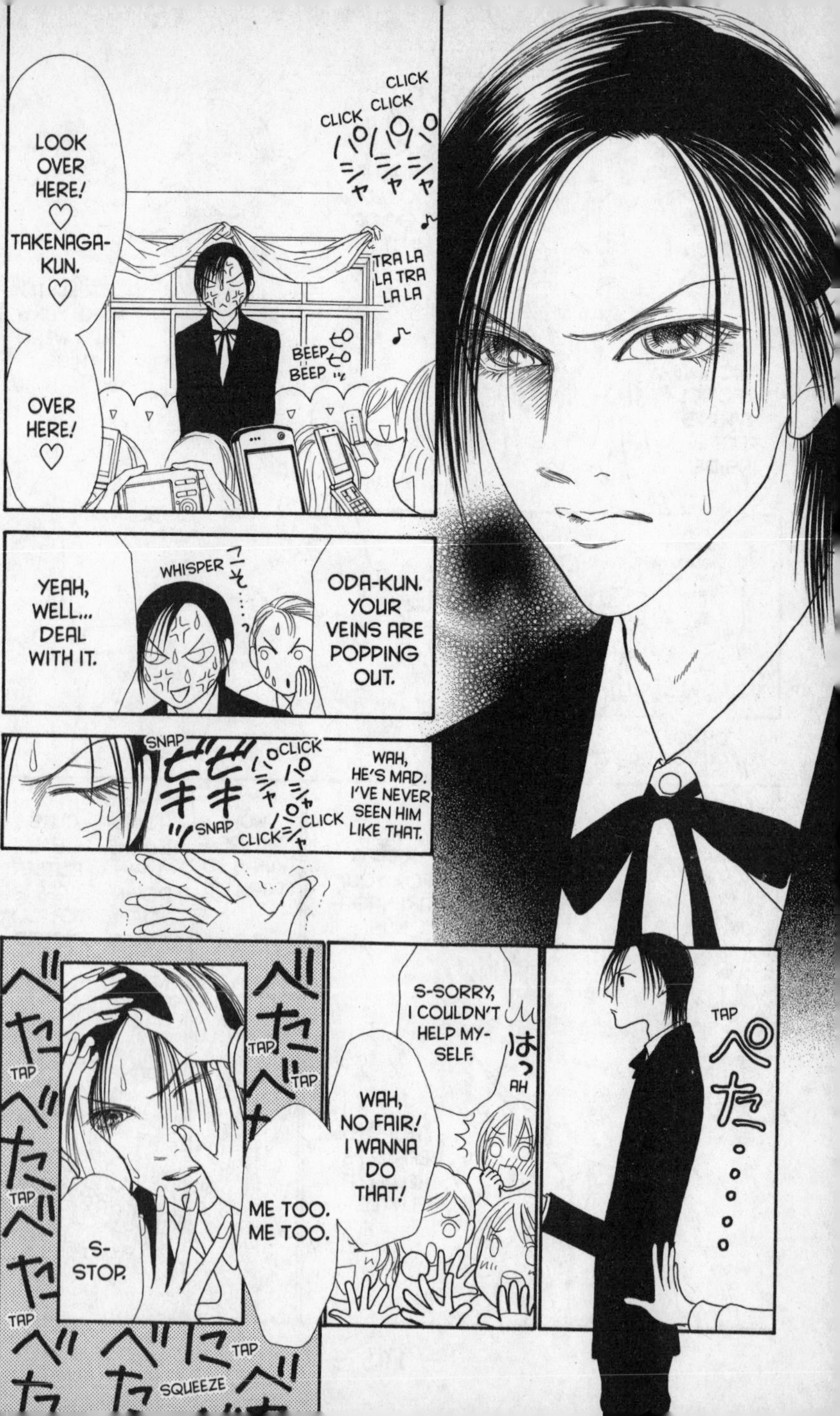
CLICK CLICK
CLICK CLICK
パシャパシャパシャ
TRA LA LA TRA LA LA
BEEP BEEP
ピロピロッ
LOOK OVER HERE! ♡ TAKENAGA-KUN. ♡
OVER HERE! ♡
ODA-KUN. YOUR VEINS ARE POPPING OUT.
WHISPER
YEAH, WELL... DEAL WITH IT.
WAH, HE'S MAD. I'VE NEVER SEEN HIM LIKE THAT.
CLICK
CLICK
CLICK
SNAP
SNAP
TAP
ぺた・・・・・
S-SORRY, I COULDN'T HELP MY-SELF.
はっ
AH
WAH, NO FAIR! I WANNA DO THAT!
ME TOO. ME TOO.
TAP
TAP
TAP
TAP
TAP
TAP
S-STOP.
SQUEEZE

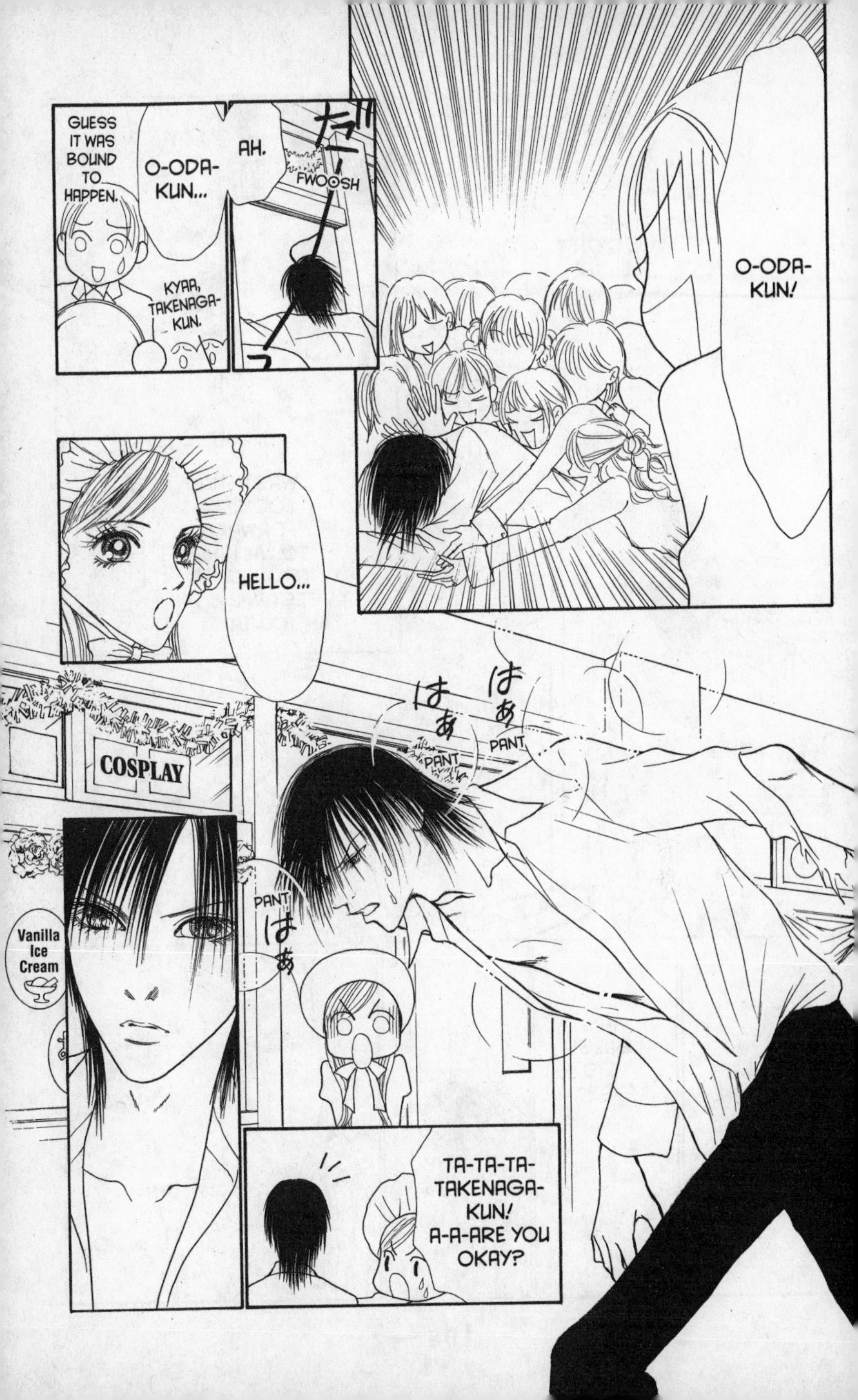
O-ODA-KUN!
AH.
FWOOSH
KYAA, TAKENAGA-KUN.
O-ODA-KUN...
GUESS IT WAS BOUND TO HAPPEN.
HELLO...
はあ
PANT
はあ
PANT
COSPLAY
PANT
はあ
Vanilla Ice Cream
TA-TA-TA-TAKENAGA-KUN! A-A-ARE YOU OKAY?

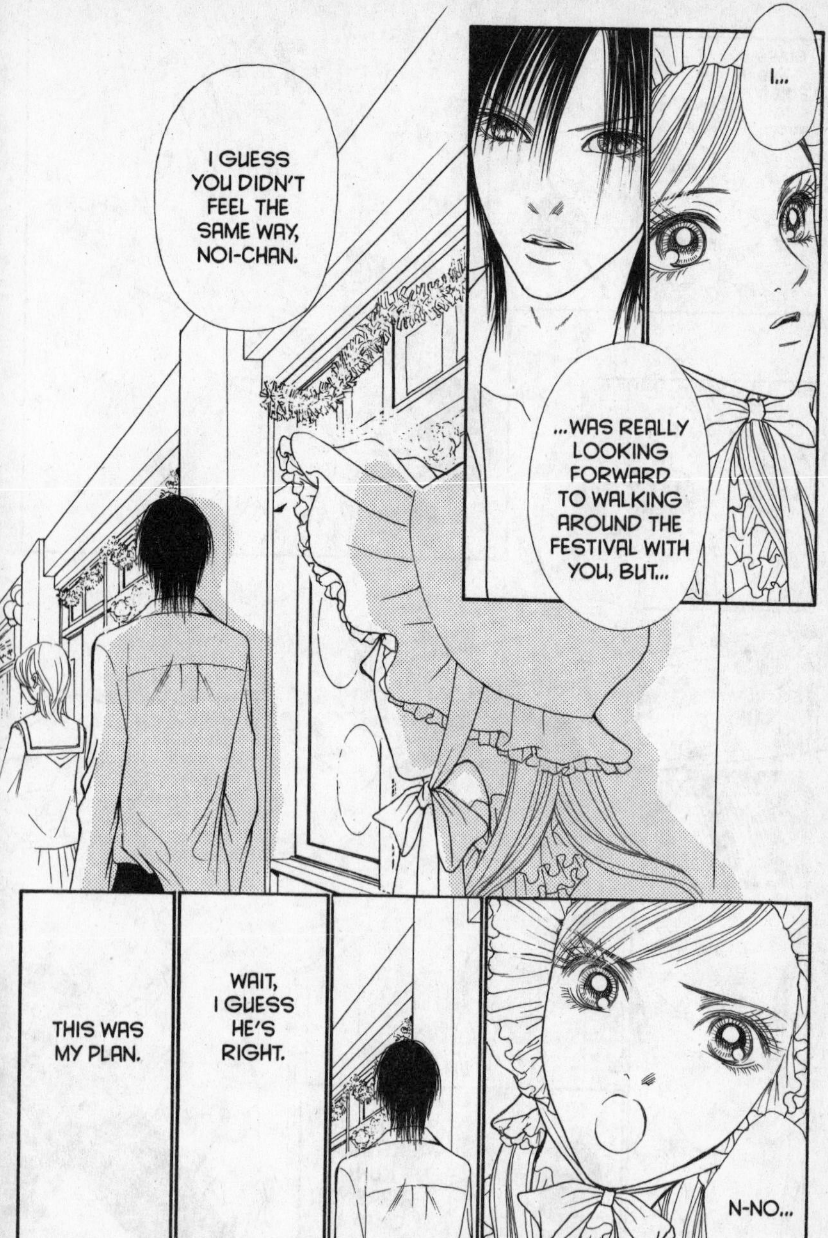
I...
...WAS REALLY LOOKING FORWARD TO WALKING AROUND THE FESTIVAL WITH YOU, BUT...
I GUESS YOU DIDN'T FEEL THE SAME WAY, NOI-CHAN.
N-NO...
WAIT, I GUESS HE'S RIGHT.
THIS WAS MY PLAN.

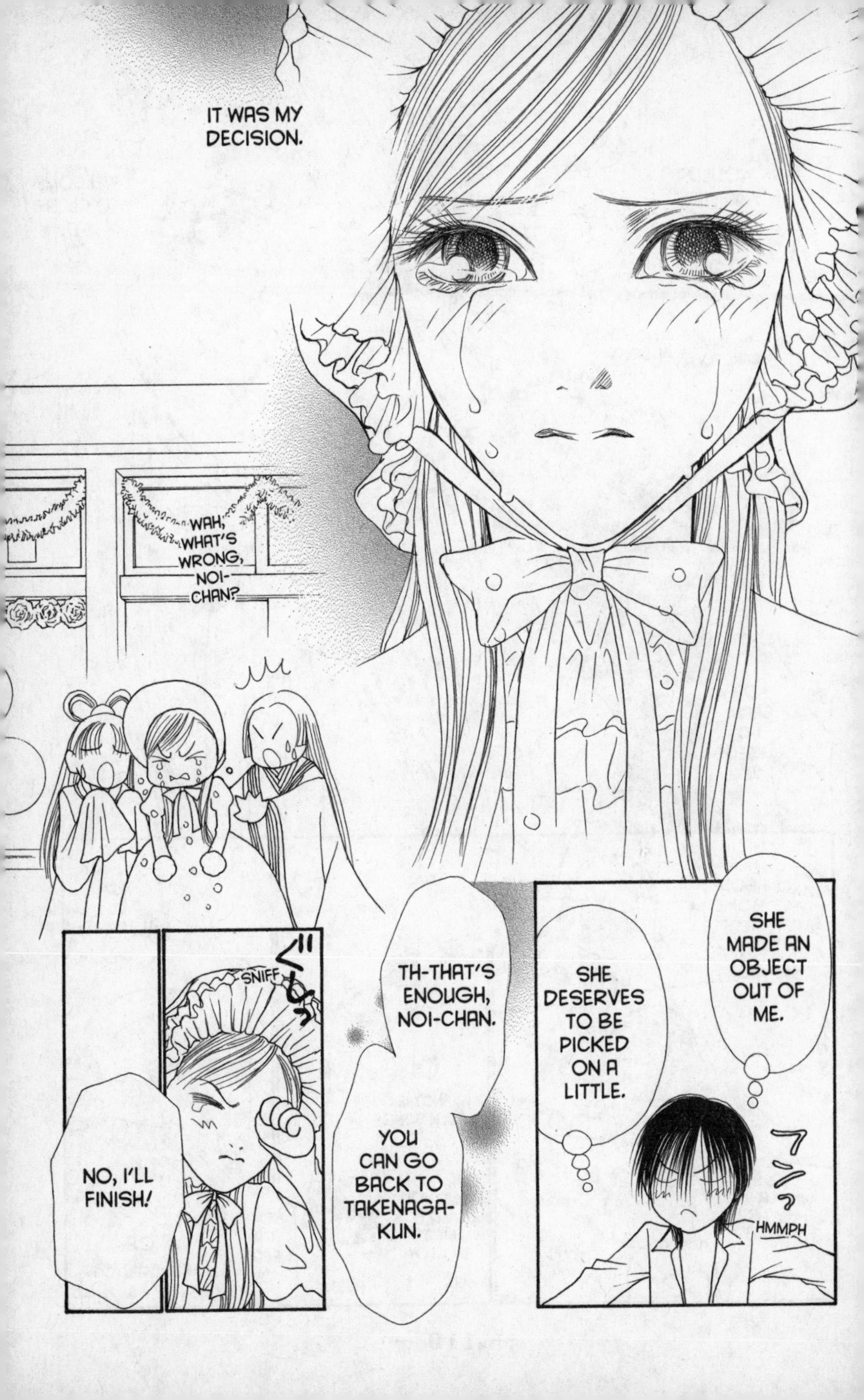
IT WAS MY DECISION.
WAH, WHAT'S WRONG, NOI-CHAN?
SHE MADE AN OBJECT OUT OF ME.
SHE DESERVES TO BE PICKED ON A LITTLE.
HMMPH
TH-THAT'S ENOUGH, NOI-CHAN.
YOU CAN GO BACK TO TAKENAGA-KUN.
SNIFF
NO, I'LL FINISH!

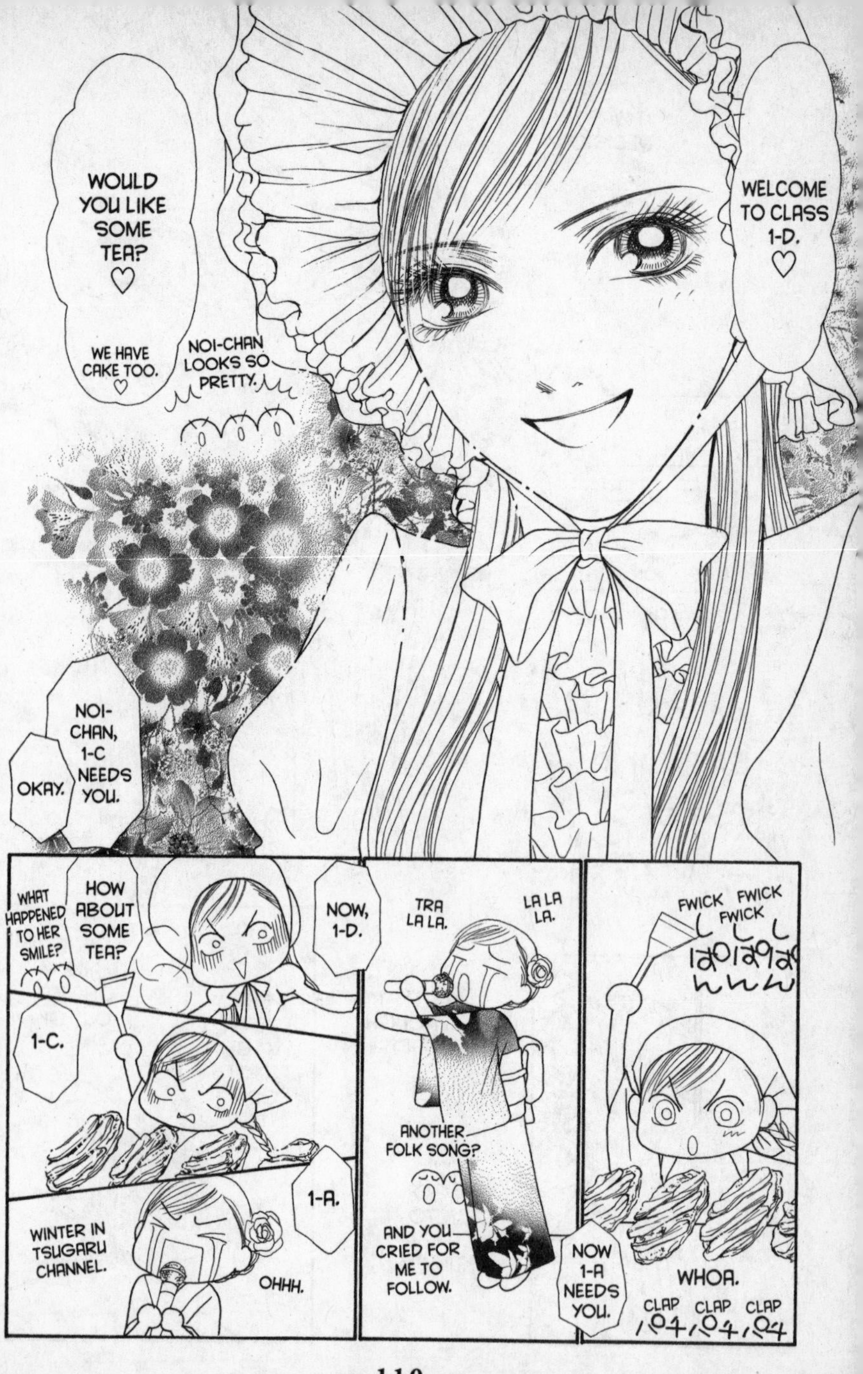
WELCOME TO CLASS 1-D. ♡
NOI-CHAN LOOKS SO PRETTY.
WOULD YOU LIKE SOME TEA? ♡
WE HAVE CAKE TOO. ♡
NOI-CHAN, 1-C NEEDS YOU.
OKAY.
FWICK FWICK FWICK
WHOA.
NOW 1-A NEEDS YOU.
CLAP CLAP CLAP
パチパチパチ
LA LA LA.
TRA LA LA.
ANOTHER FOLK SONG?
AND YOU CRIED FOR ME TO FOLLOW.
NOW, 1-D.
HOW ABOUT SOME TEA?
WHAT HAPPENED TO HER SMILE?
1-C.
1-A.
WINTER IN TSUGARU CHANNEL.
OHHH.

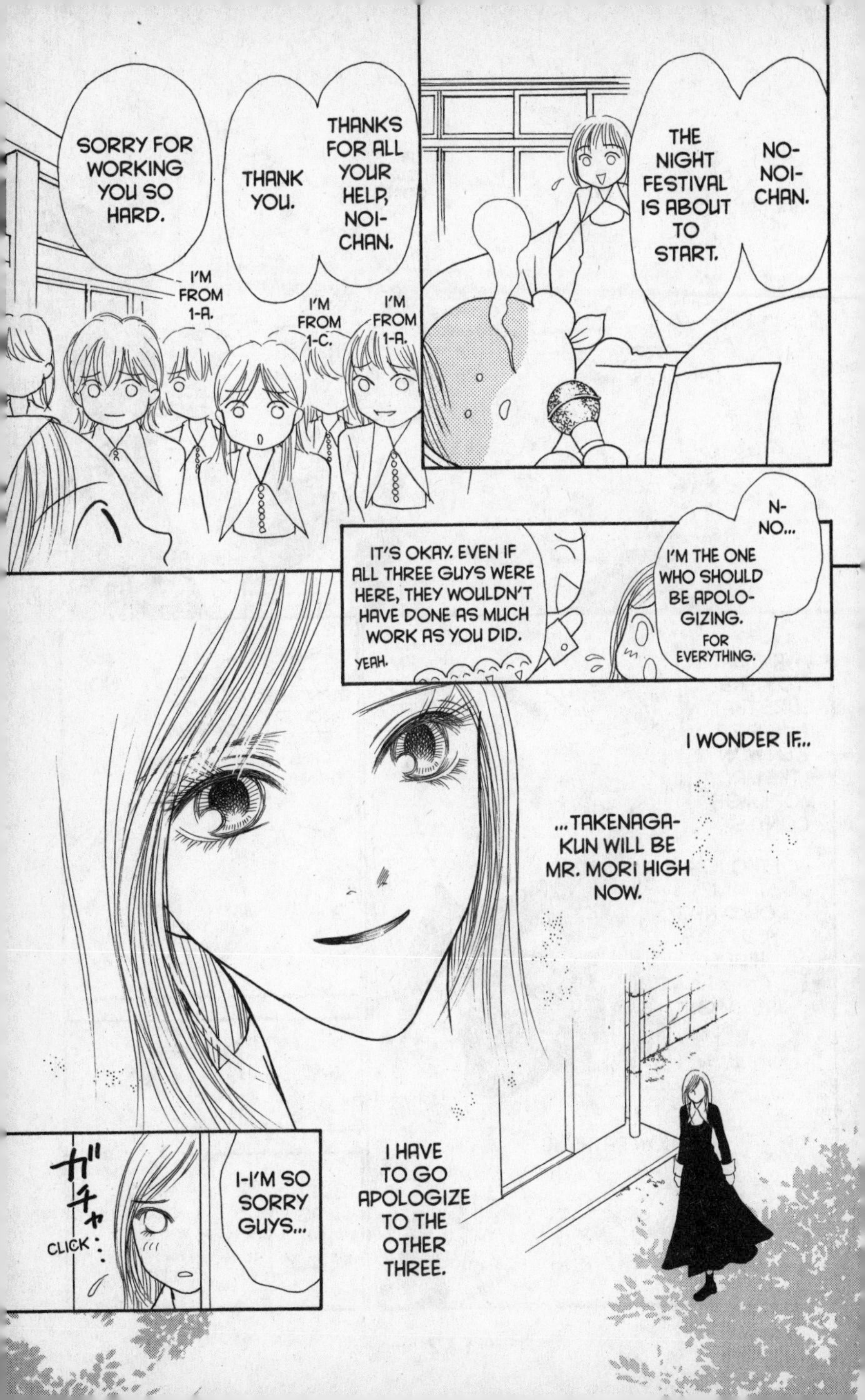
NO-NOI-CHAN.
THE NIGHT FESTIVAL IS ABOUT TO START.
THANKS FOR ALL YOUR HELP, NOI-CHAN.
THANK YOU.
SORRY FOR WORKING YOU SO HARD.
I'M FROM 1-A.
I'M FROM 1-C.
I'M FROM 1-A.
N-NO...
I'M THE ONE WHO SHOULD BE APOLO-GIZING.
FOR EVERYTHING.
IT'S OKAY. EVEN IF ALL THREE GUYS WERE HERE, THEY WOULDN'T HAVE DONE AS MUCH WORK AS YOU DID.
YEAH.
I WONDER IF...
...TAKENAGA-KUN WILL BE MR. MORI HIGH NOW.
I HAVE TO GO APOLOGIZE TO THE OTHER THREE.
I-I'M SO SORRY GUYS...
ガチャ
CLICK

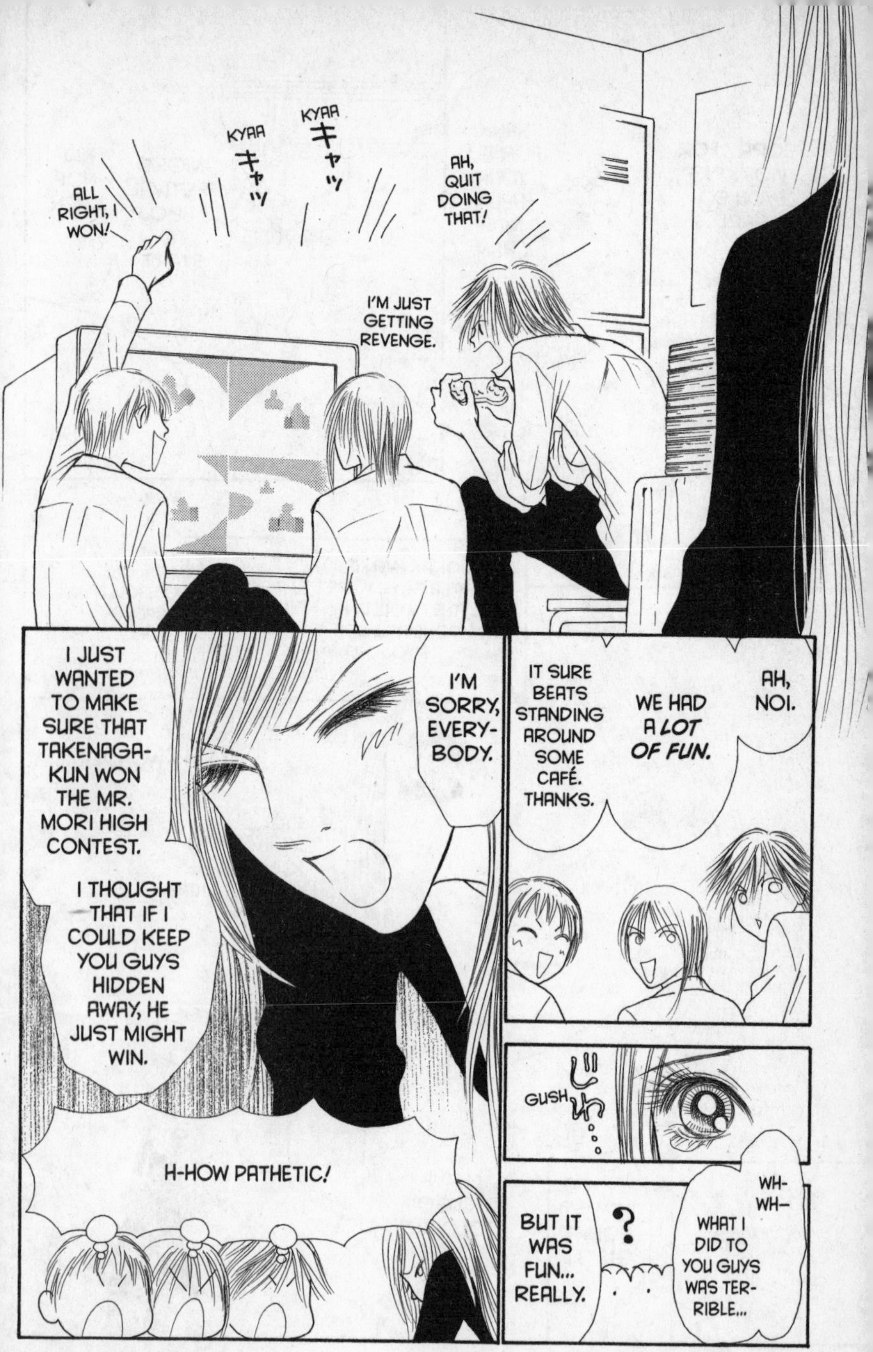
KYAA キャッ
AH, QUIT DOING THAT!
KYAA キャッ
ALL RIGHT, I WON!
I'M JUST GETTING REVENGE.
AH, NOI.
WE HAD A *LOT OF FUN.*
IT SURE BEATS STANDING AROUND SOME CAFÉ. THANKS.
GUSH じわ…
WH- WH- WHAT I DID TO YOU GUYS WAS TERRIBLE...
?
BUT IT WAS FUN... REALLY.
I'M SORRY, EVERYBODY.
I JUST WANTED TO MAKE SURE THAT TAKENAGA-KUN WON THE MR. MORI HIGH CONTEST.
I THOUGHT THAT IF I COULD KEEP YOU GUYS HIDDEN AWAY, HE JUST MIGHT WIN.
H-HOW PATHETIC!

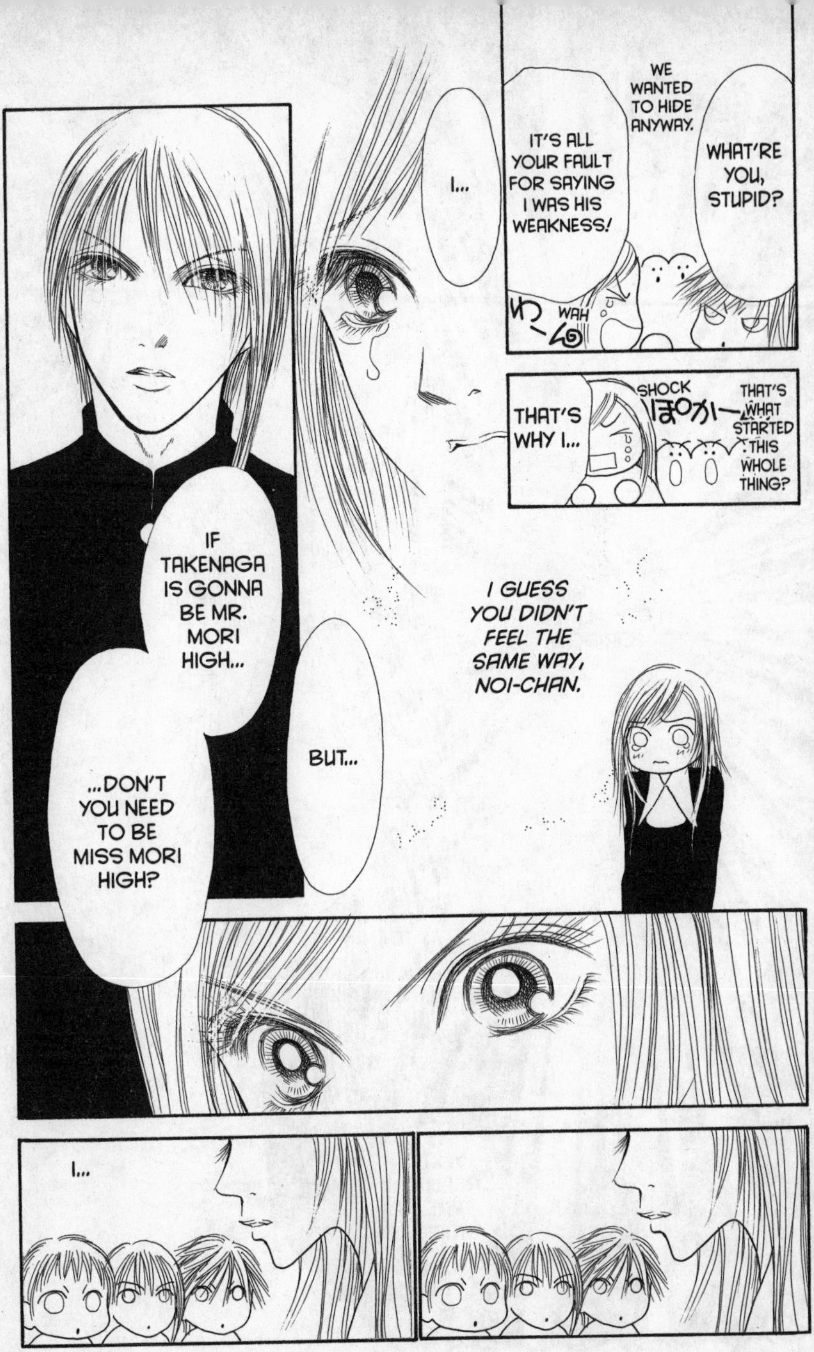
WHAT'RE YOU, STUPID?
WE WANTED TO HIDE ANYWAY.
IT'S ALL YOUR FAULT FOR SAYING I WAS HIS WEAKNESS!
WAH
わーん
THAT'S WHAT STARTED THIS WHOLE THING?
SHOCK
ぽかーん
THAT'S WHY I...
I...
I GUESS YOU DIDN'T FEEL THE SAME WAY, NOI-CHAN.
BUT...
IF TAKENAGA IS GONNA BE MR. MORI HIGH...
...DON'T YOU NEED TO BE MISS MORI HIGH?
I...

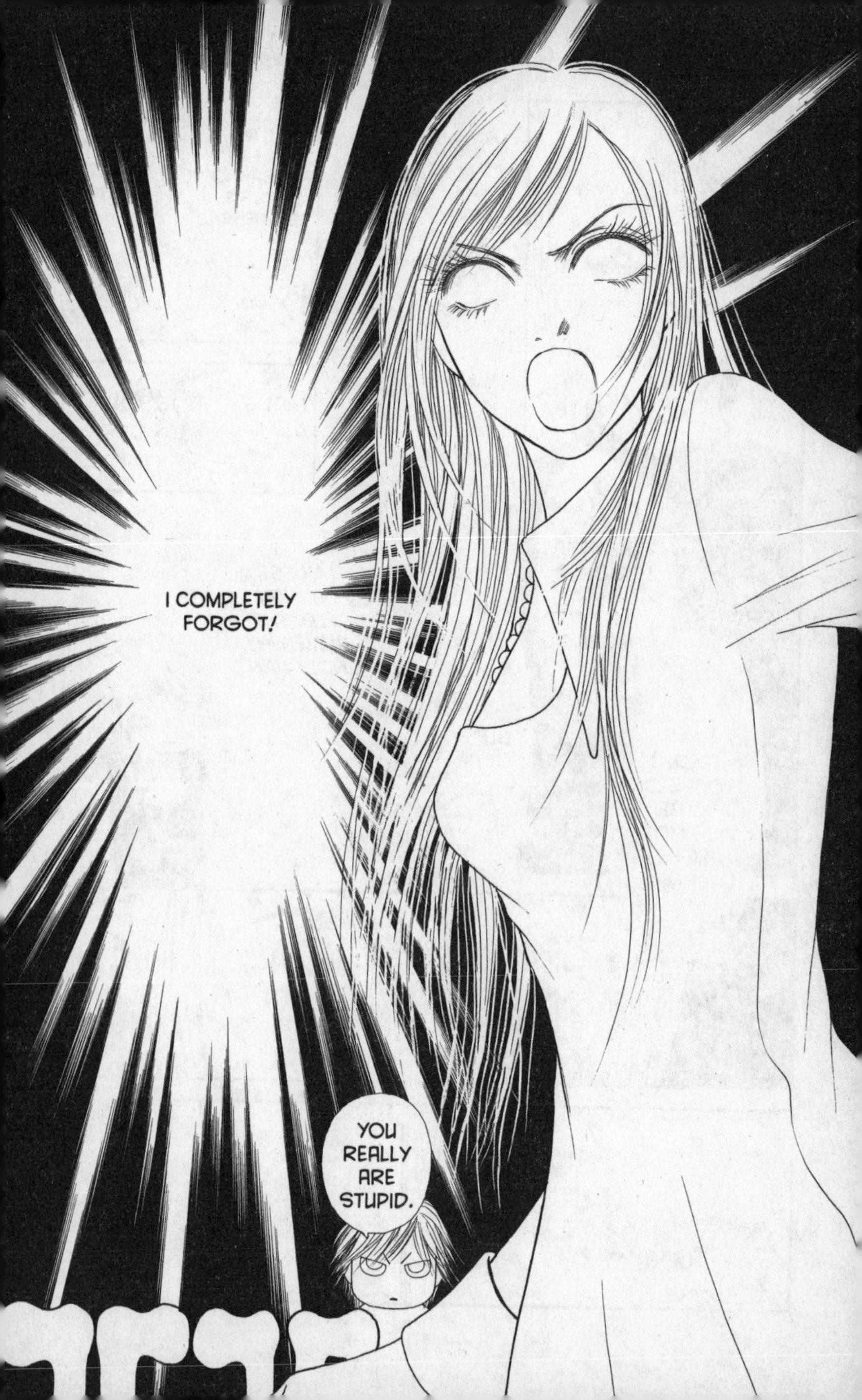
I COMPLETELY FORGOT!
YOU REALLY ARE STUPID.

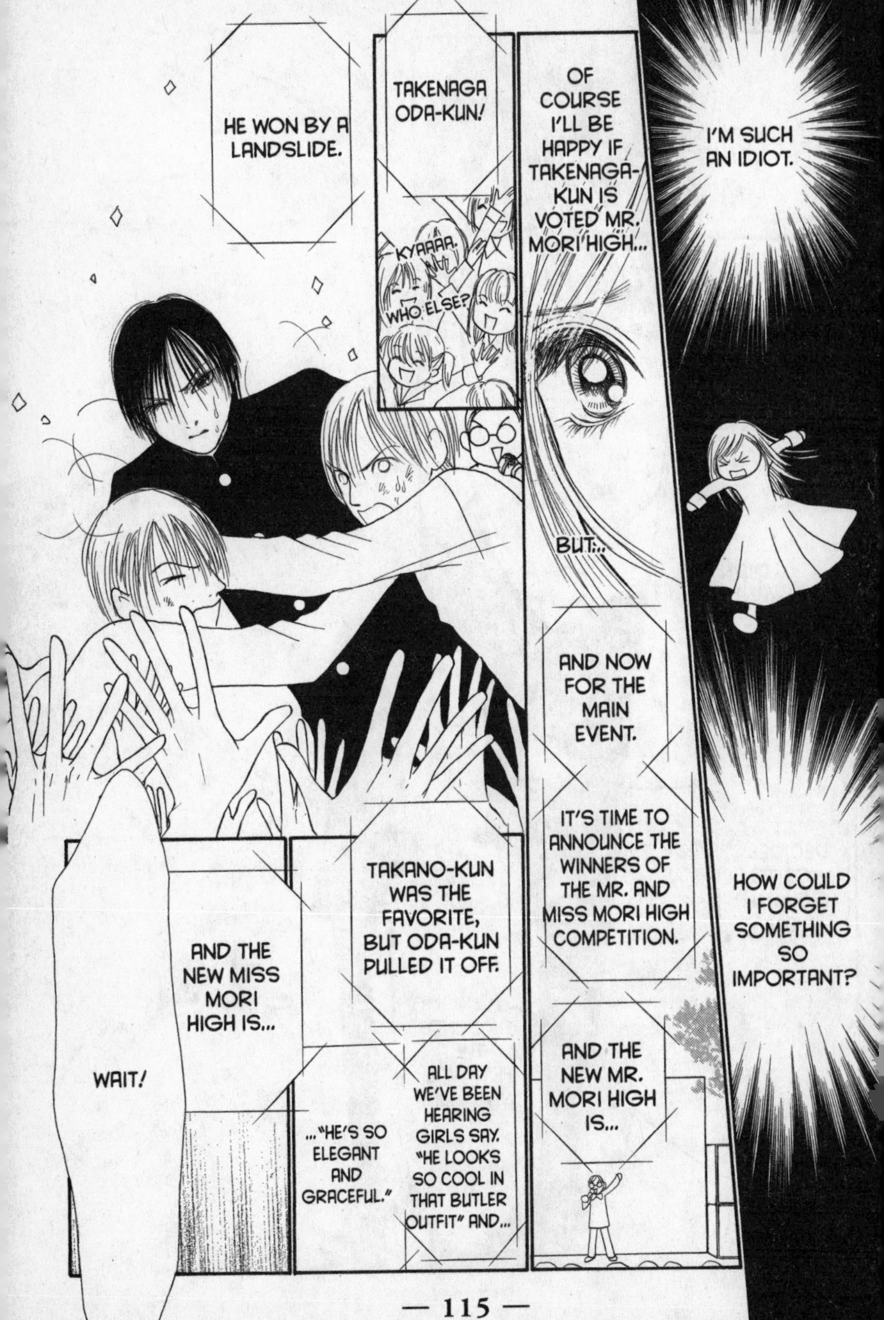
I'M SUCH AN IDIOT.
HOW COULD I FORGET SOMETHING SO IMPORTANT?
OF COURSE I'LL BE HAPPY IF TAKENAGA-KUN IS VOTED MR. MORI HIGH...
BUT...
AND NOW FOR THE MAIN EVENT.
IT'S TIME TO ANNOUNCE THE WINNERS OF THE MR. AND MISS MORI HIGH COMPETITION.
AND THE NEW MR. MORI HIGH IS...
TAKENAGA ODA-KUN!
KYAAAA.
WHO ELSE?
HE WON BY A LANDSLIDE.
TAKANO-KUN WAS THE FAVORITE, BUT ODA-KUN PULLED IT OFF.
ALL DAY WE'VE BEEN HEARING GIRLS SAY. "HE LOOKS SO COOL IN THAT BUTLER OUTFIT" AND...
..."HE'S SO ELEGANT AND GRACEFUL."
AND THE NEW MISS MORI HIGH IS...
WAIT!

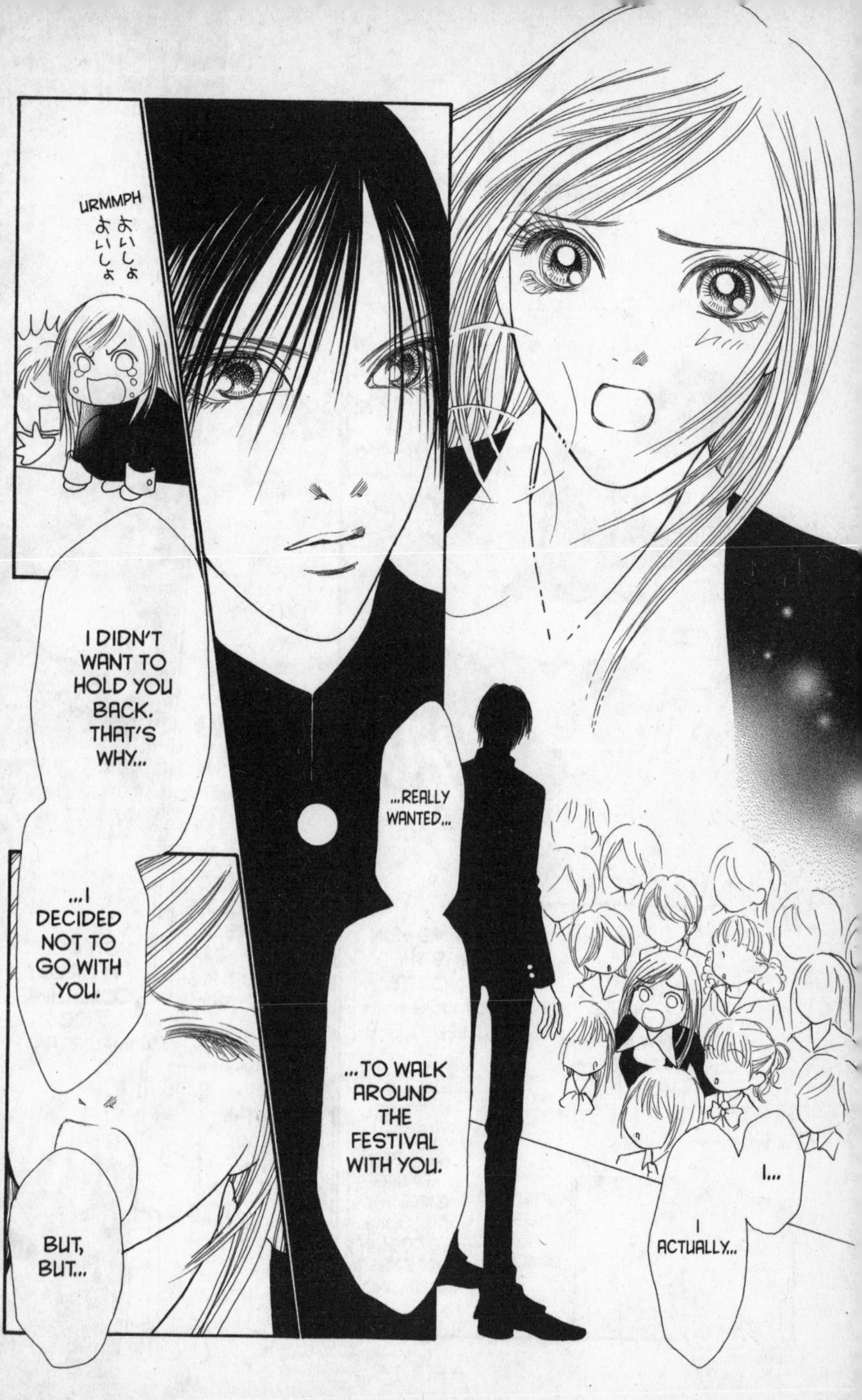
I...
I ACTUALLY...
...REALLY WANTED...
...TO WALK AROUND THE FESTIVAL WITH YOU.
URMMPH
おいしょ おいしょ
I DIDN'T WANT TO HOLD YOU BACK. THAT'S WHY...
...I DECIDED NOT TO GO WITH YOU.
BUT, BUT...

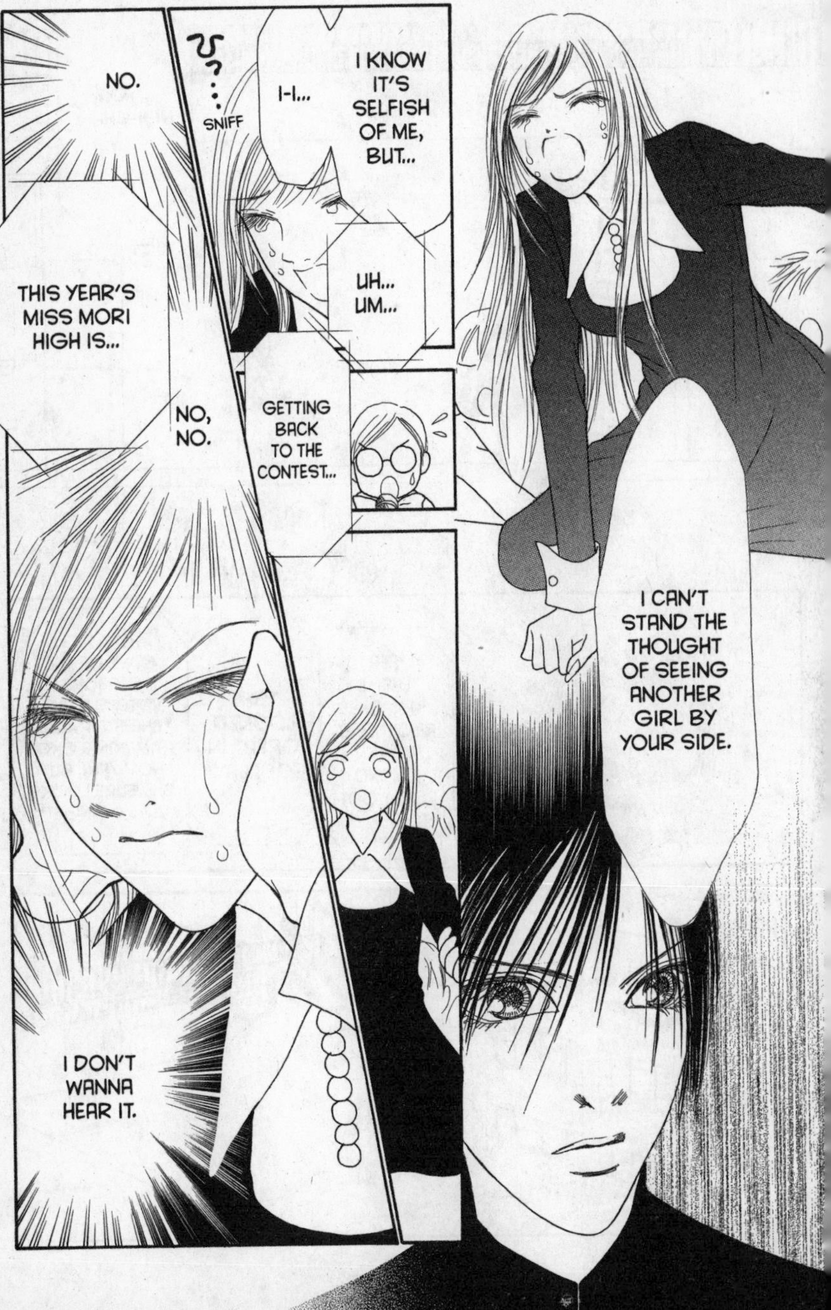
I CAN'T STAND THE THOUGHT OF SEEING ANOTHER GIRL BY YOUR SIDE.
I KNOW IT'S SELFISH OF ME, BUT...
I-I...
SNIFF
UH... UM...
GETTING BACK TO THE CONTEST...
NO.
THIS YEAR'S MISS MORI HIGH IS...
NO, NO.
I DON'T WANNA HEAR IT.

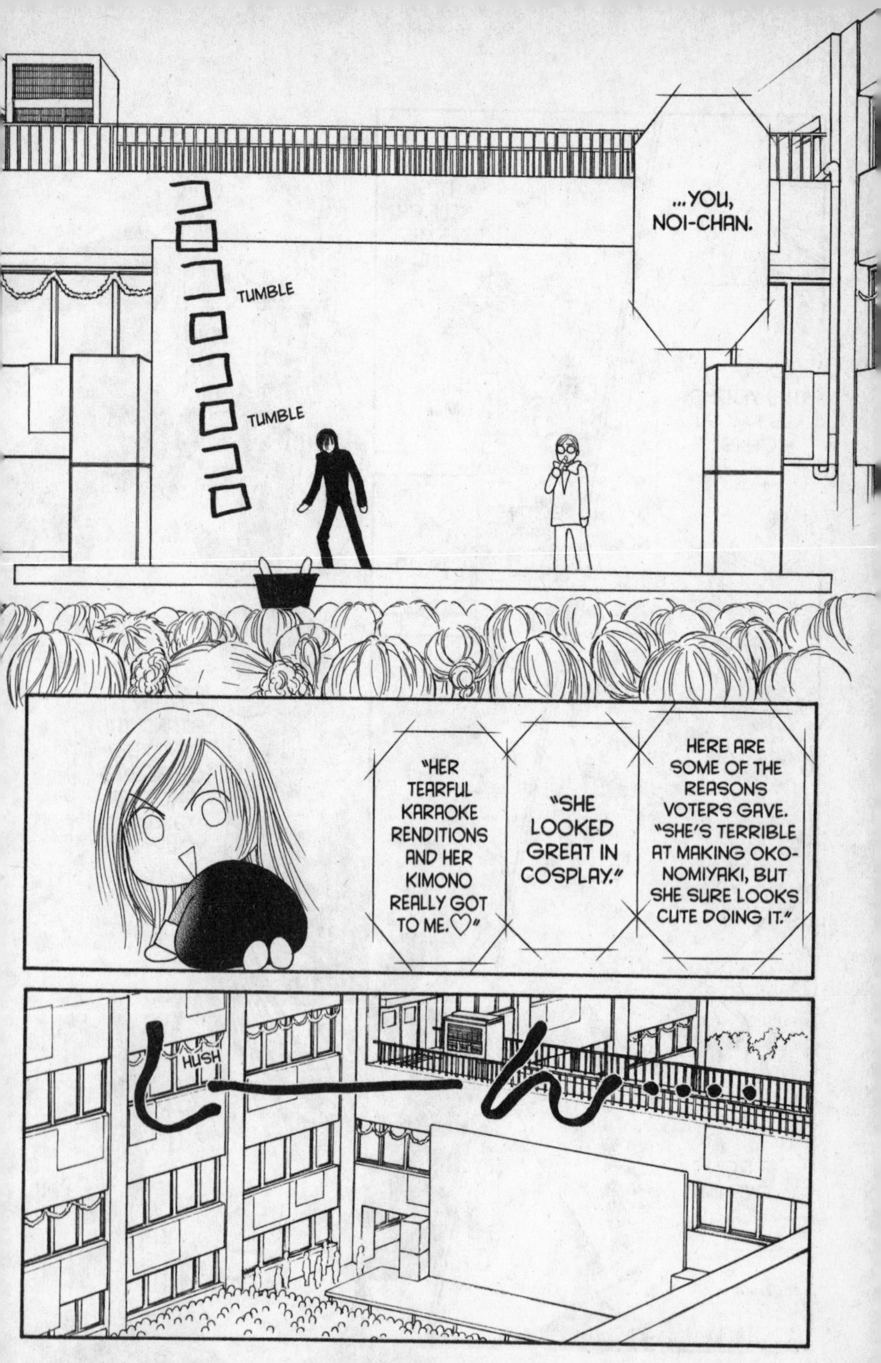
...YOU, NOI-CHAN.
コロコロコロコロ
TUMBLE
TUMBLE
HERE ARE SOME OF THE REASONS VOTERS GAVE. "SHE'S TERRIBLE AT MAKING OKONOMIYAKI, BUT SHE SURE LOOKS CUTE DOING IT."
"SHE LOOKED GREAT IN COSPLAY."
"HER TEARFUL KARAOKE RENDITIONS AND HER KIMONO REALLY GOT TO ME.♡"
しーん....
HUSH

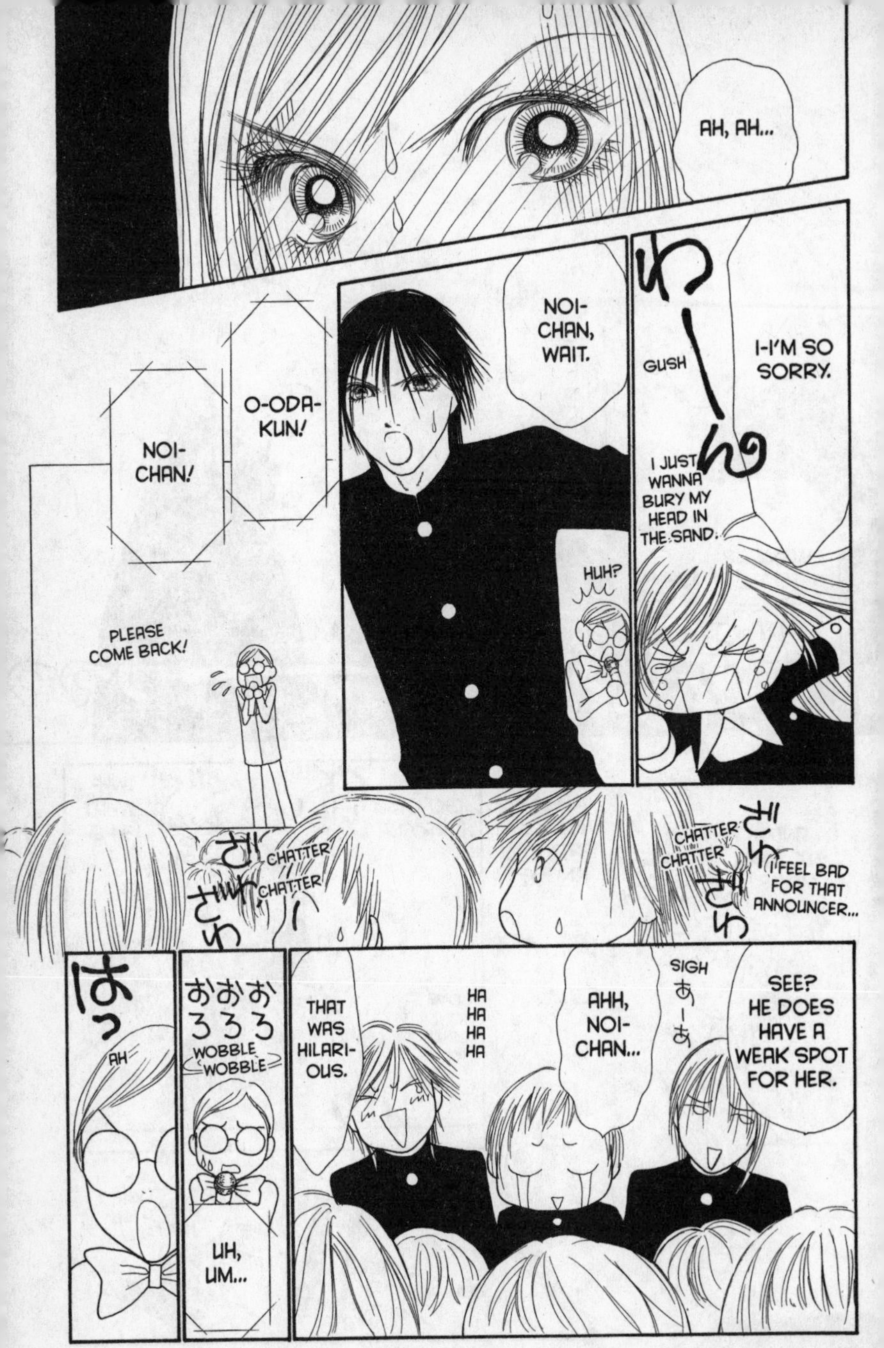
AH, AH...
わーん
GUSH
I-I'M SO SORRY.
I JUST WANNA BURY MY HEAD IN THE SAND.
HUH?
NOI-CHAN, WAIT.
O-ODA-KUN!
NOI-CHAN!
PLEASE COME BACK!
ざわ ざわ
CHATTER CHATTER
I FEEL BAD FOR THAT ANNOUNCER...
ざわ ざわ
CHATTER CHATTER
SEE? HE DOES HAVE A WEAK SPOT FOR HER.
SIGH
あーあ
AHH, NOI-CHAN...
HA HA HA HA
THAT WAS HILARI-OUS.
おおおろろろ
WOBBLE WOBBLE
UH, UM...
はっ
AH

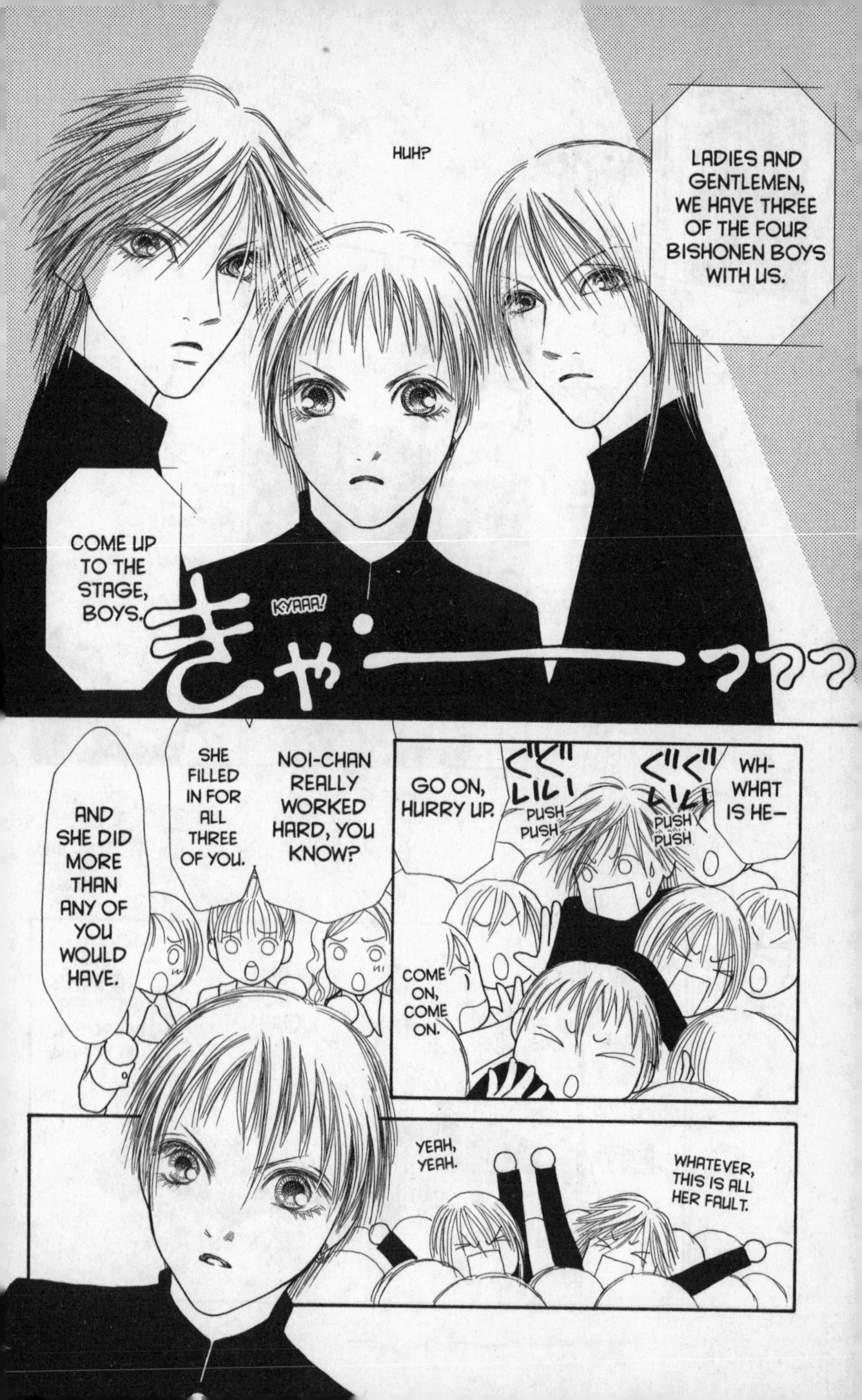
LADIES AND GENTLEMEN, WE HAVE THREE OF THE FOUR BISHONEN BOYS WITH US.
HUH?
COME UP TO THE STAGE, BOYS.
KYAAA!
WH- WHAT IS HE—
PUSH PUSH
PUSH PUSH
GO ON, HURRY UP.
COME ON, COME ON.
NOI-CHAN REALLY WORKED HARD, YOU KNOW?
SHE FILLED IN FOR ALL THREE OF YOU.
AND SHE DID MORE THAN ANY OF YOU WOULD HAVE.
WHATEVER, THIS IS ALL HER FAULT.
YEAH, YEAH.

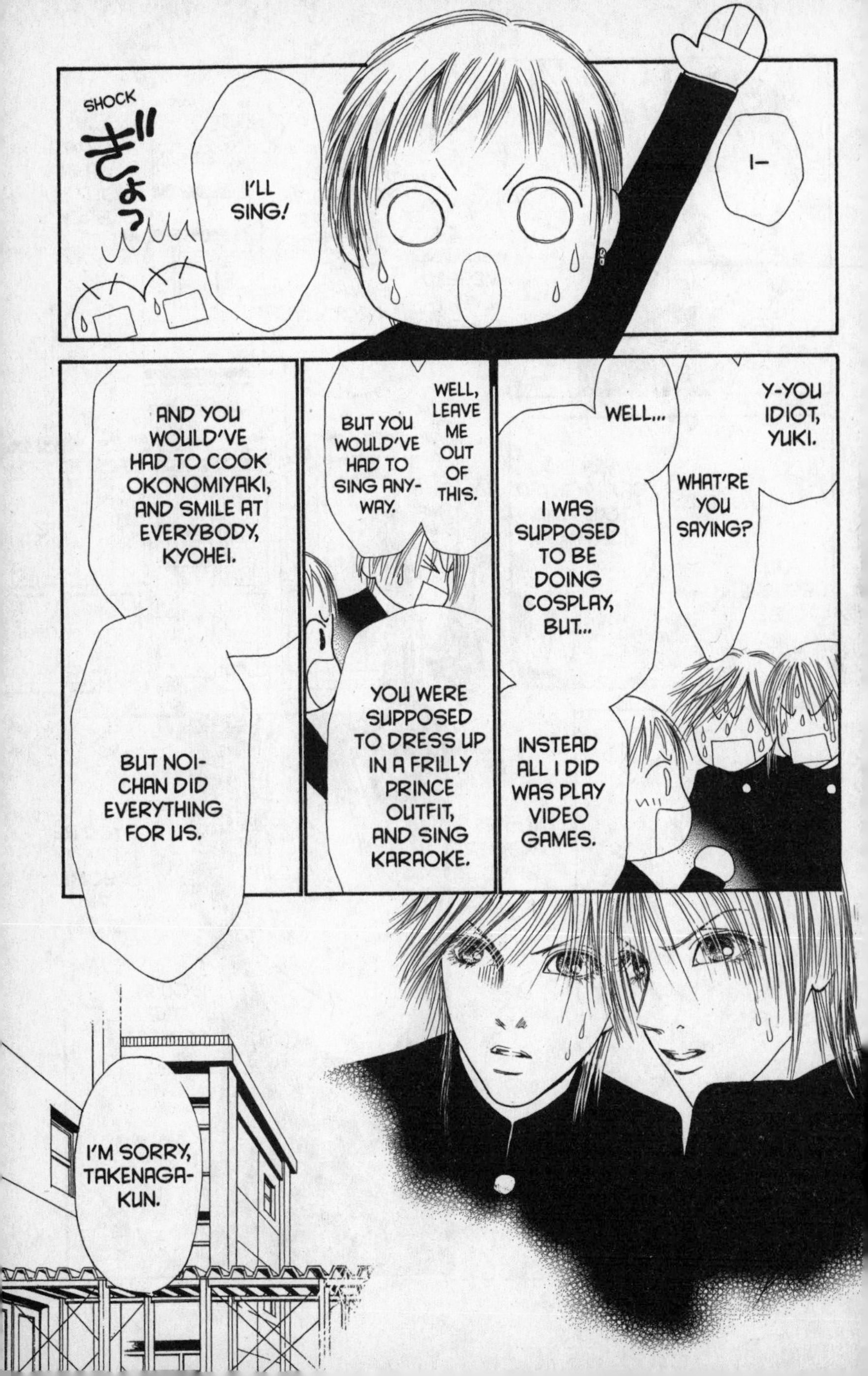
I—
I'LL SING!
SHOCK
ぎょっ
Y-YOU IDIOT, YUKI.
WHAT'RE YOU SAYING?
WELL...
I WAS SUPPOSED TO BE DOING COSPLAY, BUT...
INSTEAD ALL I DID WAS PLAY VIDEO GAMES.
WELL, LEAVE ME OUT OF THIS.
BUT YOU WOULD'VE HAD TO SING ANY-WAY.
YOU WERE SUPPOSED TO DRESS UP IN A FRILLY PRINCE OUTFIT, AND SING KARAOKE.
AND YOU WOULD'VE HAD TO COOK OKONOMIYAKI, AND SMILE AT EVERYBODY, KYOHEI.
BUT NOI-CHAN DID EVERYTHING FOR US.
I'M SORRY, TAKENAGA-KUN.

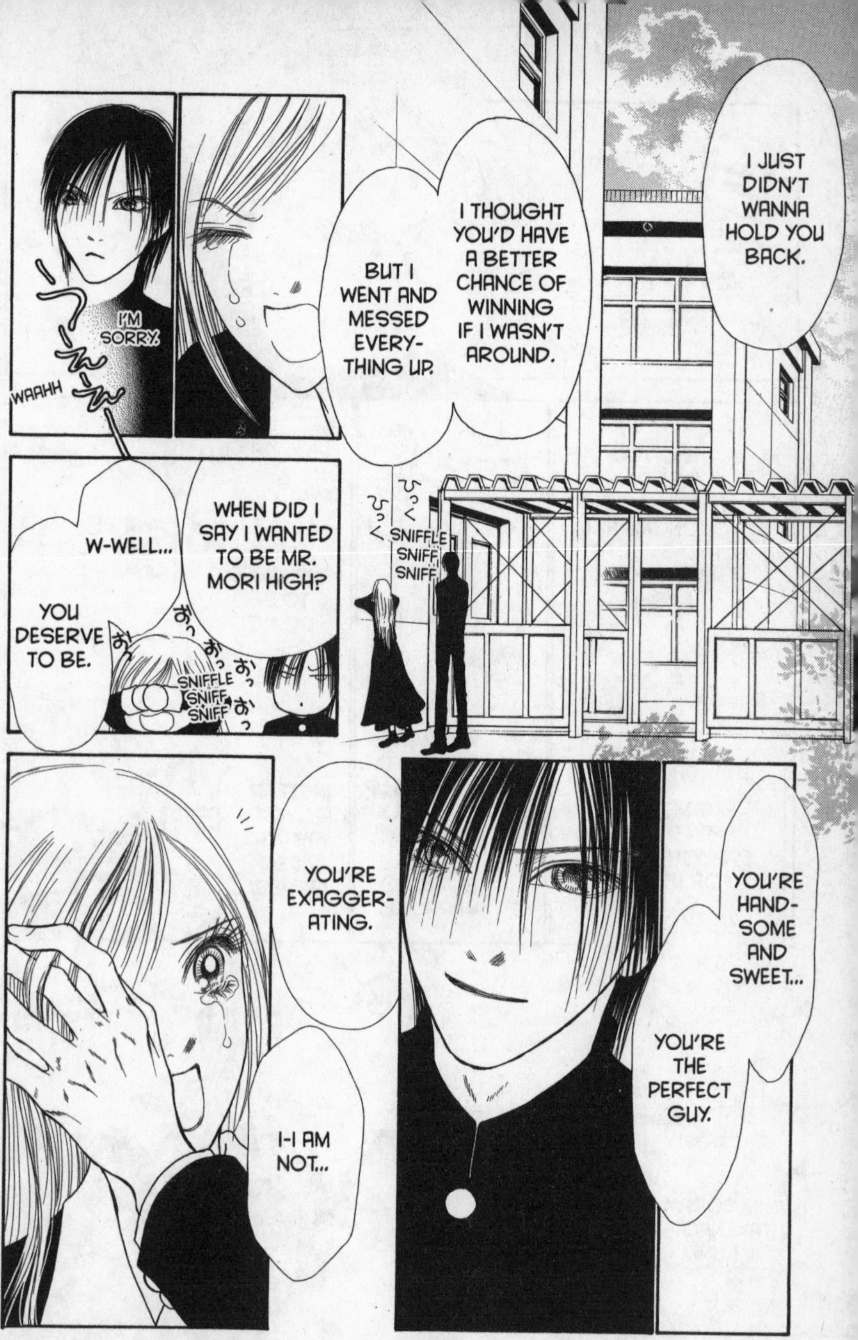
I JUST DIDN'T WANNA HOLD YOU BACK.
I THOUGHT YOU'D HAVE A BETTER CHANCE OF WINNING IF I WASN'T AROUND.
BUT I WENT AND MESSED EVERY-THING UP.
ひっく ひっく
SNIFFLE SNIFF SNIFF
I'M SORRY.
WAAHH
WHEN DID I SAY I WANTED TO BE MR. MORI HIGH?
W-WELL...
YOU DESERVE TO BE.
おっ おっ おっ おっ おっ
SNIFFLE SNIFF SNIFF
YOU'RE HAND-SOME AND SWEET...
YOU'RE THE PERFECT GUY.
YOU'RE EXAGGER-ATING.
I-I AM NOT...

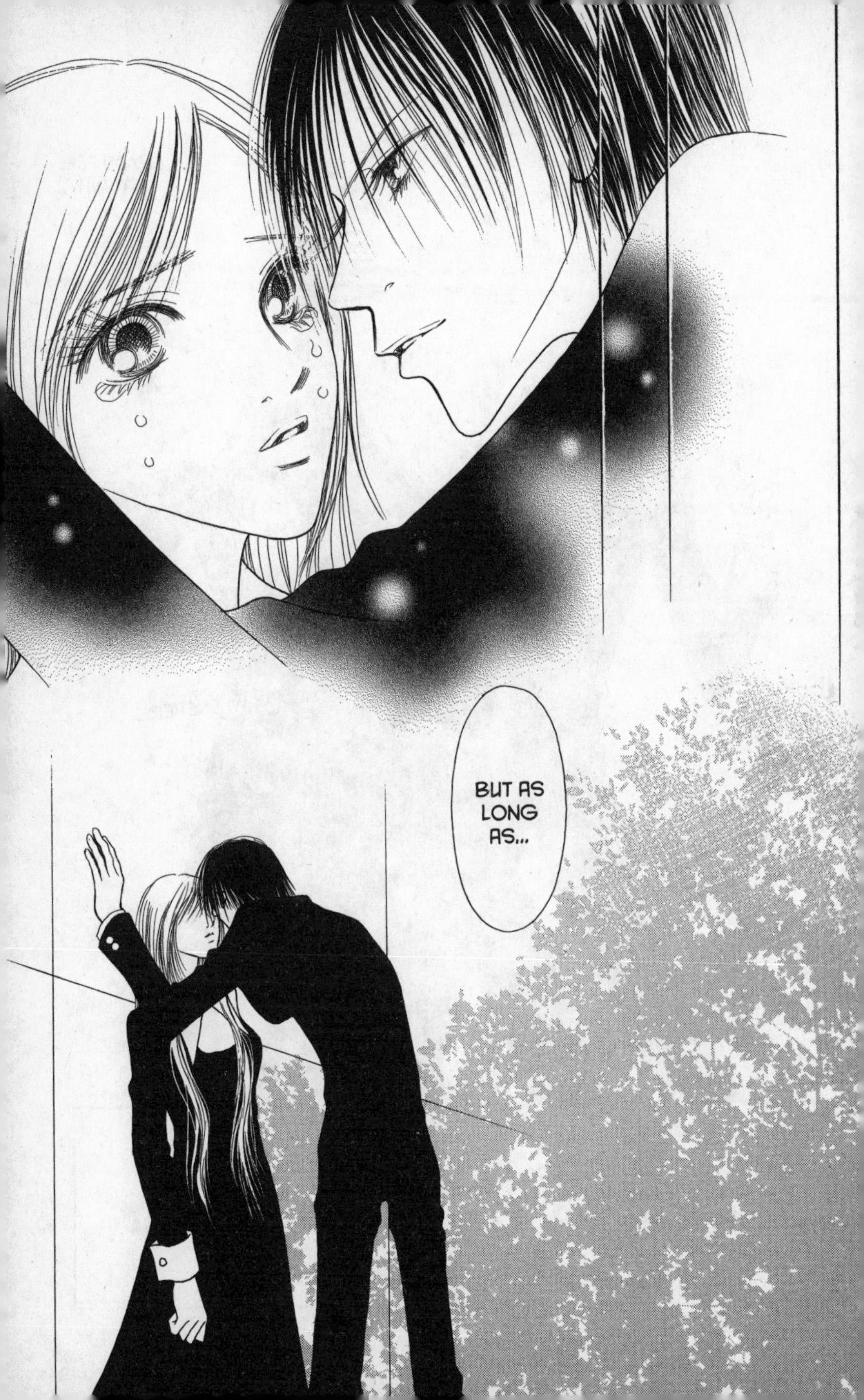
BUT AS LONG AS...

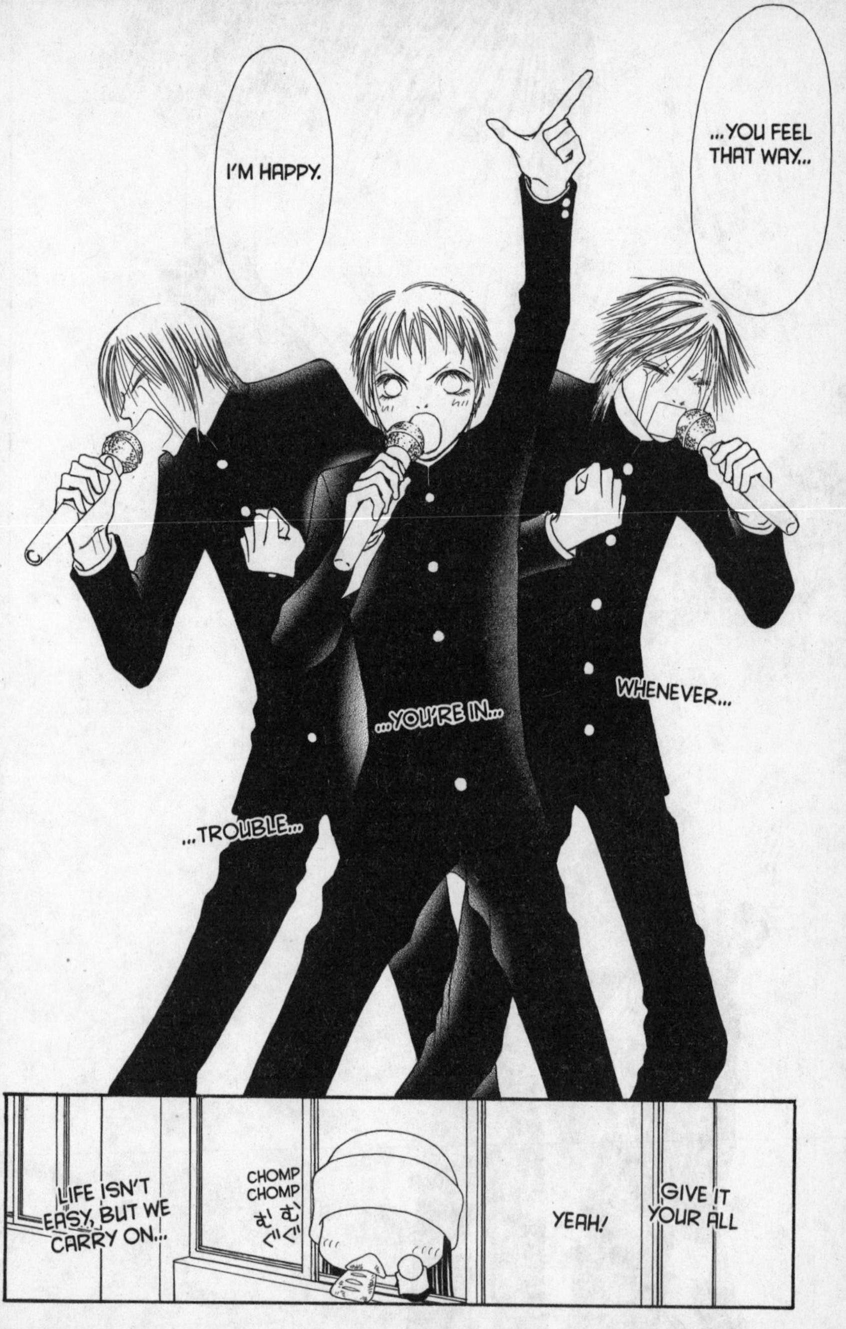
...YOU FEEL THAT WAY...
I'M HAPPY.
WHENEVER...
...YOU'RE IN...
...TROUBLE...
GIVE IT YOUR ALL
YEAH!
CHOMP CHOMP
むぐむぐ
LIFE ISN'T EASY, BUT WE CARRY ON...

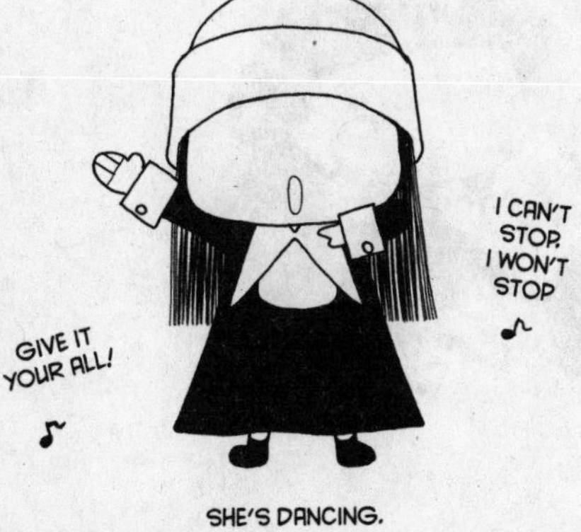
I CAN'T STOP. I WON'T STOP
GIVE IT YOUR ALL!
SHE'S DANCING.

# Chapter 82

## THE JAPANESE NEW YEAR

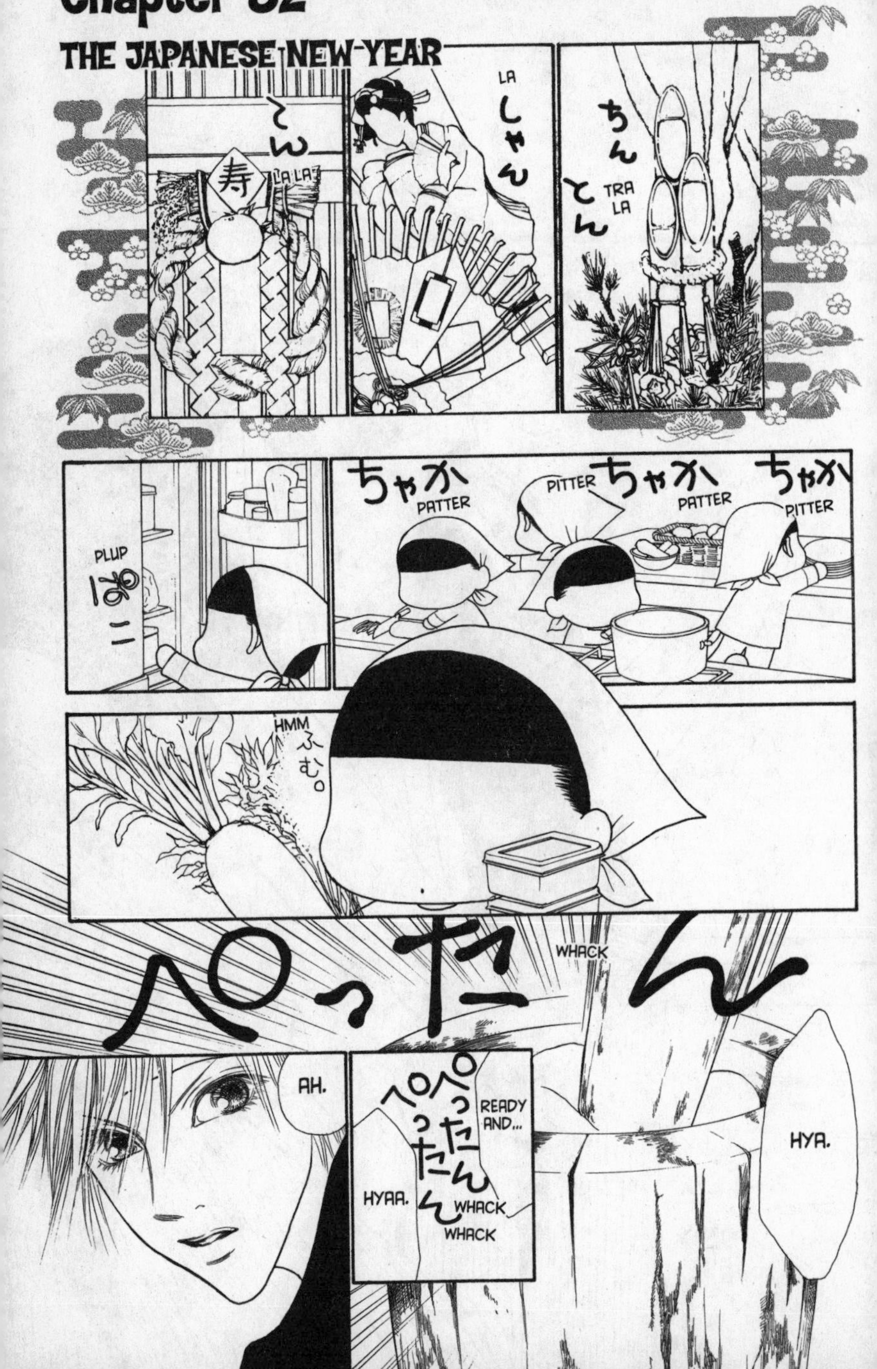
ちんとん
TRA LA
しゃん
LA
てん
LA LA
ちゃか
PITTER
ちゃか
PATTER
PITTER
ちゃか
PATTER
PLUP
ぽこ
HMM
ふむ。
ぺったん
WHACK
HYA.
READY AND...
ぺぺったんったん
WHACK
WHACK
HYAA.
AH.

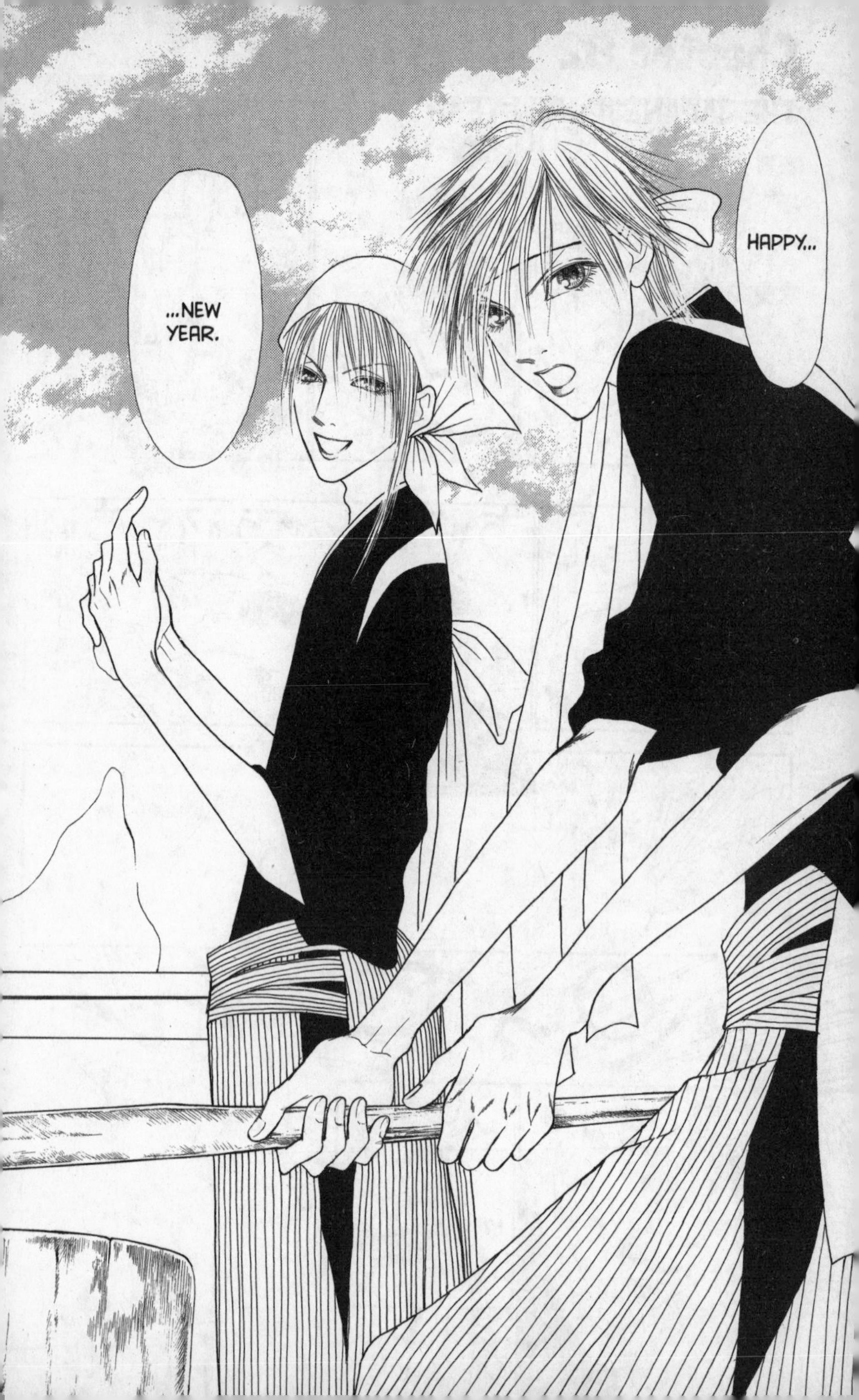
HAPPY...
...NEW YEAR.

# Chapter 82
## THE JAPANESE NEW YEAR

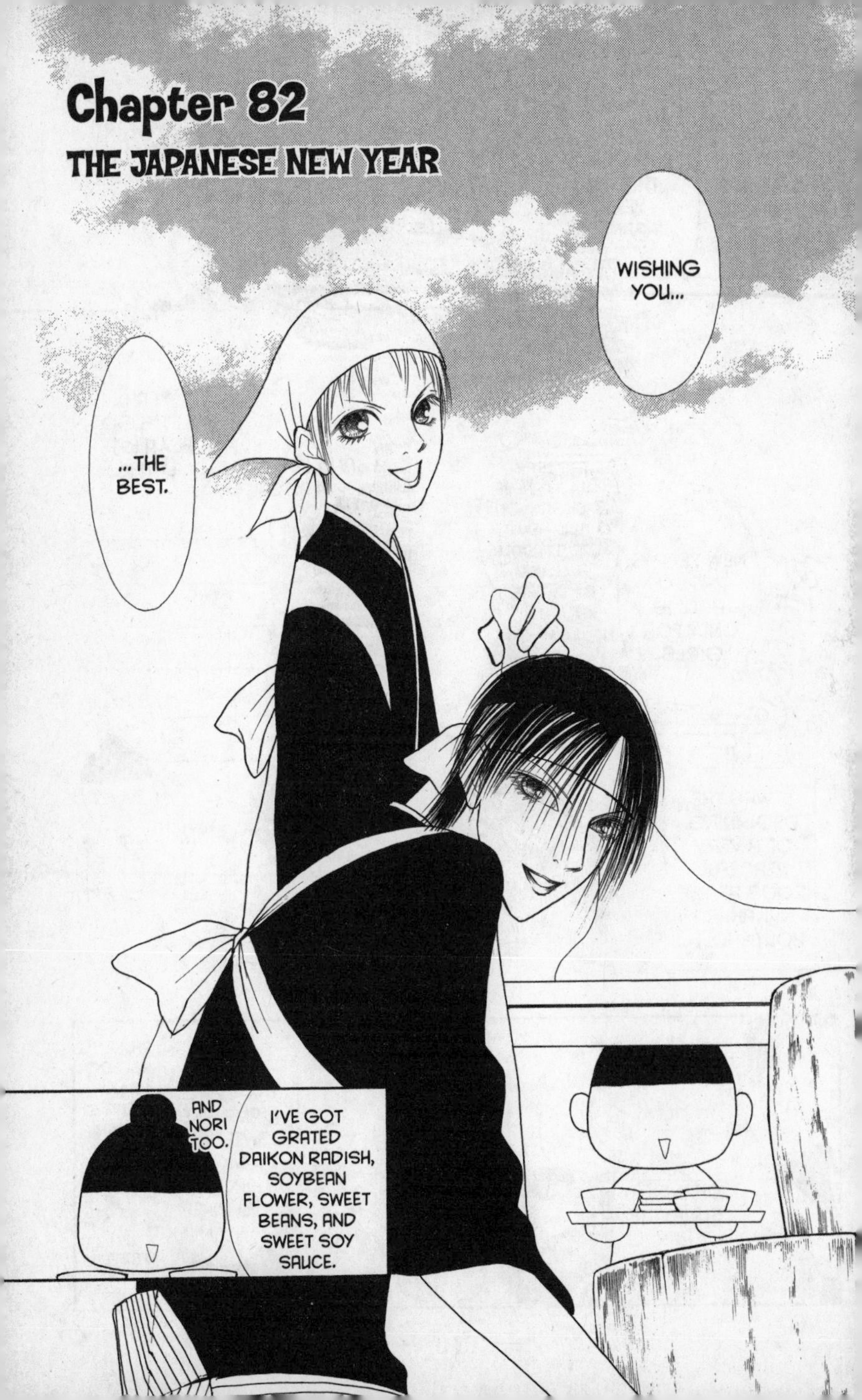
WISHING YOU...
...THE BEST.
I'VE GOT GRATED DAIKON RADISH, SOYBEAN FLOWER, SWEET BEANS, AND SWEET SOY SAUCE.
AND NORI TOO.

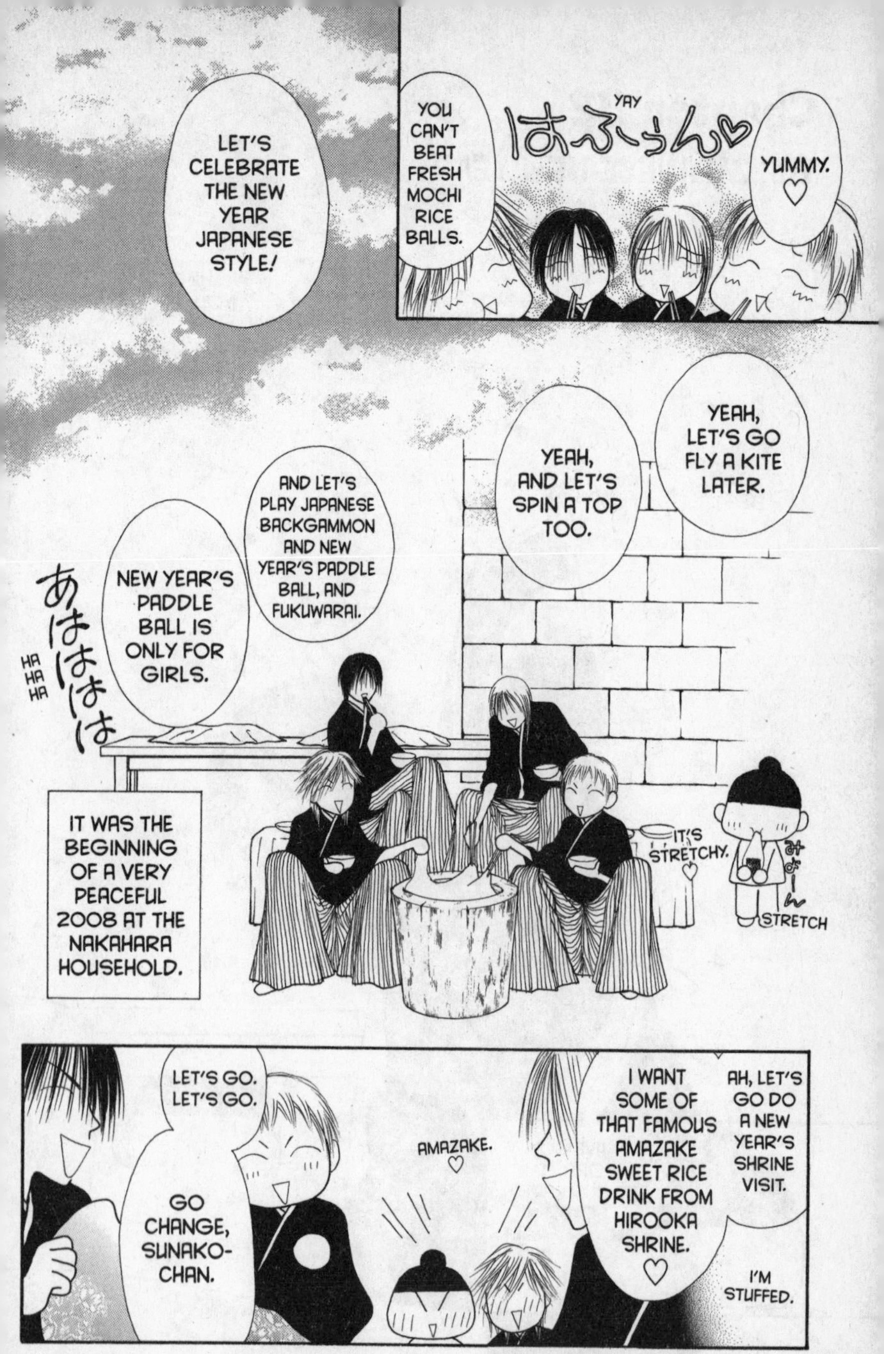

YUMMY. ♡
YAY
はふ〜うん♡
YOU CAN'T BEAT FRESH MOCHI RICE BALLS.
LET'S CELEBRATE THE NEW YEAR JAPANESE STYLE!
YEAH, LET'S GO FLY A KITE LATER.
YEAH, AND LET'S SPIN A TOP TOO.
AND LET'S PLAY JAPANESE BACKGAMMON AND NEW YEAR'S PADDLE BALL, AND FUKUWARAI.
NEW YEAR'S PADDLE BALL IS ONLY FOR GIRLS.
あははは
HA HA HA
IT'S STRETCHY. ♡
みよ〜ん
STRETCH
IT WAS THE BEGINNING OF A VERY PEACEFUL 2008 AT THE NAKAHARA HOUSEHOLD.
AH, LET'S GO DO A NEW YEAR'S SHRINE VISIT.
I'M STUFFED.
I WANT SOME OF THAT FAMOUS AMAZAKE SWEET RICE DRINK FROM HIROOKA SHRINE. ♡
AMAZAKE. ♡
LET'S GO. LET'S GO.
GO CHANGE, SUNAKO-CHAN.

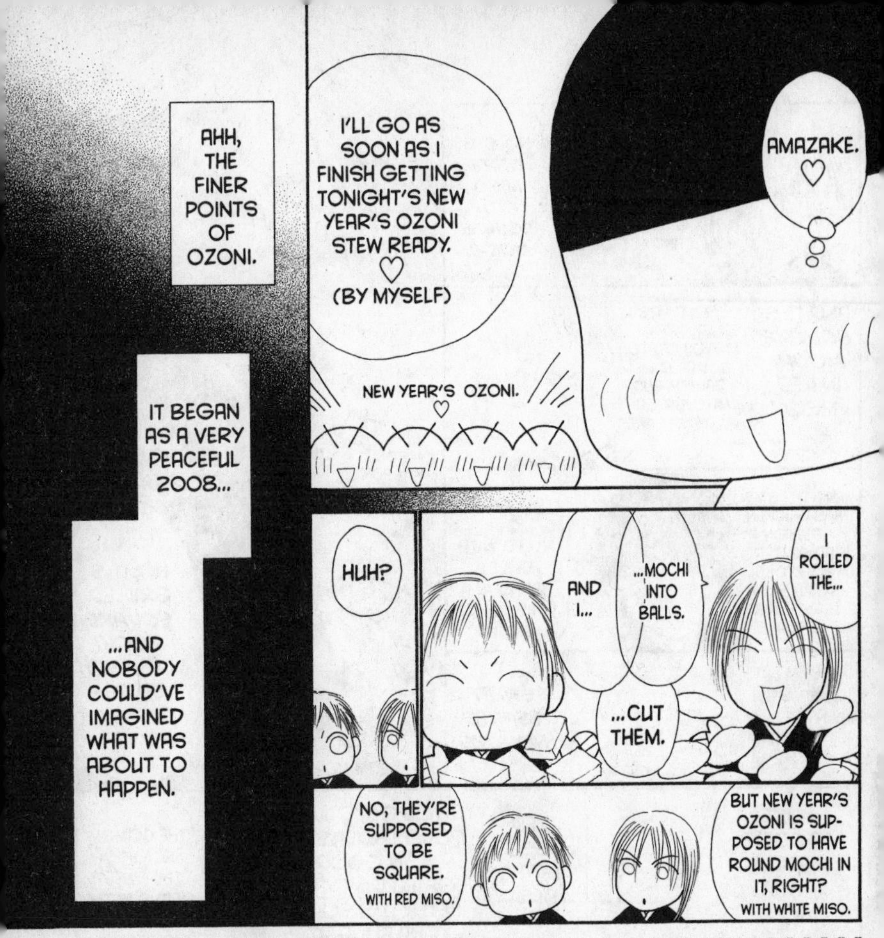
AMAZAKE. ♡
I'LL GO AS SOON AS I FINISH GETTING TONIGHT'S NEW YEAR'S OZONI STEW READY. ♡ (BY MYSELF)
NEW YEAR'S OZONI. ♡
I ROLLED THE...
...MOCHI INTO BALLS.
AND I...
...CUT THEM.
HUH?
BUT NEW YEAR'S OZONI IS SUP-POSED TO HAVE ROUND MOCHI IN IT, RIGHT? WITH WHITE MISO.
NO, THEY'RE SUPPOSED TO BE SQUARE. WITH RED MISO.
AHH, THE FINER POINTS OF OZONI.
IT BEGAN AS A VERY PEACEFUL 2008...
...AND NOBODY COULD'VE IMAGINED WHAT WAS ABOUT TO HAPPEN.

***BEHIND THE SCENES***

MY WORK WAS SO BUSY THAT I COULDN'T GO SEE KIYOHARU-SAMA IN CONCERT FOR SIX WHOLE MONTHS. ♥♥♥ BUT I FINALLY MADE IT. KYAAA! ♥♥♥

HE'S JUST SO COOL. ♥♥♥ I SAID IT BEFORE, AND I'LL SAY IT AGAIN. HE'S THE ***HOTTEST MAN ON EARTH.*** ♥♥♥ HIS NEW ALBUM IS FANTASTIC. ♥ KIYOHARU-SAMA'S SONGS ARE ALWAYS SO AMAZING THAT THEY BRING TEARS TO MY EYES. BUT THIS ONE REALLY MADE ME CRY. THE SONGS ALONE ARE ENOUGH TO MAKE YOU CRY, AND THEN ADD IN HIS VOICE, AND . . . WAH, IT'S TOO MUCH.

HE'S JUST TOO HOT FOR WORDS. ♥ EVERYTHING ABOUT HIM . . . HIS MUSIC, HIS LYRICS, HIS FACE . . . EVERYTHING . . . ♥♥♥ HE'S BEEN AROUND SO LONG, YET SOMEHOW HE STAYS COOL. ♥ HE WAS COOL WHEN HE WAS IN KUROYUME, AND HE WAS COOL WHEN HE WAS IN SADS . . . HE'S ALWAYS COOL. ♥♥♥

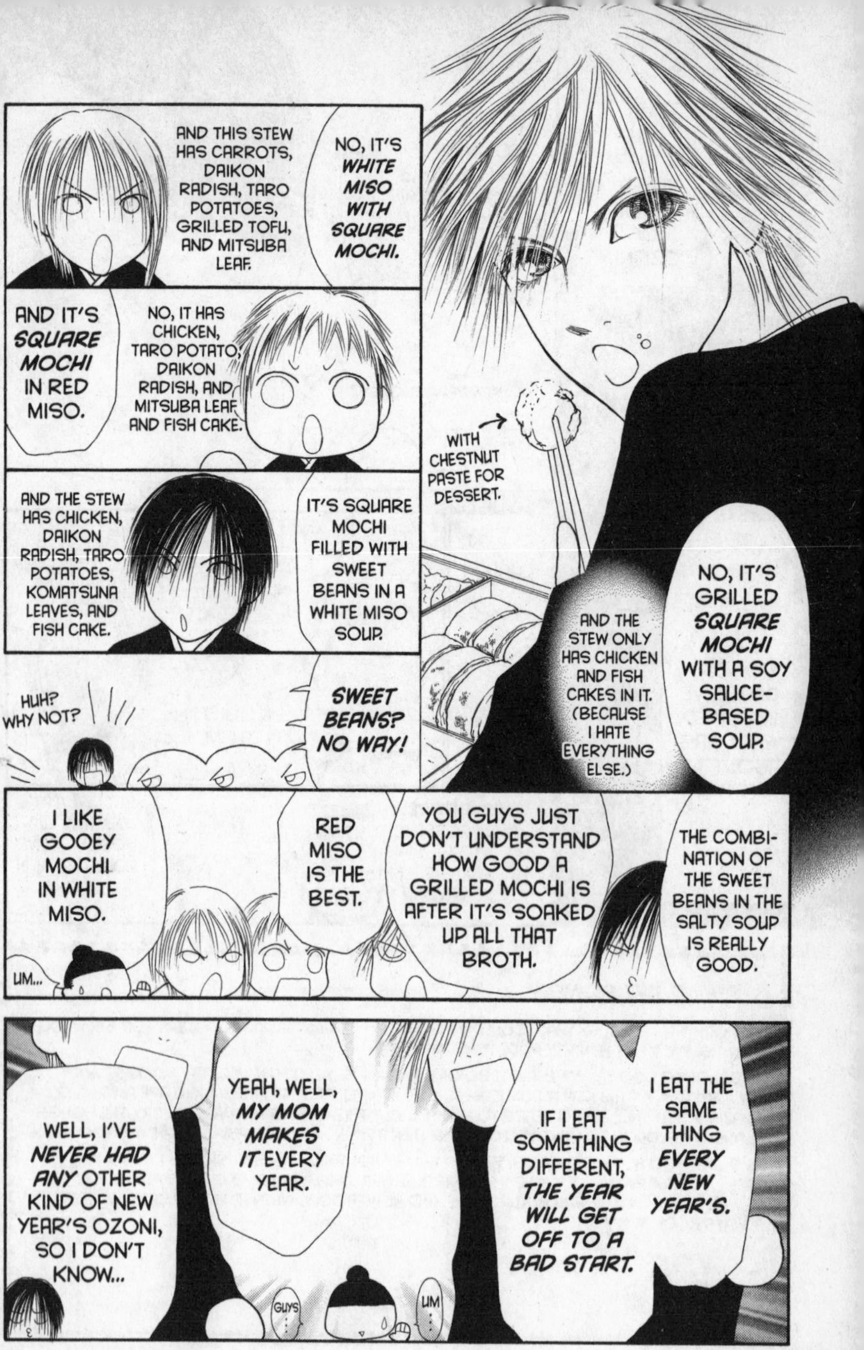
NO, IT'S GRILLED SQUARE MOCHI WITH A SOY SAUCE-BASED SOUP.
AND THE STEW ONLY HAS CHICKEN AND FISH CAKES IN IT. (BECAUSE I HATE EVERYTHING ELSE.)
WITH CHESTNUT PASTE FOR DESSERT.
NO, IT'S WHITE MISO WITH SQUARE MOCHI.
AND THIS STEW HAS CARROTS, DAIKON RADISH, TARO POTATOES, GRILLED TOFU, AND MITSUBA LEAF.
NO, IT HAS CHICKEN, TARO POTATO, DAIKON RADISH, AND MITSUBA LEAF AND FISH CAKE.
AND IT'S SQUARE MOCHI IN RED MISO.
IT'S SQUARE MOCHI FILLED WITH SWEET BEANS IN A WHITE MISO SOUP.
AND THE STEW HAS CHICKEN, DAIKON RADISH, TARO POTATOES, KOMATSUNA LEAVES, AND FISH CAKE.
SWEET BEANS? NO WAY!
HUH? WHY NOT?
THE COMBINATION OF THE SWEET BEANS IN THE SALTY SOUP IS REALLY GOOD.
YOU GUYS JUST DON'T UNDERSTAND HOW GOOD A GRILLED MOCHI IS AFTER IT'S SOAKED UP ALL THAT BROTH.
RED MISO IS THE BEST.
I LIKE GOOEY MOCHI IN WHITE MISO.
UM...
I EAT THE SAME THING EVERY NEW YEAR'S.
IF I EAT SOMETHING DIFFERENT, THE YEAR WILL GET OFF TO A BAD START.
UM
YEAH, WELL, MY MOM MAKES IT EVERY YEAR.
GUYS
WELL, I'VE NEVER HAD ANY OTHER KIND OF NEW YEAR'S OZONI, SO I DON'T KNOW...

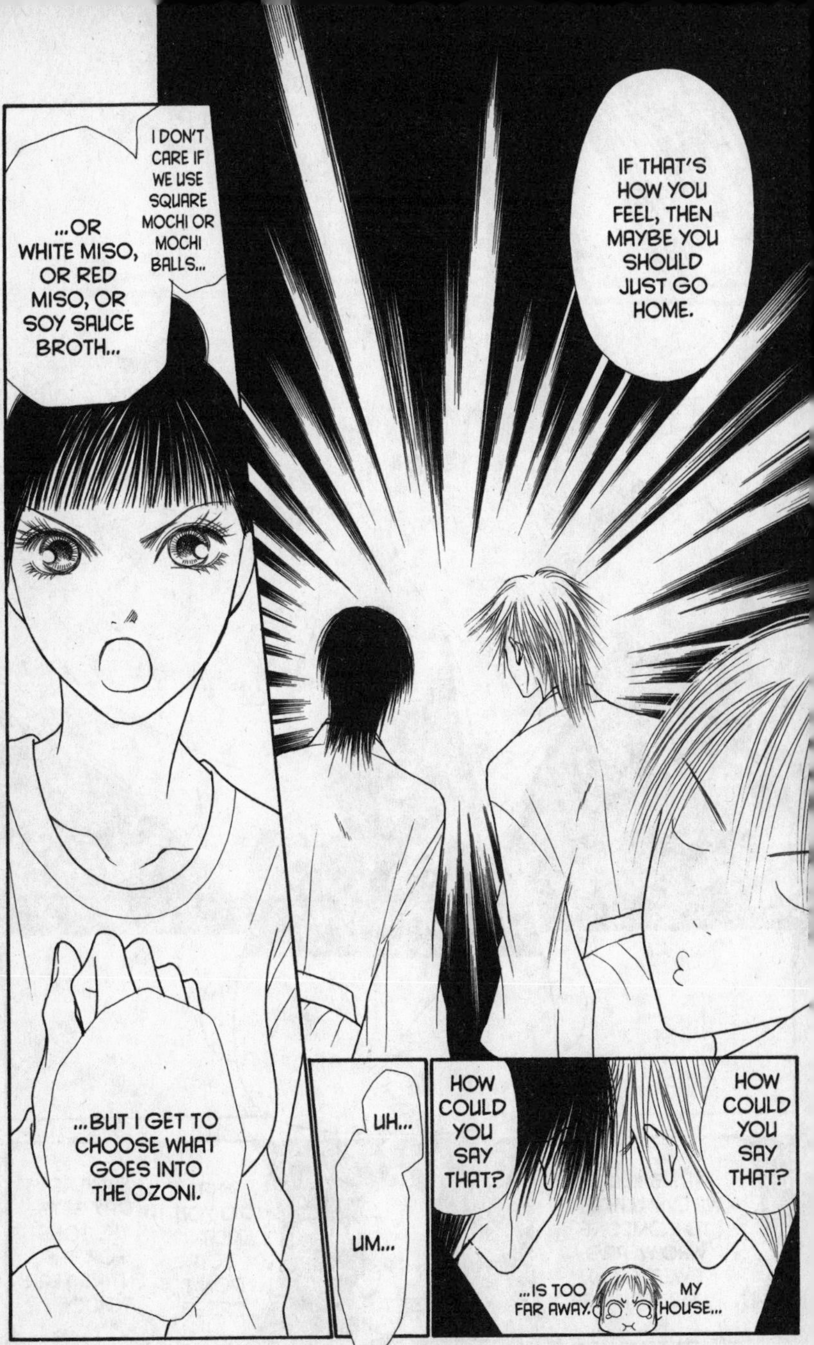
I DON'T CARE IF WE USE SQUARE MOCHI OR MOCHI BALLS...
...OR WHITE MISO, OR RED MISO, OR SOY SAUCE BROTH...
...BUT I GET TO CHOOSE WHAT GOES INTO THE OZONI.
IF THAT'S HOW YOU FEEL, THEN MAYBE YOU SHOULD JUST GO HOME.
HOW COULD YOU SAY THAT?
HOW COULD YOU SAY THAT?
MY HOUSE...
...IS TOO FAR AWAY.
UH...
UM...

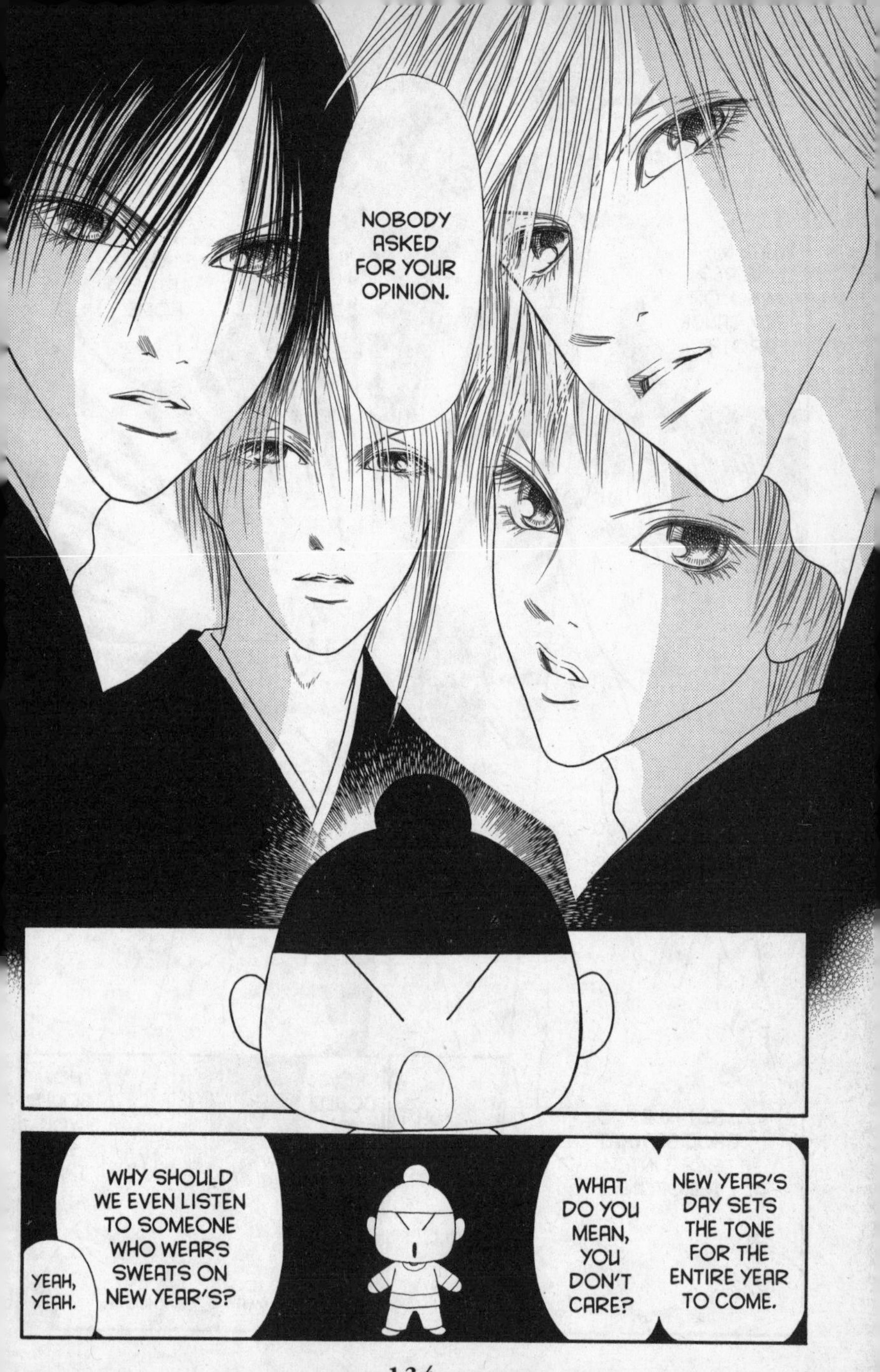
NOBODY ASKED FOR YOUR OPINION.
NEW YEAR'S DAY SETS THE TONE FOR THE ENTIRE YEAR TO COME.
WHAT DO YOU MEAN, YOU DON'T CARE?
WHY SHOULD WE EVEN LISTEN TO SOMEONE WHO WEARS SWEATS ON NEW YEAR'S?
YEAH, YEAH.

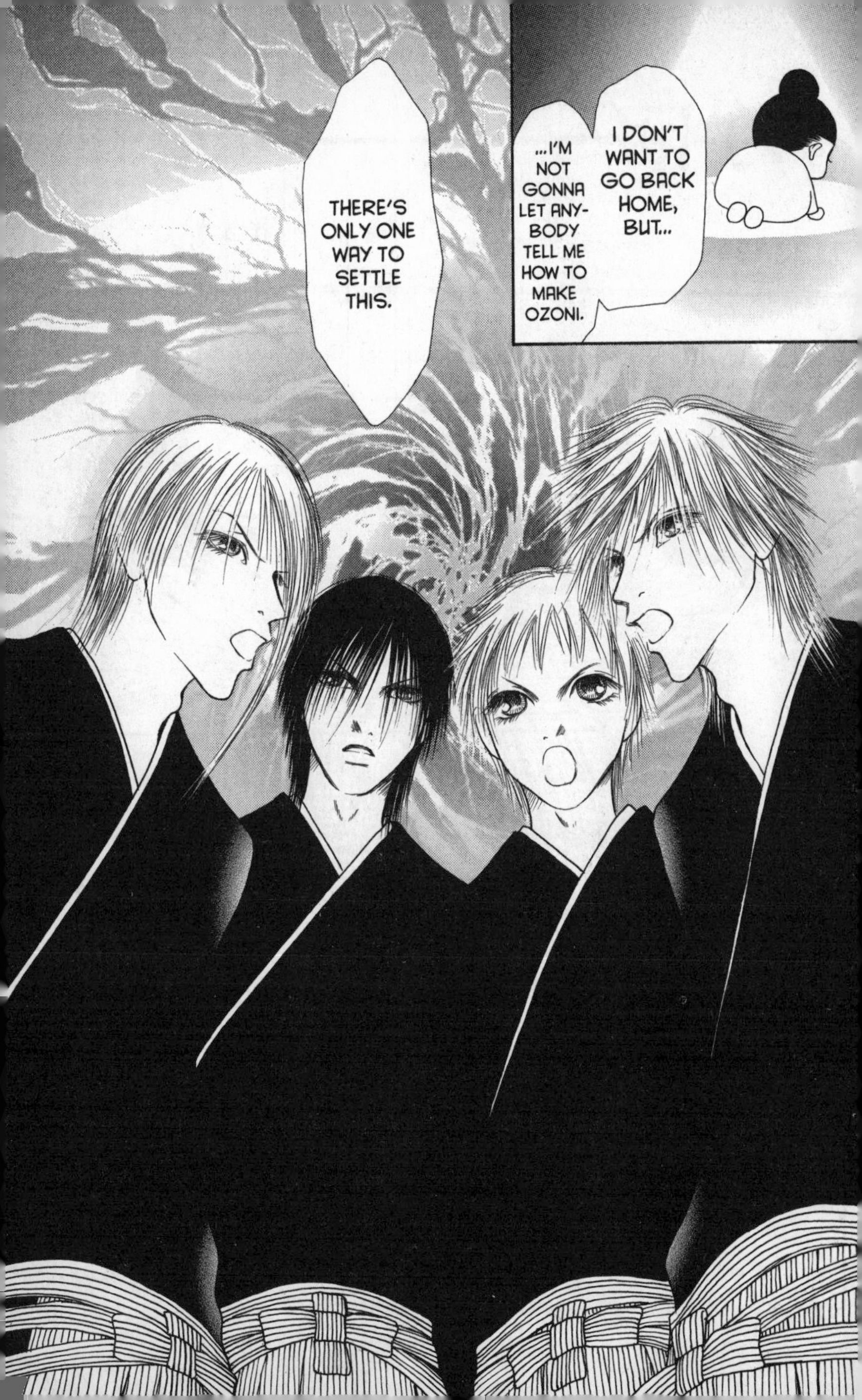
I DON'T WANT TO GO BACK HOME, BUT...
...I'M NOT GONNA LET ANYBODY TELL ME HOW TO MAKE OZONI.
THERE'S ONLY ONE WAY TO SETTLE THIS.

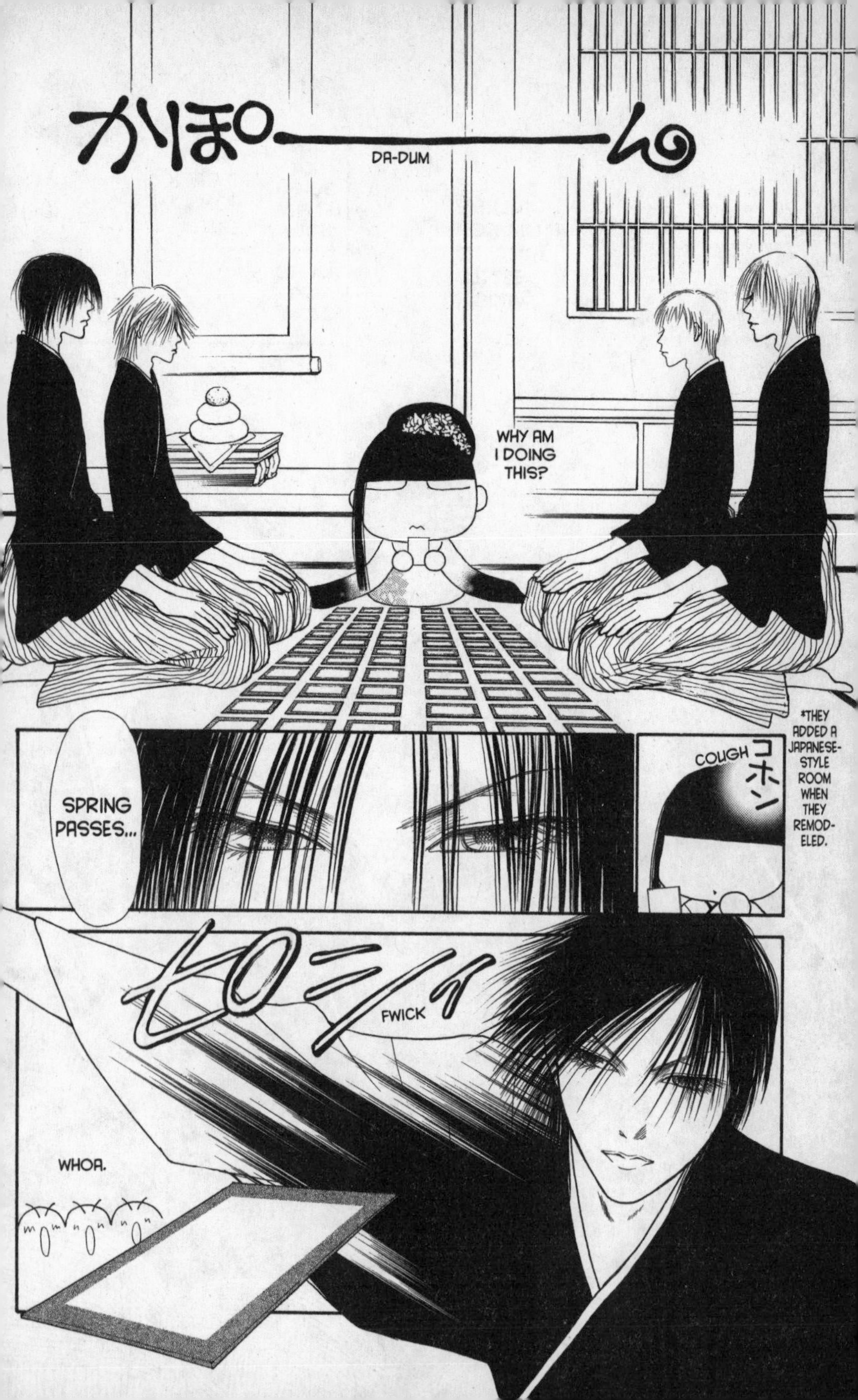
かぽーん
DA-DUM
WHY AM I DOING THIS?
COUGH
コホン
SPRING PASSES...
ヒュン
FWICK
WHOA.
*THEY ADDED A JAPANESE-STYLE ROOM WHEN THEY REMODELED.

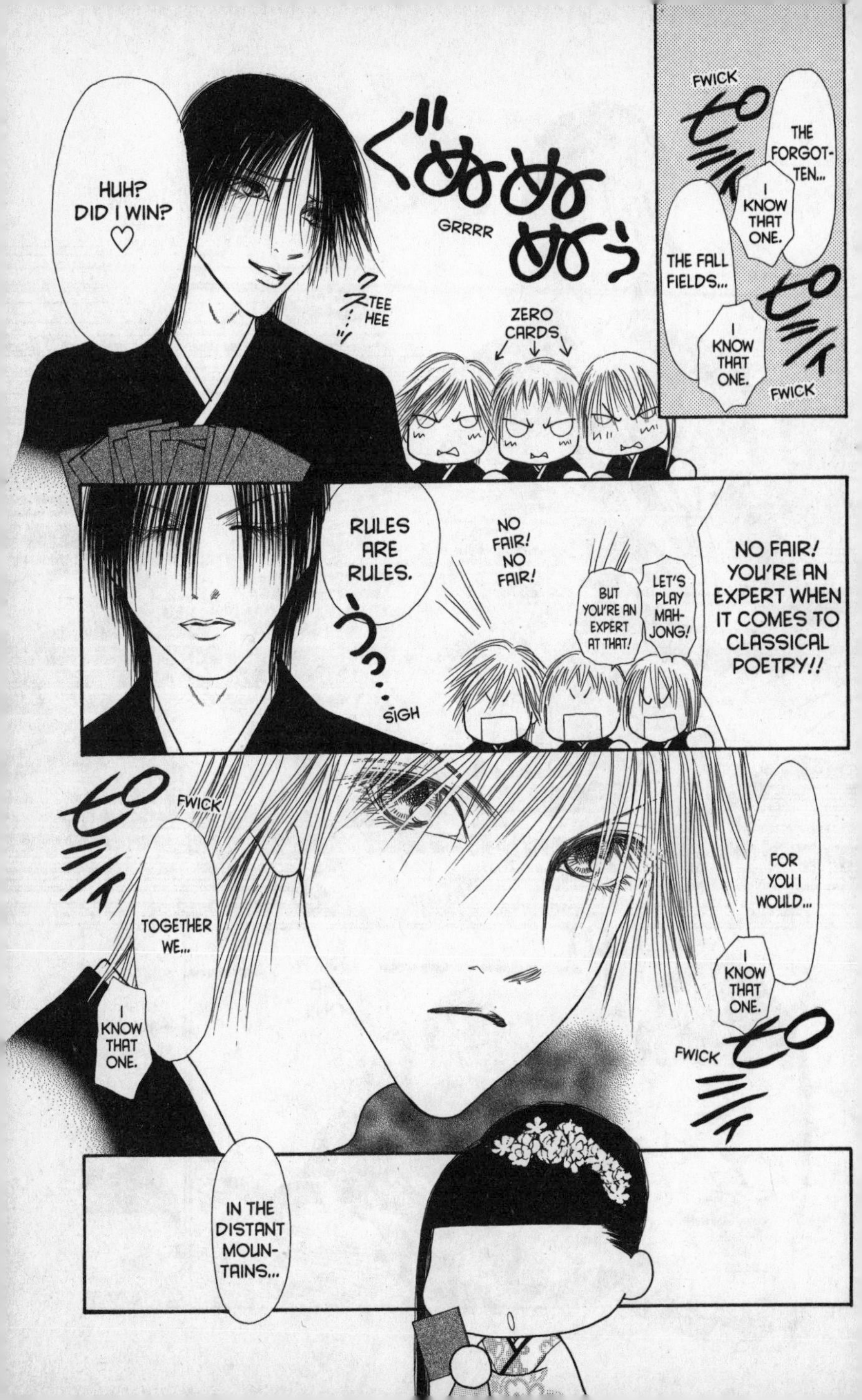
FWICK
THE FORGOT-TEN...
I KNOW THAT ONE.
THE FALL FIELDS...
I KNOW THAT ONE.
FWICK
GRRRR
TEE HEE
ZERO CARDS
HUH? DID I WIN? ♡
NO FAIR! YOU'RE AN EXPERT WHEN IT COMES TO CLASSICAL POETRY!!
LET'S PLAY MAH-JONG!
BUT YOU'RE AN EXPERT AT THAT!
NO FAIR! NO FAIR!
RULES ARE RULES.
SIGH
FOR YOU I WOULD...
I KNOW THAT ONE.
FWICK
TOGETHER WE...
I KNOW THAT ONE.
FWICK
IN THE DISTANT MOUN-TAINS...

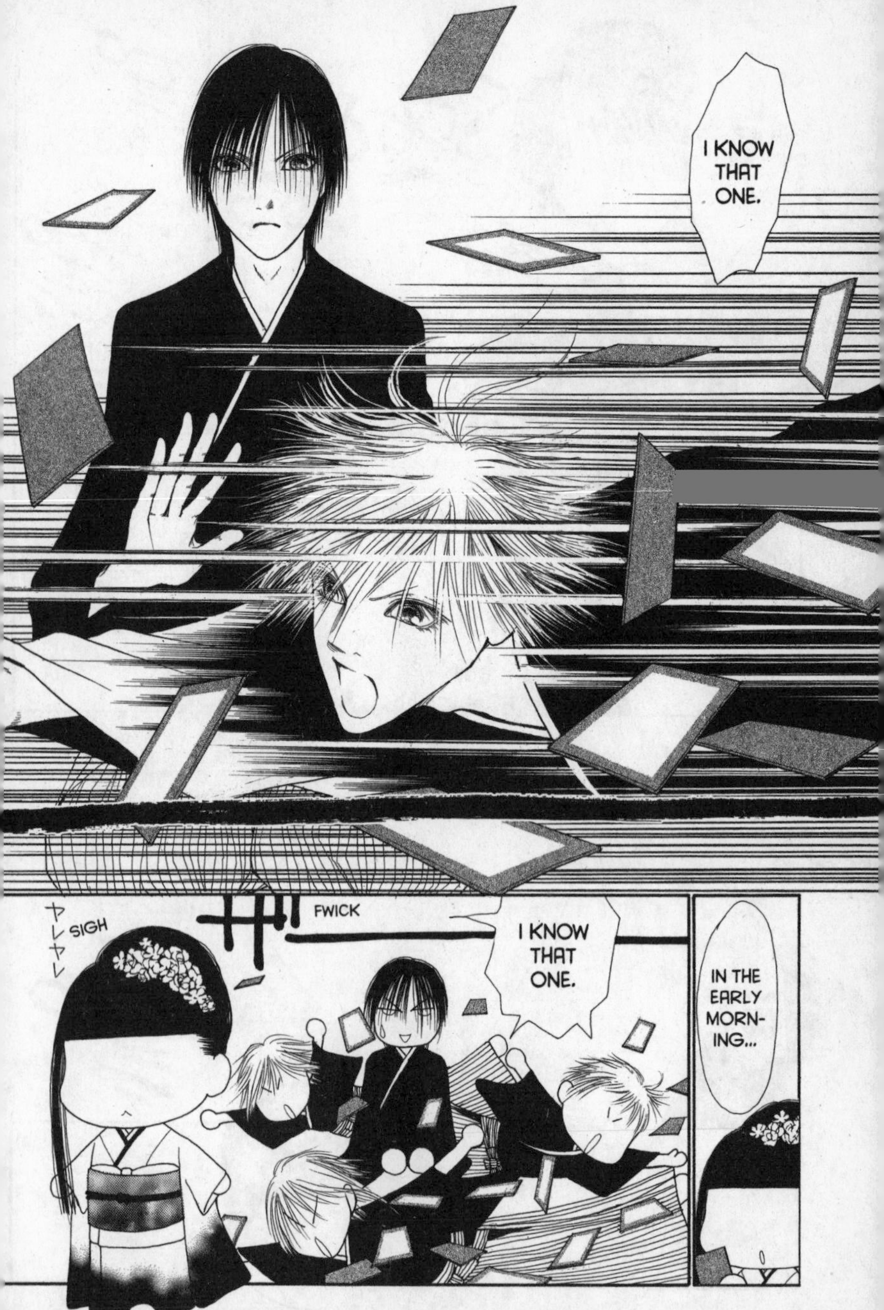
I KNOW THAT ONE.
IN THE EARLY MORNING...
I KNOW THAT ONE.
FWICK
ヤレヤレ
SIGH

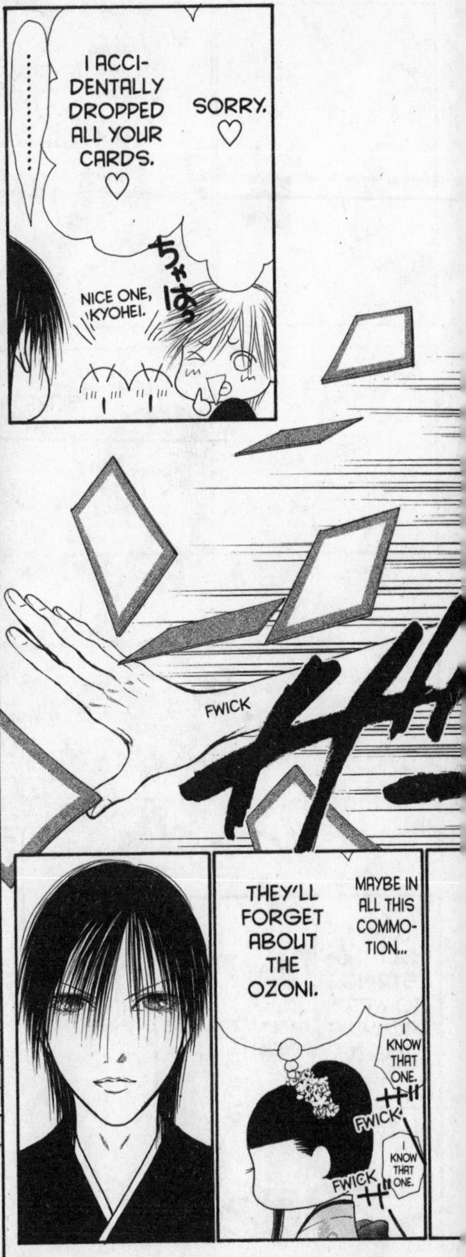
SORRY. ♡
I ACCIDENTALLY DROPPED ALL YOUR CARDS. ♡
......
ちゃはっ
NICE ONE, KYOHEI.
FWICK
MAYBE IN ALL THIS COMMOTION...
THEY'LL FORGET ABOUT THE OZONI.
I KNOW THAT ONE.
FWICK
I KNOW THAT ONE.
FWICK

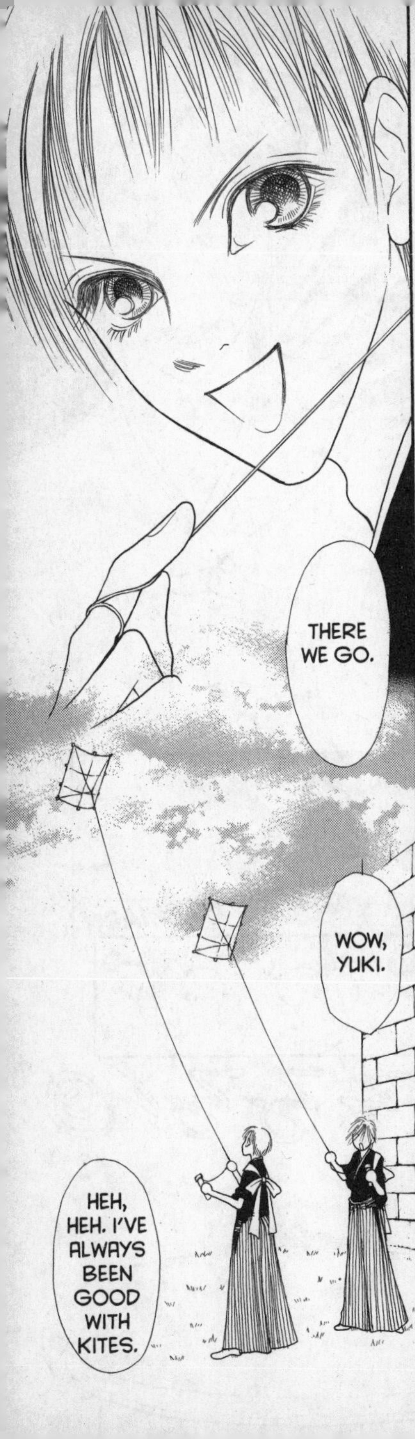
THERE WE GO.
WOW, YUKI.
HEH, HEH. I'VE ALWAYS BEEN GOOD WITH KITES.

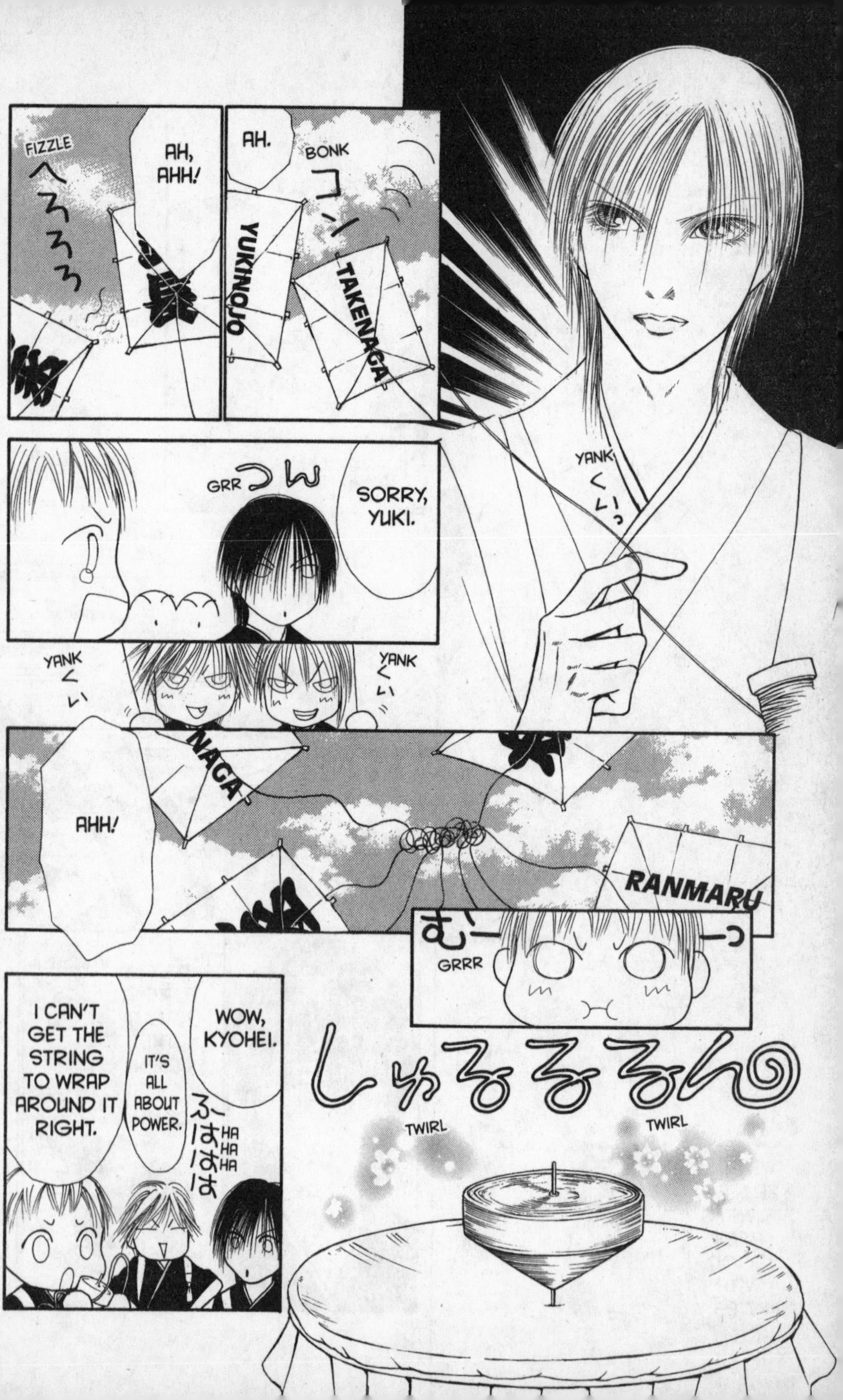
YANK
くいっ
AH.
BONK
コン
YUKINOJO
TAKENAGA
FIZZLE
へろろろ
AH, AHH!
SORRY, YUKI.
GRR
つん
YANK
くい
YANK
くい
RANMARU
NAGA
AHH!
むーっ
GRRR
しゅるるるん
TWIRL
TWIRL
WOW, KYOHEI.
IT'S ALL ABOUT POWER.
ふははは
HA HA HA
I CAN'T GET THE STRING TO WRAP AROUND IT RIGHT.

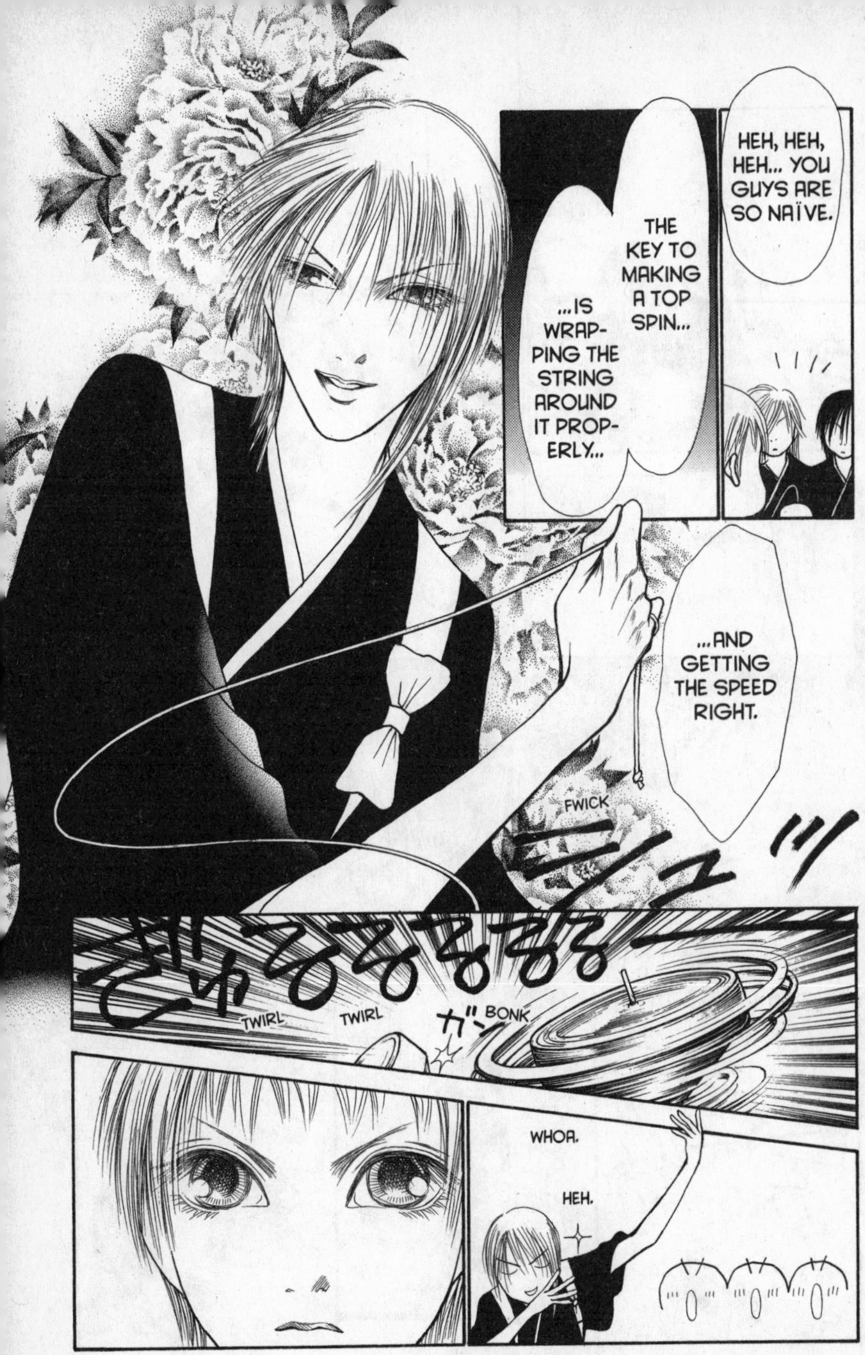
HEH, HEH, HEH... YOU GUYS ARE SO NAÏVE.
THE KEY TO MAKING A TOP SPIN...
...IS WRAPPING THE STRING AROUND IT PROPERLY...
...AND GETTING THE SPEED RIGHT.
FWICK
TWIRL
TWIRL
BONK
WHOA.
HEH.

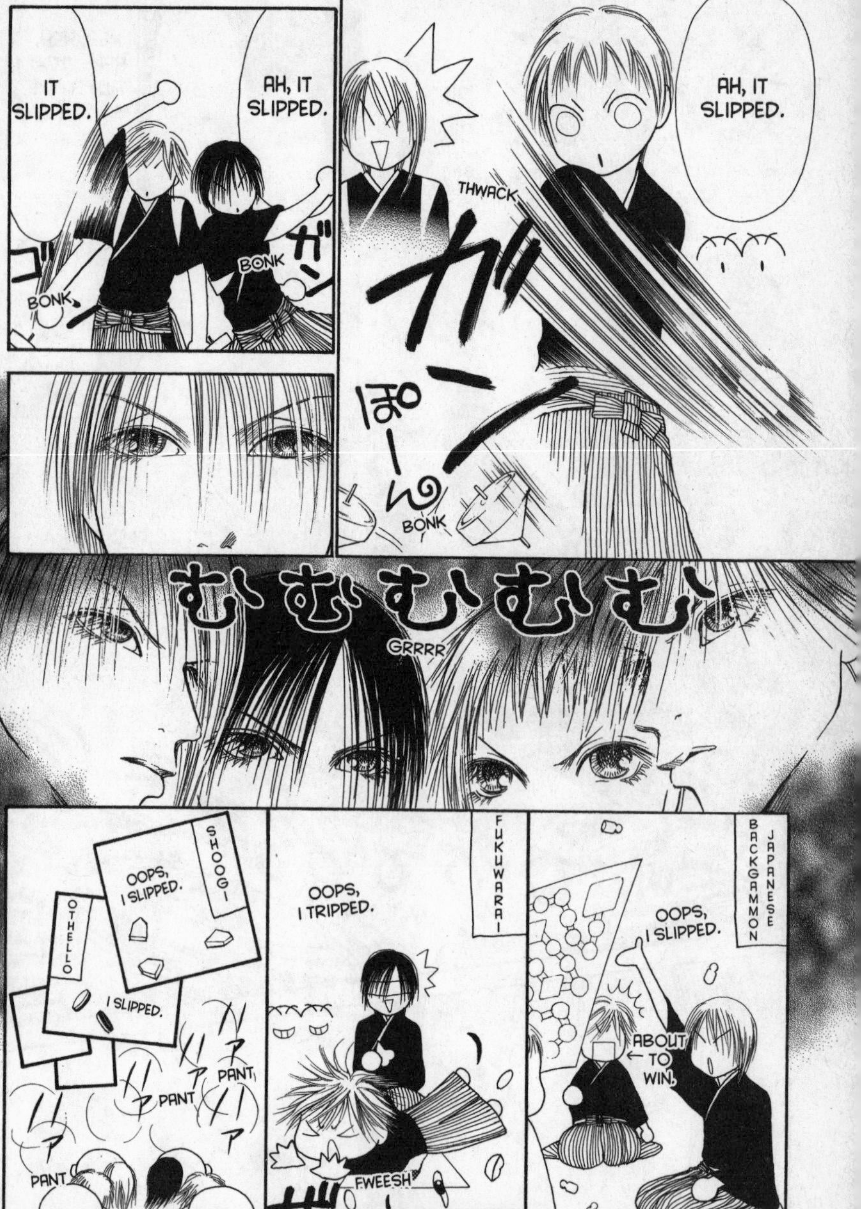
AH, IT SLIPPED.
THWACK
BONK
AH, IT SLIPPED.
IT SLIPPED.
BONK
BONK
GRRRR
JAPANESE BACKGAMMON
OOPS, I SLIPPED.
ABOUT TO WIN.
FUKUWARAI
OOPS, I TRIPPED.
FWEESH
SHOOGI
OOPS, I SLIPPED.
OTHELLO
I SLIPPED.
PANT
PANT
PANT

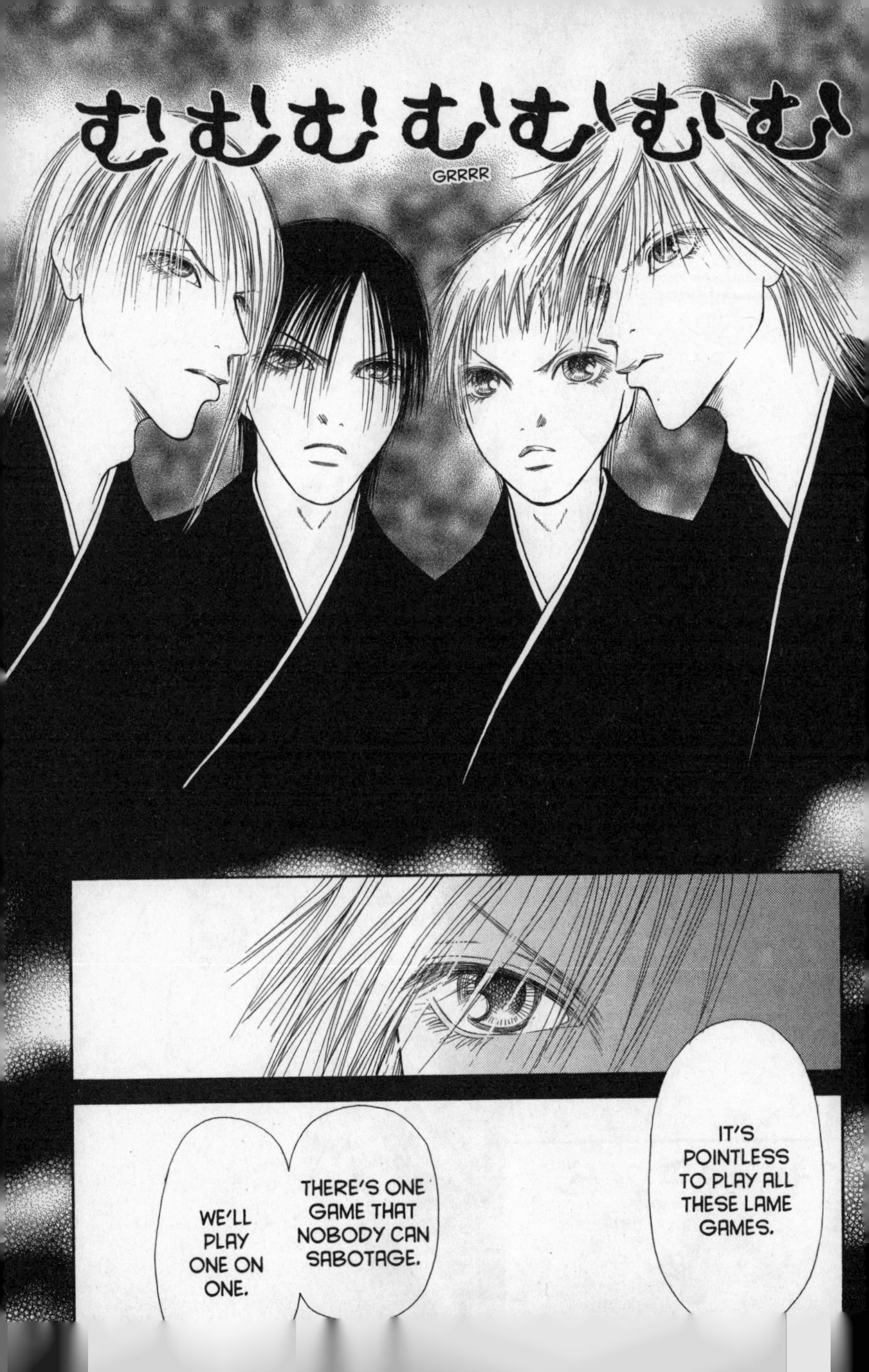
むむむむむむむ
GRRRR
IT'S POINTLESS TO PLAY ALL THESE LAME GAMES.
THERE'S ONE GAME THAT NOBODY CAN SABOTAGE.
WE'LL PLAY ONE ON ONE.

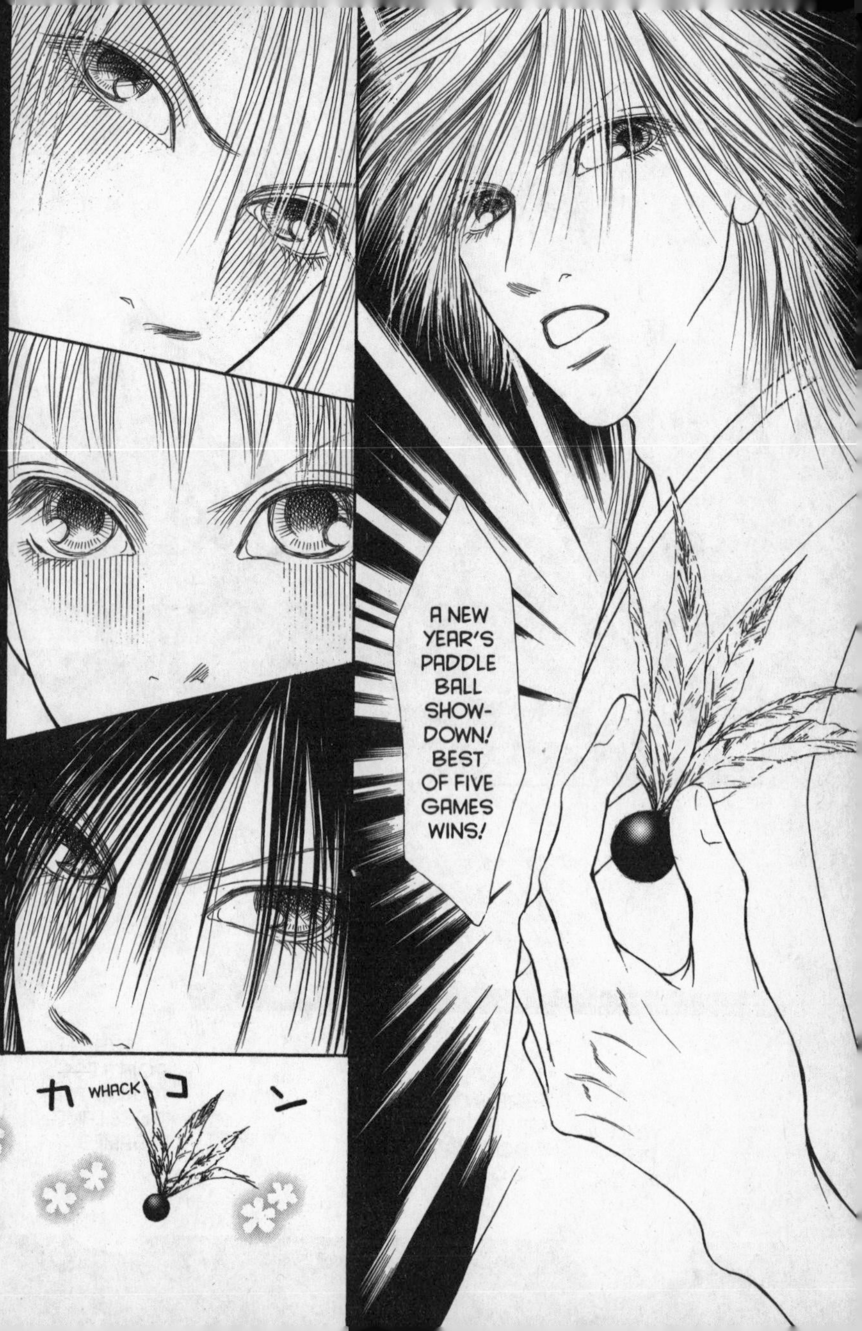
A NEW YEAR'S PADDLE BALL SHOW-DOWN! BEST OF FIVE GAMES WINS!
カコン WHACK

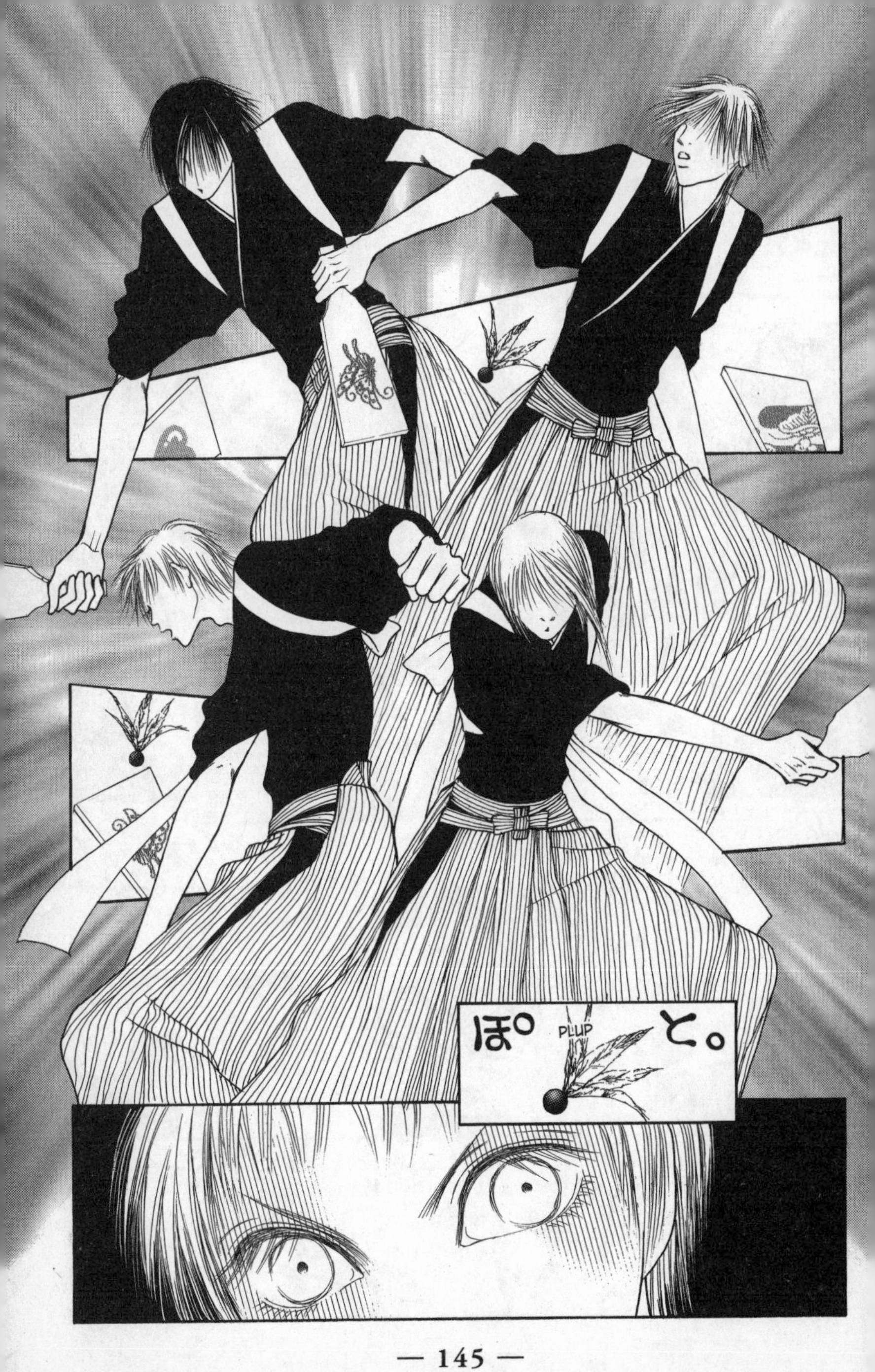
ぽ PLUP と。

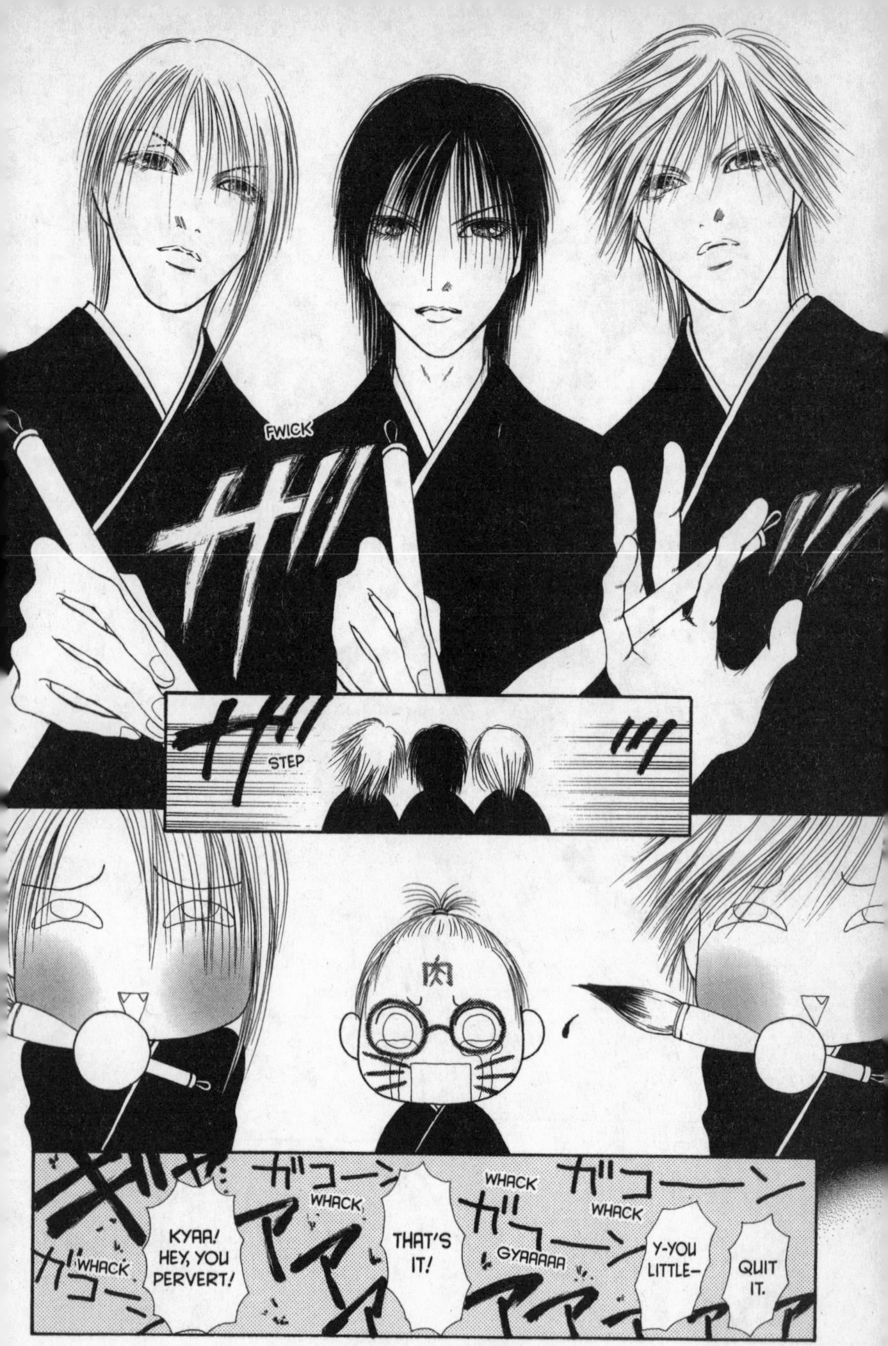
FWICK
STEP
QUIT IT.
Y-YOU LITTLE–
WHACK
WHACK
GYAAAAA
THAT'S IT!
WHACK
KYAA! HEY, YOU PERVERT!
WHACK

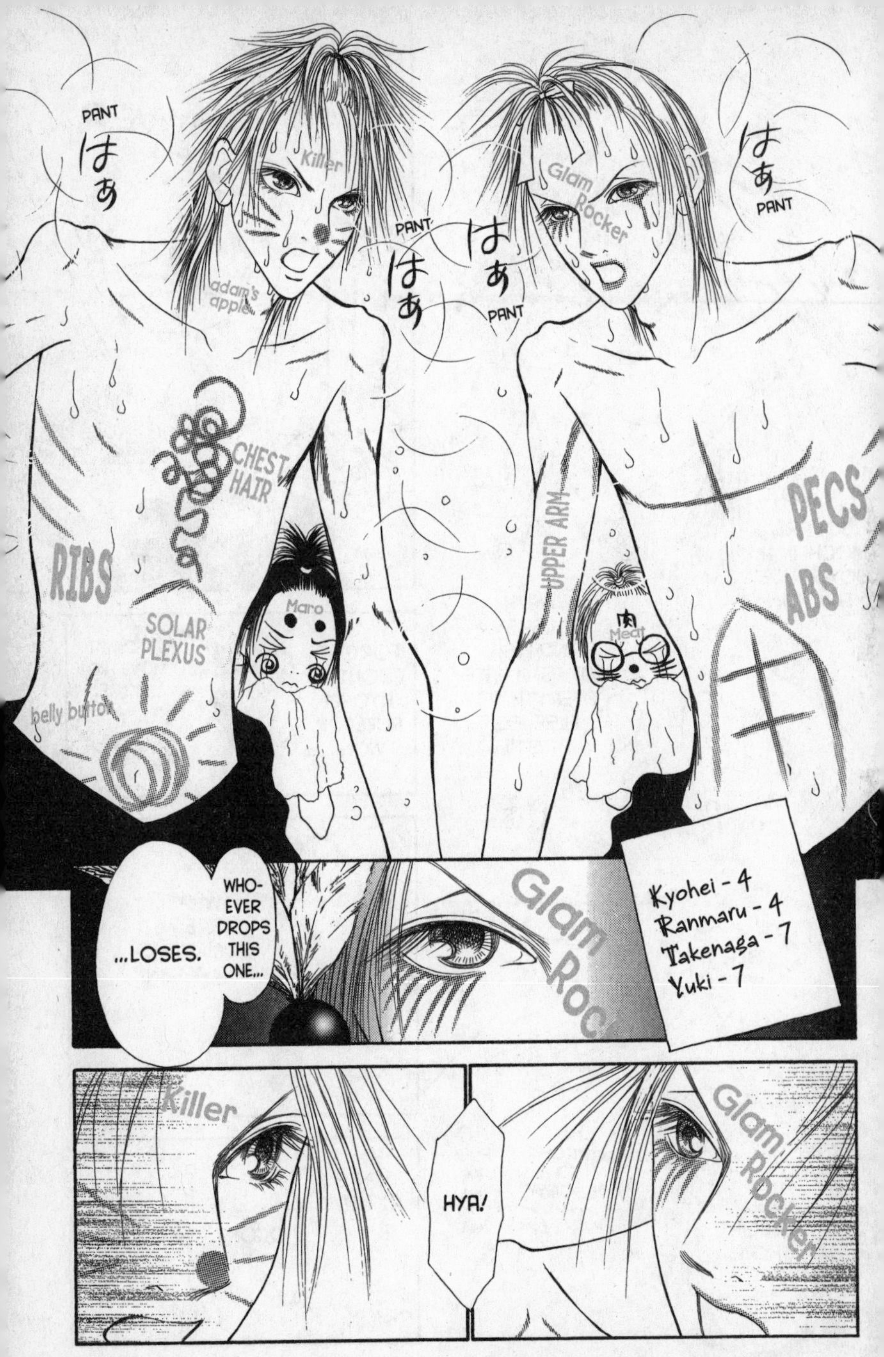
はぁ
PANT
Glam Rocker
はぁ
PANT
PANT
はぁ
Killer
PANT
はぁ
adam's apple
PECS
ABS
UPPER ARM
肉
Meat
CHEST HAIR
Maro
RIBS
SOLAR PLEXUS
belly butto
Kyohei - 4
Ranmaru - 4
Takenaga - 7
Yuki - 7
Glam Rock
WHO-EVER DROPS THIS ONE...
...LOSES.
Glam Rocker
HYA!
Killer

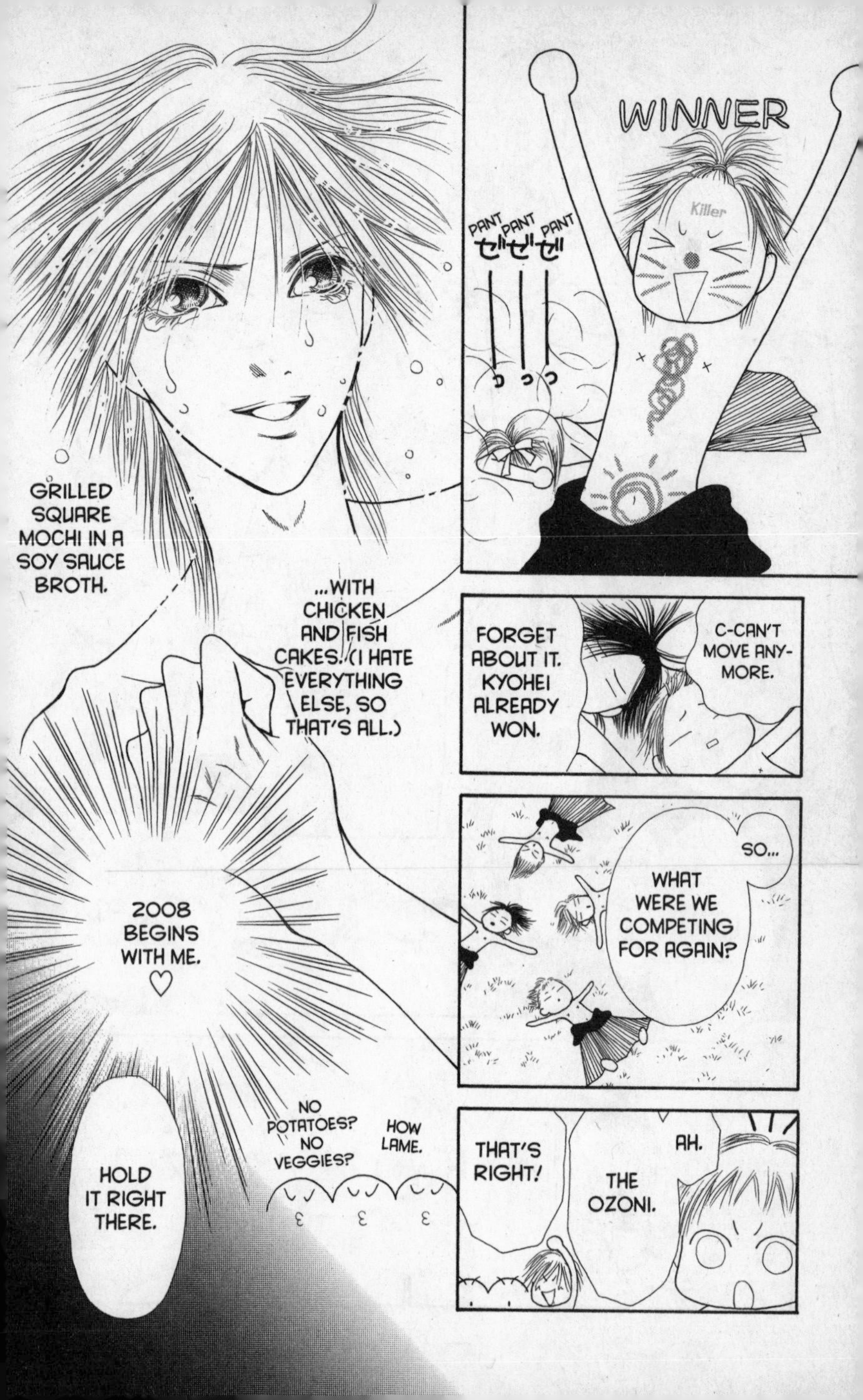
WINNER
PANT PANT PANT
ぜぜぜ
Killer
C-CAN'T MOVE ANY-MORE.
FORGET ABOUT IT. KYOHEI ALREADY WON.
SO...
WHAT WERE WE COMPETING FOR AGAIN?
AH.
THE OZONI.
THAT'S RIGHT!
GRILLED SQUARE MOCHI IN A SOY SAUCE BROTH.
...WITH CHICKEN AND FISH CAKES. (I HATE EVERYTHING ELSE, SO THAT'S ALL.)
2008 BEGINS WITH ME. ♡
HOW LAME.
NO POTATOES? NO VEGGIES?
HOLD IT RIGHT THERE.

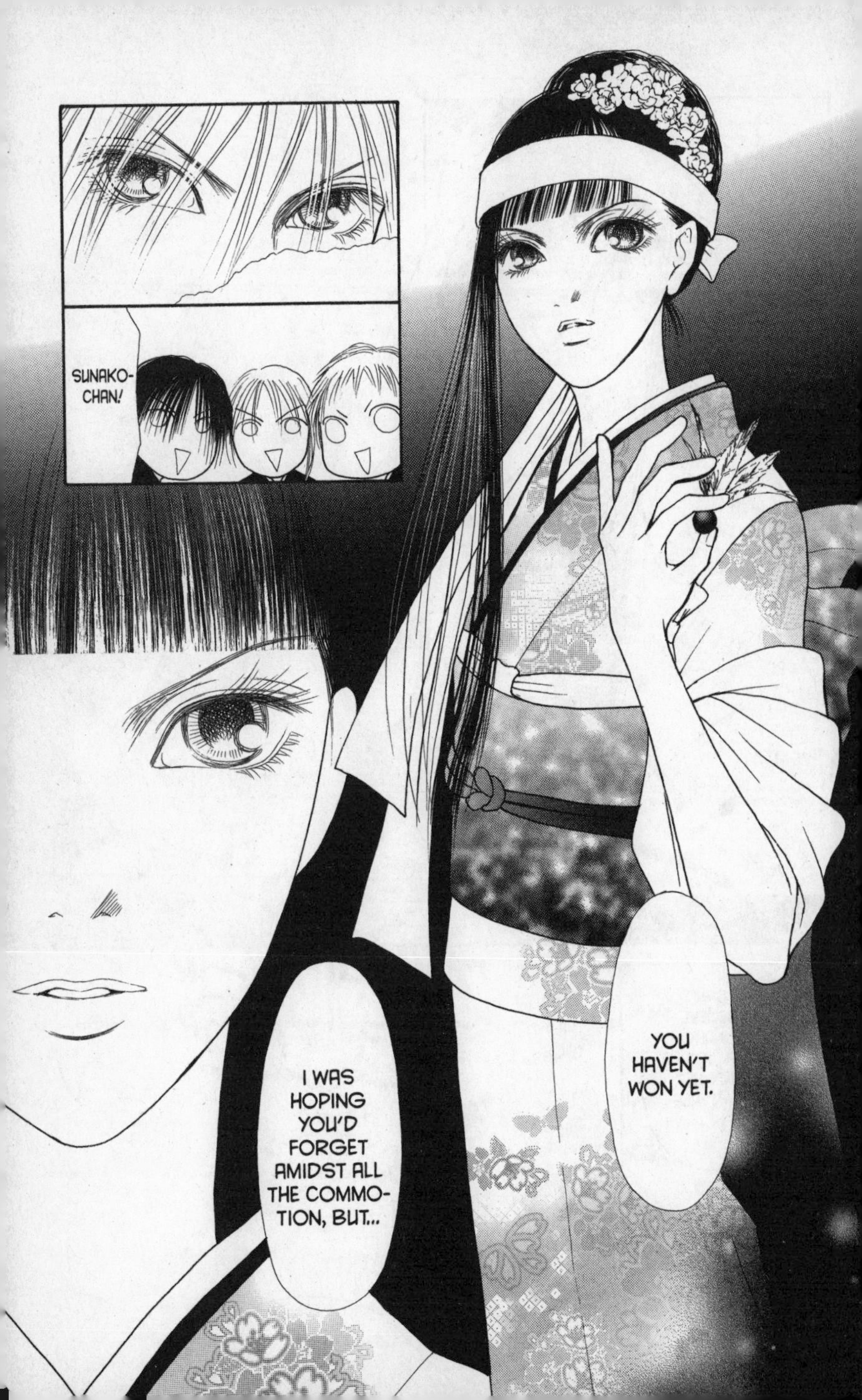
YOU HAVEN'T WON YET.
SUNAKO-CHAN!
I WAS HOPING YOU'D FORGET AMIDST ALL THE COMMOTION, BUT...

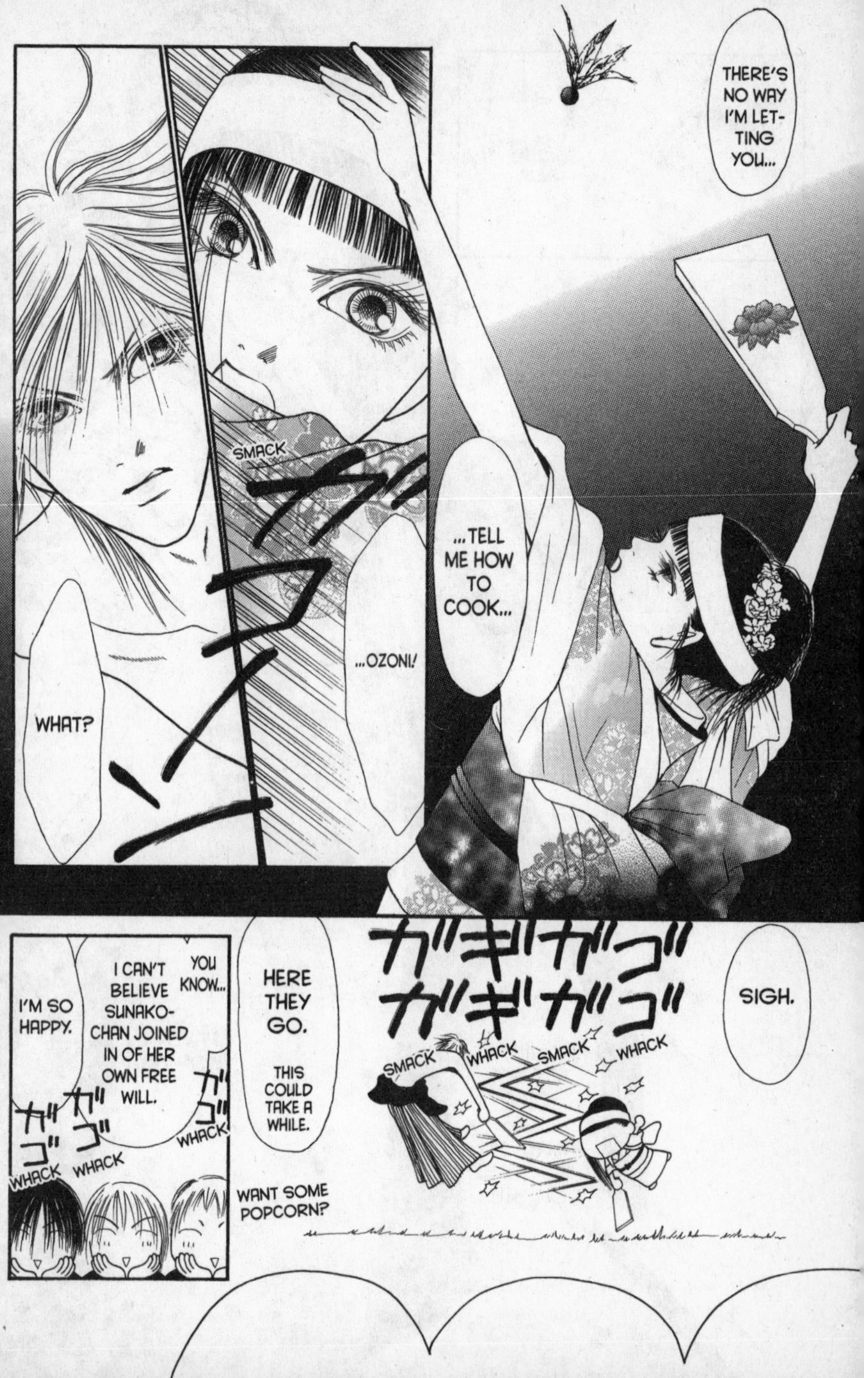
THERE'S NO WAY I'M LET-TING YOU...
...TELL ME HOW TO COOK...
SMACK
...OZONI!
WHAT?
SIGH.
ガギガゴ
ガギガゴ
SMACK WHACK SMACK WHACK
HERE THEY GO.
THIS COULD TAKE A WHILE.
YOU KNOW...
I CAN'T BELIEVE SUNAKO-CHAN JOINED IN OF HER OWN FREE WILL.
I'M SO HAPPY.
ガゴ WHACK
ガゴ ガゴ WHACK WHACK
WANT SOME POPCORN?

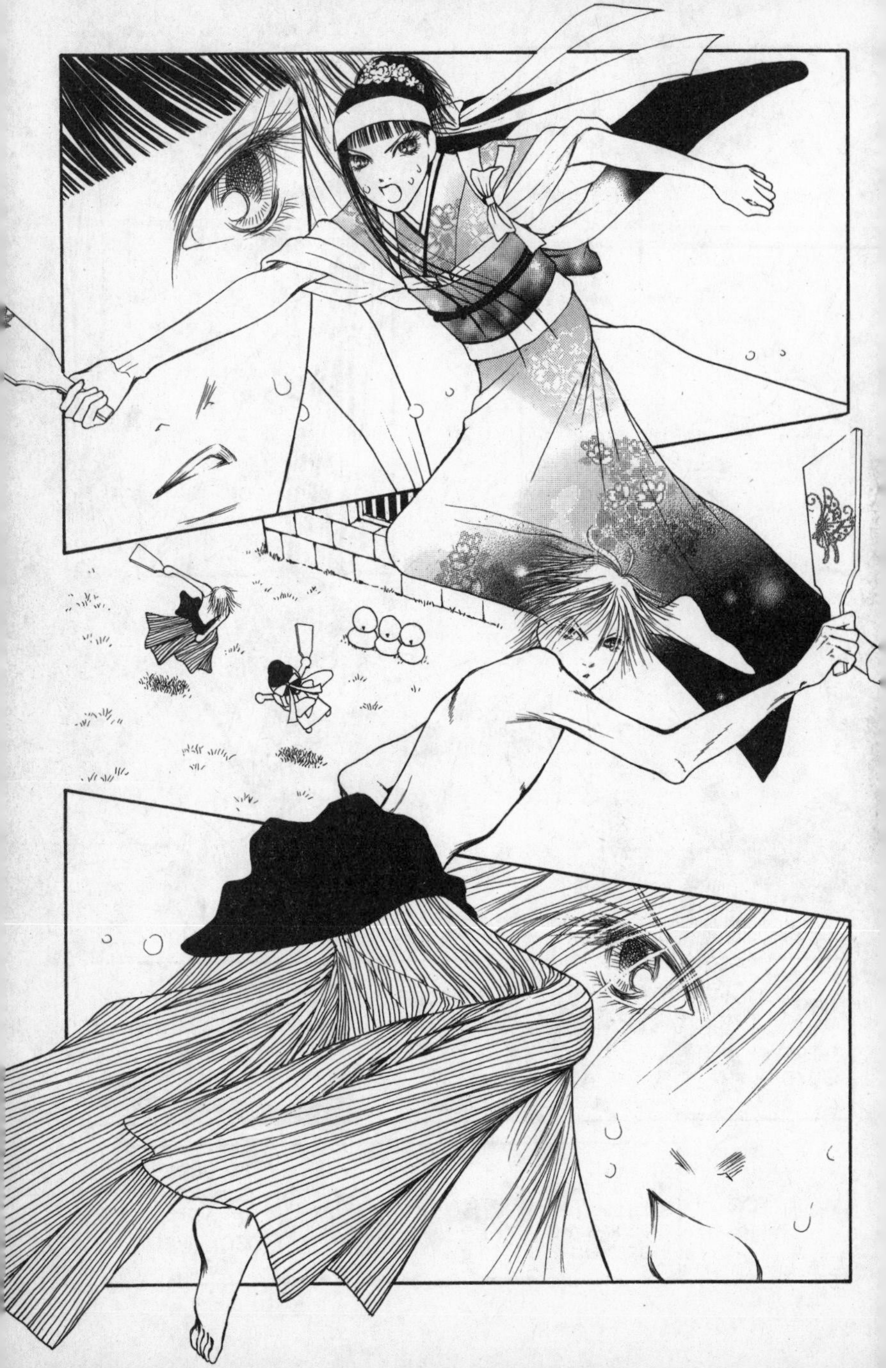

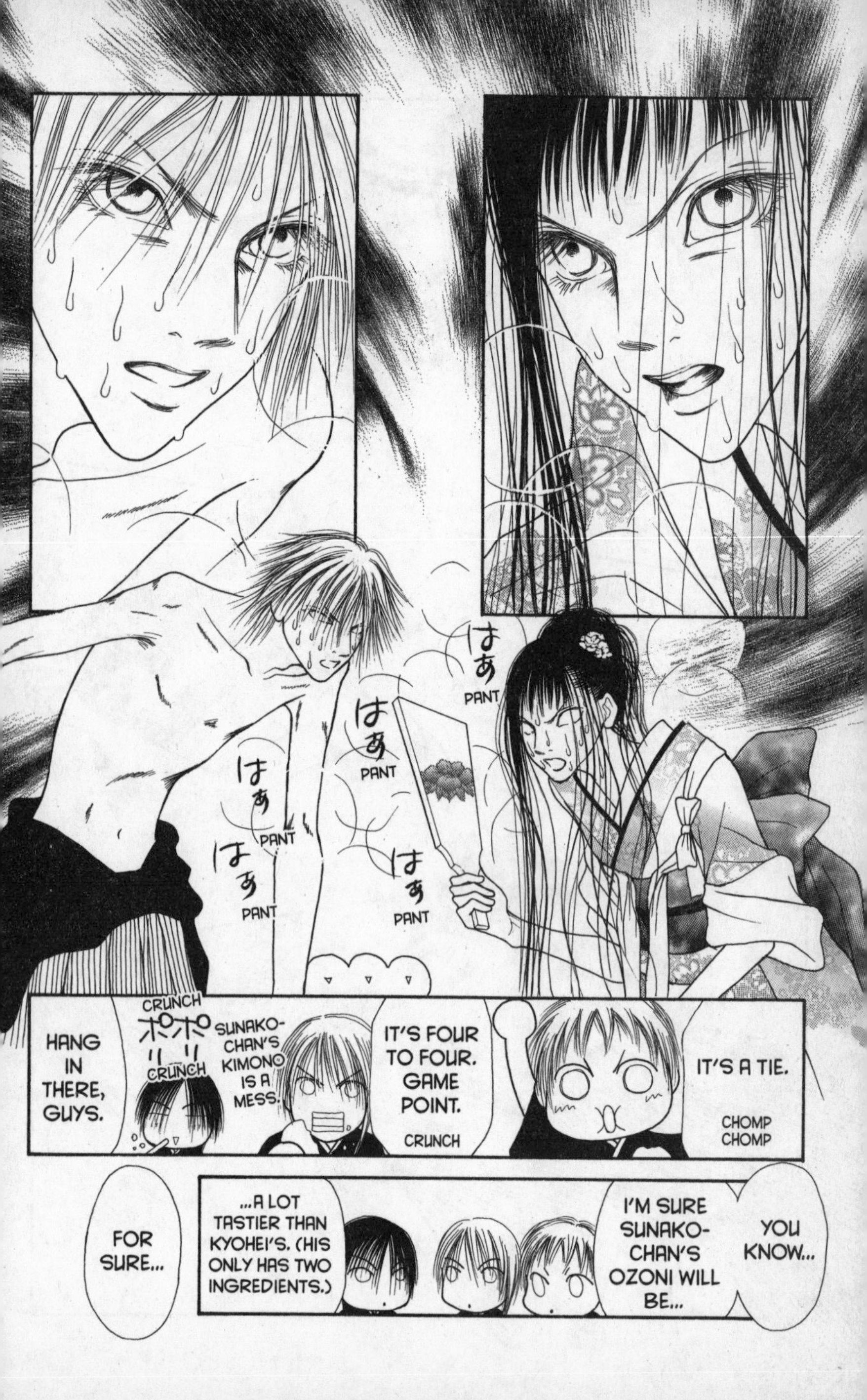
はあ
PANT
はあ
PANT
はあ
PANT
はあ
PANT
はあ
PANT
IT'S A TIE.
CHOMP CHOMP
IT'S FOUR TO FOUR. GAME POINT.
CRUNCH
SUNAKO-CHAN'S KIMONO IS A MESS.
CRUNCH
ポリポリ
CRUNCH
HANG IN THERE, GUYS.
YOU KNOW...
I'M SURE SUNAKO-CHAN'S OZONI WILL BE...
...A LOT TASTIER THAN KYOHEI'S. (HIS ONLY HAS TWO INGREDIENTS.)
FOR SURE...

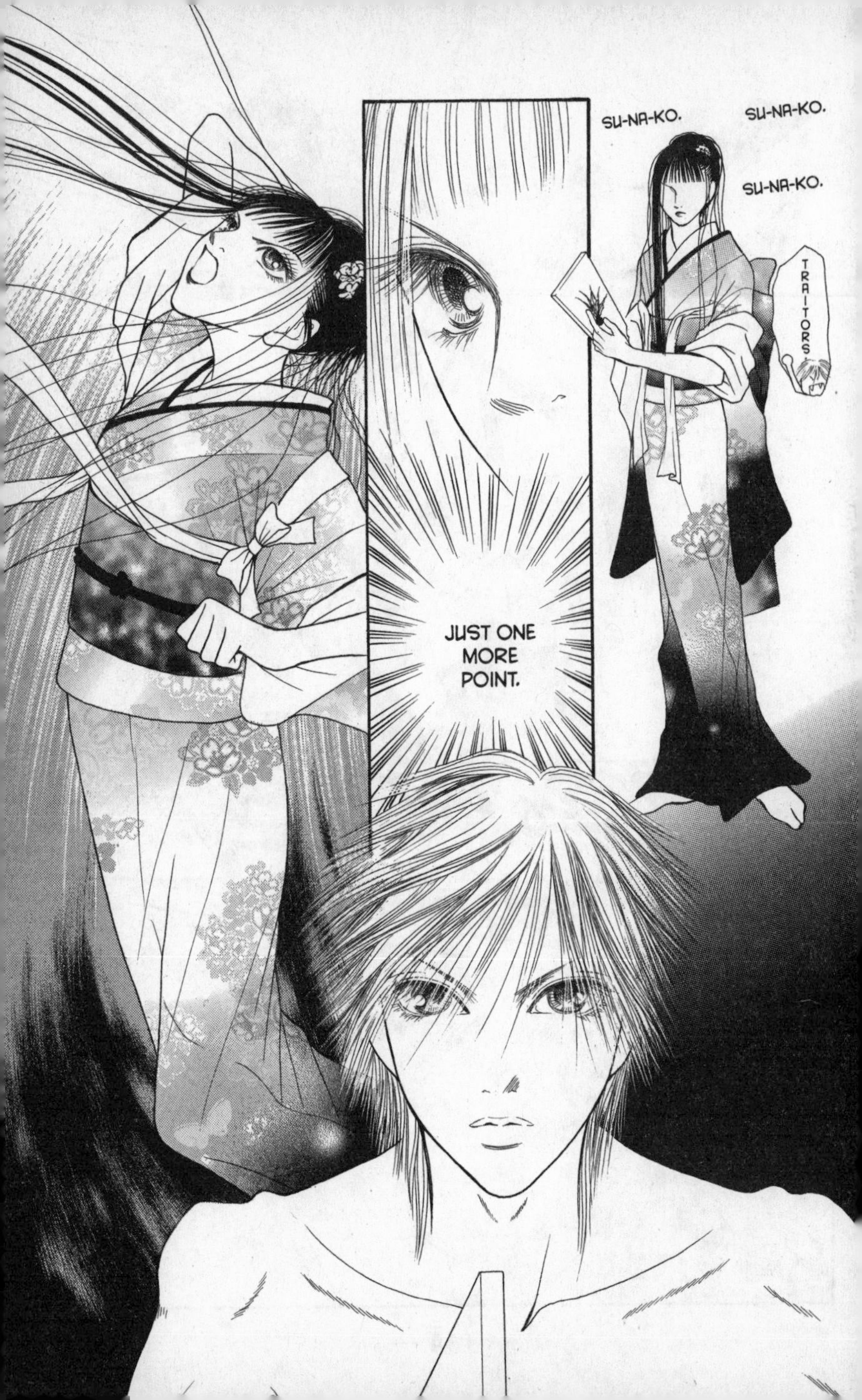
SU-NA-KO.
SU-NA-KO.
SU-NA-KO.
TRAITORS
JUST ONE MORE POINT.

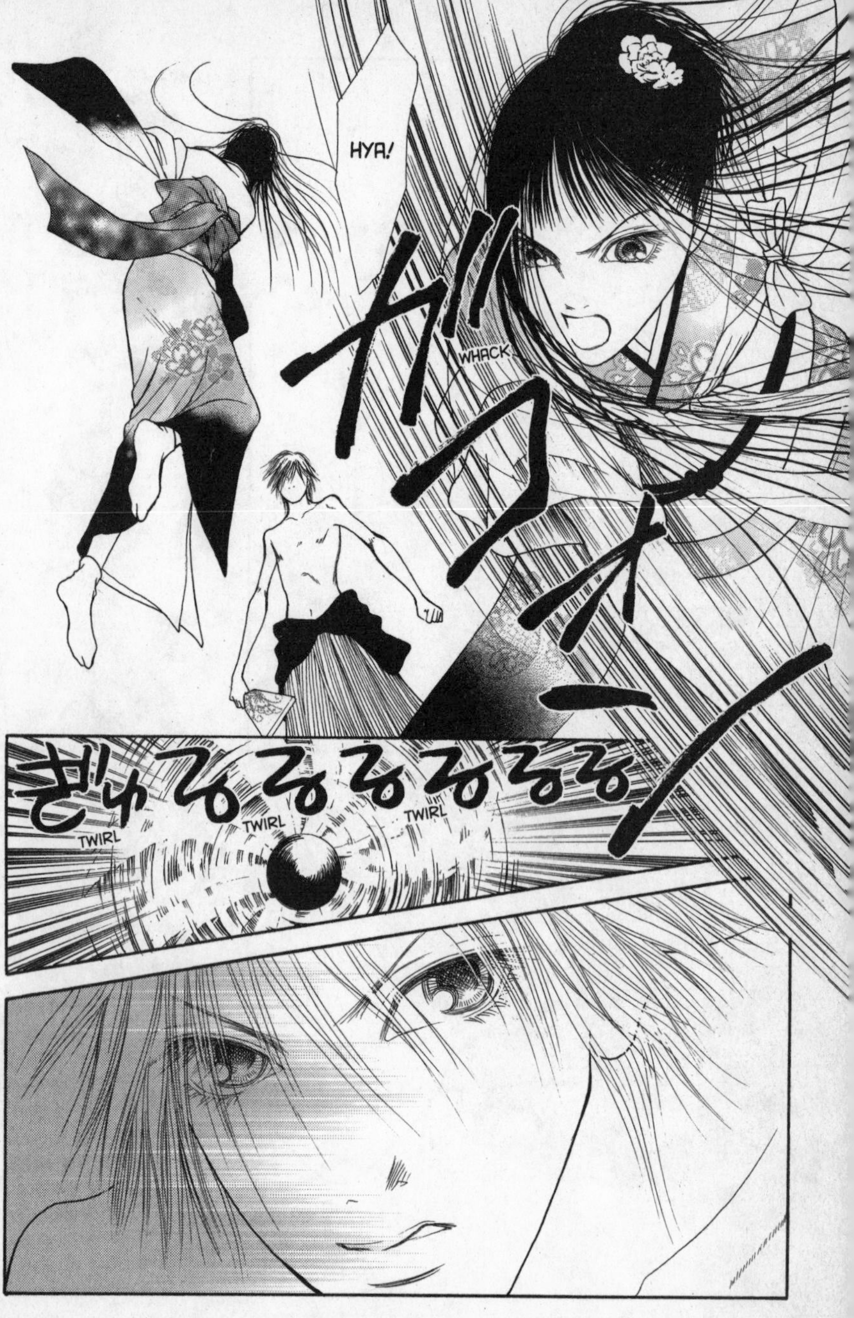
HYA!
WHACK
TWIRL
TWIRL
TWIRL

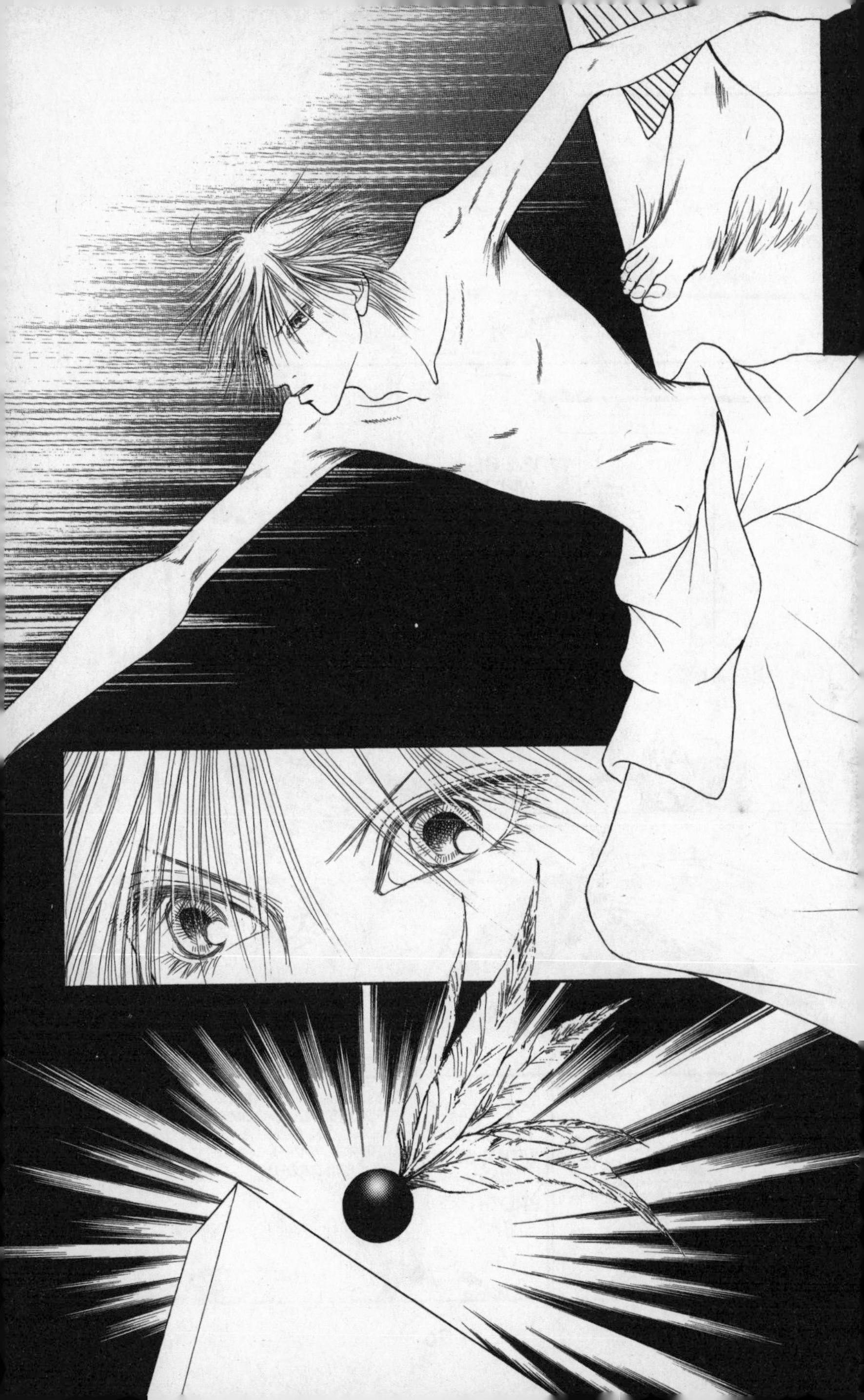

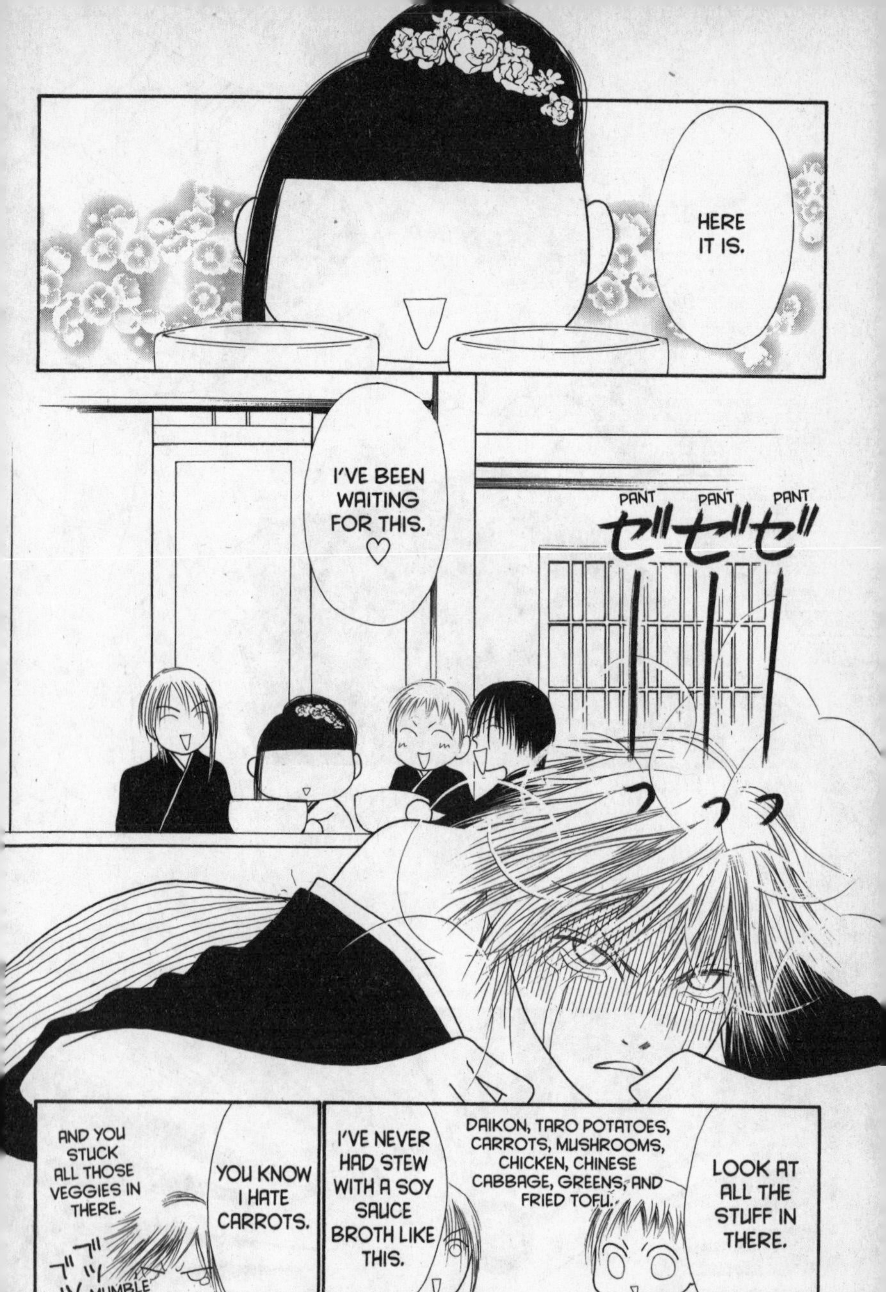
HERE IT IS.
I'VE BEEN WAITING FOR THIS. ♡
PANT PANT PANT
ゼゼゼ
LOOK AT ALL THE STUFF IN THERE.
DAIKON, TARO POTATOES, CARROTS, MUSHROOMS, CHICKEN, CHINESE CABBAGE, GREENS, AND FRIED TOFU...
I'VE NEVER HAD STEW WITH A SOY SAUCE BROTH LIKE THIS.
YOU KNOW I HATE CARROTS.
AND YOU STUCK ALL THOSE VEGGIES IN THERE.
MUMBLE MUMBLE

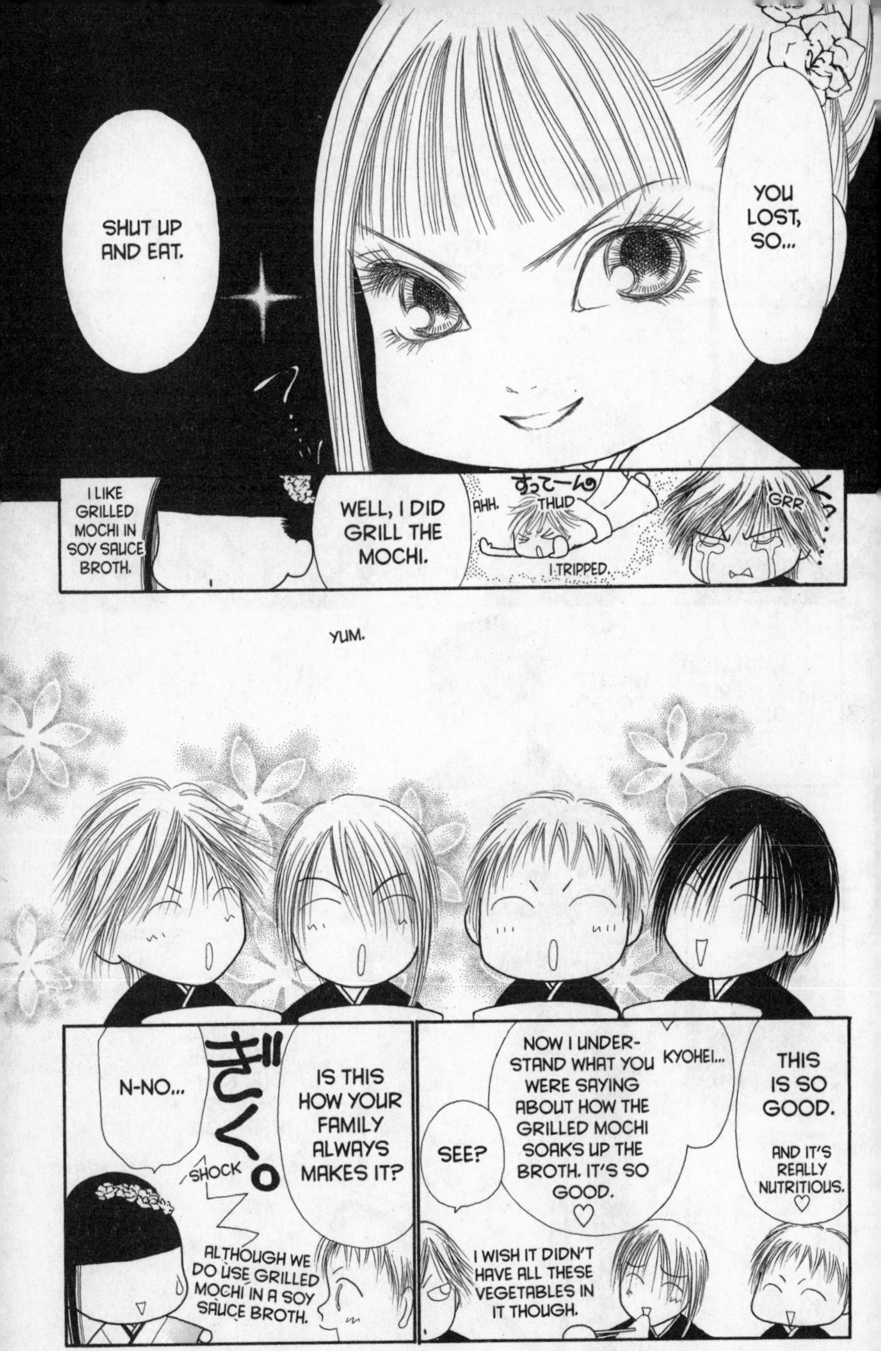

YOU LOST, SO...
SHUT UP AND EAT.
GRR
THUD
AHH.
I TRIPPED.
WELL, I DID GRILL THE MOCHI.
I LIKE GRILLED MOCHI IN SOY SAUCE BROTH.
YUM.
THIS IS SO GOOD.
AND IT'S REALLY NUTRITIOUS.
KYOHEI...
NOW I UNDER-STAND WHAT YOU WERE SAYING ABOUT HOW THE GRILLED MOCHI SOAKS UP THE BROTH. IT'S SO GOOD.
SEE?
I WISH IT DIDN'T HAVE ALL THESE VEGETABLES IN IT THOUGH.
IS THIS HOW YOUR FAMILY ALWAYS MAKES IT?
SHOCK
N-NO...
ALTHOUGH WE DO USE GRILLED MOCHI IN A SOY SAUCE BROTH.

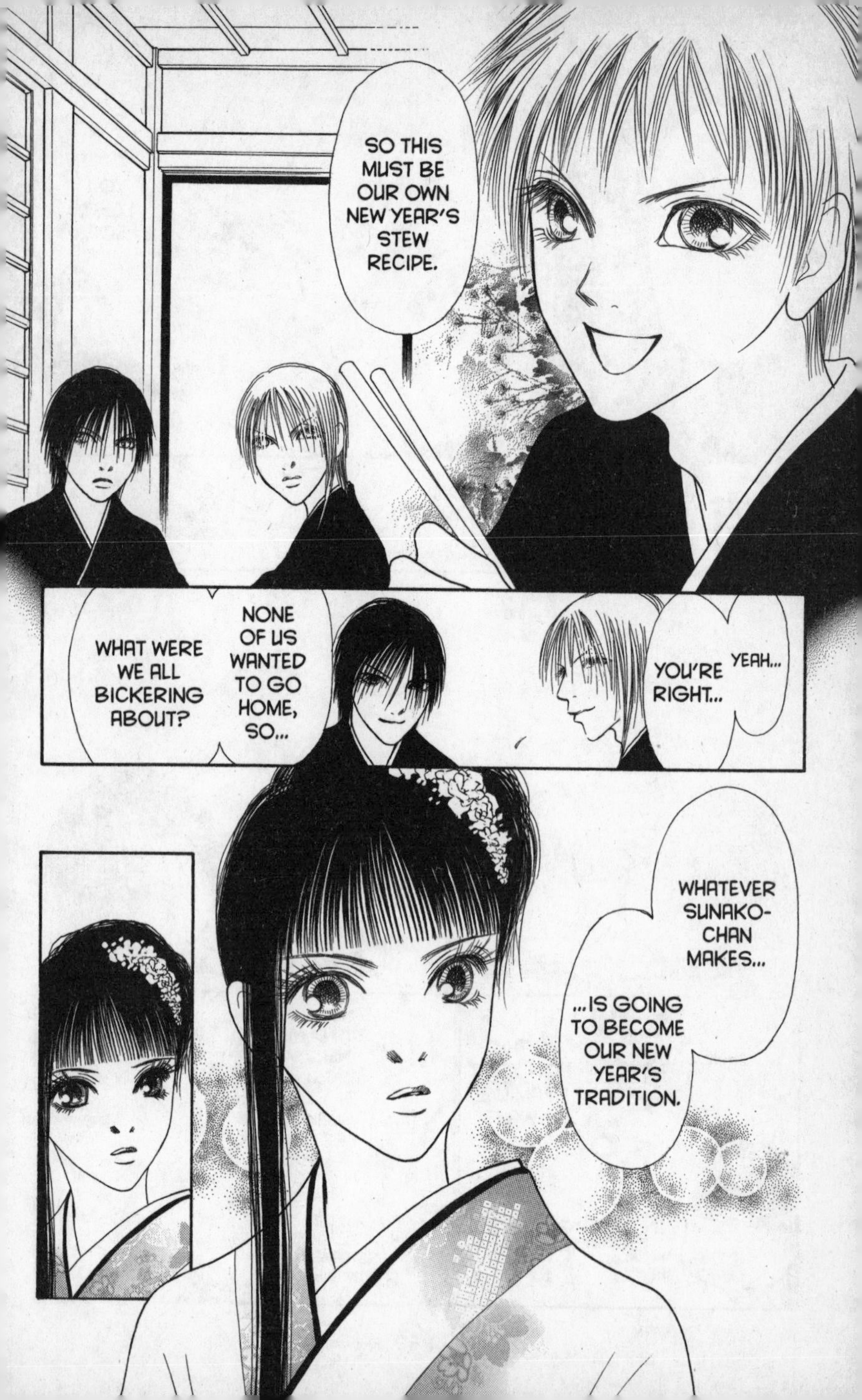
SO THIS MUST BE OUR OWN NEW YEAR'S STEW RECIPE.
YEAH...
YOU'RE RIGHT...
NONE OF US WANTED TO GO HOME, SO...
WHAT WERE WE ALL BICKERING ABOUT?
WHATEVER SUNAKO-CHAN MAKES...
...IS GOING TO BECOME OUR NEW YEAR'S TRADITION.

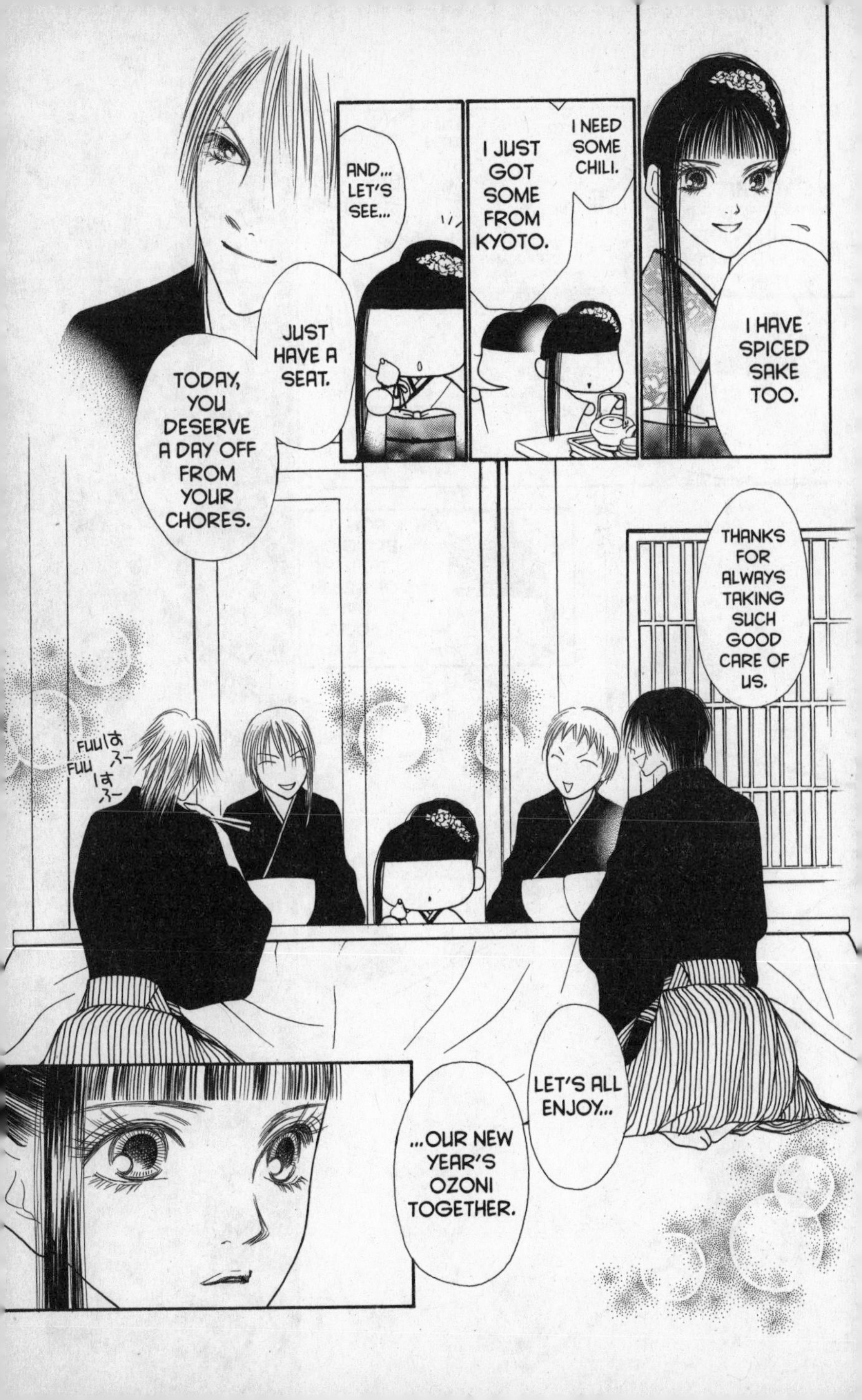
I HAVE SPICED SAKE TOO.
I NEED SOME CHILI.
I JUST GOT SOME FROM KYOTO.
AND... LET'S SEE...
JUST HAVE A SEAT.
TODAY, YOU DESERVE A DAY OFF FROM YOUR CHORES.
THANKS FOR ALWAYS TAKING SUCH GOOD CARE OF US.
FUU はふー
FUU はふー
LET'S ALL ENJOY...
...OUR NEW YEAR'S OZONI TOGETHER.

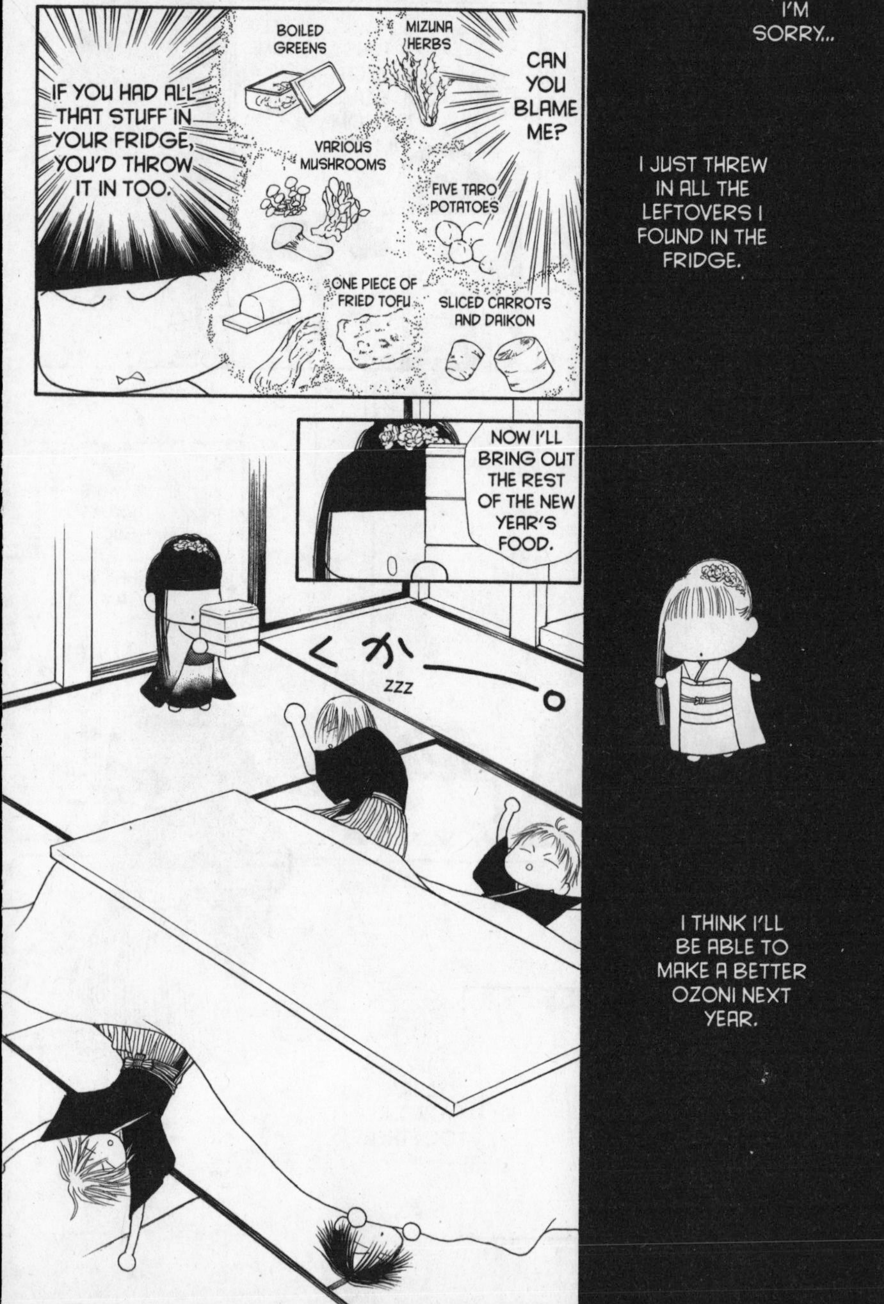
I'M SORRY...
I JUST THREW IN ALL THE LEFTOVERS I FOUND IN THE FRIDGE.
I THINK I'LL BE ABLE TO MAKE A BETTER OZONI NEXT YEAR.
CAN YOU BLAME ME?
MIZUNA HERBS
BOILED GREENS
IF YOU HAD ALL THAT STUFF IN YOUR FRIDGE, YOU'D THROW IT IN TOO.
FIVE TARO POTATOES
VARIOUS MUSHROOMS
SLICED CARROTS AND DAIKON
ONE PIECE OF FRIED TOFU
NOW I'LL BRING OUT THE REST OF THE NEW YEAR'S FOOD.
くかー。
ZZZ

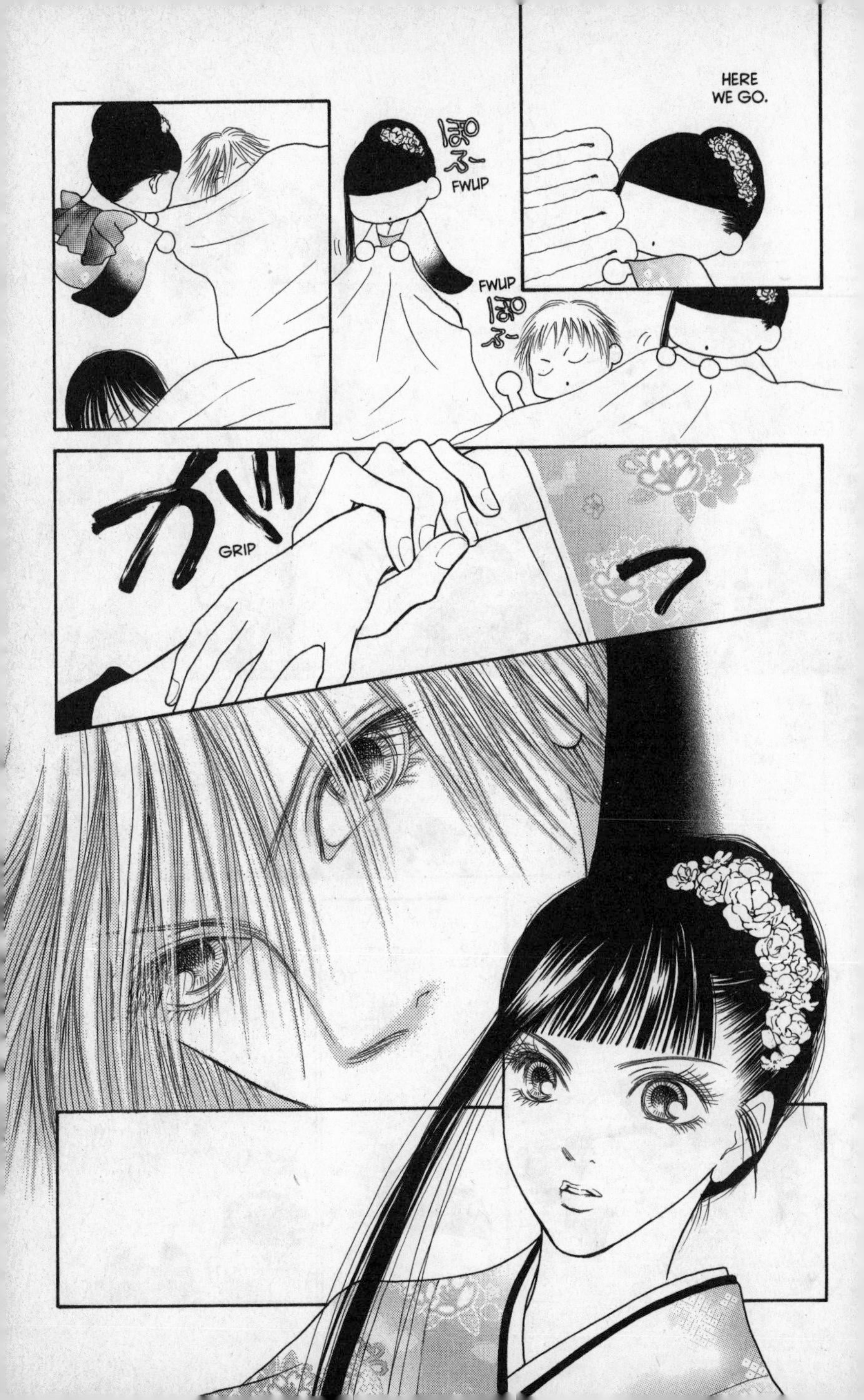
HERE WE GO.
ぽふ~
FWUP
FWUP
ぽふ~
GRIP

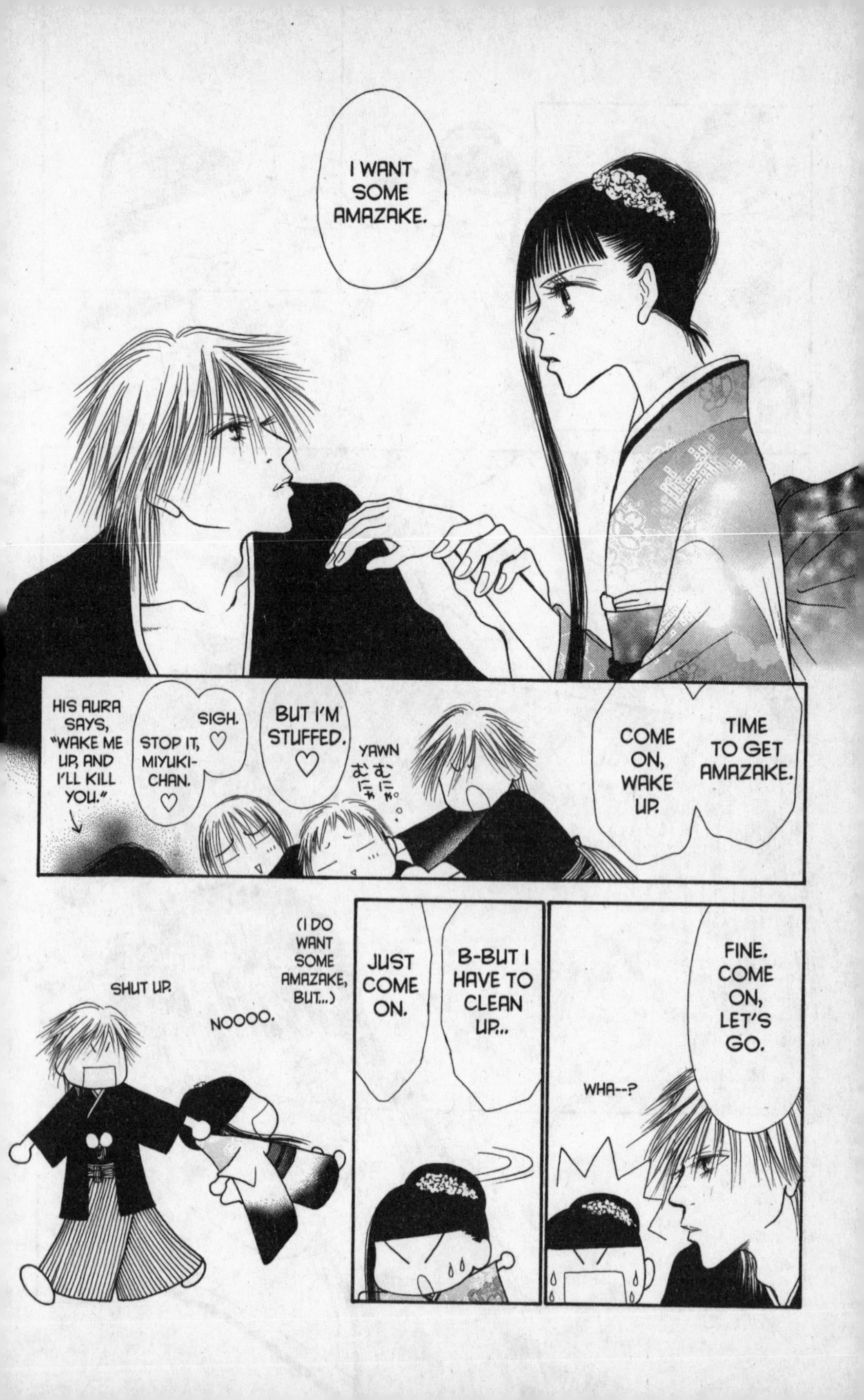
I WANT SOME AMAZAKE.
TIME TO GET AMAZAKE.
COME ON, WAKE UP.
YAWN
むにゃむにゃ。
BUT I'M STUFFED. ♡
SIGH. ♡
STOP IT, MIYUKI-CHAN. ♡
HIS AURA SAYS, "WAKE ME UP, AND I'LL KILL YOU."
FINE. COME ON, LET'S GO.
WHA--?
B-BUT I HAVE TO CLEAN UP...
JUST COME ON.
(I DO WANT SOME AMAZAKE, BUT...)
NOOOO.
SHUT UP.

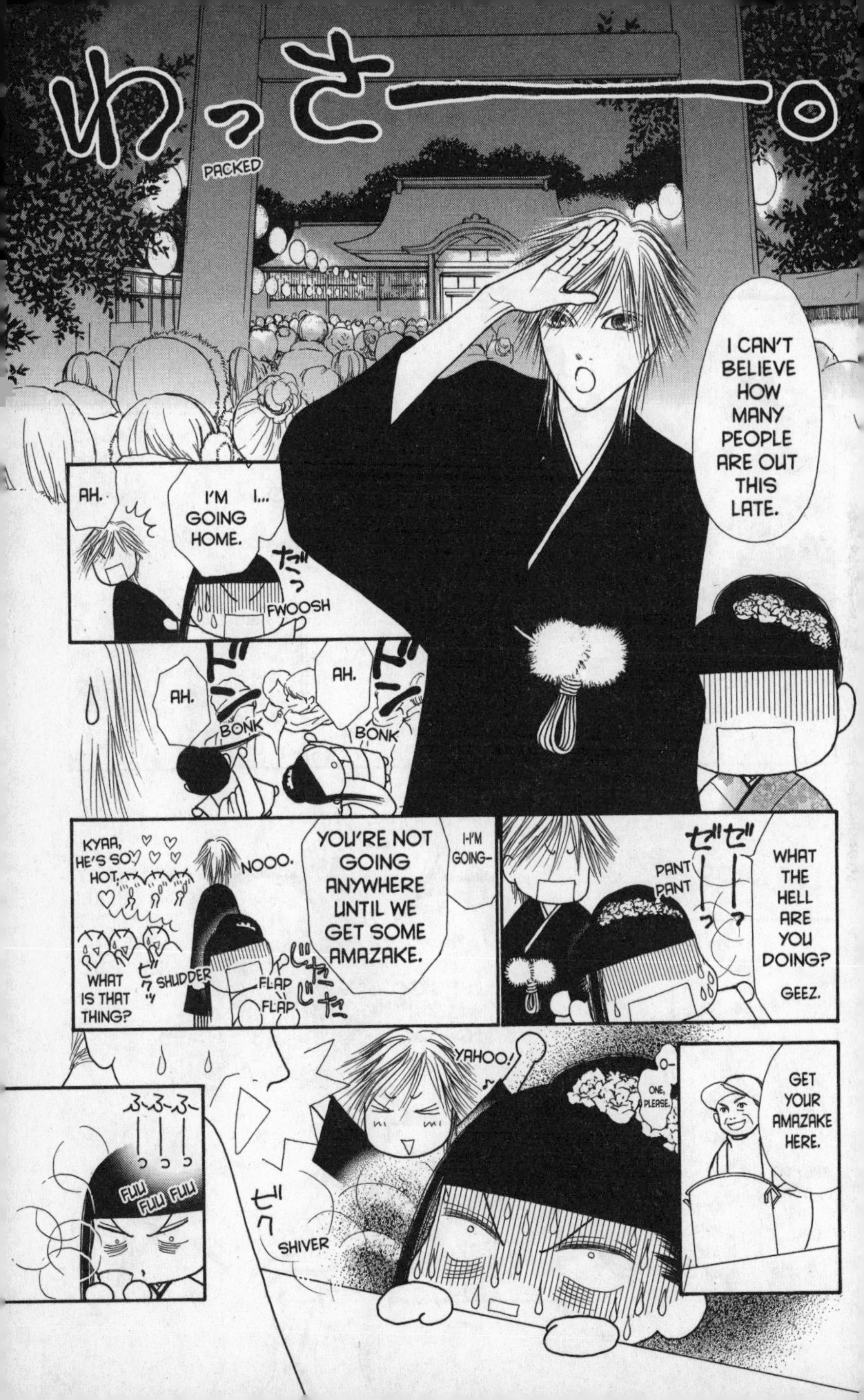

わっさー。
PACKED
I CAN'T BELIEVE HOW MANY PEOPLE ARE OUT THIS LATE.
I...
I'M GOING HOME.
AH.
FWOOSH
AH.
BONK
AH.
BONK
WHAT THE HELL ARE YOU DOING?
GEEZ.
PANT PANT
I-I'M GOING-
YOU'RE NOT GOING ANYWHERE UNTIL WE GET SOME AMAZAKE.
FLAP FLAP
NOOO.
KYAA, HE'S SO HOT.
SHUDDER
WHAT IS THAT THING?
GET YOUR AMAZAKE HERE.
O-ONE, PLEASE.
YAHOO!
SHIVER
ふーふーふー
FUU FUU FUU

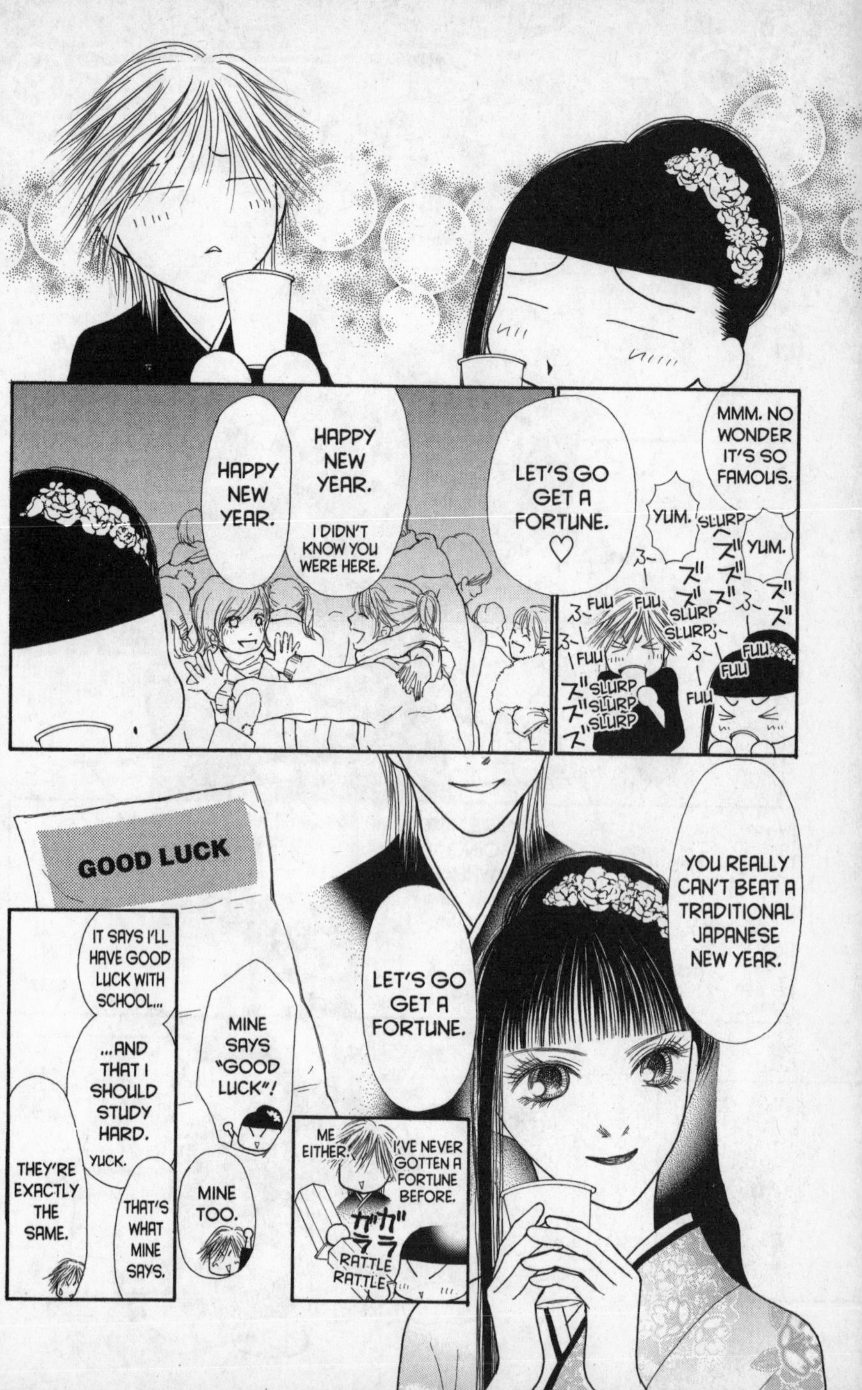
MMM. NO WONDER IT'S SO FAMOUS.
YUM.
YUM.
SLURP
SLURP
SLURP
FUU
FUU
FUU
FUU
FUU
FUU
SLURP
SLURP
SLURP
LET'S GO GET A FORTUNE. ♡
HAPPY NEW YEAR.
I DIDN'T KNOW YOU WERE HERE.
HAPPY NEW YEAR.
YOU REALLY CAN'T BEAT A TRADITIONAL JAPANESE NEW YEAR.
LET'S GO GET A FORTUNE.
I'VE NEVER GOTTEN A FORTUNE BEFORE.
ME EITHER.
ガガ
ララ
RATTLE
RATTLE
GOOD LUCK
MINE SAYS "GOOD LUCK"!
IT SAYS I'LL HAVE GOOD LUCK WITH SCHOOL...
...AND THAT I SHOULD STUDY HARD.
YUCK.
MINE TOO.
THAT'S WHAT MINE SAYS.
THEY'RE EXACTLY THE SAME.

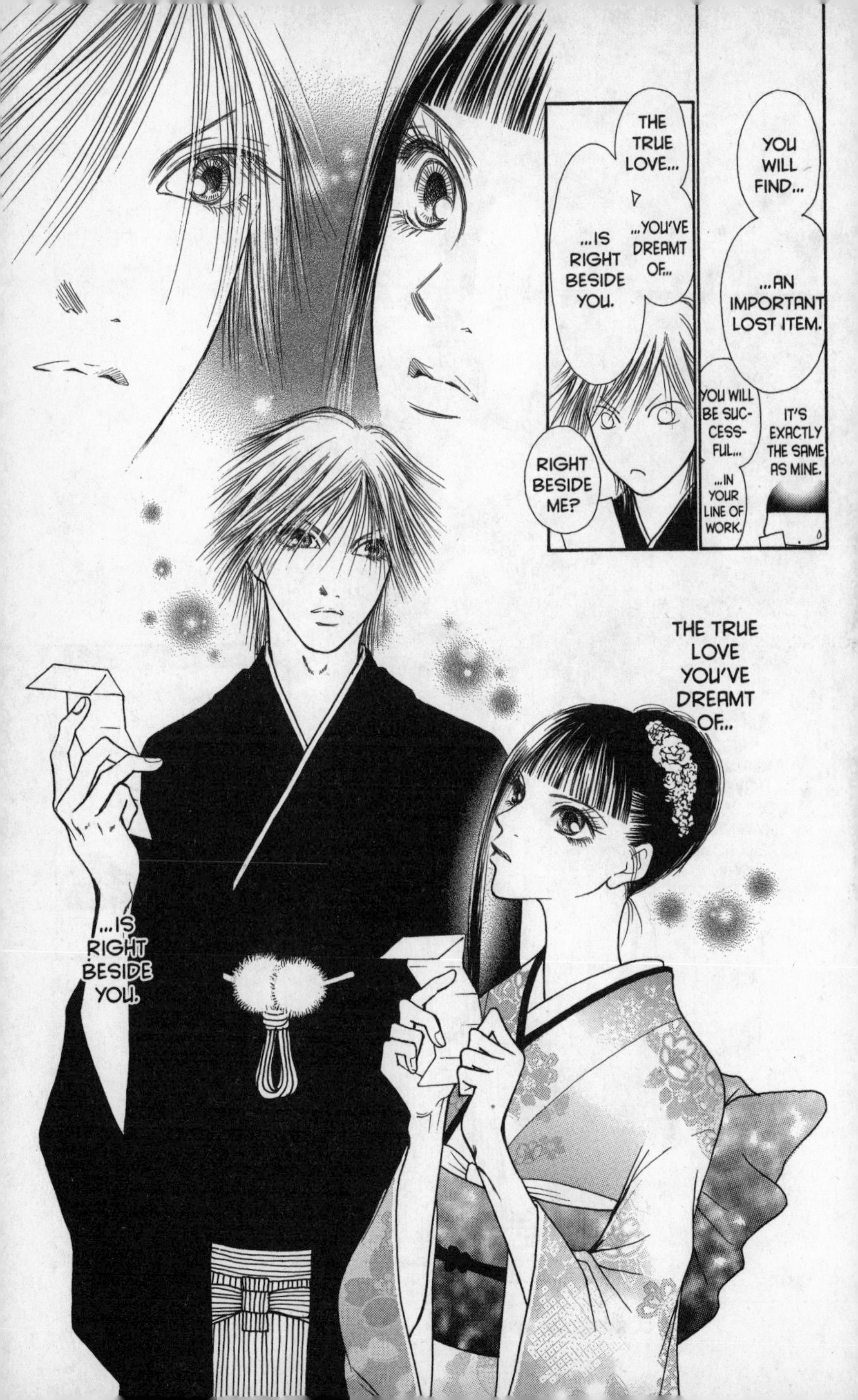
YOU WILL FIND...
...AN IMPORTANT LOST ITEM.
YOU WILL BE SUCCESSFUL...
...IN YOUR LINE OF WORK.
IT'S EXACTLY THE SAME AS MINE.
THE TRUE LOVE...
...YOU'VE DREAMT OF...
...IS RIGHT BESIDE YOU.
RIGHT BESIDE ME?
THE TRUE LOVE YOU'VE DREAMT OF...
...IS RIGHT BESIDE YOU.

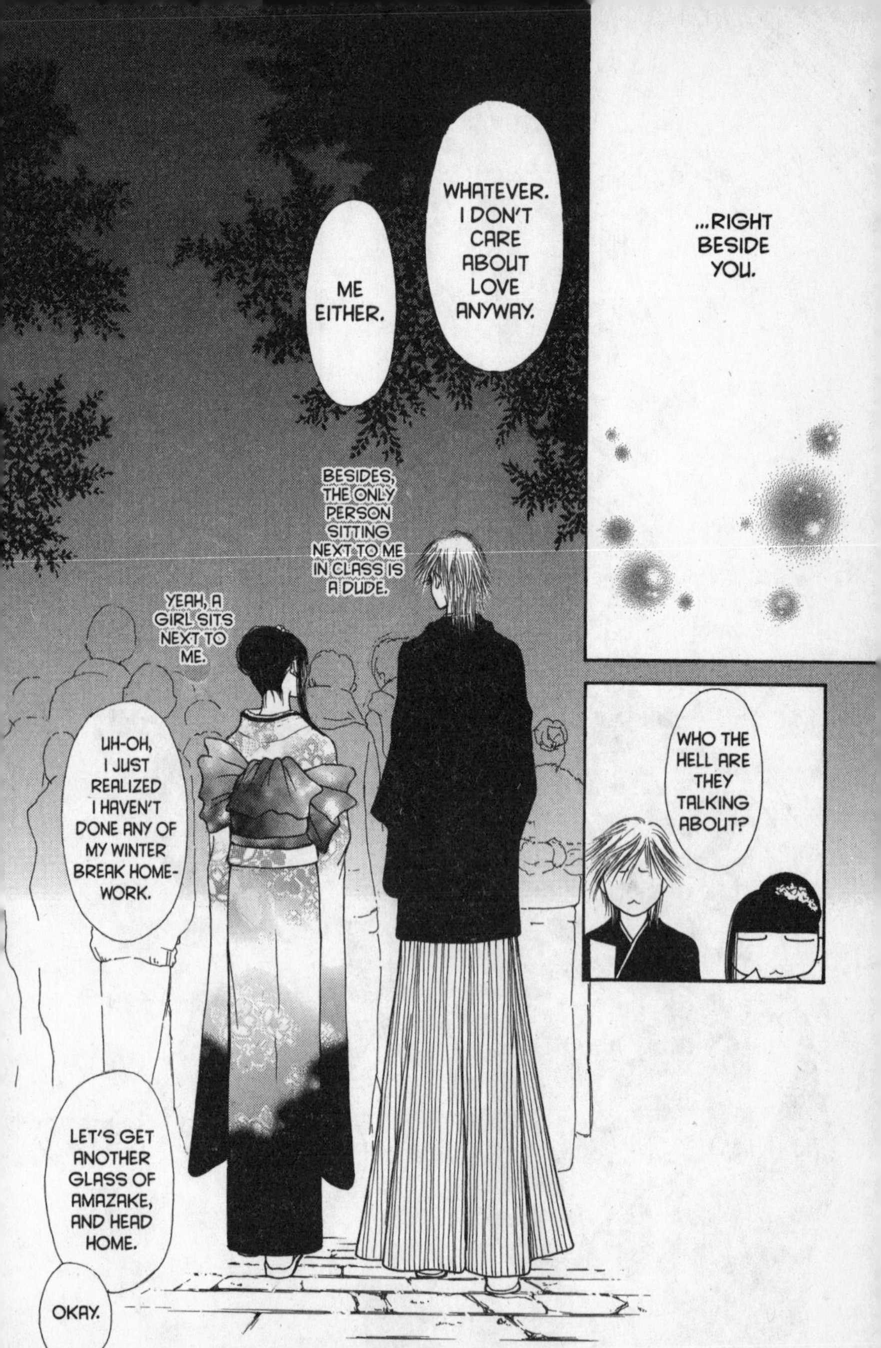
...RIGHT BESIDE YOU.
WHO THE HELL ARE THEY TALKING ABOUT?
WHATEVER. I DON'T CARE ABOUT LOVE ANYWAY.
ME EITHER.
BESIDES, THE ONLY PERSON SITTING NEXT TO ME IN CLASS IS A DUDE.
YEAH, A GIRL SITS NEXT TO ME.
UH-OH, I JUST REALIZED I HAVEN'T DONE ANY OF MY WINTER BREAK HOME-WORK.
LET'S GET ANOTHER GLASS OF AMAZAKE, AND HEAD HOME.
OKAY.

CONTINUED IN *WALLFLOWER* BOOK 21♥

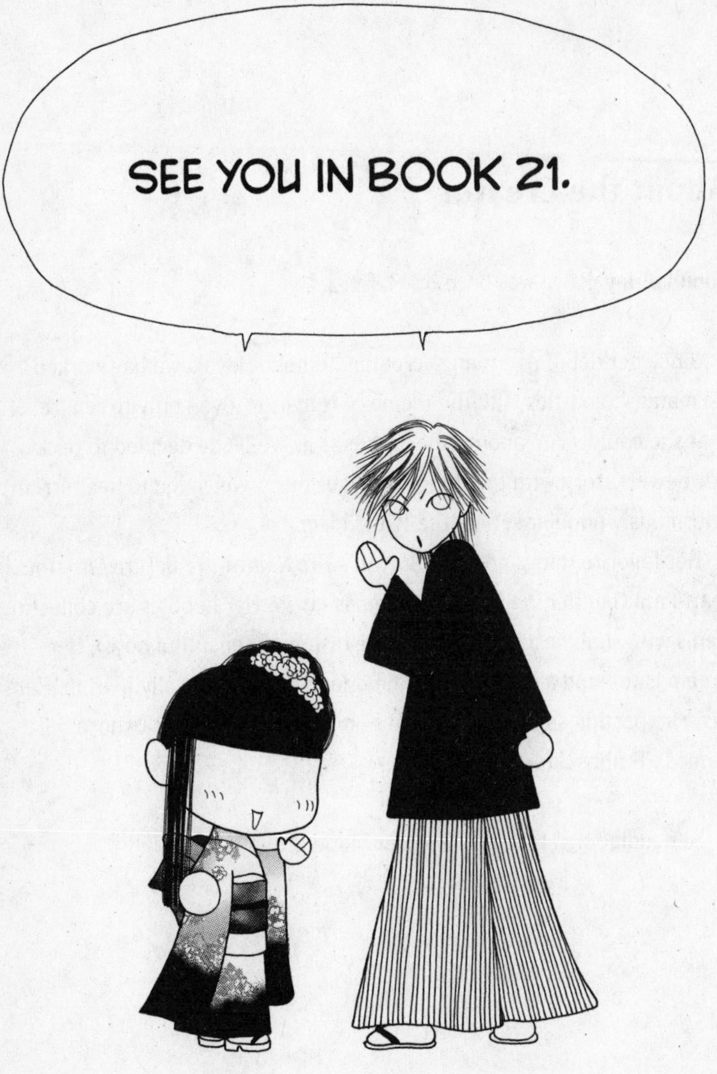
SEE YOU IN BOOK 21.

# About the Creator

Tomoko Hayakawa was born on March 4.

Since her debut as a manga creator, Tomoko Hayakawa has worked on many shojo titles with the theme of romantic love—only to realize that she could write about other subjects as well. She decided to pack her newest story with the things she likes most, which led to her current, enormously popular series, *The Wallflower*.

Her favorite things are: Tim Burton's *The Nightmare Before Christmas*, Jean-Paul Gaultier, and samurai dramas on TV. Her hobbies are collecting items with skull designs and watching bishonen (beautiful boys). Her dream is to build a mansion like the one the Addams family lives in. Her favorite pastime is to lie around at home with her cat, Ten (whose full name is Tennosuke).

Her zodiac sign is Pisces, and her blood group is AB.

# Translation Notes

Japanese is a tricky language for most Westerners, and translation is often more art than science. For your edification and reading pleasure, here are notes on some of the places where we could have gone in a different direction in our translation of the work, or where a Japanese cultural reference is used.

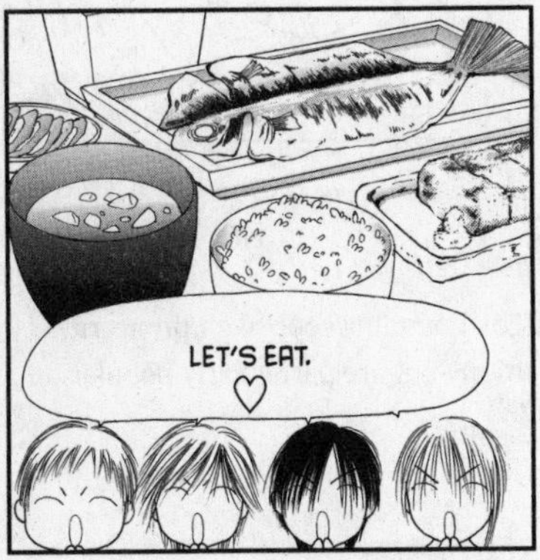
LET'S EAT. ♡

## Natto, page 6

Natto is the Japanese term for fermented soy beans. A foul-smelling, yet delectable food often eaten for breakfast and valued for its vitamin content.

## Curry Pan, page 49

Curry bread is a popular snack sold at Japanese bakeries. It's a deep-fried donut-type of pastry, stuffed with Japanese-style curry.

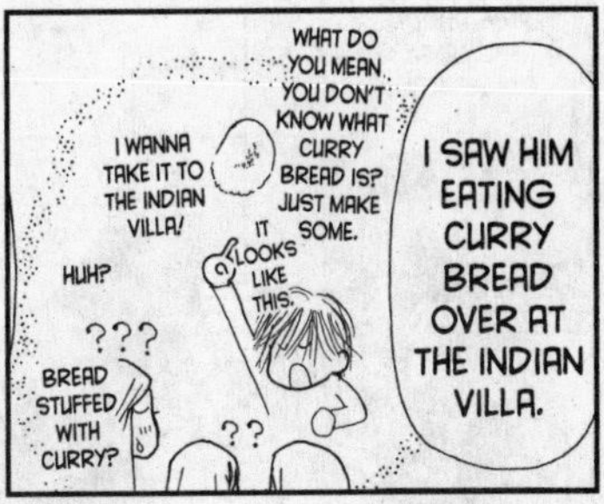
I SAW HIM EATING CURRY BREAD OVER AT THE INDIAN VILLA.
WHAT DO YOU MEAN YOU DON'T KNOW WHAT CURRY BREAD IS? JUST MAKE SOME.
I WANNA TAKE IT TO THE INDIAN VILLA!
IT LOOKS LIKE THIS.
HUH?
???
BREAD STUFFED WITH CURRY?
??

## School Festival, page 85

School festivals are generally held once a year at Japanese schools. Each class usually puts together some kind of activity such as a play or a dance. Some classes open up food stalls or cafés.

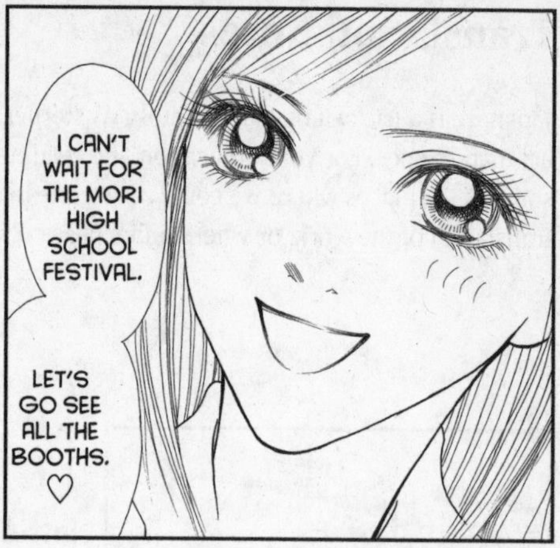
I CAN'T WAIT FOR THE MORI HIGH SCHOOL FESTIVAL.
LET'S GO SEE ALL THE BOOTHS. ♡

## Mochi Tsuki, page 128

The guys are making mochi, or "rice balls," by pounding cooked glutinous rice into doughy balls. Mochi are eaten all year long but are particularly popular on New Year's.

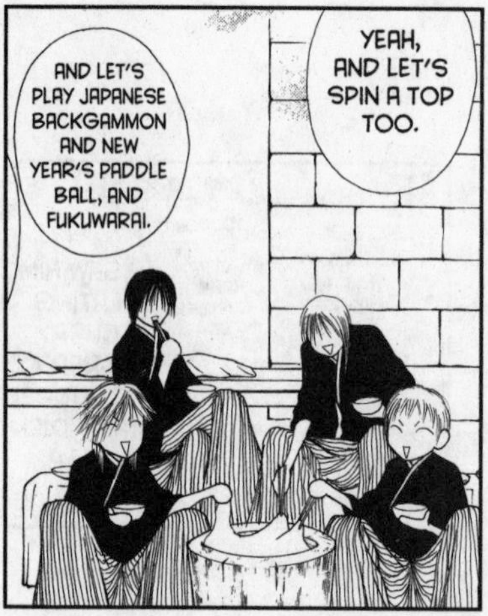
YEAH, AND LET'S SPIN A TOP TOO.
AND LET'S PLAY JAPANESE BACKGAMMON AND NEW YEAR'S PADDLE BALL, AND FUKUWARAI.

## New Year's games, page 130

Japanese New Year's festivities often consist of playing several games. Kite flying and spinning tops are popular New Year's activities, as is Sugoroku ( a board game similar to backgammon). Hanetsuki, which we translated as New Year's paddle ball, is played by young girls. They use ornately designed wooden paddles to hit something like a badminton birdie. The object is to keep the birdie from falling to the ground. Fukuwarai is similar to pin the tail on the donkey; however in Fukuwarai, one sticks facial features, such as the eyes, nose, and mouth, to a featureless face.

## Hatsumode, page 130

It is a tradition to visit a shrine on New Year's day. Popular shrines can become incredibly crowded from late New Year's Eve through New Year's day.

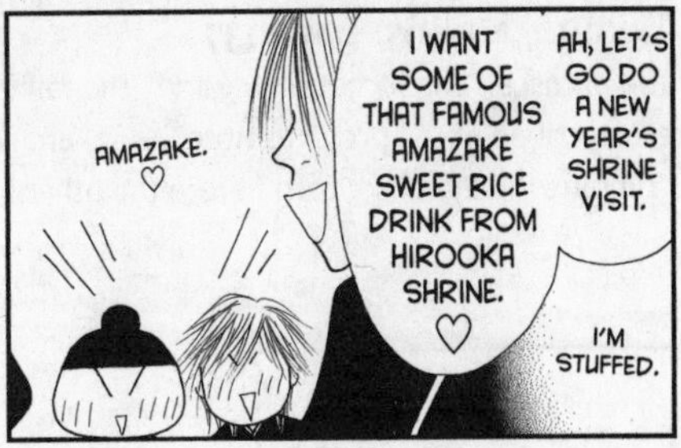
AH, LET'S GO DO A NEW YEAR'S SHRINE VISIT.
I WANT SOME OF THAT FAMOUS AMAZAKE SWEET RICE DRINK FROM HIROOKA SHRINE. ♡
I'M STUFFED.
AMAZAKE. ♡

## Amazake, page 131

Amazake is a warm, sweet, non-alcoholic beverage made from fermented rice. It is often served at shrines and temples during the cold winter months.

## Ozoni, page 131

Ozoni is a Japanese stew that is eaten on New Year's Eve. Recipes and styles of Ozoni vary by region and familial tradition, but ozoni almost always contains mochi of some kind.

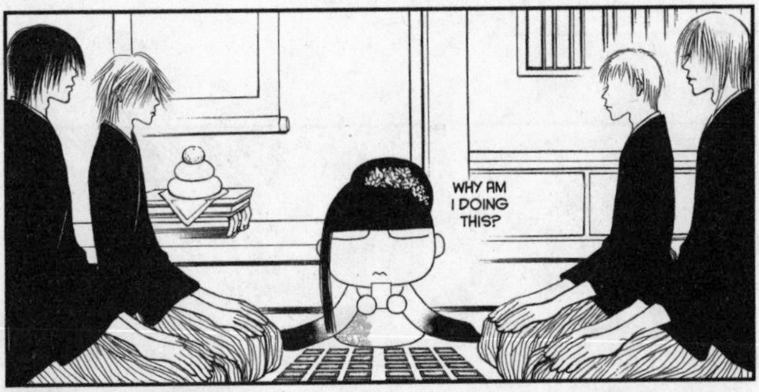
WHY AM I DOING THIS?

## Uta-garuta, page 136

The gang is playing Uta-garuta. Uta-garuta is another traditional New Year's game played with a deck of cards. The deck is made up of two groups. One group of cards contains the first line of a three-line Japanese Tanka-style poem. The second group of cards contain the remaining two lines of the poems. Somebody reads the first line of the poem, and the goal of the game is to be the first to find the card with the subsequent lines that finish the poem. The person who collects the most cards wins. Of course, Takenaga the intellectual excels at this game.

### Takenaga wins, page 137

The phrases "The forgotten..." and "The fall fields"....are the first lines of poems as described in the previous note. As Takenaga yells out "I know that one," he is grabbing the matching card before the other guys can get to it.

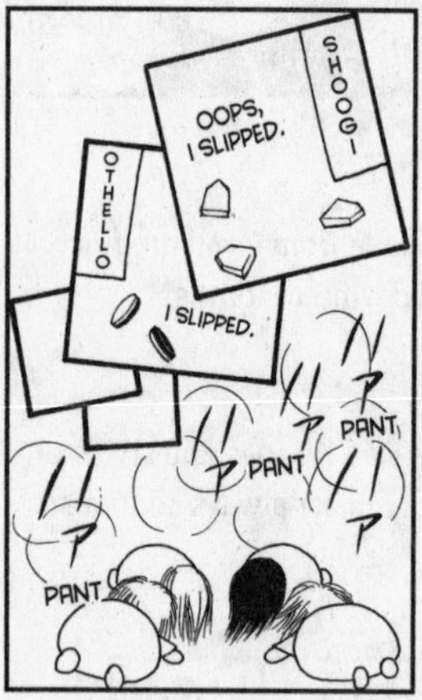
SHOOGI
OOPS, I SLIPPED.
OTHELLO
I SLIPPED.
PANT
PANT
PANT

### Shoogi, page 142

Shoogi is another Japanese board game which is similar to Chess.

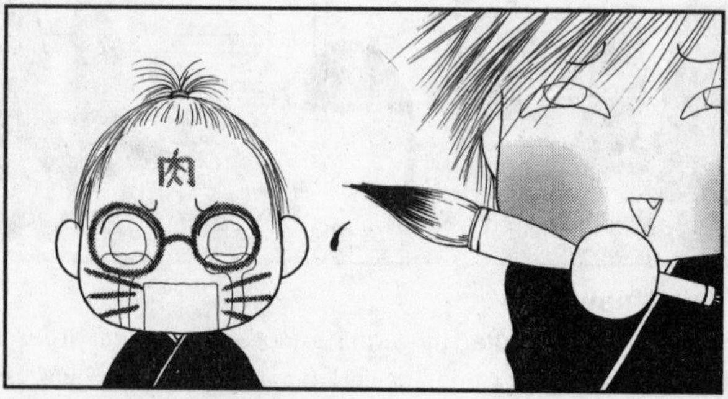
肉

### Draw on the Loser, page 146

Traditionally, the loser at a Japanese paddle ball game gets his face painted. Here, Yuki has the kanji for meat scribbled on his forehead. This is a reference to the popular manga character Kinniku man, who also has the character for meat on his forehead.

**Maro, page 147**

The guys have drawn on Takenaga to make him look like he's from ancient times, and have written the word "maro" on his forehead. In ancient Japan, the term maro was added as a suffix to people's names to show respect.

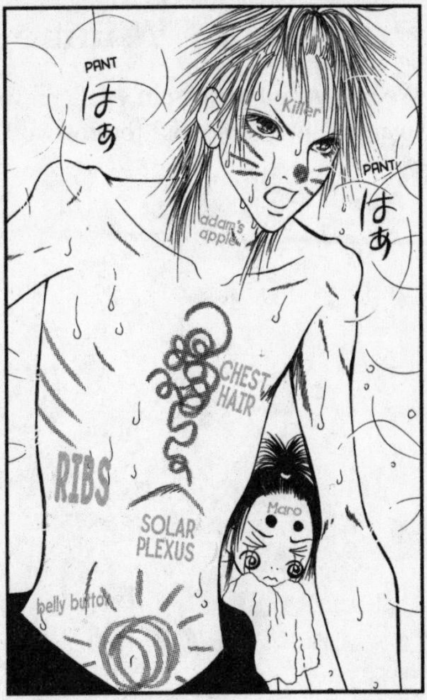
PANT
はあ
Killer
PANT
はあ
adam's apple
CHEST HAIR
RIBS
SOLAR PLEXUS
Maro
belly button

**Omikuji, page 165**

Shrines sell paper fortunes called omikuji. It is a New Year's tradition to buy omikuji. Sunako and Kyohei both picked a fortune which bore the characters "Daikichi," meaning Excellent Luck. The worst fortune possible is "Daikyo," meaning Cursed Luck.

# Preview of Volume 21

We're pleased to present you a preview from volume 21. This volume is available in English, but for now you'll have to make do with Japanese!

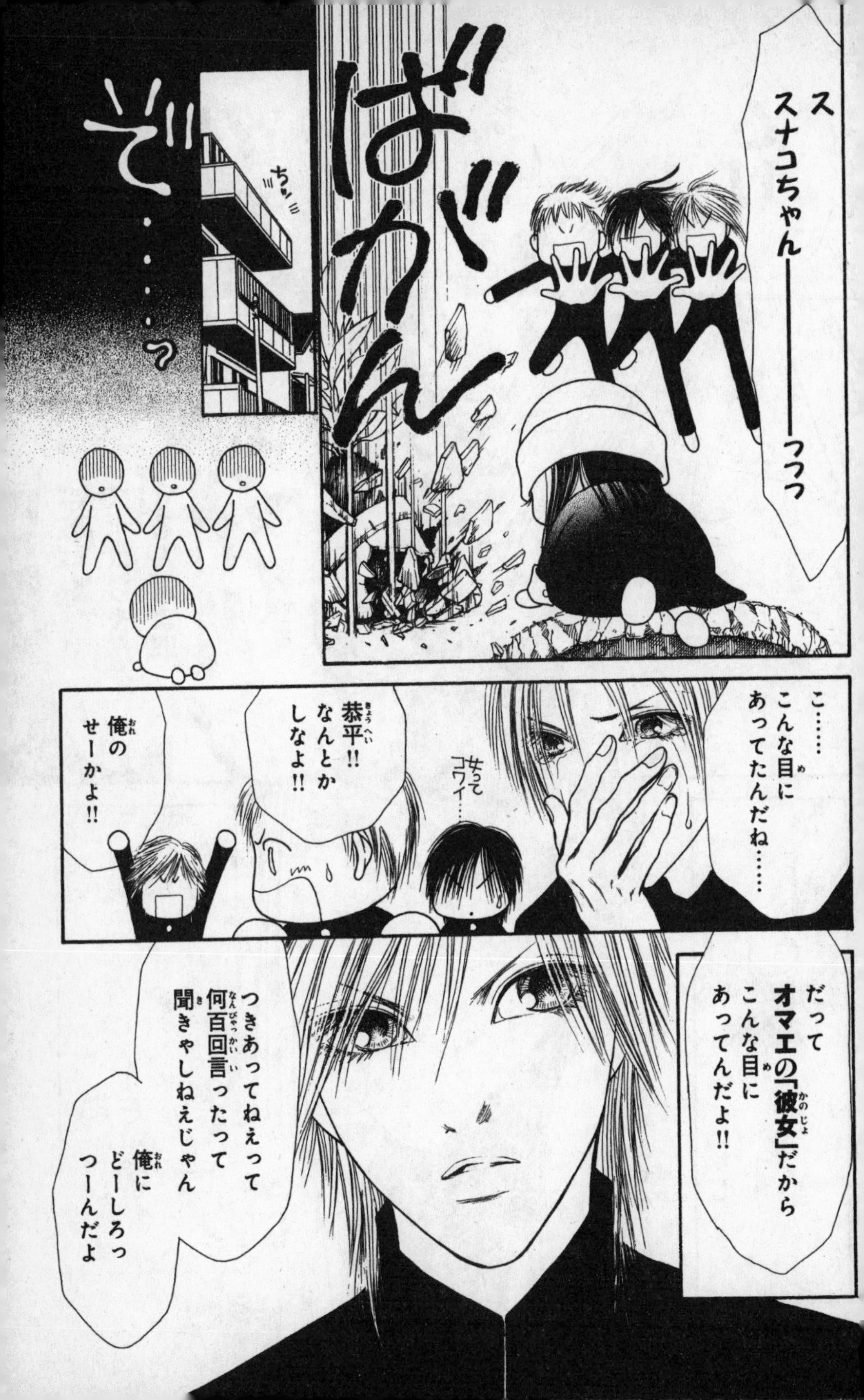
ス
スナコちゃん――――っつつ
ばがん
で……っ
こ……
こんな目に
あってたんだね……
女って
コワイ……
恭平!!
なんとか
しなよ!!
俺の
せーかよ!!
だって
オマエの「彼女」だから
こんな目に
あってんだよ!!
つきあってねえって
何百回言ったって
聞きゃしねえじゃん
俺に
どーしろっ
つーんだよ

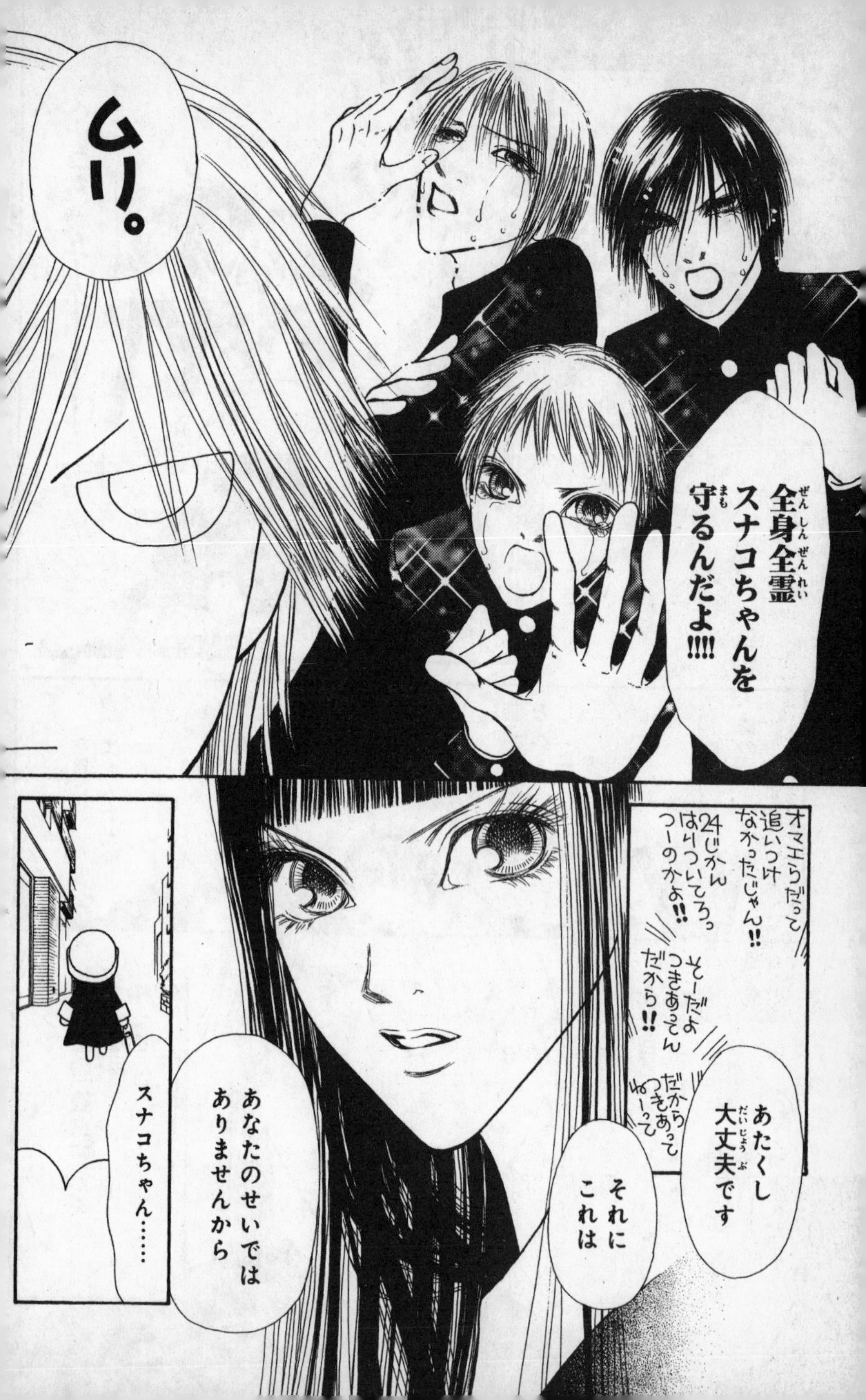

全身全霊スナコちゃんを守るんだよ!!!!
ムリ。
オマエらだって追いつけなかったじゃん!!
24じかんはりついてろっつーのかよ!!
そーだよつきあってんだから!!
だからつきあってねーって
あたくし大丈夫です
それにこれは
あなたのせいではありませんから
スナコちゃん……

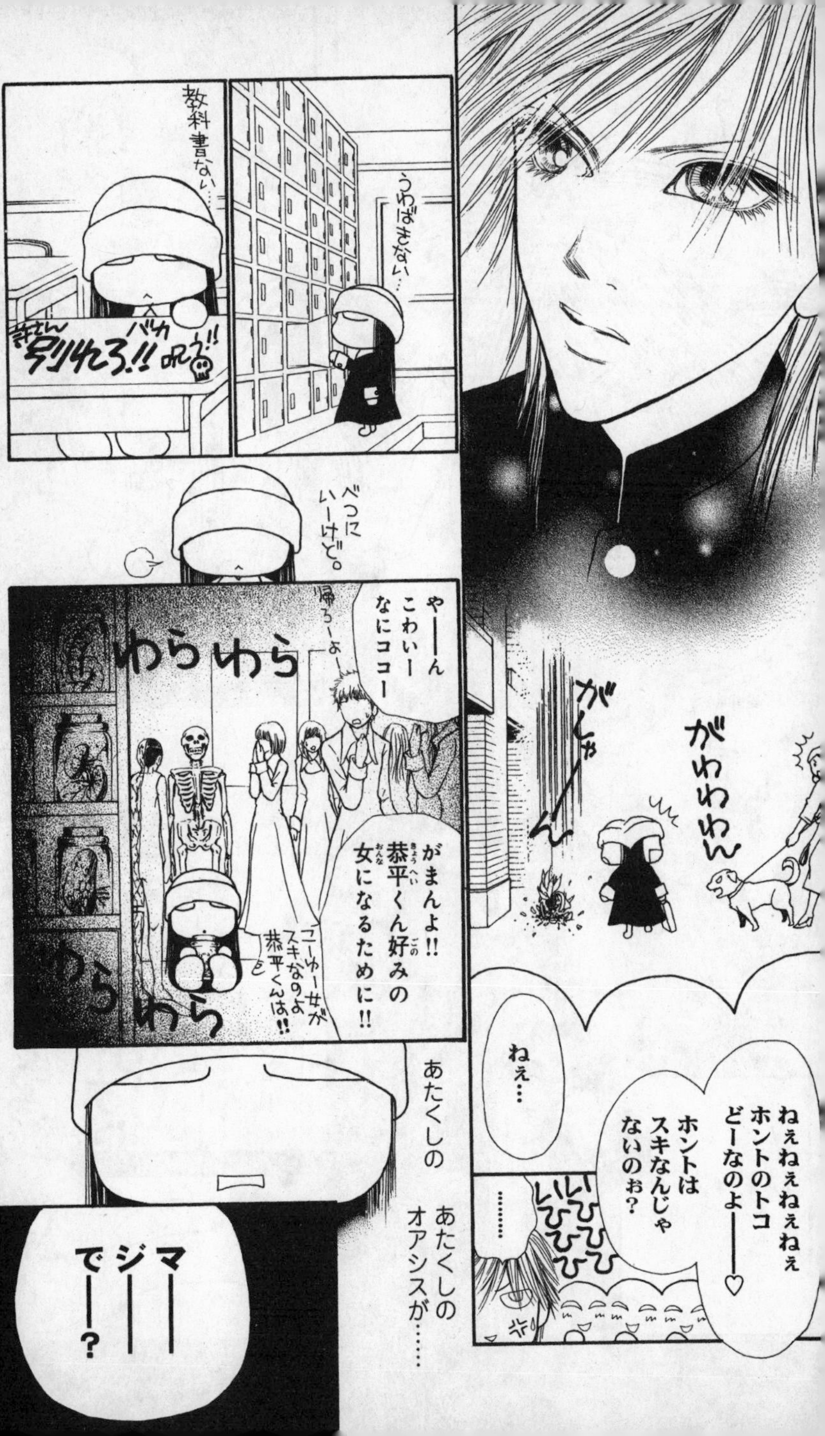

がわわわん
がしゃーん
ねぇねぇねぇねぇ ホントのトコ どーなのよーー♡
ホントは スキなんじゃ ないのぉ?
ねぇ…
……
いひひひ ひひひひ
うわばきない…
教科書ない…
許さん 別れろ!! バカ 呪う!!
べつに いーけど。
やーーん こわいー なにココー
帰ろーよー
わらわら
がまんよ!! 恭平くん好みの女になるために!!
コーゆー女がスキなのよ 恭平くんは!!
わらわら
あたくしの
あたくしの オアシスが……
マージーでーー?

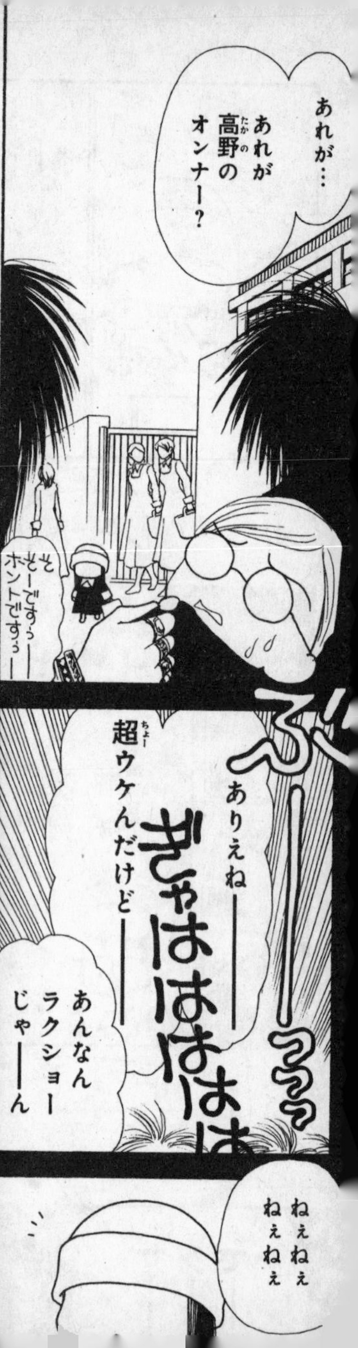
あれが…
あれが高野のオンナー？
そ
そーですぅ
ホントですぅーー
ぶーーーっっっ
ぎゃはははは
ありえねーー
超ウケんだけどーー
あんなんラクショーじゃーーん
ねぇねぇねぇ
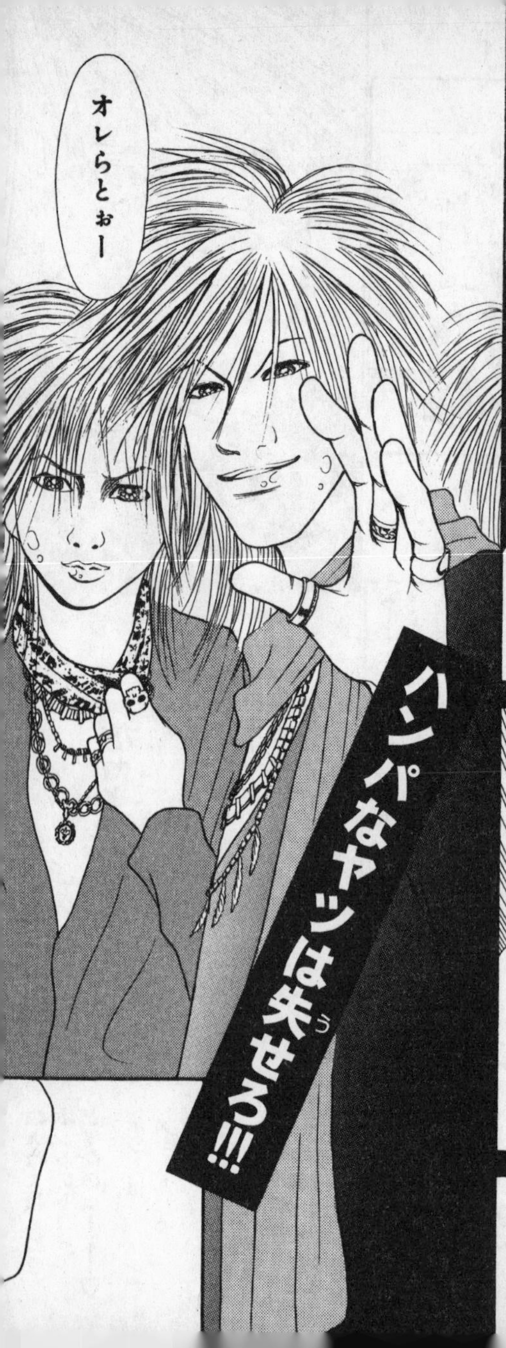
オレらとぉー
ハンパなヤツは失せろ!!!

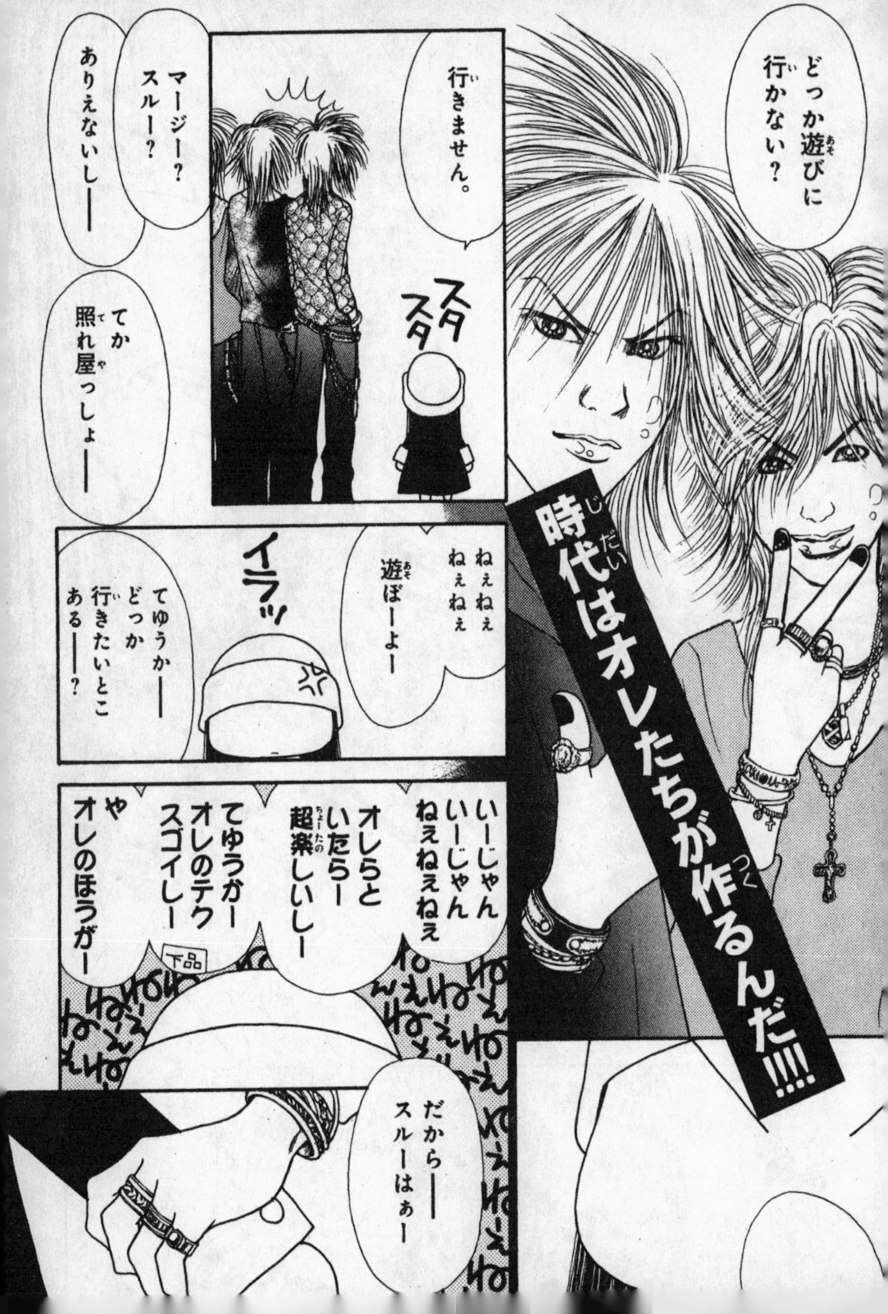

どっか遊びに行かない？
時代はオレたちが作るんだ!!!!
行きません。
スタスタ
マージー？スルーー？
ありえないしー――
てか照れ屋っしょー――
ねぇねぇねぇねぇ遊ぼーよー
イラッ
てゆうかー――どっか行きたいとこある――？
いーじゃんいーじゃんねぇねぇねぇ
オレらといたらー超楽しいしー
てゆうかーオレのテクスゴイしー
下品
やオレのほうがー
だから――スルーーはぁー

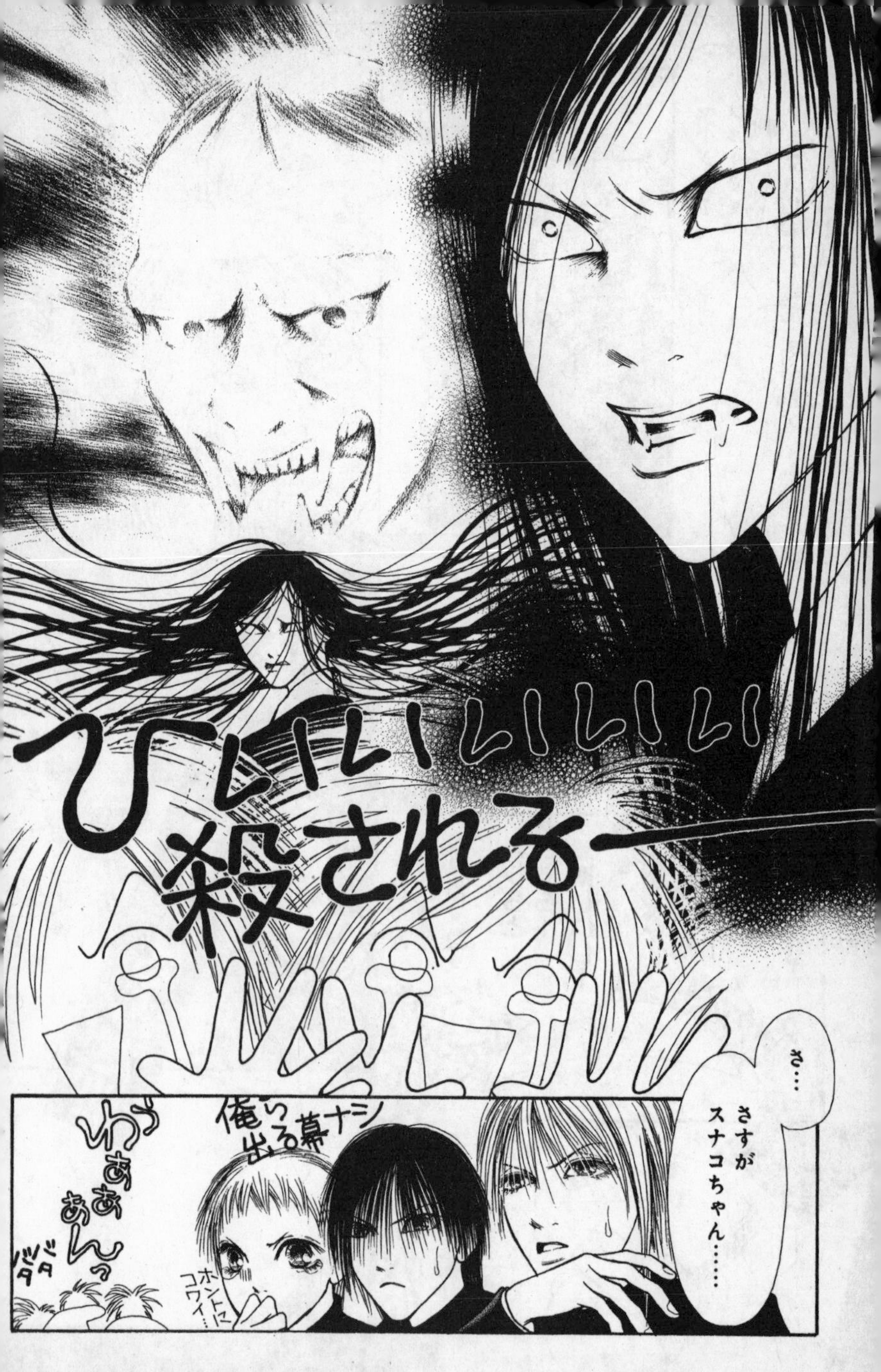
ひぃいいいいいい
殺されるー
さ……
さすがスナコちゃん……
俺ら出る幕ナシ
ホントにコワイ…
わぅあああんっ
バタバタ